HMS HOOD

HMS HOOD

PRIDE OF THE ROYAL NAVY

DANIEL KNOWLES

FONTHILL

Dedicated to the men of HMS Hood

Fonthill Media Language Policy

Fonthill Media publishes in the international English language market. One language edition is published worldwide. As there are minor differences in spelling and presentation, especially with regard to American English and British English, a policy is necessary to define which form of English to use. The Fonthill Policy is to use the form of English native to the author. Daniel Knowles was born and educated in the United Kingdom; therefore, British English has been adopted in this publication.

Fonthill Media Limited
Fonthill Media LLC
www.fonthillmedia.com
office@fonthillmedia.com

First published in the United Kingdom and the United States of America 2019

British Library Cataloguing in Publication Data:
A catalogue record for this book is available from the British Library

Copyright © Daniel Knowles 2019

ISBN 978-1-78155-723-5

Typeset in 10.5pt on 13pt Sabon
Printed and bound in England

Acknowledgements

There are a number of people without whose assistance this book would not be possible. In the first instance, I would like to thank the archivists at the National Archives, the Tyne and Wear Archives, Churchill College, the Royal Navy Library Portsmouth, and at the University of Glasgow Archives as without their assistance in navigating the vast collections of the archives, the production of this book would have been so much harder to write.

A special thank you must go to Jeannie Hounslow of the City of Vancouver Archives for her invaluable assistance with information on the photographs contained within the archives. Another special acknowledgement must be made to James Warrand, Frank Allen, and Barry Roberts of the HMS *Hood* Association. Other individuals who deserve to be thanked for their assistance with photographs and information relating to photographs are David L. Mearns, Susan Kennedy of the City of Sydney Archives, Carol Smith and Pena Atanasoff of the State Library of Western Australia, Lisa Crunk of the Naval History and Heritage Command, Washington, Catherine Lavoie of the Bibliothèque et Archives Nationales du Québec, Harco Gijsbers of Beeldbank WO2, and Greg Swinden of the Sea Power Centre.

Thanks must be extended to Jay Slater and everyone at Fonthill Media who brought this book to publication. Finally, I would like to thank my family, especially my parents, Tracey and Gary; my sister, Natalie; my grandparents, Eddie and Iris; and my close friends, Jake Dorrell and David Osborne, for their continued support and encouragement.

Contents

The *Hood*'s recovered bell on display at the Royal Navy Museum Portsmouth.

Introduction

On 7 December 2017, the aircraft carrier HMS *Queen Elizabeth* was commissioned into the Royal Navy at Portsmouth. In attendance at the commissioning ceremony were Queen Elizabeth II and Princess Anne. During the course of the ceremony, Queen Elizabeth II delivered a speech and described the new vessel as 'The most powerful and capable ship ever to raise the White Ensign, she will in the years and decades ahead represent this country's resolve on the global stage'.[1] HMS *Queen Elizabeth* joined the fleet as the largest ship ever commissioned by the Royal Navy. The words delivered by Queen Elizabeth II could, however, have been attributed to another vessel, one which until the commissioning of the *Queen Elizabeth* held the mantle of being the largest warship ever commissioned into service with the Royal Navy—the battlecruiser HMS *Hood*.

A year and a half earlier, on 24 May 2016, veterans and the descendants of those who served aboard the *Hood* gathered at Portsmouth Historic Dockyard. At Portsmouth Historic Dockyard, Princess Anne unveiled the bell of the *Hood* to mark the seventy-fifth anniversary of her sinking. At midday, the Princess Royal struck the bell eight times in memorial before it was carried by a Royal Navy Guard and put on display at the Royal Navy Museum Portsmouth.

Alongside such ships as HMS *Victory* and unmatched in her beauty and charisma, the *Hood* is one of history's great warships and one of the most famous vessels to ever fly the White Ensign. For more than twenty years, 'The Mighty Hood' (as she was affectionately referred) toured the world as the largest and most powerful warship in the world. Engaging in many diplomatic exercises during her career, the *Hood* was the pride of the Royal Navy. She was a phoenix rising out from the ashes of the Battle of Jutland—the only ship of her class to be constructed, following the loss of British battlecruisers in action with the German High Seas Fleet, with her design having been revised and improved. Despite this, she had one fatal flaw: her deck armour. With her long, low hull and finely balanced silhouette, and armed with eight powerful 15-inch guns, in many ways, the *Hood* was the embodiment of the big-gun era of sea power.

The *Hood* was the product of the First World War, the war that was supposed to end all wars. As the last battlecruiser ever built for the Royal Navy and with most of the Grand Fleet destined for scrapyards, for over twenty years during the twilight years of the British Empire, she toured the world as the most iconic warship in the Royal Navy, showing the flag as a symbol of British power.

She lacked an essential full modernisation that, combined with her reputation, meant that she was ill-prepared to fight more modern and capable capital ships. When first commissioned, she was capable of destroyer-like speeds; however, by the time of the Second World War, her speed had been reduced and newer more capable vessels had been built and commissioned. Despite being built for a different war, the *Hood*'s service during the Second World War was relentless. As the Royal Navy's show ship, the *Hood* came to command a special place in the hearts and minds of the British public. A much-loved ship in the Royal Navy, the *Hood* was an icon. Such was the regard for HMS *Hood* that her destruction in the Denmark Strait on the morning of 24 May 1941 by the German battleship *Bismarck* created dismay across the world. Within minutes of entering battle, 'the Mighty *Hood*' was destroyed by a catastrophic explosion which had echoes of Jutland a quarter of a century earlier. Out of a crew of 1,418, only three survived. The sinking of the *Hood* was the single largest disaster ever sustained by the Royal Navy and marked a major turning point in the history of imperial Britain.

What follows is the story of HMS *Hood*—the life and death of a legendary battlecruiser. It is a story of both peace and war, yet it is not just the story of a ship, but of many men and an era. The initial chapters of this book are dedicated to the conception of the battlecruiser and focus on the deployment of battlecruisers during the First World War. In particular, the initial chapters focus on the first battlecruiser—HMS *Invincible*—for it is only through understanding the first battlecruiser that the Royal Navy's final battlecruiser may be understood. As Alan Coles has written, to 'understand the fate of HMS *Hood* is to understand the indecision of her planning and building, the clash of opinions in the Royal Navy, the failure of the Admiralty to implement suggestions to improve her and their inability to heed the lessons of Jutland. She was conceived too early, developed too late and died in battle outmoded by her enemies'.[2] The remainder of this book is dedicated to the career of HMS *Hood* and her service history with a focus on such events as her cruises around Europe and farther afield, notably the cruise of the Special Service Squadron, the Invergordon Mutiny, her service during the Second World War, and her catastrophic loss.

Over the course of the following pages, many of the ship's movements will be referenced, taken from the ship's logs held at the National Archives. For the sake of space and simplicity, every movement made by the *Hood* has not been referenced. These documents are, however, recorded in the bibliography.

1

From the *Dreadnought* to the *Invincible*

Following the routing of the combined French and Spanish Fleet at Trafalgar in 1805, the Royal Navy entered a period of over 100 years as the world's pre-eminent naval force. Such was the dominance of the Royal Navy that in the period between the Congress of Vienna—the conference of ambassadors of European States chaired by the Foreign Minister of the Austrian Empire, Klemens Wenzel von Metternich, held in Vienna from November 1814 to June 1815, designed to provide a long-term peace plan for Europe by the settling of issues that arose from the French Revolutionary and Napoleonic wars—and the turn of the century, the Royal Navy was engaged in one fleet battle (the Battle of Navarino, fought on 20 October 1827 during the Greek War of Independence) and one war (the Crimean). As such, by the time Britain declared war on Germany on 4 August 1914, it had been well over half a century since the Royal Navy had joined battle with another major power.[1]

During the second half of the nineteenth century, the British people began to take on a romantic pride in the Royal Navy, a pride that, according to David Howarth, 'had rather lapsed since the end of Napoleon's war'.[2] Indeed, the end of the nineteenth century was to be a great age for naval songs and verses; songs that glorified sailors. The age witnessed such compositions as 'Land of Hope and Glory', 'Rule Britannia', 'Drake's Drum', 'Admirals All', and 'The Old Superb'. These songs became popular numbers for gentlemen in musical events, in ladies' drawing rooms, and to working-class men in pubs.

However, Britain was coming to delude itself with regards to the Royal Navy. Britannia appeared to have ruled the waves for such a length of time that some drifted towards the idea that Britain had always ruled the waves and that she always would. As time passed by, 'people began to have blind faith in the navy's invincibility, and the blind faith infected the navy too. But as the century passed, the navy's supremacy was resting more and more on past prestige, and less on present power'.[3] It was during this period that the Royal Navy entered what has been described as a period of 'atrophy, marginalised by politicians and starved of funds during the years of peace and unchallenged British global supremacy'.[4] A sense of inertia prevailed, which was compounded by the prevailing attitudes of the upper echelons of the Navy. The Admiralty and the senior officers of the Royal Navy, weighed down by tradition and past successes, held continuity in much higher regard than ingenuity.

On 13 January 1901, then Vice-Admiral Sir John 'Jackie' Fisher wrote to the First Sea Lord, Lord Selborne, bemoaning the situation and complained that 'one of our cleverest and most experienced officers would be frightened to move a yard without orders in wartime'.[5] Such was the sense of inertia in the upper echelons of the Navy that in one instance when a practical suggestion was presented to a Sea Lord by a young lieutenant, the response was indignation: 'On what authority does this lieutenant forward such a proposal?'[6] The lieutenant in question would become Admiral Sir Doveton Sturdee, who would gain prominence thanks largely to the decisive victory of the Royal Navy over the Imperial German Navy on 8 December 1914 at the Battle of the Falkland Islands. The rise of Sturdee and officers like him demonstrated the move towards bold, initiative-taking officers that were championed by Fisher.

Fisher was a master of administration, a skill that was demonstrated during his tenure as the Director of Naval Ordnance, Admiral Superintendent of Portsmouth Dockyard, and then as Controller of the Navy. Fisher's skill was also adept at sea and was demonstrated in his operational roles first as Commander-in-Chief of the North American and West Indies Station, and then as commander of the Navy's most prestigious command: the Mediterranean.[7] According to Admiral Lord Beresford, during his tenure as Commander-in-Chief of the Mediterranean, Fisher transformed the Royal Navy squadron based there 'from a 12-knot Fleet with numerous breakdowns' into a '15-knot Fleet without breakdowns'.[8] Surrounded by a group of like-minded officers, Fisher set about implementing the kind of innovations that would serve to revolutionise the Royal Navy over the coming years, such as high-speed steaming exercises and gunnery trophies to increase accuracy.[9]

In 1902, Fisher was promoted to the position of Second Sea Lord where he gained direct responsibility for the training of the Navy's future officers. It was in this role in which he oversaw the opening of the first shore-based, custom-built training facility in the history of the Navy: Britannia Royal Naval College at Dartmouth. It was to be here that Fisher intended technical education to be improved and for the officer corps to become more flexible.

Further modifications were to follow, which included the development of wireless communications technology, the gunnery director finding system, the development of the submarine as a naval weapon and the establishment of a naval wing of the Royal Flying Corps. Nevertheless, despite these developments, it was to be the introduction of a new type of battleship that came to symbolise the reforms initiated by Fisher and which really caught the imagination of the public: the *Dreadnought*.

Laid down on 2 October 1905, and launched on 10 February 1906, christened with a bottle of Australian wine by King Edward VII, HMS *Dreadnought* was constructed at HM Dockyard, Portsmouth, which at the time was regarded as the fastest-building shipyard in the world. Fisher had set the goal of constructing the *Dreadnought* in a single year. In order to meet this goal, material needed for construction was stockpiled and a great deal of prefabrication undertaken before she was formally laid down on 2 October 1905. A year and a day after being formally laid down, HMS *Dreadnought* was taken to sea on 3 October 1906 for steam trials. Fifteen months after she was laid down, at a cost of £1,783,883, she was commissioned on 11 December 1906.[10] HMS *Dreadnought* was the first ship of her class and was the realisation of Fisher's ideas—an all big-gun warship that was faster and more powerful than any other vessel afloat. Armed with 12-inch guns and with belt armour up to 11 inches thick, she was capable of sailing at a very impressive 21 knots. The *Dreadnought* revolutionised battleship design and single-handedly rendered all other battleships constructed hitherto obsolete. HMS *Dreadnought* was not, however, the only all big-gun, fast capital ship under construction for the Royal Navy at the time.

During the spring of 1906, the first of three vessels sporting the same big-gun design as the dreadnought-type, but with significantly more speed was launched. This increase in speed was achieved by and large via the virtue of the removal of much of the armour plating that had been incorporated in the design of the *Dreadnought* and led to these vessels being referred to as fast armoured cruisers, and later as battlecruisers.

Admiral Sir John Fisher. (*Library of Congress, LC-B2- 3330-5*)

Fisher was obsessed with speed. In a letter dated 5 January 1901 to Lord Selborne, he stated that 'It is clearly necessary to have superiority of speed in order to compel your opponent to accept battle, or enable you to avoid battle and lead him away from his goal till it suits to fight him'.[11] Later that same month, Fisher again demonstrated his fondness for innovation and speed in a letter written to naval journalist and friend, Arthur White, regarding the potential offer of a directorship at Armstrong Whitworth's shipyard in Elswick, Newcastle that he had received:

> It's a place I should revel in, and I should immediately set to work to revolutionise the battleship, cruiser and destroyer on revolutionary principles—oil fuel, turbine propulsion, equal gunfire all round, greater speed than any existing vessel of their class ...[12]

Fisher was not alone in his adoration of speed. The editor of *Fighting Ships*, Fred T. Jane, argued in a paper presented at the Royal United Services Institute on 6 June 1902 that 'to cook our hare we have to catch him. Hence it logically follows that speed is more essential to us than any nation. We must have it at all costs, surely!'[13]

In order to understand the fascination that Fisher had with speed, one must first understand the strategic role then occupied by the Royal Navy. Britain was a nation reliant upon trade and had a global trading empire—the largest empire in history covering approximately a third of the world's surface. At the time, Britain was more active than any other power in exerting her will over extra-European regimes by means other than that of direct colonial role, or through her financial and commercial pre-eminence, such as in Argentina between 1880 and 1939. Indeed, no 'other colonial power aspired to the same degree of global influence or had enjoyed it. No other country derived such extensive benefits from its empire or undertook such far-flung military burdens to protect it'.[14] Coupled with this, Britain possessed the largest mercantile fleet afloat, which had to be protected. As such, the Royal Navy needed ships that were capable of overhauling and destroying any potential raiders and challengers to Britain's global supremacy.[15]

With the design and construction of HMS *Invincible*, a type of vessel had been created that, in essence, placed the guns of a battleship onto the hull of a cruiser. This enabled the *Invincible* to be fast enough to catch any raider harassing British shipping and to be powerful enough to sink said raider—with the exception of a battleship. A general breakdown of the *Invincible*'s specifications can be viewed in Chapter 4. Specifically, the battlecruiser was envisaged to undertake four roles: heavy reconnaissance; close support for the battle fleet; pursuit; and commerce protection. Owing to their power, the ships of the *Invincible*-class and subsequent battlecruisers could undertake a heavy reconnaissance, sweeping away the screen of enemy cruisers and close in and observe an enemy battle fleet before using their superior speed to retire. Within the Royal Navy's battle fleet, the battlecruisers could also be stationed at the end of the battle line where they would provide close support for the fleet, stopping enemy cruisers from harassing friendly battleships while also, if conditions permitted, harassing the enemy's battleships if they were engaged with battleships.

Therein lay the issue that was to envelope the battlecruiser for its entire existence; it was an issue that was succinctly and prophetically articulated in 1907 edition of the *Brassey Naval Annual*:

> The *Invincible* class have been given the armament of a battleship, their superiority in speed being compensated for by lighter protection … an admiral having *Invincibles* in his fleet will be certain to put them in the line of battle, where their comparatively light protection would be a disadvantage, and their high speed of no value.[16]

Not everyone, however, was so convinced. Those in favour of the battlecruiser concept countered claims such as that made above with two points: the first, since all capital ships were vulnerable to new weapons such as the torpedo, armour plating had lost some of its validity; second, because of the greater speed possessed by a battlecruiser, an Admiral could control the range from which he engaged the enemy.[17]

From early on, confusion surrounded the terminology used to refer to the new battleship-size cruisers. In late 1905, before construction had begun on the *Invincible*-class, a Royal Navy memorandum made reference to 'large armoured ships' as a term to classify both battleships and large cruisers. From October 1906, however, the Admiralty began to classify all armoured cruisers and post-*Dreadnought* battleships as 'capital ships'. The confusion was further compounded by Fisher who used the term 'dreadnought' to refer to both battleships pre- and post-*Dreadnought* and armoured cruisers together. Furthermore, the *Invincible*-class were, at the same time, themselves referred to as 'cruiser-battleships' and 'dreadnought cruisers'. The term 'battlecruiser' was first used by Fisher in 1908. Clarification was finally gained on 24 November 1911 when Admiralty Weekly Order No. 351 was issued. Order No. 351 stipulated that 'All cruisers of the "Invincible" and later types are for the future to be described and classified as "battle cruisers" to distinguish them from the armoured cruisers of earlier date'.[18]

In a letter to King Edward VII dated 4 October 1907, Fisher revealed the esteem in which he regarded the *Invincible*, remarking 'England has 7 Dreadnoughts and 3 "*Invincibles*" (In my opinion better than Dreadnoughts)'.[19] It was clear that Fisher regarded the *Invincible*, and indeed the battlecruiser as a whole, as crucial to the future success of the Royal Navy. With this in mind, it becomes necessary to analyse the design of HMS *Invincible* and the *Invincible*-class of battlecruisers in greater detail.

Fisher held armour with little regard, nor did he hold those who championed armour over speed and firepower in high regard, a view demonstrated in 1911 in a letter to the then First Lord of the Admiralty, Winston Churchill (including his own emphasis):

The first desideratum is <u>speed</u>! Your fools don't see it. They are always running around to see where they can put on a little more armour! ... You hit him first, you hit him hard and you keep on hitting. <u>That's your safety</u>! You don't get hit back! Well! That's the improved 13.5-inch gun! But disassociated from <u>dominating speed,</u> that gun is futile.[20]

Although armour was not paramount, the little armour that adorned the battlecruisers had to be of the highest quality. Around the turn of the century, a new, innovative type of armour plate was developed by the German firm Krupp. Krupp's innovation—cemented armour—represented a 25 per cent improvement over the previous Harvey armour thanks in large part to the addition of nickel-chrome steel alloys.[21]

A letter was sent on 24 November 1898 to Krupp written by Sir Andrew Noble, the director of Armstrong's, enquiring 'whether you are at liberty to communicate to us the Krupp system of manufacture, and, if so, upon what terms'.[22] Armstrong's took up production of cemented armour and it was fitted to all subsequent vessels, including HMS *Invincible*. The fact that the ships of the British Grand Fleet that faced those of the German High Seas Fleet at the Battle of Jutland had Krupp armour fitted to them was but only one example of the close pre-war relationship that existed between British and German industries; another was the use of Krupp fuses in some British shells, which were manufactured under a 1902 licencing agreement.[23]

It is clear that Fisher was not overly concerned with armour. In addition to his fascination with speed, he asserted: 'Hitting is the thing, not armour'.[24] As mentioned earlier, the *Invincible* and the *Invincible*-class of battlecruisers were fitted with far less armour plating than contemporary battleships. The *Invincible*'s belt (side) armour, was up to six inches thick, whereas the deck was only covered by up to two and a half inches of armour. The *Invincible*'s gun turrets were covered by seven inches of armour on the face side, but only two and a half inches on top. The barbette protection, which covered the trunk of the gun down into the ship, was covered by several inches of armour.[25]

What can be ascertained from these figures is that HMS *Invincible*, along with her sister ships, was substantially better protected against incoming fire from the side as opposed to plunging fire (fire from above). This was something that was in keeping with naval doctrine that had saw projectiles being fired into the sides of vessels—a tradition that dated back to the earliest days of naval warfare. However, given the extended range of newer, larger calibre guns, shells were more likely to hit a target from a higher angle. Projectiles fired in this manner had a greater velocity upon impact and, therefore, caused more damage. This combined with the thinner deck armour represented a significant problem with the *Invincible*'s design. This susceptibility to plunging fire was to have catastrophic repercussions when the ships of the Royal and Imperial German Navies met at Jutland in 1916.

In order to facilitate the high speeds that Fisher demanded, a revolutionary new type of engine was designed and fitted to the battlecruisers, which achieved the desired effect. On Tuesday, 4 August 1908, the *Invincible*'s sister ship, HMS *Indomitable*, arrived in Canada carrying His Royal Highness The Prince of Wales, later King George V. HMS *Indomitable* had begun the cruise straight from the builders' yard and would be fully completed upon her return.

The cruise provided the opportunity to test the speed of the new class of battlecruiser, and the Prince was so delighted with the *Indomitable*'s performance that he even took a turn at stoking, extolling that she was 'a grand success in every way. She is indeed a grand ship and the finest steamer I have ever seen'.[26] The *Indomitable*'s average speed of 21 knots beat the previous record for a warship, set in 1905, and was largely regarded as a triumph of the Parsons' turbines that equipped the ship.[27] Furthermore, Fisher journeyed to Chatham to check both the ship's logs and register to confirm the achievement for himself, and, such was his personal interest, even penned a letter to Parsons, congratulating him on the *Indomitable*'s performance.[28]

Parsons had first developed his marine steam turbine in the 1880s; however, it was not until the 1897 Naval Review held in celebration of Queen Victoria's Diamond Jubilee that it first came to the attention of the Royal Navy, and, indeed, the nation as a whole.

Designed by Charles Parsons in 1894, the *Turbinia* was an experimental craft constructed in order to demonstrate the potential of Parsons' steam turbines. With a long, narrow hull 100 feet long by 9 feet tall, the *Turbinia* was equipped with a single 1,000-hp steam turbine, which was expected to propel the vessel along at 30 knots or more. Launched on 2 August 1894, trials with the *Turbinia* started on 14 November. Initial testing produced disappointing results as the *Turbinia* only reached 19.7 knots. The source of this disappointment lay in the propeller, which it was found could not perform efficiently at 200 rpm. Two years of intensive work followed, during which time the effects of cavitation on high-speed propellers was discovered and overcome. The *Turbinia* was refitted to carry three steam turbines, each of which drove three propellers. The results were impressive, trials in December 1896 saw the *Turbinia* reach 29.6 knots. Following a number of slight modifications, she reached a speed of 32.7 knots in April 1897, making her the fastest vessel in the world.

The *Turbinia*'s most iconic moment occurred at the June 1897 Naval Review where she demonstrated the speed advantage accorded by steam turbines by travelling at over 30 knots between the lines of warships.[29] One of those who witnessed the display put on by the *Turbinia* at the Naval Review was naval architect Eustace Tennyson d'Eyncourt, who described the ship as 'appearing to be leaping from one wave to another' and making 'a tremendous impression on the Queen and everyone there, none of whom had seen anything like it before'.[30] The performance advantage of the *Turbinia* impressed the Admiralty, which placed orders for two turbine-powered torpedo boat destroyers HMS *Cobra* and *Viper*. The success of these vessels paved the way for the introduction of steam turbines the world over. The launching of HMS *Dreadnought* in 1906 saw her become the world's first turbine-powered battleship.[31] The predominance of steam turbine

The *Turbinia* on display at the Discovery Museum, Newcastle-upon-Tyne. (*Author's collection*)

power had arrived. While powering HMS *Dreadnought*, Parsons' turbines would also equip HMS *Invincible*, HMS *Indomitable*, and HMS *Inflexible* as well as some of the world's largest ocean liners.

In addition to a revolutionary propulsion system, the *Invincible* also sported a revolutionary all-big-gun format. She was armed with the same eight 12-inch guns carried by HMS *Dreadnought*. The eight guns were arranged in pairs in four turrets: one forward; one aft; and two amidships, slightly echeloned. While a successful and reliable weapon, the 12-inch calibre gun was quickly succeeded by the 13.5-inch gun, which equipped vessels of the *Lion*-class onwards.

The ability of the 12-inch gun to pierce enemy armour was, however, hampered by defects with the shells. If British shells hit armour obliquely, as was more often than not the case, they had a propensity to detonate prematurely, before fully piercing the armour.[32] Although this issue would later be rectified, the solution would come too late for the Battles of the Falkland Islands and Jutland.

Due to slower shell hoists, the *Invincible* had a slower rate of fire than German vessels. In an effort to increase the rate of fire, it became commonplace for charges to be left at various points between the magazine and the turret. In addition, magazine doors were often left open in combat, propped open by sacks of cordite.[33] The combination of poor charge handling practices and the highly flammable modified cordite used in British shells combined with the poorer deck and turret roof armour left the *Invincible* and the other ships of her class dangerously exposed—a vulnerability that would be demonstrated with devastating effects at Jutland.

Launched on 13 April 1907, HMS *Invincible* was constructed by Armstrong's Elswick Works in Newcastle-upon-Tyne.[34] Indeed, Armstrong's Elswick Works where the *Invincible* was constructed was located barely 3 miles from where Parsons' turbines were manufactured. A number of vessels that were to see action at Jutland were built along the banks of the Tyne including the battleships *Agincourt*, *Hercules*, and *Malaya*, the battlecruiser *Queen Mary*, and the cruiser *Hampshire* to name but a few.

The Elswick Works were not immune to the poor industrial relations that were endemic in heavy industry at the time. At the time of the *Invincible*'s launching, the north-east coast was facing the worst depression to hit the engineering and shipbuilding industries for fifteen years; the year 1908 would see tonnage levels down by nearly 30 per cent.[35] Strike action taken by shipwrights, drillers, and joiners, followed later by an engineers' strike caused the construction of *Invincible* to be delayed and can be seen to be lamented in the board minutes of the Elswick yard.[36] Such were the effects of the strike that a meeting of north-east shipbuilding employers came to the conclusion that unless the strikers resumed work, the strike-affected shipyards would have to close.[37]

Such was the gravity of the situation that the President of the Board of Trade, and future Prime Minister, David Lloyd-George was called in to negotiate a settlement to the dispute. The situation was further complicated by the number of different unions involved in the action, which made a single, comprehensive settlement much more difficult.[38] Finally, the strikers accepted a reduction in pay and returned to work.[39] The minutes from the Elswick Works describe the *Invincible* as having undergone the whole of its trials with most satisfactory results, and the ship was handed over to the Royal Navy on 15 February 1909 where she completed a twenty-four-hour trial with the Admiralty before proceeding to Portsmouth on 17 February.[40]

The Imperial German Navy took a keen interest in the construction of the *Invincible* and began designing its own battlecruiser. The *Von Der Tann* was laid down at the Blohm & Voss shipyard in Hamburg on 21 March 1908 and possessed several key advantages over the ships of the *Invincible*-class. The armour belt of the *Von Der Tann* was up to 10 inches thick, and with the addition of further armour plating on important areas (including the turrets), the ship's armour weighed in at 5,693 tons, compared to the 3,735 tons that the *Invincible* carried.[41]

The main armament of the *Von Der Tann* consisted of eight 11-inch guns. Due to her extra armour plating, she was to be slightly slower than the ships of the *Invincible*-class. However, the decision to sacrifice a small amount of speed and to equip smaller calibre guns proved to be a price worth paying to accommodate the extra armour as it resulted in the *Von Der Tann* being a better all-round vessel than the *Invincible*.[42]

The first battlecruiser: HMS *Invincible* was launched at Armstrong's Elswick Works on 13 April 1907. (*Author's collection*)

HMS *Invincible*. (*Author's collection*)

By the time that the *Von Der Tann* was launched in March 1909, it was too late to do anything to alter the next class of British battlecruisers that were under construction, the *Indefatigable*-class. The ships of the *Indefatigable*-class would carry the same armament as the ships of the *Invincible*-class, and because Fisher did not like to 'handicap a racehorse' as he put it, they were also equipped with the same levels of armour as the *Invincible*-class.[43] This pattern would continue, with the British believing in speed as the key to defence, and the Germans sacrificing a knot or two in return for better armour protection throughout subsequent classes of battlecruisers.

These differences in design ethos are something that will be examined further over the course of the next chapter, and how the design of the British and German battlecruisers contributed to the outcome of events at the Battle of Jutland.

2

The Battles of
the Falkland Islands and Jutland

It was at 6.33 p.m. on 31 May 1916 that a huge explosion erupted deep inside HMS *Invincible*, which tore the ship in half and sent the shattered remnants of the vessel and over 1,000 British sailors to their final resting place at the bottom of the North Sea. Having only just entered the fray, the loss of the mighty battlecruiser came as a shock to the British, although, as will become apparent, the loss of the *Invincible* had not been the first shock of the day.

The destruction of the *Invincible* came at the height of the battlecruiser action in what would prove to be by far the largest naval confrontation of the First World War, the Battle of Jutland. Eighteen months earlier, however, in December 1914, the *Invincible* and her sister ship the *Inflexible* had successfully engaged and destroyed a German naval squadron in the South Atlantic, and had suffered minimal damage in the process.

Over the course of this chapter, the confrontation in the South Atlantic around the Falkland Islands and Jutland will be explored to provide a clear understanding of the differing circumstances that led to both success and failure.

Having considered the conception, design and construction of HMS *Invincible*, it is now necessary to assess her performance, and that of the *Invincible*-class, in battle. In order to do this, two different battles will be examined: the Battle of the Falkland Islands, which occurred on 8 December 1914, and the Battle of Jutland, which took place between 31 May and 1 June 1916. It should be noted, however, that these two battles were not the only confrontations involving battlecruisers during the Great War; other engagements such as the Battle of Dogger Bank, which took place on 24 January 1915, provide an equally interesting study. However, it is the contrast in mission, tactics, and the outcome of the Battles of the Falkland Islands and Jutland that ultimately render them as the most rewarding comparative study.

The Battle of the Falkland Islands can be regarded as a brilliant naval victory for the British, achieved thanks to the deployment of the appropriate assets as well as to the use of considered tactics. This is not to say that the engagement was faultless, however, as this chapter will address some of the failings. Nevertheless, it was a decisive victory. At Jutland, by contrast, the loss of three battlecruisers

Vice-Admiral Sir David Beatty, commander of the Battlecruiser Squadron at Jutland. In December 1916, Beatty would succeed Jellicoe as the Commander-in-Chief of the Grand Fleet.

in relatively quick succession, with them having withstood relatively little punishment, sent shockwaves throughout the Royal Navy, the Admiralty in London, and the country at large. The loss of the second battlecruiser, the then pride of the Royal Navy HMS *Queen Mary* with the loss of 1,266 lives, prompted Admiral David Beatty, on the bridge of HMS *Lion*, to turn to his flag captain, Ernle Chatfield, and remark, 'There must be something wrong with our bloody ships today!'[1] One of the aims of this chapter is to consider whether or not this much-quoted remark was, in fact, accurate. Was there something wrong with the Royal Navy's battlecruisers that particular day?

An examination of both of these battles will provide a clearer insight into the chain of events that led to both the great success and great failure of the battlecruisers, allowing conclusions to be drawn regarding deficiencies in armour, problems with cordite storage, and shell effectiveness, as well as the tactical deployment of the battlecruisers as a whole.

On 1 November 1914, the British West Indies Squadron, under the command of Rear-Admiral Sir Christopher Craddock, was patrolling off the coast of Chile. Consisting of the armoured cruisers HMS *Good Hope* (Craddock's flagship) and HMS *Monmouth*, the light cruiser HMS *Glasgow*, and the armed merchantman HMS *Ontario*, Craddock's West Indies Squadron was hunting the German East Asia Squadron under the command of Vice-Admiral Maximillian von Spee. Von Spee commanded a formidable force of five modern vessels, which included the two armoured cruisers SMS *Gneisenau* and *Scharnhorst*, and the light cruisers *Dresden*, *Leipzig*, and *Nürnberg*.

Craddock and von Spee's squadrons joined battle with each other off the Chilean coast near the city of Coronel. Outmatched and outgunned, the West Indies Squadron was annihilated. A large number of British sailors, including Craddock, lost their lives, with only HMS *Glasgow* and HMS *Ontario* making good their escape. After the battle, von Spee sailed the German East Asia Squadron into the Chilean port of Valparaiso in order to exact repairs. Despite the adulation from German expatriates, von Spee was far from jubilant. A great naval victory had been won, but at what cost? Having expended a large amount of ammunition that he could not replace, and knowing that the British were certain to send a more powerful squadron to hunt down his own squadron and to avenge Craddock, von Spee remarked, somewhat prophetically, that the flowers presented to him by the locals would do nicely for his grave.[2]

It was at the same time that, in London, Fisher, now aged seventy-four, was re-appointed First Sea Lord. Back in this position, Fisher's first act was to remove Vice-Admiral Doveton Sturdee from his position as Chief of the Naval Staff, snarling:

> You, Sturdee, were responsible for this whole bloody mess, now you can go and clean it up. And don't come back until your orders have been carried out to the letter—until von Spee and his squadron have been wiped off the face of the earth![3]

Sturdee subsequently raised his flag in the *Invincible* whereupon, along with HMS *Indomitable*, he proceeded towards the South Atlantic on 10 November at the impressive mean speed of 18 knots.[4] Rendezvousing with the other ships that were to make up his squadron, Sturdee proceeded to steam to the Falkland Islands where they arrived on 7 December, and commenced coaling prior to beginning the search for von Spee and the German East Asia Squadron.

In addition to the *Invincible* and the *Indomitable*, Sturdee had the armoured cruisers *Carnarvon*, *Cornwall*, and *Kent*, as well as the light cruisers *Bristol* and *Glasgow* at his disposal. Moreover, the old, pre-dreadnought battleship HMS *Canopus* had been grounded in Port Stanley as a guard ship. The *Canopus* had been grounded in a position where she was out of sight, but was able to fire her 12-inch guns over the headland and out to sea.

The German decision to attack the Falkland Islands was aimed at depriving the Royal Navy of a valuable coaling station and harbour in which to take on supplies and to conduct minor repairs. During the morning of 7 December, von Spee received a message from a German agent in Port Stanley that the harbour was empty of warships. At the time that the message was transmitted, the intelligence contained within it was true, but unfortunately for von Spee, this was no longer to be the case upon his arrival.[5]

On the morning of 8 December, as the *Gneisenau* approached Port Stanley, her gunnery commander reported seeing tripod masts over the headland. Julius Maerker, the *Gneisenau*'s captain, knew that tripod masts meant one of only two things: the presence of dreadnoughts or battlecruisers. Confident that there were no dreadnoughts south of the Mediterranean, Maerker dismissed the sighting, reporting to von Spee the probable presence of three *County*-class cruisers, one light cruiser, and two possibly pre-dreadnought battleships.[6]

Conscious of his lack of a friendly port in which to repair possible battle damage, von Spee ordered Maerker to rejoin the squadron, confident that they could easily outrun the lumbering British ships. It was only when the British ships emerged from the harbour and took up the chase that the Germans noticed that two of the British vessels were gaining ground. With all binoculars trained on the pursuing ships, the unmistakable shapes of the *Invincible* and the *Indomitable* loomed into view and the challenge presented to the German sailors became painfully apparent, as Commander Pochhammer of the *Gneisenau* noted with some despondency:

> The possibility, even probability, that we were being chased by English battlecruisers ... this was a bitter pill to swallow. We choked a little ... the throat contracted and stiffened, for it meant a life and death struggle, or rather a fight ending in honourable death.[7]

Such was his confidence in victory, Sturdee ordered his men to lunch; he would engage von Spee on his own terms, when good and ready.[8] The British had a weight of shell of 5,100 pounds, compared to the German 1,957 pounds, and held the advantage in speed, which enabled them to stay within their maximum range of 9.31 miles, but outside the maximum range of the Germans, which was 7.6 miles.[9] This served to allow Sturdee to use his battlecruisers as Fisher had intended when the battlecruiser concept was first conceived, using their powerful guns to destroy the enemy while using their superior speed to pick and choose the terms of engagement.

Von Spee was more than aware that he could not outrun the British battlecruisers; therefore, in what can be described as a valiant attempt to save part of his squadron, he ordered his cruisers to make good their escape while the *Gneisenau* and the *Scharnhorst* turned to engage the British. The result was as predicted as the *Scharnhorst*, followed two hours later by the *Gneisenau*, succumbed to the pounding unleashed by the British, slowly capsized, and sank. In due course, the light cruisers of von Spee's East Asia Squadron were in turn hunted down and sunk by the British, albeit three months after the Battle of the Falkland Islands in the case of the *Dresden*.[10]

Despite appearing to be, on the face of it, an overwhelming military success for the British, the Battle of the Falkland Islands did, in fact, yield some worrying questions that were in need of answers. Both the *Scharnhorst* and the *Gneisenau* were armed with 8-inch guns and were fitted with 6 inches of belt and between 1.5 and 2.5 inches of deck armour. During the course of the battle, both the *Invincible* and the *Indomitable* expended almost 600 shells out of a complement of 640.[11] This raises the question as to why so many 12-inch shells were needed to sink two relatively poorly armoured vessels. Range finding by British gunners serves to explain the expenditure of some of the shells. Another possible explanation for the high number of shells expended by the British could also be attributed to the incredible amount of smoke that was being produced by the two pursing battlecruisers.

The British ships added fuel oil to the coal when steaming full ahead, and as such, produced copious amounts of thick black smoke. This smoke, while not interfering with the sight of the foremost 'A' turret, did, however, cause serious issues for 'P', 'Q' and 'X' turrets. In a telegram sent to the Admiralty on 2 January 1915, Sturdee reported that '*Inflexible* much hindered by *Invincible* funnels smoke, and [that] control over fire in both ships was seriously hampered by smoke from battle cruisers necessitating alteration of course'.[12] Upon receiving the telegram, a subcommittee concluded that the excessive smoke that was being produced was due to 'untrained staff', as opposed to the practice of adding fuel oil to coal, and subsequently suggested that training should be improved and that the Commander-in-Chief of the Grand Fleet should release a brief statement on its use.[13]

Although the issues regarding British shells have been examined in the previous chapter, it is nevertheless worth exploring why the German ships did not explode under such a tremendous barrage of fire. At least part of the answer lies in the type of powder charge used, and the brass cartridges in which it was housed.

One key difference that existed between German and British powder was that German powder tended to burn when receiving fire, not to explode as British powder did. Furthermore, German charge cases were made of brass whereas British charge cases were made out of silk. This meant that an impact such as that which was to result in the sinking of HMS *Invincible* may not have proved fatal in the case if a German vessel. A case in point is the damage inflicted to the German battlecruiser SMS *Seydlitz* at the Battle of Dogger Bank. Having been hit by a British heavy shell, hot fragments of metal penetrated her magazine and ignited a fire that killed everyone in the magazine. Crucially, however, the charges did not explode; a similar hit on a British vessel would almost certainly have resulted in its destruction.[14]

Providing further weight to the argument, survivors of the *Gneisenau* stated that although shocking injuries had occurred on the main and upper decks, such as heads and limbs being blown clean off, no fires whatsoever occurred on board, and no shells penetrated the engine or boiler rooms.[15]

Given this disparity, there were indeed lessons to be learned from the battle. A report produced for the Naval Ordnance Department remarked that the direction and fire discipline of the Germans was excellent, and that plunging fire was very effective at long range.[16] Moreover, it was proposed to issue a Gunnery Order at once 'to the effect that experience has shewn [*sic.*] the greatest danger of allowing cordite to cumulate in gun positions and causing severe fires, this accumulation should on no account be allowed'.[17] Whether or not the recommendations were operationalised is something that shall be analysed.

The *Invincible* and the *Inflexible* seen from HMS *Kent* during the pursuit of Von Spee's squadron in the Battle of the Falkland Islands. Note the thick black smoke that is beginning to build up during the chase.

The *Invincible* giving chase during the Battle of the Falkland Islands. Note the copious amounts of thick black smoke resulting from the practice of adding fuel oil to coal. While not hindering 'A' turret, the smoke would hinder 'P', 'Q', and 'X' turrets. (*BritishBattles.com*)

Regardless of the debate surrounding the strategic outcome of the Battle of Jutland, the destruction of three battlecruisers was a cause of both great shock and concern for the Admiralty. In the aftermath of the battle, both the official report of the battle and the subsequent commissions sought to establish the reasons behind the losses and attempted to put in place systems to prevent them from being repeated. The manifestation of these processes was HMS *Hood*, the fate of which served as a litmus test for the changes made to battlecruiser design and to the future viability of the battlecruiser as a whole.

In this, it is necessary to investigate and understand the reports of the officers involved in the Battle of Jutland. Therefore, it is necessary to examine the reports of Admiral John Jellicoe, Beatty, d'Eyncourt, and Chatfield alongside statements made by the survivors of the *Invincible* and the *Queen Mary*, as well as those of the commanding officers of HMS *Indomitable* and HMS *Inflexible* in order to produce a more complete understanding of the battlecruiser action.

In the wake of the Battle of Jutland, a number of reports were commissioned on a variety of subjects including battlecruiser deployment, actions when meeting enemy forces, and design and protection from plunging fire, culminating in recommendations for design alterations to be made to future battlecruisers. These reports, their conclusions, and the orders issued as a result of the recommendations made in the reports are something that will be examined alongside the issues surrounding the storage of cordite and its use.

In Admiral Jellicoe's report to the Admiralty, his praise for the actions of his officers and men was lavish: 'The conduct of the officers and men throughout the day and night actions were entirely beyond praise … On all sides it was reported to me that the glorious traditions of the past were most worthily upheld'.[18]

Subsequently, Jellicoe went on to make some interesting points. The ships of the 5th Battle Squadron which were attached to Beatty's Battlecruiser Squadron had a top speed of 24 knots, making them the fastest battleships in the world at the time. However, while sailing away from the German battleships *König* and *Kaiser* to lead them into the Grand Fleet, they were unable to increase the distance between themselves and the enemy despite the German ships being reported as having a top speed not in excess of 21 knots. This 'unpleasant surprise' was recognised by Jellicoe to have 'considerable effect on the conduct of future operations'.[19]

Jellicoe, after making this statement, went on to tackle the brutal truth that in the initial action, five German battlecruisers were able to successfully engage six British battlecruisers, successfully managed to hold their own when the British battlecruisers were joined by four *Queen Elizabeth*-class battleships, and successfully managed to sink two British battlecruisers without loss to themselves. In this initial report, Jellicoe attributed this fact to 'indifferent armour protection, particularly regarding turret armour and deck plating', as well as the 'disadvantageous lighting conditions' faced by Beatty's ships.[20]

Both the accuracy and rate of fire of the German vessels impressed Jellicoe, especially during the night action, leading him to remark, 'I am reluctantly compelled to the opinion that under night conditions we have a good deal to learn

Above: HMS *Invincible* blowing up at the Battle of Jutland. (*Author's collection*)

Right: Admiral Sir John Jellicoe, the Commander-in-Chief of the Grand Fleet from 4 August 1914 to November 1916 when he was appointed as the First Sea Lord. (*Library of Congress, LC-B2- 6462-7*)

Badly damaged and with her bow almost submerged as a result of shell and torpedo hits, the German battlecruiser *Seydlitz* limps home following the battle of Jutland. (*NH 59637, US Naval History and Heritage Command*)

The *Seydlitz* at Wilhelmshaven following Jutland. Jellicoe would later remark on the ability of five German battlecruisers to successfully engage six British battlecruisers and four battleships while being able to hold their own and sink two British battlecruisers without loss.

from them'.[21] In reply, the Admiralty was in agreement with Jellicoe's appraisal of the battle and lavished praise upon him, his officers and his sailors.[22]

What was perhaps crucial, however, Jellicoe reported that while there was no evidence that deficient armour resulted in enemy shells penetrating the magazines, there could be no doubt that the amount of cordite that lay exposed aboard the ships was enormous. He went on to attribute this lax handling to the lack of efficient control of ammunition parties due to the unavoidable stringency in officers.[23] This statement from Jellicoe implies that had there been more officers then perhaps the cordite would not have been stowed in such an unsafe manner, thus appearing to attribute the loss of the ships, in contradiction to his earlier praise, to the unprofessional behaviour of the men.

Finally, Jellicoe argued that 'the most unfortunate result of the battle has possibly been to give rise to the false idea as to the necessity and value of armour protection'.[24] In making this remark, Jellicoe revealed himself to be a follower of Fisher's doctrine of speed over armour as the best form of defence, and as such, he did not blame the design of the ships, but the poor cordite handling for their loss.

The Director of Naval Construction, Sir Eustace Tennyson d'Eyncourt, in his report argued against what he saw as the prevailing impression throughout the Fleet that the battlecruisers were lost due to shells penetrating the magazine. In particular, d'Eyncourt took issue with the report made by the commander of the First Battlecruiser Squadron, Rear-Admiral Osmond de Beauvoir Brock, which stated that the *Queen Mary* was destroyed by plunging fire that penetrated her magazine. In defence against Rear-Admiral Brock's report and the prevailing impression throughout the navy, d'Eyncourt argued that there were very few cases of shells, or parts of shells, penetrating protected areas such as the machinery, despite these areas covering much greater areas than the magazines.[25] In summation, d'Eyncourt was concerned, as was Jellicoe, that this misconception would lead to additional armour being fitted to ships, which went against the traditional maxim of British warship design—that the best defence was a superior offence.[26] D'Eyncourt's support for maintaining the status quo regarding the design of British warships was hardly surprising given his role in overseeing their production—a role that would later include the construction of HMS *Hood*.

Beatty, in his report, detailed the actions of the battlecruisers and escort vessels under his command. In an attempt to gain a more accurate picture of the enemy's strength, the light cruiser HMS *Galatea* launched a seaplane to investigate. Such use of aviation provides an insight into the beginnings of naval air power and the benefits of modern technology in the navy—a fact that was not lost on Beatty, who remarked 'seaplanes under such circumstances are of distinct value'.[27]

Beatty reported that, at 4 p.m., HMS *Indefatigable* was hit by three shells falling together on the outer edge of the upper deck in line with the aft turret. Following an explosion, the *Indefatigable* fell out of line, where she was struck once more, capsized, and disappeared beneath the waves.[28] Beatty went on to note how eight minutes after the loss of the *Indefatigable*, at the extreme range of 20,000 yards, the 5th Battle Squadron opened fire, causing the enemy fire to slacken.[29]

Sir Eustace Tennyson d'Eyncourt
(*Library of Congress, LC-B2- 5921-6*)

Given the effectiveness of this fire, the distance to which the 5th Battle Squadron had been allowed to fall behind seems unfortunate. Admiral Sir Reginald Bacon went further; he held Beatty's failure to consolidate his forces responsible for the battlecruisers paying a heavy price, and the nation missing what should have been an annihilating victory.[30]

At 4.26 p.m., Beatty reported a violent explosion erupting from the *Queen Mary*, enveloping the ship in grey smoke, after which it disappeared beneath the waves. According to Captain Henry Pelly of HMS *Tiger*, the *Queen Mary* was struck by a salvo abreast of 'Q' turret directly preceding the explosion, and when the *Tiger* passed through the smoke some thirty seconds later, nothing remained of the *Queen Mary*.[31] The speed at which the *Queen Mary* sank suggests that the ship was subjected to an explosion of such catastrophic power that only the detonation of one or more of the magazines could be responsible. This theory is supported by the highest ranking of the seventeen survivors from the *Queen Mary*—Midshipman Jocelyn Latham Storey, who had been stationed inside 'Q' turret and reported a gap of approximately four minutes between the initial impact and explosion of 'Q' turret, and a second, far larger explosion that threw him into the water and left nothing of the ship.[32]

Captain Chatfield, Beatty's Flag-Captain aboard HMS *Lion*, in listing the officers and men he deemed worthy of special praise, singled out, among others, the commanders of 'A', 'B', and 'X' turrets for their ability to keep the guns firing at an impressive rate throughout the course of the battle, firing 321 rounds in total.[33] The importance placed upon rate of fire is consistent with the previously discussed naval doctrine of the time. It is, however, the exploits of Major Francis Harvey that received Chatfield's praise above all others. In his remarks, Chatfield readily acknowledged that had Harvey not acted as he did then the *Lion* would have been lost.[34] The *Lion* was struck by a German shell that penetrated 'Q' turret and blew the face plate off the face of the turret, which served to kill or wound everyone inside. The shell started a fire that ignited eight propellant charges. Harvey, recognising the danger posed by the flames, ordered the magazine to be flooded. The charges burned violently and killed most of the magazine and shell room crews. The gas pressure severely buckled the magazine doors and it is likely that had the magazine not been flooded then it too would have detonated.

Commander Hubert E. Dannreuther was the highest ranking of the six survivors from the sinking of the *Invincible*. Dannreuther observed that no appreciable damage had been inflicted on the ship until a shell struck 'Q' turret, bursting inside and blowing the turret roof off. However, it was the second, far larger explosion that sealed the *Invincible*'s fate, indicating as it did the detonation of 'Q' magazine, which resulted in the ship breaking in half and sinking within ten to fifteen seconds.[35] That the second explosion was not instantaneous implies that the shell itself did not penetrate the magazine—something that supports d'Eyncourt's report in which he denied that enemy shells were capable of breaching the magazines of the battlecruisers—but that the detonation of the shell caused a flash that travelled down to the magazine. Such was the catastrophic force of the second explosion that, when the smoke and mist cleared, the bow and stern sections of the shattered *Invincible* could be seen protruding from the water, standing as if to attention on the seabed.

Several key issues were raised by the reports of those involved in the battlecruiser action at Jutland. Firstly, it is clear that the technical specifications of the German vessels attributed by the Admiralty was incorrect. The underestimation of speed that the German vessels possessed presented a serious tactical problem to the British, as the future attachment of fast battleships such as the 5th Battle Squadron to the battlecruiser fleet would nullify the battlecruisers' best defence: their speed. The removal of the extremely well-armed and protected 5th Battle Squadron would deprive the battlecruiser squadrons of much-needed support when engaging enemy battlecruisers—a point that was underlined by Beatty when he remarked, 'There is the unfortunate fact that our ships blow up after only a short period of punishment whereas the enemy's ships never do'.[36]

Secondly, the issue of cordite storage was raised by Jellicoe, and the consequences of the resultant flash were reported by Beatty, Storey and Dannreuther. These were issues that were to be addressed following Jutland, although to what degree of success these issues were addressed will be addressed shortly.

Finally, the issue of insufficient armour protection was not regarded by any of the officers in their reports as being of paramount importance. Indeed, Jellicoe and d'Eyncourt went so far as to say that they hoped that the addition of supplementary armour would not take place. In the aftermath of Jutland, the Admiralty convened a conference entitled 'Tactical and Strategical Questions Arising from the Action on 31 May 1916'.[37] One of the reports that the conference brought forth was entitled 'Action to be taken by Battlecruiser Fleet on Meeting Enemy Forces'.[38] It was the wording, and the apparent implications of this report, that was to provoke a furious debate between Beatty on the one side and Jellicoe and the Admiralty on the other:

> The Battlecruiser Fleet and any vessels attached to it when ordered South, is to avoid becoming seriously engaged with superior forces until the Battlefleet is within supporting distance, unless the Admiralty consider the circumstances sufficiently urgent to render a different course necessary, in which case their Lordships will give instructions directly to Vice-Admiral Commanding, Battlecruiser Fleet.[39]

In a letter to Jellicoe, Beatty demonstrated his frustration with what he considered to be confusing and unnecessary orders. He queried exactly what was meant by the term 'superior force', and in what conditions would an engagement be acceptable.[40] He went on to argue the case for the 5th Battle Squadron to remain attached to the Battlecruiser Fleet, as to do so would lessen the risk to the battlecruisers.

To further urge the point, Beatty claimed that had it not been for the presence of the 5th Battle Squadron at Jutland, then the battlecruisers would 'either have been destroyed or had to haul off'.[41] Finally, Beatty contested that it was prescriptive orders such as these that had allowed the SMS *Goeben* to escape the shadowing HMS *Indefatigable* and *Indomitable* and to reach the Dardanelles during the very early days of the war.[42] Beatty believed that his judgement and discretion were under question, and that the orders from the Admiralty could result in the loss of opportunities of the greatest value, which might never occur again.[43]

In reply, Jellicoe again reiterated to Beatty that the safety of the Battlecruiser Fleet lay in its speed, and as such the addition of the 5th Battle Squadron would 'present a source of distinct embarrassment and risk'.[44] He argued that it was, in fact, this speed that allowed the Battlecruiser Fleet to remain engaged with the German scouting forces while staying out of range of their battleships.[45] Then, in what appeared to be a damming rebuke, Jellicoe suggested that perhaps any misconceptions on Beatty's part were due to the use of the term 'Battlecruiser Fleet' to describe the force under his command:

> This nomenclature may be taken to imply that it is a force distinct from, and not an adjunct to, the battlefleet and that, owing to its advanced position, it is expected to fulfil the role of a fast battle squadron and not that of a powerful scouting force possessing a speed which enables it to accept or refuse action with an enemy possessing no force of equal power which can compel it to accept action.[46]

The argument was ultimately settled by the Admiralty, which came down overwhelmingly in Jellicoe's favour, stating that the order freed Beatty from subsequent criticism if he decided not to engage a superior force.[47] That the Battlecruiser Fleet was not to act as an independent force, nor travel too far ahead of the main battle fleet served to annul the tactical principles upon which Beatty had always acted.[48]

For such a debate to have occurred between two of the most senior officers in the Navy demonstrates that even in 1916, two years into the Great War, the most effective tactical deployment of Britain's battlecruisers was still a highly contested issue.

Following the loss of the battlecruisers at Jutland, changes were made to both the tactics and design to be used on both existing and future vessels. With regards to the design, the catastrophic manner in which the three battlecruisers were destroyed meant that this was more than sheer bad luck; a fundamental problem existed with Britain's battlecruisers. This was not, however, one individual problem, but a series of issues that, once combined, led to such grievous losses.

The penetration of the turret armour, combined with the resultant flash, the copious amounts of cordite stored outside of the magazines, and the lack of flash protection were all issues that needed to be addressed. As was reported by d'Eyncourt, the magazines were relatively safe from plunging fire, but not invulnerable. It is known, however, that as the charges could only be passed to the handling room with the magazine door open, the doors were often kept permanently open during action in order to expedite a rapid rate of fire.[49] In light of the sinking of the battlecruisers, charges were no longer allowed to be removed from the magazine until it was absolutely necessary, and magazine doors were to remain closed when possible.[50]

In their final conclusion, the Admiralty authorised the installation of old-fashioned fearnought (fireproof) shutters in the turret trunks.[51] Finally, 1 inch of extra armour was to be fitted over the middle deck armour above the magazines.[52]

In conclusion, three main problem areas were cited as existing with the battlecruisers: flash protection, cordite handling procedures, and armour. As a result, both technical and tactical changes were made to the Battlecruiser Fleet in the weeks and months following the Battle of Jutland.

Although other battlecruisers entered service after Jutland, such as those of the *Renown*- and *Courageous*-classes, it was with HMS *Hood* that the lessons of Jutland were to become apparent.

3

Construction

The contract for constructing the battlecruiser that would become HMS *Hood* was awarded to the John Brown Works at Clydebank. The John Brown Works is a contender for the title of the world's most famous shipyard. During its lifetime, the John Brown yard produced numerous ships, the names of which resonate to this day and include the battlecruisers *Hood*, *Tiger*, and *Renown*, the aircraft carrier HMS *Indefatigable* and the battleships *Barham*, *Duke of York*, and *Vanguard* to name but a small selection. To this list of warships can be added the names of liners like the RMS *Aquitania*, *Windsor Castle*, *Empress of Britain*, and *Lusitania*, and of course the Cunard queens—the *Queen Mary*, *Queen Elizabeth*, and *Queen Elizabeth 2*.

The story of John Brown & Co. began in Anderston in 1847 when the brothers James and George Thomson opened the Clyde Bank Foundry. Four years after opening the Foundry, the brothers opened what they called the Clyde Bank Iron Shipyard at nearby Cessnock and launched their first ship the SS *Jackal* the following year. The Clyde Bank Iron Shipyard quickly established a reputation in building prestigious passenger ships. The brothers suffered an acrimonious split that saw George take over the shipbuilding end of the association while James Thomson started a new business. George Thomson died in 1866 at the age of fifty and was subsequently succeeded by his sons, James and George. The two brothers were faced with the compulsory purchase of their shipyard by the Clyde Navigation Trust, which wanted the land to construct the new Princes' Dock (now the Pacific Quay) whereupon they established a new shipyard down river at Barns O'Clyde near the village of Dalmuir. This was an inspired site for a shipyard, sitting at the confluence of the River Cart with the River Clyde which allowed for the launching of large ships. The Thomson iron foundry and engineering works soon moved to the site and James Thomson became the first provost of Clydebank.

The company faced intermittent financial difficulties but succeeded in developing a reputation based on engineering quality and innovation. The shipyard grew rapidly, which, combined with its ancillary works, and the construction of housing for the workers, resulted in the creation of a new town that took its name from the shipyard from which it grew: Clydebank. In 1899, the Sheffield steelmaker

John Brown bought the Clydebank yard for £923,255 3s 3d (approximately £108,069,184.94 today).[1] So began a new chapter in the yard's history under the name John Brown and Company. The Works comprised two main areas: the shipyard, which employed somewhere in the region of 7,000 men; and the engine works where the propulsion machinery and engines were constructed. At the engine works, John Brown employed between 3,000 and 4,000 people.

The immediate origins of HMS *Hood* can be traced back to before Jutland—to a note sent by the Controller of the Navy, Admiral Sir Frederick Tudor, to d'Eyncourt in October 1915. In the note, Tudor requested a series of designs for an experimental battleship based on the *Queen Elizabeth*-class, incorporating the latest advances in underwater protection and seakeeping. Central to the brief on the experimental battleship was a higher freeboard and a shallower draught than previous vessels, features that it was believed would permit more effective operation under wartime loads, but which would at the same time lessen the threat to the vessel posed by underwater damage.

The most prevalent problem that the designers sought to overcome was the combination of low freeboard and high draught. Owing to increased wartime loads resulting from ships being loaded out with extra provisions, fuel, ammunition, and personnel, many vessels were operating at a heavier weight than had originally been envisaged. This additional weight resulted in several issues. Owing to the increase in weight, many ships now sat much lower in the water with the result that in heavy seas, their secondary armament batteries were frequently awash. This in turn often made the guns unusable and reduced the vessel's firepower. Another unwanted result was that the vessel became poor at seakeeping as vast amounts of seawater penetrated the hull around the openings for the gun batteries. The water inside the hull had the negative effect of increasing the weight of the ship thus causing it to ride still lower in the water. The high draught that resulted from the increases in weight seriously degraded the ability of some vessels to operate in shallower waters. As a result, d'Eyncourt and his design team were instructed to ensure that the new vessel incorporated a high freeboard, low draught, and had a secondary armament that was mounted high up. To further compound the work of the designers, the new vessel had to be capable of sailing at 30 knots and was to be armed with 15-inch guns. The design was to 'take the armament, armour and engine power of *Queen Elizabeth* as the standard and build around them in a hull which would draw as little water as was considered practicable and safe, and which should embody all the latest protection and improvements against underwater attack'.[2]

Between November 1915 and January 1916, d'Eyncourt oversaw the evolution of five designs, the most promising of which had a greatly enlarged hull and beam, necessary in order to ensure the required reduction in draught. These studies were rejected by Jellicoe in a lengthy memorandum in January 1916. While the Royal Navy had a marked superiority over the German High Seas Fleet, it did not, in fact, have an answer to the High Seas Fleet's large, 13.8-inch gun *Mackensen*-class of battlecruiser, which, at the time, were under construction. Accordingly,

February 1916 saw six further designs produced that, while based on earlier studies highlighting an enlarged hull and beam to reduce draught, emphasised speed over protection. Of the six designs produced in February 1916, one was selected for further development, which in itself resulted in a further two designs being produced in March. It was the second of these designs, 'Design B', which received the approval of the Admiralty on 7 April 1916, and upon which the ship that was to become HMS *Hood* was based.[3]

The design approved by the Admiralty was named the *Admiral*-class battlecruiser. On 13 April, the Admiralty agreed to the production of four *Admiral*-class vessels, to be named 'Anson', 'Hood', 'Howe', and 'Rodney'. The order for the vessel that would become HMS *Hood* was acquired by John Brown at Clydebank. The below table outlines the basic details of the ships of the *Admiral*-class including their namesake, the contracted builder, and the year the keel was laid.

Ship	Builder	Namesake	Laid Down
The *Anson*	Armstrong Whitworth, Elswick	Admiral of the Fleet George Anson	9 November 1916
The *Hood*	John Brown & Co., Clydebank.	Admiral Samuel Hood	1 September 1916
The *Howe*	Cammell Laid, Birkenhead	Admiral of the Fleet Richard Howe	16 October 1916
The *Rodney*	Fairfield, Govan	Admiral George Brydges Rodney	9 October 1916

The *Hood* was a large warship; indeed, at the time of her construction, she was the largest warship ever built for the Royal Navy and was the largest ship in the world. At 860 feet 7 inches (262.3 metres) in length, she would be the largest ship to serve with the Royal Navy until the commissioning of the *Queen Elizabeth*-class aircraft carrier HMS *Queen Elizabeth* in 2017. Designed to incorporate the lessons learned from Jutland, she was considered the very embodiment of British naval might.[4]

It has often been written that the keel of the vessel that would become HMS *Hood* was laid just as Beatty's battlecruisers sailed into action at Jutland. This is, however, nothing more than a legend. In fact, work did not begin on ship No. 460, as she was referred to, until 1 September 1916. Then, as now, the building of a capital ship was a challenging endeavour and was a process that required the skills and labour of countless men and women across Britain.

As will have previously been noted, the design of the ship began with a brief from the Admiralty to the Director of Naval Construction who, with the assistance

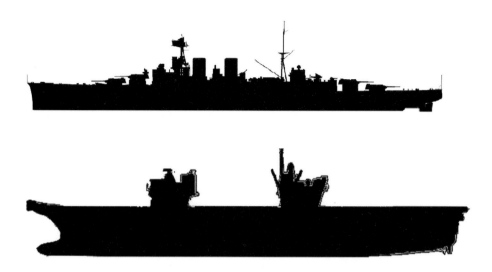

Comparison in size between HMS *Hood* and HMS *Queen Elizabeth*. (*Author's collection*)

of his team, began to calculate the proportions and characteristics of the hull as well as the balance of the armament, armour, and propulsion that would all govern the design. After a provisional hull design had been worked out, a model was produced that was subjected to tank tests at the Admiralty Experimental Works at Halsar, near Portsmouth. From these tests, the centres of gravity, metacentric heights, buoyancy, wave resistance along with the optimum shape of the propellers and underwater surfaces were all measured and calculated. Following this, detailed plans showing the arrangement of armour and machinery spaces alongside the structure, dimensions and projected weight of the completed vessel were produced which, when approved by the Admiralty Board, were sent to the contracted shipyard so that copies could be made and working drawings produced.[5]

With the construction of previous vessels, it had been usual for the armament and machinery contractors to produce their own working drawings. In the case of the *Hood*, however, things were different as the Admiralty placed a greater reliance on the draughtsmen at John Brown and Co. than had hitherto been the norm. Work on ship No. 460 began in the mould loft in John Brown's shipyard, a room over 375 feet in length, on the floor of which the frames for the ship were traced in full size on to black scrieve boards. Each scrieve board contained not only the shape of the frame but also had marked the positions of every bolt, rivet, buttock line, sheer line and deck to which it would attach. The scrieve boards were taken to the plate shops where metal for frames was selected, measured, and cut before being heated and bent until their shape conformed perfectly to the prescribed shapes. With this completed, ship fitters began the process of punching holes in the plates so that ever bar and frame reached the No. 3 slipway ready to be riveted into place. Meanwhile, beams were imported into the correct shape and moulds produced for major components.

Despite the assertion from senior officers that the battlecruiser did not require increased armour, just a matter of weeks after the Battle of Jutland, d'Eyncourt authorised a series of changes to the design of the *Hood*.[6] D'Eyncourt submitted a revised version of 'Design B' on 5 July 1916, which was accepted on 4 August. While the main armament was to remain unchanged, the main changes were to be with regards to armour protection. Belt armour was increased from 8 inches to 12 inches, while armour over the barbettes was increased from 9 to 12 inches. The angled 12-inch belt armour now provided the equivalent of 15 inches of horizontal armour while a 460-foot-long bulge packed with steel tubing offered protection against a torpedo attack that was the equal of any prior to the Second World War. Vertical protection, however, saw relatively little improvement, and was no more than 2.5-inches, despite an addition of 3,100 tons to the *Hood*'s displacement. This protection might have proved sufficient had the magazines not been placed over the shell room as was the norm in British designs at the time.[7]

Jutland and the loss of the *Indefatigable*, the *Queen Mary*, and the *Invincible* had made designers aware of the need to 'trunk off' magazines to the open air so that explosive gases would be blasted outward, rather than causing havoc in the hull. The Admiralty, however, did not see things in the same light as the designers, and insisted that to 'trunk off' the magazines was defeatism and should not be considered in the designs of British warships because 'enemy shells are meant to remain outside British magazines'.[8] Due to the view of the Admiralty, even in light of the events at Jutland, explosion trunks were not built into the *Hood*.[9]

Following the laying of the keel on 1 September 1916, the next stage of construction saw transverse and longitudinal frames joined to the keel in order to form watertight compartments. In total, the *Hood* would be divided into twenty-five watertight sections. Longitudinal strength was preserved with girders that ran the length of the ship that were pierced for the funnel uptakes and main armament turrets and barbettes. While frames were riveted to the keel to form watertight compartments, the forecastle and upper decks formed the upper part of what amounted to a slope-sided box to which ultimately the ship would owe her structural integrity. At the same time, the blacksmiths' shop turned out forgings of every different dimension as electricians began to lay the first of what were hundreds of miles of cabling. Following all of this, the shafts, screws, bulges, and bilge keels were installed before squads of men were dispatched from the paint shop to apply coats of red lead paint.[10]

The strength of the ship relied heavily on the quality of the teams of riveters and caulkers who followed them.

[Riveting parties] could be either machine or hand squads. A hand squad comprised a right and a left handed riveter to alternatively hammer the rivet, a 'holder on' who was positioned behind the plate to hold the heated rivet in place with a tool called a 'hobey', and a 'heater boy'—who could be 50 or 60 years of age. The heater boy was important as he had to arrange his fire in such a fashion that he had an adequate

The box construction of the hull to which the ship would owe her structural integrity. (*Author's collection*)

supply of different types of rivet likely to be required properly heated and ready for use ... In confined or awkward spaces an additional member of the squad known as a catch boy, who could be employed to insert the rivet. Where a riveting machine was used, the squad comprised a riveter to operate the machine, a holder on and a heater boy. When the riveters had completed their work, the caulkers took over. They finished the shell by caulking each plate overlap with a pneumatic caulking machine to ensure an absolutely watertight seam.[11]

It is worth briefly acknowledging that although built at the John Brown & Company shipyard on the Clyde, the *Hood* was the product of works across Britain. From across the length and breadth of Britain, 40,000,000 tons of material from hardened plate to cabinetry were sent to John Brown's shipyard via ship, rail and lorry from workshops, forgeries, mines, mills and factories across the country. The *Hood*'s rudder frame was constructed at William Beardmore's Parkhead Forge in Glasgow while her four propellers were constructed at the Manganese Bronze & Brass Co of London. Each propeller weighing over 20 tons was transported 400 miles from the Manganese Bronze & Brass Co. to John Brown's shipyard by traction engines supplied by Messrs H. Bentley & Co. of Bradford.

The *Hood*'s propellers during their 400-mile journey from the Manganese Bronze & Brass Co. to the John Brown & Co. shipyard in 1918. (*Author's collection*)

On 2 November 1916, a report from John Brown & Co noted:

> Sufficient information is gradually being obtained from the Admiralty to enable more material to be ordered for this vessel and to employ a few more men on her construction, but in view of the alteration in her design, comparatively slow progress can only be made until the beginning of next year.[12]

On 1 March 1917, John Brown & Co. was encouraged to press on with the construction of the *Hood*; however, the unrestricted German submarine offensive against merchant shipping aimed at starving Britain into submission and the resulting pressing need for merchant vessels prevented the yard from devoting its entire resources to the project. Nevertheless, construction work continued and satisfactory progress was reported on 22 June 1917. However, work on the hull was somewhat hindered by a shortage of manpower. No additional reports on the *Hood*'s construction are available until January 1919. This lack of reportage is perhaps best explained by the need to preserve secrecy surrounding the new vessel.

In early 1917, it was reported that the *Hood* would be ready for sea trials in November 1918; however, the Admiralty appeared to be having second thoughts about the other *Admiral*-class vessels for on 9 March 1917, it was imitated that work on them was not to be given priority. On 27 February 1919, the Admiralty cancelled the construction of the *Hood*'s three sister ships.[13] While the Admiralty were having second thoughts regarding the completion of the *Hood*'s sister ships, the Director of Naval Ordnance, Rear-Admiral Morgan Singer, was taking a keen interest in the development of the *Hood*. Singer became concerned that

The *Hood*'s hull while under construction. Note the forward barbette of what would become 'B' turret. (*Author's collection*)

the 15-inch and 5.5-inch magazines were directly above the shell rooms. Singer therefore obtained a reversal of the positions in the forward section of the *Hood*, yet was, somewhat surprisingly, satisfied with the layout aft. Aft, the magazines remained above the shell rooms because Singer thought it essential that at the lowest end of the ship, the higher positions were an inbuilt defence against mines and torpedoes.

Beatty entered the armour debate in June 1917 and averred that the armour protection equipping the *Hood* was too weak, and that turret roofs should be armoured up to 6 inches. It was, however, too late to invoke Beatty's recommendation that turret roofs be armoured up to 6 inches as they had already been manufactured. Only one of Beatty's proposals would ultimately be accepted—that all sliding doors on bridge decks should be altered to be hinged.[14]

By this time, word was spreading throughout the Royal Navy that the *Hood* was a waste of money for she did not appear superior to the ships of the *Queen Elizabeth*-class. While having improved deck armour, the major factor in the *Hood*'s favour was her speed; she was to be over 6 knots faster than the *Queen Elizabeth*-class battleships. Test firings against plates representing the 5-inch-thick roof armour and 1-inch-thick magazine crowns were made on 10 January 1918. At Beatty's insistence, the tests were undertaken with 13.5-inch armour piercing shells and with new, secret Vickers 15-inch shells. The tests highlighted the inadequacy of the armour, and after the second of the three tests, it was decided that the magazine crown armour should be doubled to 2 inches. Further modifications were agreed, including moving the foremast 12 feet and lowering the bridge by 6 feet two weeks prior to the *Hood*'s launching. Additional shell tests in 1919 were made against the 2-inch armour that was to be incorporated into the magazine crowns. These tests were to be the most revealing of all. In conditions similar to a range of 10¾ miles a 15-inch shell was fired at the replica armour plate. The shell tore through the 7-inch armour, the 1-inch backing and also the plates representing the 2-inch sloping main deck and 3-inch bulkhead. Worse still was the fact that the shell burst 31 feet behind the 7-inch protection. This was to be the final confirmation that the armour of HMS *Hood* was woefully weak. Some 3-inch armour was equipped to the sides of the main deck while the plating of the barbettes was increased to 5 inches. This increased barbette protection was an especially significant modification given that it was the turrets of the *Invincible* and the other battlecruisers that had proved to be a significant weakness in their designs. More shell tests were carried out and resulted in the shells fired being deflected. To counteract the additional weight resulting from the additional armour plating, it was agreed that four of the 5.5-inch guns would be removed. Nevertheless, these modifications did not improve protection over the magazines.

D'Eyncourt, whose opinion on the matter of further armour was sought, was wholeheartedly in favour of more armour being placed on the main deck, which would have increased the weight of the *Hood* still further by 440 tons. Meanwhile, additional gunnery tests to determine the penetrating power of 16-inch shells were carried out after which it was determined that an additional thousand tons of steel would have to be added. It was, however, impossible to balance the equipping of more armour by shedding more 'fittings' like guns. As such, from this stage, the designers of the *Hood* and the specialists forgot the problems of perfect armour protection, if such a thing were possible.[15]

Despite all the modifications and additional armour plating, the *Hood* did not have an armoured deck and herein lay the fatal weakness in her design, regardless of how superior her design when compared to her predecessors. As the historian Bruce Taylor has written, 'Though occasionally classified as a fast battleship, by later standards the *Hood* failed to make the transition from a battlecruiser and ultimately proved incapable of meeting the requirement that had sooner or later to be made of any man-o'-war: the ability to withstand punishment from ships armed to the same standard as herself'.[16]

Meanwhile, construction work on the hull continued. At 1.05 p.m. on 22 August 1918, the *Hood* was launched by Lady Hood, the widow of Rear-Admiral Horace Hood who had been killed in the *Invincible* when she sank at Jutland, and who was a great-grandson of Admiral Samuel Hood (1724–1816), whose

The *Hood*'s hull on the slipway. Note the unfinished side armour. (*Author's collection*)

The hull of the *Hood* on the slipway at John Brown & Co., Clydebank. (*Lord Hood, HMS Hood Association*)

'On 22 August 1918 the *Hood* rattled down the slipway at Clydebank following being launched by Lady Hood'. This image shows the moment the *Hood* entered the Clyde during her launch. (*Lord Hood, HMS Hood Association*)

namesake the *Hood* bore. Having been launched by Lady Hood, the *Hood* spent the next year and a half at John Brown & Co. being fitted out. On 12 September 1918, the first barbette armour was added to the ship. This was followed on 28 October by the installation of the first of the ship's turbines. By 27 February 1919, the deck area over the forward engine room had been completed. In addition to this, the second funnel and part of the conning tower had been shipped. Around this time, work began on the laying of deck planking on the forward portion of the forecastle. A month later a shipyard report noted that good progress was being made in the fitting of the ship's side armour and that progress had been made on the armoured walls of the conning tower. The report went on to detail the work that was beginning on the bridge area and noted that the fourth set of turbines was scheduled to arrive within a few days for fitting in April. By May 1919, the fourth set of turbines had been successfully fitted and work had begun on replacing the decks over the turbine spaces. At the same time, shipwrights were making notable progress with the forecastle deck planking and work had begun on the construction of the shelter deck.

The *Hood*'s main mast being hoisted prior to being placed into position. (*Author's collection*)

On 2 May, the mainmast was shipped while later in the month, a further increase in deck armour in the vicinity of the magazines was authorised by the Admiralty. It was around this time in the *Hood*'s fitting out that tragedy struck the ship when on 19 May, there was an explosion in one of the watertight compartments beneath the Carpenter's heavy store. Two civilian engineers, thirty-two-year-old James McGregor and twenty-five-year-old John Morton, were killed in the explosion while a third engineer escaped with injuries. In the wake of the explosion and the deaths of Morton and McGregor, a fatal accident enquiry was held at Dumbarton Sheriff Court in July, which failed to find an obvious cause for the explosion. Experts who were called in to examine what happened presented the view that the explosion was most likely the result of a build-up of gas in the compartment. Despite the deaths of Morton and McGregor, work on the ship continued.

By June 1919, the *Hood*'s side armour had all been fitted. In July, additional modifications concerning the armour protection over the magazines were made to the plans but the changes were never implemented. On 7 August, the first of the *Hood*'s 15-inch gun turrets, 'X' turret, was installed. On 12 September, the *Hood* was towed out into the Clyde for shipping barbette plates. This occurred four days later on the 16th.

On 6 September 1916, the Ship's Badges Committee approved the seal pattern for the *Hood*'s badge. Designed by Major Charles Ffoulkes, the badge was derived

Above: A 15-inch turret under construction. (*Author's collection*)

Left: The foremast being hoisted into position. (*Author's collection*)

from the crest of Admiral Sir Samuel Hood, 1st Viscount Hood, and showed a Cornish clough holding on to a gold anchor. The motto *Ventis Secundis* meaning 'With favouring winds', which was used by Viscount Hood, was also used. On occasion, the ship's badge included the year 1859 below the Clough and anchor. This year alluded to the first ship commissioned as HMS *Hood*, a second-rate ship of the line which was launched in 1859 as HMS *Edgar* but renamed 'Hood'. With the navy crown removed, the badge would be adorned on the ship's boats and the tampions. The badge could be seen in other areas of the ship, also including in the commander's lobby and on the bridge.

By the end of October, the second 15-inch turret had been installed on the *Hood* and work had begun on aligning the ship's shafting and on connecting the engines. As this work began, progress was being made by an army of joiners and electricians on the living quarters in the after portion of the ship. Throughout November, work proceeded inside the ship with significant progress being made on the electrical and ventilation systems. The masts and derricks were rigged and many of the mechanical systems were set up. In addition to this, the third 15-inch gun turret was completed. On 9 and 10 December, the *Hood* began basin trials. On the 11th, she was visited by His Royal Highness Prince Albert, who would later go on to reign as King George VI. Shortly before Christmas 1919, the fourth and final main battery turret was completed and plans were being made to take the *Hood* from Clydebank in early January.

The *Hood*'s badge.

Taken while the *Hood* was at Gibraltar, her forward guns and the tampions are adorned with the ship's badge in the muzzle of the guns. (*Beeldbank WO2, NIOD*)

The *Hood* during her fitting-out period, taken from the ship's starboard side looking forward. (*Author's collection*)

A team of men at work laying the deck planking on the *Hood*'s quarterdeck.

Taken while being fitted out, this photo was also taken from the ship's starboard side looking forward. Note the significant progress that has been made compared to the image on page xxx. (*Author's collection*)

The *Hood*'s forecastle towards the end of her fitting out to John Brown & Co. (*Author's collection*)

The *Hood* at the end of her fitting-out period at John Brown & Co. (*Author's collection*)

Anatomy of a Ship

HMS *Hood* was significantly larger than her predecessors, the ships of the *Renown*-class (the *Renown* and the *Repulse*) and the vessels of the *Courageous*-class.[1] Completed, the *Hood* had an overall length of 860 feet 7 inches (262.3 metres); a maximum beam of 104 feet 2 inches (31.8 metres); and a draught of 32 feet (9.8 metres) at deep load.[2] With a complete double bottom, the *Hood* had a metacentric height of 4 feet 2 inches (1.3 metres) at deep load, which minimised her tool and made her a steady gun platform.[3] The below table shows how the *Hood* stacked up against other prominent British battlecruisers.

Ship	HMS *Invincible*	HMS *Tiger*	HMS *Renown*	HMS *Hood*
Class	*Invincible*-class	*Tiger*-class[4]	*Renown*-class	*Admiral*-class
Length	567 feet (173 m)	704 feet (214.6 m)	794 feet 1.5 inches (242 m)	860 feet 7 inches (262.3 m)
Beam	78 feet 5 inches (23.9 m)	90 feet 6 inches (27.6 m)	90 feet 1.75 inches (27.5 m)	104 feet 2 inches (31.8 m)
Draught	30 feet (9.1 m)	32 feet 5 inches (9.9 m)	31 feet 9 inches (9.7 m)	32 feet (9.8 m)
Displacement (Deep Load)	20,750 tons	33,790 tons	32,740 tons	47,430 tons
Speed (Knots)	25.5	28	31	32
Range	3,560 miles (5,729.26 km)	3,800 miles (6,100 km)	6580 miles (10,590 km)	6,140 miles (9,870 km)
Main Armament	Eight BL 12-inch MK X guns	Eight BL 13.5-inch MK V guns	Six BL 15-inch MK I guns	Eight BL 15-inch MK I guns[5]
Maximum Main Armament Range	10.22 miles (16.44 km)	13.48 miles (21.71 km)	13.48 miles (21.70 km)	17.14 miles (27.59 km)
Complement	781	1,112 (September 1914) 1,459 (April 1918)	1,223 (1919) 953 1,200 (1939)	1,433 (1919) 1,325 (1934) 1,418 (1941)

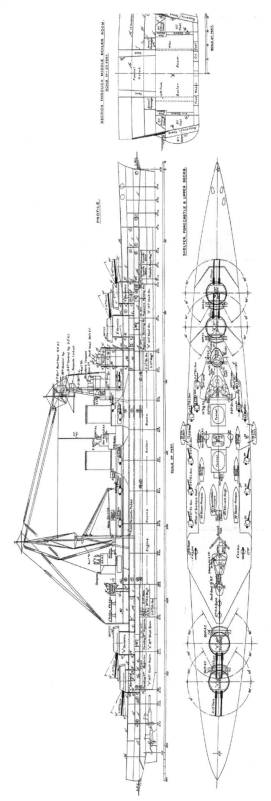

Plans of the *Hood*.

Armament

Unlike in other ships, the *Hood* originally had her magazines placed above rather than below the shell rooms that were situated in the very bottom of the ship before Rear-Admiral Singer gained an approval for the reversal of the forward magazines. Each magazine for the 15-inch guns contained approximately 50 tons of cordite.[6] The *Hood* was armed with eight BL 15-inch Mark I guns in four turrets. The BL 15-inch Mk I was the successor to the 13.5-inch gun, which equipped the *King George V-* (1911), *Iron Duke-*, and *Orion*-classes of dreadnought battleships as well as the battlecruisers *Queen Mary* and *Tiger*, and those of the *Lion*-class. The BL 15-inch was the first British 15-inch gun design and would go on to be one of the most widely used and longest lasting of any British designs, being deployed on numerous capital ships from 1915 until 1959. The weapon is perhaps the most efficient heavy gun to ever be developed for the Royal Navy and earned praise in an American report produced after the Second World War, which heralded the weapon as the most reliable and accurate battleship main armament of the war, though other guns and mountings possessed superior individual features.[7] The BL 15-inch Mk I was specifically designed to arm the *Queen Elizabeth*-class battleships as part of the Royal Navy's response to the new generation of dreadnoughts being constructed for the Imperial German Navy prior to the outbreak of the First World War.

The *Hood* had her Mk I guns housed in a unique mounting referred to as the Mk II. It may be noted that the *Hood* was the only ship to have Mk I guns housed in the specially designed Mk II mountings. The Mk II mounting incorporated experience drawn from the Battle of Jutland described in an official Admiralty document:

These mountings, known as 'Mark II', are arranged generally on the same lines as those of 'Mark I' for the *Queen Elizabeth* and *Royal Sovereign* classes, but they have certain new and distinguishing features which may be enumerated as follows:
1. The Maximum Elevation of the guns is 30 degrees, the gear being the same in principle as before with the elevating cylinder lengthened to suit. Further, the trunnion bearings for the elevating cylinder and the plate structure supporting these bearings have been greatly stiffened up. There is a hydraulically operated stop which prevents elevation beyond 20 degrees when the breech is open, and an intercepting valve to prevent the gun loading hoist being raised until the breech is fully open.
2. The 'Run-Out' Gear is pneumatic and the air pressure, 1,000 lbs. per square inch, is provided by means of suitable connections to the air blast system of the turret. 'Run-Out' Control is by means of valves fitted into the pistons of the recoil buffers, and separate self-contained buffers for the end of the run-out stroke. "Run-in" can be obtained by reducing the pressure in the 'Run-Out' cylinder and elevating the gun; under these conditions the gun runs in by gravity.
3. A 'Flash Door' in the gun loading hoist well completely separates the gun house from the working chamber. The door is operated hydraulically in conjunction with

the hoist and is arranged so that it must be fully open before the cage is raised or lowered and that it will close again after the cage has passed.

4. In the Handling Room a Cordite Hopper is fitted to the Trunk and the hopper is provided with buckets so arranged that when loaded they can be rotated immediately to a flash proof position. The buckets can only be completely rotated to discharge the cordite into the central cage when the cage itself is right down.

5. The Cordite Cage is also provided with rotating flash proof buckets and when the cage comes to the bottom of the hoist of the bucket are brought automatically to the receiving position. When the cage has been loaded the hand telegraph gear is put to 'Cage Ready' and the buckets rotate to the Flash Proof Position. The cage ascends with the buckets flash proof and at the top of the hoist they automatically discharge the cordite into the waiting trays in the working chamber.

6. The bearings for the worm shaft of the training gear are fitted with forced lubrication.

7. The Pump in the Working Chamber is provided with electric drive only; hand gear is not fitted.

8. Telescope Sights are provided:

(a). In the centre position they are carried on a bracket and operated by a connecting rod secured to the trunnion arm, and

(b). In the side position they are carried in the trunnion pins and operated by a bracket bolted to the trunnion arm.

9. Anti-Surging Stops, adjustable to suit varying lengths of shell, are fitted to the hoist cages, bogies, and waiting trays.[8]

Each gun had a rate of fire of two rounds every thirty seconds (four rounds per turret per minute), and could be depressed to minus 5 degrees and elevated to 30 degrees. At maximum elevation, a 15-inch shell weighing 1,920 pounds (870 kg) could be fired 17.14 miles (27.6 kilometres). From the bow, the turrets were designated 'A', 'B', 'X', and 'Y'. A total of 120 rounds for each gun was carried aboard.[9]

The secondary armament of the *Hood* was twelve BL 5.5-inch Mk I guns. The BL 5.5-inch Mk I was developed at the Coventry Ordnance Works in 1913 and was first offered to the Greek Navy as the main armament for two cruisers being built on its behalf at Cammell Laird on Merseyside. With the onset of the First World War, the two cruisers were purchased by the Royal Navy and pressed into service as HMS *Birkenhead* and HMS *Chester*. On the whole, the Royal Navy was pleased with the performance of the gun; it was significantly lighter than the standard 6-inch gun that equipped Royal Navy ships and fired a 37-kg shell as opposed to the 45-kg shell fired by the 6-inch weapon that gave it a higher rate of fire with little loss in terms of hitting power.

The *Hood*'s BL 5.5-inch Mk I guns were fitted along the upper deck and on the forward shelter deck on shield single pivot mounts. Owing to their high position on the ship, the guns could be worked during heavy weather and were less affected by sea spray and waves when compared to the secondary armaments

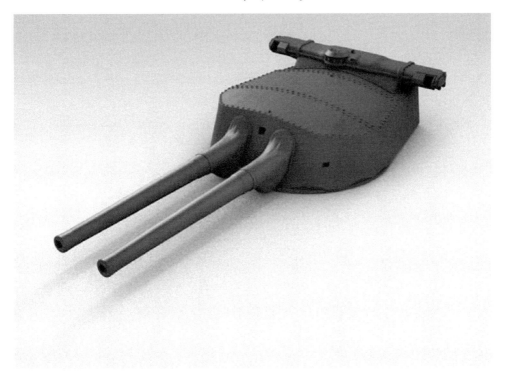

A 3D model of the face of a BL 15-inch Mk I gun of the type fitted to *Hood*. (*Author's collection*)

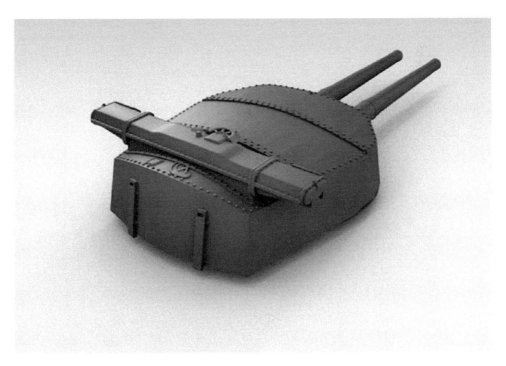

A 3D model showing the back of a BL 15-inch Mk I gun (*Author's collection*)

'A' and 'B' turrets pointing forward. Note the tompions adorning the ship's badge. (*Author's collection*)

The *Hood*'s main armament trained to starboard in July 1932. Note the sighting port on the turret. (*Richard Toffolo*)

Above left: A 3D model of a BL 5.5-inch Mk I gun of the type fitted to the *Hood*.

Above right: A 3D model showing the breach side of a BL 5.5-inch Mk I gun.

fitted to capital ships constructed earlier.[10] Each gun was provided with 200 rounds, and could fire between eight and twelve rounds per minute.[11] Capable of being elevated to 30-degrees or depressed to minus 5-degrees, the BL 5.5-inch Mk I could fire a 37-kg shell 10.5 miles (16.9 kilometres).[12]

Two of the *Hood*'s 5.5-inch guns, located on the forward shelter deck, were temporarily removed in 1937 and were replaced by single barrel 4-inch guns. In May 1940, all of the BL 5.5-inch Mk I guns and mounts aboard the *Hood* were removed and were sited in key areas as coastal defence guns around Dover, Folkestone, the Coalhouse Fort, Tilbury, and on Ascension Island. Two of the guns that equipped the *Hood* are still in existence today on Ascension Island where they make up the Hood Battery. The guns on Ascension Island saw service during the Second World War when on 9 December 1941 they participated in a bombardment which helped to drive away the German U-boat *U-124*, which approached the island.

The *Hood*'s BL 5.5-inch Mk I secondary armament was replaced by seven QF 4-inch Mk XVI dual purpose guns. Four Mk XVI guns were first fitted to the *Hood*'s shelter deck in 1937, and were followed by an additional three that were fitted to the shelter deck in 1940. Three guns were fitted on each side of the ship before a final mount was fitted at the very end of the shelter deck on the centreline.

The Mk XVI superseded the QF 4-inch Mk V naval gun on many Royal Navy vessels during the 1930s and 1940s. The Mk XVI fired a heavier shell than the Mk V at 30.28 kg against 25 kg. Although technically dual purpose as their high angle capability allowed them to be used to engage aircraft while their low angle capability enabled the guns to be used against surface targets, the Mk XVI was better suited to the role of anti-aircraft gun than it was to being a surface battery. The QF 4-inch Mk XVI could be elevated to 80 degrees, which allowed the gun to fire shells up to 40,000 feet. At an angle of 45 degrees, the Mk XVI could fire a shell 12.1 miles (19.47 km) and had a maximum rate of fire of between sixteen and eighteen rounds per minute.

During her lifetime, the *Hood* was equipped with a wide range of weapons for anti-aircraft defence. From her completion until her 1939 refit, the *Hood* was equipped with up to eight Mk V High Angle 4-inch anti-aircraft guns, which were located on the shelter deck. The Mk V High Angle 4-inch anti-aircraft gun was a single barrel weapon which could fire between eight and thirteen 14.25-kg shells per minute. The High Angle 4-inch anti-aircraft gun could fire a shell up to 28,750 feet and over a distance of 9.26 miles (14.9 km).

In 1931, the *Hood* was first fitted with two Mk VIII 2-pounder eight-barrel pom-pom anti-aircraft guns. The pom-pom anti-aircraft guns fired 1.6-inch shells up to a maximum range of 2.15 miles (3.47 kilometres) and could be trained 360-degrees. Of the first two mounts, the starboard mounting was officially designated 'Pom-pom 1' but was nicknamed 'Sally' while the port mount, officially referred to as 'Pom-pom 2', was nicknamed 'Peter' by the crew. In late 1937, at the

The starboard shelter deck in either late 1940 or early 1941. Three QF 4-inch Mk XVI dual purpose guns can be seen. Two are facing forward while one (back of the photograph) is trained out to starboard and elevated. Behind the foremost 4-inch gun, a UP launcher can be seen under a cover. Note the various boats under cover on the deck. (*Leonard Eaves Photograph Collection, HMS Hood Association*)

One of the Mk V high angle 4-inch anti-aircraft guns on the *Hood*'s starboard side during firing exercises in 1932. (*Author's collection*)

This photograph shows 'Pom-Pom 3', nicknamed 'Auntie', the aft Mk VIII 2-pounder eight-barrel pom-pom anti-aircraft gun. In this photo, the gun crew appear to be engaged in a gunnery drill. Below and behind the gun crew is the aft 4-inch gun mount and splinter shielding. (*Ken Bridges/HMS Hood Association*)

end of the shelter deck, a third mount was fitted. Due to its position aft, the gun, officially designated 'Pom-pom 3' was nicknamed 'Auntie'.

In 1933, around the area of the conning tower, the *Hood* was fitted with two Mk III 0.5-inch guns, effectively a quadruple-mount of Vickers machine guns used for anti-aircraft defence. Typically, the guns were mounted in groups of four. The mount featured a 200-round magazine that wrapped the ammunition belt around the magazine drum, which, in turn, provided a maximum rate of fire of 700 rounds per minute per gun. Vickers claimed that together, the four guns could fire 800 rounds in a period of twenty seconds and could then be reloaded in a further thirty seconds. The mount had its guns adjusted so as to provide a spread of fire which amounted to 60 feet wide and fifty feet high. In service, the guns proved insufficiently powerful in the short-range anti-aircraft role against all-metal aircraft and was subsequently superseded during the Second World War by the 20-mm Oerlikon cannon.

Capable of being trained 360 degrees, the guns had a maximum range of 0.85 miles (1.37 km) and could be elevated to 80 degrees or depressed to minus 10 degrees. The first two mountings fitted to the *Hood* in late 1933 were designated M1 (starboard) and M2 (port). These guns also acquired unofficial nicknames from the crew. The port gun was referred to as 'Pip' while the starboard mount was referred to as 'Squeak'. In late 1937, two more mounts were added abreast the rear superstructure. The starboard mount, M3, became known as 'Simon' while the port mount, M4, was nicknamed 'Paul'. The mounts equipped to the *Hood* were fitted with gun shields and had ready-use lockers sited nearby.

In addition to these traditional anti-aircraft guns, the *Hood* was outfitted with five 7-inch Naval wire barrage, unrotating projectile (UP) rocket launchers in 1940. Each launcher contained twenty tubes which fired a rocket 7-inches in diameter and 32-inches long. At the tip of the rocket was an 8-oz (0.14-kg) aerial mine. Capable of being trained 360 degrees, the launchers could fire a projectile up to 1,000 feet.

The *Hood* was outfitted with five of the mounts in 1940. One of the launchers was fitted atop 'B' turret while the remaining four were situated on the shelter deck. In general, the unrotating projectile launcher was an unsuccessful attempt at creating an aerial minefield. When hostile aircraft were detected the operator, known as a layer, would manually launch a spread of ten rockets. Upon reaching 1,000 feet, the rockets would detonate and expel mines attached to three parachutes. The idea was that low flying enemy aircraft would snag the cables and would pull the mines into themselves where they would explode bringing down the enemy aircraft. In practice, the unrotating projectile launcher concept was cumbersome. The minefield created by the projectiles was clearly visible to approaching aircraft and were easily avoidable. Furthermore, the rockets were volatile, something recognised in July 1941 by the Admiralty which led to the mothballing of the projectiles:

> U.P. ammunition generally does not come up to the accepted standards of safety normally insisted on for Naval Service ... The stowage of this ammunition, the

Above left: A 7-inch Naval Wire Barrage Unrotating Projectile Rocket Launcher of the type fitted to *Hood* in 1940. (*Author's collection*)

Above right: An UP launcher firing a barrage of rockets. (*Author's collection*)

The *Hood*'s starboard side amidships. The above water torpedo tubes are clearly visible with the doors open.

balance of which is not required for Ready Use, has to be stowed apart from other magazines and between decks on the deck below the weather, is a constant source of anxiety.[13]

There was a real risk of the mines floating back onto the launching ship. There are no records showing that unrotating projectiles succeeded in bringing down any enemy aircraft, and it is likely that the system resulted in more injuries and deaths to British servicemen than it did to enemy personnel.

In addition to her gun armament, the *Hood* was also equipped with torpedo tubes and was capable of firing 21-inch Mk IV and Mk V torpedoes. The range of the torpedoes varied depending on their speed. If set to cruise at 25 knots, they had a range of 7.67 miles (12.34 km). If set to travel at a less practical 40 knots, the range of the torpedoes was reduced to 2.84 miles (4.5 km). The *Hood* was equipped with two submerged torpedo tubes (one port, one starboard) just forward of 'A' turret. These tubes were removed in 1937. These tubes were supplemented by four Mk V above water tubes, divided two per side, which were located parallel with the main mast approximately halfway between the waterline and shelter deck. These torpedo tubes remained on the ship through to her sinking.

Gunnery Direction and Fire Control

The *Hood* was equipped with a number of directors to control her range of weapons. The main fire control directors are outlined below.

The primary directors for the main armament were the 15-foot range finders located above the spotting top and the 30-foot rangefinder located atop the conning tower. In addition to these primary directors, each gun turret was fitted with a 30-foot rangefinder as well as open director sites. Should the primary rangefinders be disabled, secondary fire control was carried out through the 'B' turret sites. In the case of divided fire, 'B' turret would control the forward turrets while 'X' turret was responsible for directing the fire of the aft turrets. Finally, if the need arose, each turret was capable of being fired independently and could rely on its own rangefinder and sites. The rangefinders were augmented by auxiliary fire control equipment which included tripod directors and Evershed bearing transmitters. In 1941, the *Hood*'s fire control systems were bolstered by the incorporation of Type 284 gunnery radar and Type 279M radar systems. It may be noted that when the Type 284 radar was fitted, the spotting top rangefinder was removed. Inputs from these devices could be fed into the Mk V Dreyer fire control tables located in the 15-inch transmitting stations, which allowed for coordinated fire control.

The BL 5.5-inch guns were primarily controlled by the 5.5-inch directors, which consisted of 9-foot rangefinders. Evershed bearing indicators allowed for additional inputs to be made. Inputs from the various rangefinders and indicators were fed to the 5.5-inch transmitting station, which then used the figures to

The *Hood* on 12 June 1924 off Honolulu, Hawaii. 'A' and 'B' turrets are visible with their prominent rangefinders protruding at the rear. Directly behind 'B' turret is the conning tower atop which is the main fire-control director with its own rangefinder. On top of the spotting top, on the tripod foremast, the secondary director can be seen. Also of note is the disassembled aircraft platform. (*NH 60450, US Naval History and Heritage Command*)

coordinate gunfire. Additionally, it may be noted that the 5.5-inch guns could be manually aimed and directed.

The *Hood*'s anti-aircraft guns were controlled by a simple high-angle 6-foot 7-inch rangefinder mounted on the aft control position, which was fitted between 1926 and 1927.[14] During the 1929–31 refit, a High-Angle Control System (HACS) Mk I director was fitted to the rear searchlight platform and two positions for the pom-pom anti-aircraft directors were added at the rear of the spotting top, although it may be noted that only one director was initially fitted.[15] In 1934, the pom-pom directors were moved to the former locations of the 5.5-inch control positions on the spotting top while the 9-foot rangefinders for the 5.5-inch control positions were reinstalled on the signal platform. In 1936, in an effort to keep them clear of the funnel gases, the pom-pom directors were moved to the rear corners of the bridge. An additional pom-pom director was added on the rear superstructure in 1938 abaft of the HACS director. Two HACS Mk III directors were added to the aft end of the signal platform in 1939 and the Mk I director located aft was replaced by a Mk III director.[16]

The *Hood*'s torpedoes were directed using Mk III Deflection Sites. Two were located in the after torpedo control tower, four on the bridge and a final two were located in the conning tower. In the conning tower, 15-foot rangefinders were used, which were removed in 1937. Following her refit in 1940, the former 12-foot rangefinders for the 5.5-inch guns were used as the torpedo rangefinders.

Armour

The armour scheme of the *Hood* was originally based on that of HMS *Tiger* with an 8-inch-thick waterline belt. Unlike HMS *Tiger*, the *Hood*'s waterline armour was angled outwards at an angle of twelve-degrees from the waterline in order to increase its relative thickness in relation to flat trajectory shells. At the same time, however, this increased the ship's vulnerability to plunging fire as it exposed more of the ship's vulnerable deck armour. During her construction, additional armour was fitted to the *Hood* based on the experience gained at the Battle of Jutland. When she was finally completed, the *Hood*'s armour would account for 33 per cent of her total displacement—a high percentage by British standards, but less than the percentage in contemporary German designs of the time. A comparative example of this is the German battlecruiser SMS *Hindenburg* whose armour accounted for 36 per cent of her total displacement.[17]

The armoured belt of the *Hood* consisted of face-hardened Krupp Cemented armour arranged in three strakes. At the waterline, between the barbettes of 'A' and 'Y' turrets, the belt armour was 12 inches thick. The next strake directly above had a maximum thickness of 7 inches over the same area while the upper belt was approximately 5 inches thick amidships.[18] It is worth noting that the main waterline armour belt thinned from 12 inches to between 5 and 6 inches towards each end of the ship but did not reach either the bow or the stern.

The gun turrets and barbettes were protected by between 11 and 15 inches of Krupp Cemented armour. With a maximum thickness of 12 inches on the barbettes, the face of the *Hood*'s main battery turrets was fitted with 15 inches of armour. The side of the turrets had armour that was between 11 and 12 inches in thickness while the rear of the turret also had 11-inch-thick armour. The turret roofs, were, however, only 5 inches thick. The *Hood*'s decks were made of high-tensile steel; the forecastle deck ranged between 1.75 and 2 inches in thickness while the main deck was an inch thick except over the magazines where the armour was 3 inches thick. A 2-inch slope of armour was to be found where the deck met the bottom of the main belt. On the lower deck, the armour was 3 inches thick over the propeller shafts, 2 inches thick over the magazines, and an inch thick everywhere else. The 3-inch plating on the main deck was added to the *Hood* late on during the construction process and led to the aft 5.5-inch guns and their hoists being removed in partial compensation while firing tests led to the decision to increase the armour over the forward magazines to 5 inches and to 6 inches over the aft magazines in July 1919.

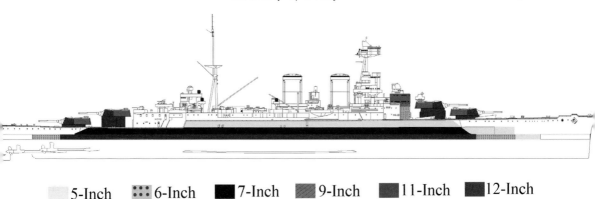

5-Inch   6-Inch   7-Inch   9-Inch   11-Inch   12-Inch

Diagram showing *Hood*'s armour protection and thickness represented by the different blocks of colour. (*Author's collection*)

Owing to the increased weight resulting from this additional armour, the two submerged torpedo tubes and the armour for the rear torpedo warheads were removed. In addition, the armour for the aft torpedo control tower was reduced from 6 inches to 1.5 inches. However, the additional armour was never fitted to the *Hood* pending further trials with the result that she was susceptible to plunging fire.[19]

To offer her protection against torpedoes, the *Hood* was given a 7.5-foot (2.3-m) deep anti-torpedo bulge that ran the length of the ship between the forward and after barbettes. The anti-torpedo bulge was divided into an empty outer compartment and an inner compartment that was filled with five rows of water-tight 'crushing tubes', which were intended to absorb and distribute the force of an explosion resulting from a torpedo attack. The anti-torpedo bulge was backed by a 1.5-inch-thick torpedo bulkhead.

With regards the superstructure, the *Hood*'s conning tower was provided with armour that was between 9 and 11 inches in thickness and incorporated 2-inch-thick deck armour while the ship's funnel uptakes were a mere 1-inch thick.

Propulsion

The *Hood* was a steamship. Steam was supplied by twenty-four Yarrow tube drum boilers that burned fuel oil. On average, the *Hood* carried 1,200 tons of fuel, but could carry a maximum of 4,000 tons. In all, the *Hood* was equipped with four boiler rooms each of which contained six boilers, which required extensive and regular cleaning in order to remove scaling. Cleaning of the boilers usually took place in a twenty-one-day cycle with the work being undertaken by a specially assembled team. When one set of boilers was closed down for maintenance or cleaning, if the *Hood* was at sea, she would operate on the other three sets of boilers. While capable of sailing at a maximum of 32 knots, the *Hood*'s economical cruising speed was 12 knots, a speed that could be achieved without any difficulty on three sets of boilers. Each boiler room was fitted with six fans and engines. Each fan was of the enclosed forced-lubrication type and had cylinders 9 inches in diameter by 7 inches. Serving two boiler rooms each were the *Hood*'s two funnels. Each funnel was 25 feet deep and 18 feet wide with an outer casing measuring 6 inches. The distance from the lower burners on the front of the boilers to the top of the funnels was approximately 100 feet.

The *Hood*'s boilers produced steams for four sets of Brown-Curtis geared turbines, each of which served one propeller shaft. In all, the *Hood* had three engine rooms: forward, middle, and aft. The port and starboard outer shaft turbines were located in the forward engine room while the port inner shaft turbine was located in the middle engine room. Finally, the starboard inner shaft turbine was located in the aft engine room. Each set of turbines drove a propeller shaft through a single reduction gear. For cruising speeds, the *Hood* was also equipped with a Brown-Curtis cruising turbine. The cruising turbine had a separate casing and could, when required, be connected to or disconnected from the main high-pressure turbine shaft. Each of the ship's turbines was completed with its own condenser and auxiliaries and could be operated independently of the other turbines.

Each ahead high-pressure turbine rotor comprised ten wheels. In this, the first and second wheels were velocity compounded, having two rows of blades each, while the remaining eight were simple impulse wheels. The high-pressure turbine rotors were supplemented by low pressure ahead of turbine rotors which consisted of eight wheels of the simple impulse type. Each cruising speed rotor comprised four velocity-compounded wheels with three rows of blades on the first wheel and two rows on each of the others. The astern turbines for each shaft were to be found incorporated in the low-pressure head turbine casing and consisted of two velocity-compounded wheels each of which sported three rows of blades.

The *Hood*'s engines were designed to develop a total of 144,000 horsepower with 210 revolutions of the propeller and 210 pounds of pressure in the control chest. At full power, each high-pressure turbine made 1,500 revolutions per minute while each low-pressure turbine made 1,100 rpm.

Situated in the Middle and After engine rooms was the *Hood*'s distilling machinery. In each engine room two sets of distilling machinery, 'A' and 'B', were to be found. Each 'A' set distiller consisted of two 80-ton evaporators and one distiller. This combination could be used to supply water for the usage throughout the ship or to make up feed water for the boilers. Each 'B' set of distilling machinery consisted of one 80-ton evaporator with a vapour pipe connect to the auxiliary condenser in the engine room in which it was situated. Each 'B' distiller was used purely for boiler make up water.

All of this was designed with one purpose, to rotate the 28.5-inch shaft which drove the four three bladed manganese bronze screws which propelled the ship. Each screw had a diameter of 15 feet and weighed 20 tons. When driving the ship forward, each of the screws rotated outwards: clockwise on the starboard side and counter-clockwise on the port side. The screws were designed to deliver 210 revolutions per minute at full speed, which permitted the adoption of propellers of higher efficiency.

Control and Steering

The *Hood* was capable of being directly controlled from one of four positions:

1. The conning tower.
2. The after engine room.
3. The lower conning tower (Emergency position)
4. The steering compartment (Auxiliary control only).

The *Hood* was fitted with two steering engines which were situated in the after engine room. Each of the steering engines consisted of three cylinders with direct-acting engines, worked by a hydraulic telemotor. These connected to shafts which extended to the aft steering gear. Auxiliary steering was provided by a Williams-Janey type electro-hydraulic variable speed motor located in the aft steering compartment which was also connected to a telemotor.

The *Hood* was steered by a single rudder which was mounted on the centreline of the ship. Produced and issued as a Standing Order in the 1930s was a document outlining the best ways to manoeuvre the *Hood* under various conditions. This document provides an insight into the manoeuvrability of the ship and her habits at sea:

3. Points of Interest.

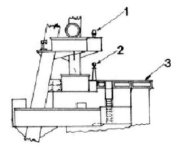

FORE BRIDGE (1920-1927)

1.   Torpedo rangefinder and platform. Note, this was removed during the 1927 refit.
2.   8ft Rangefinder.
3.   Compass platform built up and new windows provided after sea trials.

The Fore Bridge.

(a) The time required to get rudder on the ship is very considerably longer than is usual.

(b) She carries an increasingly large amount of weather helm as her speed decreases.

(c) She is sluggish in turning away from a wind before the beam. This wants watching when moving at slow speeds.

(d) She is very slow in answering Rudder when travelling at 8 knots or less. Use 20 degrees of rudder to start her swing, even for a small turn.

(e) Do not reduce speed of engines, or stop them, just before you want to use Rudder.

(f) On the other hand, an increase of revolutions as the rudder is put over increases appreciably her rate of swinging.

(g) With the execution of the condition of a strong bow wind, she can be kept under control with the rudder at very slow speed through the water as long as the Engines are moving Ahead, but once they are stopped it is often necessary to use one Engine Ahead to check or start a swing.

Wash on the rudder from either of the inner propellers moving Ahead is the secret of her manoeuvring power. This was proved when on one occasion both inner Engines were out of action: she was then very sluggish on her Rudder and moreover would not even point satisfactorily with the ship stopped.

(h) There being no wash effect on the rudder from propellers going Astern, the turning moment of going astern with one engine is not great unless Full Speed is used, but a "flick" ahead with the other engine and the Rudder hard over will gain control, and have little effect on headway.

(i) When the ship is travelling slowly she is greatly influenced in the time she will take to answer her Rudder by any slight tendency one way or the other at the moment the Rudder is put over.

A tendency of this kind may not be evident on the Compass: the eye can detect it more quickly.

(j) When running up to a berth with the Engines stopped it is useful to put the Telegraph to Slow Speed Astern and this get the Engines turning before you wish to start bringing the ship up. (See Note 3 under para.1).

(k) Slow astern Both will scarcely check her way at all.

(l) With 15 boilers (or even 12), she will pull up very quickly with Half Astern Both and 150 revolutions on the "Rev" Telegraph.

(m) When making a stern board she answers her Rudder sluggishly. A decided swing must be avoided or dealt with by using the Engines.

While with sternway, the propeller moment produced by either stopping one Engine or putting one Engine Ahead seems to be greater than that given by stopping or reversing one Engine when moving Ahead....

Like many good looking ladies she is inclined to be wilful [*sic*.], and likes surprising you. Watch her always and very closely. If the moment she gets up to mischief you give her a good hard thump with the engines and helm she will immediately behave lie [*sic*.] a perfect lady—like her sex in human form she responds to a heavy hand when she knows she has deserved it!![20]

Anchors and Cables

As completed, the *Hood* had three bow anchors. Two of these were bower anchors which weighed 9.6 tons each and were to be located on either side of the bow. In addition to these two anchors, there was a sheet anchor weighing 9.5 tons, which was situated behind the bower anchor on the starboard side. Connected to the capstan engine were two cable holders and a middle line capstan. A third cable holder was provided for the sheet cable, which was used for letting go only. In time, the sheet anchor was removed leaving her with the two bow anchors. At the stern, the *Hood* was originally fitted with a 3-ton anchor which was powered by an electric motor. The stern anchor was later moved to the shelter deck before being removed from the ship completely. At various times during her lifetime, the *Hood* carried additional anchors amidships.

The chains attached to the *Hood*'s bow anchors consisted of 1-foot 8-inch long links each of which were over 3 inches in diameter. The combined cables, when the three bow anchors were carried, consisted of forty-one shackles and had an overall combined length of 3,075 feet (937.26 m) with each of the bower cables being approximately fifteen shackles 1,125 foot (342.90 m) in length.

In addition to her anchors and the cables associated with them, the *Hood* was also equipped with Paravanes which were stored in two small structure located immediately abaft of the forward breakwater. Mounted to the forward superstructure, these torpedo-shaped devices were towed from lines on the bow and were used to detect mines or obstacles before they could damage the ship.

A line of sailors gathered to heave in the port paravane during spring 1933.

Boats

The *Hood* carried three steamboats, four motor launches, eleven sailing and pulling boats and a sufficient number of Carley floats and life rafts to evacuate the crew in the event that they had to abandon ship.

During her lifetime, the number and type of boats carried aboard the *Hood* varied. When commissioned in 1920, the *Hood* was equipped with: two 50-foot steam pinnacles; one 45-foot Admiral's barge; one 42-foot sailing launch; one 36-foot pinnacle; four 32-foot cutters; one 32-foot galley; two 30-foot Captain's gig; two 27-foot whalers; one 35-foot motor boat; two 16-foot dinghy; seven large Carley floats; two small Carley floats; and two night floats.

Throughout the 1930s, the positions of the various boats carried aboard the *Hood* changed, however, the basic composition of them remained the same. In 1941, the 50-foot steam pinnacles were replaced by 35-foot motor boats. In addition to this, the *Hood* was equipped with numerous 3-foot square Denton rafts, which were nicknamed 'biscuit floats'. Supplementing the boats, the *Hood* was equipped with life rings and life vests.

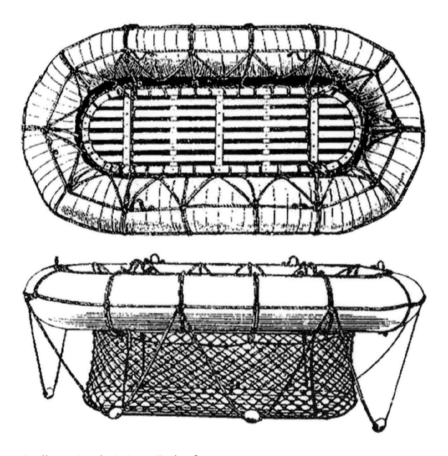

An illustration depicting a Carley float.

Above left: A close-up image of the *Hood*'s superstructure taken while the ship was anchored at Wellington, New Zealand during the Empire Cruise. A Carley float can be seen hanging on the platform behind the funnel. Note the range clock on the superstructure. (*PAColl-6304-14, Alexander Turnbull Library, Wellington, New Zealand*)

Above right: The *Hood* underway at low speed as members of the crew mill around the decks. Some of the boats carried aboard can be seen hanging amidships. (*Author's collection*)

One of the *Hood*'s steam picket boats pictured in Vancouver during the Cruise of the Special Service Squadron. (*City of Vancouver Archives, CVA 152-9.11*)

Looking forward on the starboard side, two of the *Hood*'s boats can be seen. (*City of Vancouver Archives, CVA 289-003.058*)

Right: Looking forward along
the boat deck. (*State Library of
Western Australia, 008627PD*)

Below: (*State Library of Western
Australia, 008626PD*)

Facilities

Despite being a ship, the *Hood* was akin to a small town. Aboard the *Hood*, there were 3,874 electric light fittings and six large searchlights. Each of the large searchlights produced light that was equivalent to 120 million candles. In addition to the six large searchlights, there were several smaller searchlights which were fitted with shutters to enable them to be used to flashlight signals. Inside the ship were 200 miles of cabling and wiring which in total weighed approximately 100 tons. Internal communications consisted of 380 telephones, which operated through one central exchange and several sub-exchanges.

Aboard the battlecruiser was a fully equipped medical facility. The sickbay consisted of general and isolation wards, an operating theatre, an x-ray department, and a dispensary. The medical staff consisted of two doctors, a dentist plus trained nursing staff. Below the quarterdeck, one could find the chapel. The chapel was dedicated to Our Lady and St Nicholas and was used for matins, evensong, and Holy Communion. However, church parades, when held, were conducted on the quarterdeck itself, or in bad weather, on the mess decks. When required, uniform alterations and the mending of boots and shoes would be undertaken by a rating in his spare time acting as a tailor or cobbler.

With a crew of 1,400, catering was essential. The cooking facilities aboard the *Hood* consisted of four small oil-fired ranges in the officer's galley while the galley for the bulk of the crew was equipped with three hotplate ranges, one fat frying range, two 90-gallon boiling kettles, two 120-gallon boiling kettles, two hot water tanks, three hot closets, and two wet steam cookers. Some of the equipment in the main galley was oil-fired while other items relied on steam drawn from the ship's main boilers. In her storerooms, provisions for up to four months, including one month's supply of fresh meat kept in a refrigerator, totalling 320 tons, were kept aboard.[21] In addition to the galleys, the *Hood* was equipped with a bakery. Equipped with a double-decked steam tube oven, the bakery was capable of producing approximately 250 pounds of bread in a single batch.

The crew ate on the mess decks. The *Hood* boasted larger than usual mess decks as not only were they used for eating but for many, the mess deck was where they slept. The *Hood*'s officers were provided with cabins, which were located aft, in the general area beneath the after concentrating position. The ship's captain was provided with a somewhat generous cabin on board as was the Admiral who flew his flag in the ship.

Located throughout the ship were numerous water closets, washing up spaces, urinals and baths. Aboard the *Hood*, the hot water facilities were far more outdated than those aboard the Royal Navy's 8-inch gun *County*-class heavy cruisers which were ordered in 1924 and first commissioned in 1928. In the case of the *Hood*, the gunroom bathroom boasted an antiquated hot water system in which cold water was drawn into a tank before steam was passed through the water to heat it. This method of heating water meant that only a limited quantity of hot water was available at any one time. For sanitation and the disposal of waste, the *Hood* was fitted with incinerators into which refuse was inserted while in port or in dry dock. When at sea, the ship's refuse was usually dumped overboard, leaving the ship via the midships 'gash chute'. In the 'Disinfector House' located directly behind the second funnel, medical personnel were able to cleanse bedding, clothing, medical equipment, and a multitude of other items.

The living spaces, water closets, wash places, mess decks, storerooms, and the places where the men worked were all ventilated by electrically driven exhaust fans that led directly to external vents or the open air. Around 200 electric fans pumped air through ventilation shafts around the ship that supplied the living and working spaces aboard. When the ship was sailing in cold climates, the air was often passed through a steam-powered heater to warm it up. Despite these ventilation systems, ventilation below decks was by and large quite poor.

Aircraft

As early as 1921, platforms had been fitted to 'B' and 'X' turrets in order to allow aircraft to fly off the *Hood*. The aircraft it was envisaged flying off the *Hood* were Fairey Flycatchers. The Flycatcher was a single seat biplane and is noted for being one of the earliest aircraft specifically designed for operations from aircraft carriers.[22] The Flycatcher was 23 feet (7.01 metres) long and had a wingspan of 29 feet (8.84 metres). With a top speed of 133 miles per hour (214 km/h), the Flycatcher had a range of 310 miles (499 km) and a service ceiling of 19,000 feet (5,790 metres).

The platforms for which it was intended that the Flycatchers would take off from the *Hood* consisted of ramps that could be unfolded along the gun barrels when air operations were required while the turrets were traversed into the wind to assist the aircraft in generating lift for take-off. Provisions were made aboard the *Hood* to fly off one or two Flycatchers despite there being a lack of enthusiasm from most naval officers.

The most serious attempt to provide the *Hood* with a form of air power came about during the ship's major refit of 1929–1931. By this time, the advantages of airpower at sea for the purposes of reconnaissance and gunnery spotting had been fully recognised. In response to this, the decision was taken to fit the *Hood*'s quarterdeck with the new Mk VI folding catapult and a handling crane and to provide her with a Fairy IIIF aircraft.

The Fairey III was a family of British reconnaissance biplane that was produced in both land and seaplane variants. The Fairey III first flew on 14 September 1917 and examples could still be found flying operationally during the Second World War. The Fairey IIIF first entered service in 1927 and was used by the Royal Navy as a replacement for the Fairey IIID.[23] Powered by a Napier Lion inline V-12 engine, the Fairey IIIF was 36 feet 9 inches (11.2 metres) long and had a wingspan of 45 feet 9 inches (13.95 metres). With a service ceiling of 20,000 feet (6,098 metres) and a range of 1,520 miles (2,432 km), the Fairey IIIF had a top speed of 120 mph (192 km/h) and carried a maximum crew of three. With regards armament, the Fairey IIIF was equipped with one forward firing .303-inch (7.7-mm) Vickers machine gun and one .303-inch Lewis gun that was fitted in a flexible mount for use by the aircraft's observer. In addition to this, the aircraft could carry up to 500 lb (227 kg) worth of bombs fitted under the wings.[24]

While the Fairey IIIF was a capable aircraft, its installation on the *Hood* was somewhat ill-conceived. As will be described later, the relationship between the *Hood* and her aircraft got off to a poor start when it crashed in Weymouth Bay in 1931. The additional weight that was added to the *Hood* during her refit reduced the freeboard of her quarterdeck to such an extent that the West Indies Cruise of 1932 would show the apparatus for operating an aircraft from the *Hood* to be completely unworkable at sea. So inoperable was the apparatus that S. V. Goodall of the Royal Corps of Naval Construction would record in his diary: 'the *Hood*'s catapult is a washout literally'.[25] So it was that within a few months of being installed that the catapult, the crane, and the aircraft were all removed. In 1937 the installation of a catapult atop 'X' turret was once again mooted, and again in 1940, while a planned reconstruction in 1942 was to provide the *Hood* with a double hanger and a new catapult aft of the funnel. Despite this, the *Hood* would be one of the few capital ships in the Royal Navy to enter the Second World War without the ability to launch or recover aircraft.

A Fairey IIIF on the *Hood*'s catapult, taken after the aircraft's crash a Weymouth. Note the damaged propeller. (*Author's collection*)

Additional Information

During the 1930s, members of the public could obtain a basic pamphlet about the *Hood* during visits to the ship during Navy Week. Entitled 'Notes for Visitors' and originally produced by Charpentier Ltd of Portsmouth, the end of the pamphlet contained a section entitled 'Points of Interest', which contained obscure facts about the ship. Some of the facts included on the back of the pamphlet can be read below:

> Three times round the ship is one mile.
> A normal breakfast for the ship's company is: four sides of bacon, 300lbs of tomatoes, 600lbs of bread, 75lbs of butter, and 100 gallons of tea.
> The monthly pay-roll of the ship is in the region of £6,000.
> Fuel consumption at full speed is three yards to the gallon.[26]

The crew of the *Hood* were the first in the Royal Navy to be issued with cups and saucers. Prior to her commissioning, crewmen of the Royal Navy's ships ate and drank out of bowels. In addition to this, the *Hood* had tablecloths made out of while oilcloth, which replaced the cortisone ones that were used aboard other ships.[27]

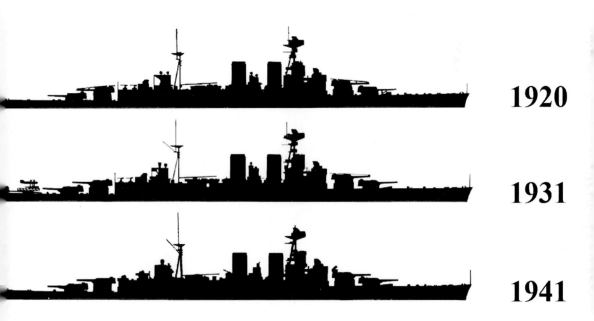

Silhouettes of the *Hood* showing the major changes in her structure between 1920 and 1941. (*Author's collection*)

5

'A Wonderful Welcome'

On Friday, 9 January 1920, flanked by tugs, the *Hood* was safely manoeuvred down the Clyde to Greenock where advanced parties of stokers and sailors from HMS *Lion* were already arriving to take up their new posting. Eight days earlier, on 1 January, Captain Wilfred Tomkinson became the first commanding officer of the *Hood*.

Tomkinson had joined the Royal Navy in 1891 and had served aboard the destroyer HMS *Fame* during the Boxer Rebellion. During the First World War, he saw service commanding the destroyer HMS *Lurcher* at the Battle of Heligoland in 1914 and at Dogger Bank in 1915. Appointed as the Senior Naval Officer, Submarines in Venice in 1915, Tomkinson was appointed as the commanding officer of the light cruiser HMS *Aurora* in 1916 before seeing action during the Zeebrugge Raid and the Ostend Raid in 1918.

Under Tomkinson's command, having been moved to Greenock, the *Hood* was first taken for steam trials off the Isle of Arran before she sailed to Rosyth on 12 January. The journey to Rosyth provided a foretaste of things to come for the sailors of the *Hood*. The journey to Rosyth was made in a Force 8 gale with waves cloaking her forecastle and quarterdeck. It was here that the *Hood*'s reputation as 'the largest submarine in the Navy' began.[1] In the high waves of heavy seas, it was not uncommon for the bow of the ship to dip into the troughs between waves. As the bow rose back up the ship would shudder. Dennis Finden was one member of the *Hood*'s crew who recalled this sea-keeping quality all too well. 'At times she'd shake like a jelly. I'm not kidding—she'd shake like a jelly.'[2] Boy Seaman Frank Pavey recalled:

> At high power she would throb like the devil. I felt sorry for the midshipmen, because their flat was right aft—the very after part of the ship, right above the screws. So they had a massage every time they turned in, I should think![3]

The high seas and dipping of the bows had a tendency to wreak havoc in places such as the latrines. Ken 'Nobby' Clark would recall how if men were sitting on one of the toilets and the bows dipped the sailors would quickly have to stand up

Above: Taken on 9 January 1920, this image shows the area around the *Hood*'s bridge and conning tower prior to the ship being manoeuvred down the Clyde to Greenock. Note the workmen on the *Hood*'s decks. (*Author's collection*)

Below: The *Hood* being manoeuvred down the Clyde to Greenock, 9 January 1920. (*Author's collection*)

lest 'they got their "own" back' or worse, someone else's. Such conditions were made worse by clogged drains which would cause the floors to be flooded by waste from the toilets, and seawater.

At Rosyth, the *Hood* was taken in hand for docking until late February when she returned to Clydebank. Having arrived at Rosyth on 13 January, the *Hood* was forced to wait in the Firth of Forth for six days until the wind conditions and the current permitted her to be drawn into the dockyard's No. 2 basin. While at Rosyth trials were carried out to establish her final displacement, which revealed the ship to be 46,680 tons at deep load, which was 1,470 tons above the 1917 legend. The vast majority of this increase in tonnage resulted from increased amounts of armour.

On 8 March, official sea trials began. These trials, conducted off the Isle of Arran, included full-power trials (18 March), steering trials (19 March), and deep-load trials (22–23 March). In addition to these trials, gunnery trials were also undertaken. Rear-Admiral Sir Roger Keyes and d'Eyncourt were both aboard the *Hood* for these trials and confirmed that they were a huge success. The advanced boiler and turbine technology that had been incorporated in the *Hood*'s design allowed her to develop more power than the ships of the *Renown*-class. During her full-power trials off the Isle of Arran, the *Hood* attained a speed of 32.07 knots, which gave her the distinction of being the most powerful ship in the world by some margin. This speed came at a price, however, as it was revealed that to maintain 32 knots, 70 tons of fuel had to be burned every hour, giving her a consumption rate of 9 feet per gallon. Speed trials revealed a mere 7 tons of fuel was required each hour to allow her to sail at the economical speed of 14 knots and that 25 knots could be attained on two-fifths power.[4]

With these trials completed, the *Hood* returned to Rosyth where a detailed examination of her hull and structure was undertaken. The final cost to the British government for constructing the *Hood* was £6,025,000 (the equivalent of £253,292,734 in 2018). This was almost double the cost of any previous ship constructed for the Royal Navy, HMS *Renown* having cost £3,117,204.

On 29 March 1920, HMS *Hood* was commissioned with a crew drawn from the battlecruiser HMS *Lion*. Early on commissioning day, fleets of lorries began arriving from barracks, ships and shore establishments. Discharged on to the jetty, the parties of men mustered in the Royal Navy Barracks before marching through the dockyard behind a seaman band and macebearer until suddenly they found themselves in the shadow of the *Hood*. Additional crewmen arrived singly or in groups, arriving from training facilities or a spell of leave. All arrived with their hammocks, kit bags, cases, and ditty boxes with which they would make their life.

At the head of the ship's brow, each man reported to the Regulating Petty Officer whom they informed whether they were a 'Grog' or 'Temperance'. 'Grog' and 'Temperance' referred to a man's decision of whether or not to take up his rum ration. Having reported to the regulating petty officer, the crewmen fell in by their divisions at their allotted spot on the upper deck. Once mustered, they were led down below by the divisional officer to stow their kit and to sling their hammocks

The *Hood* in British waters in 1920 with her main topgallant mast raised. (*NH 60402, US Naval History and Heritage Command*)

The *Hood* during her speed trials. (*Richard Toffolo*)

on the mess decks that would in all likelihood be their home for the next two or three years. The arrival of the last contingent of men aboard the *Hood* permitted the White Ensign to be hoisted and for the commissioning pendant to be run up the masthead. This done, Captain Tomkinson reported his ship commissioned with a crew of 967 to the commander-in-chief of Rosyth dockyard.[5]

From 15 April until 15 May, the *Hood* was taken in hand for docking. During this period, the 15-inch rangefinder on the spotting top was installed while the main topgallant mast was lowered. In addition to this, platforms were fitted to 'A' and 'B' turrets which would form flying-off platforms for aircraft. On 14 May, the ship was inspected by the Royal Navy and basin trials of her main engines were undertaken before she was accepted from the builders and fully commissioned as a ship of the Royal Navy on 15 May.

Having been commissioned into the Royal Navy, the *Hood* departed Rosyth for Cawsand Bay where she arrived on 17 May. The following day, the flag of the Rear Admiral Commanding Battlecruiser Squadron, Sir Roger Keyes, was hoisted before she weighed anchor and sailed to Plymouth. On 26 and 27 May, torpedo trials were undertaken before the *Hood* embarked on her first official voyage, which would largely set the tone for her career when on 29 May, in the company of HMS *Tiger* and nine destroyers headed by HMS *Spenser*, she left Portland to embark on a cruise of Scandinavia. At the time, the civil war in Russia had been raging for three years and it was apparent that the Soviets had gained the upper hand against the White movement and the Allied intervention forces (which included Britain, the United States, France, Greece, Japan, China, Italy,

The *Hood* shortly after being accepted from the builders and fully commissioned into the Royal Navy. This image was taken sometime on or shortly after 15 May 1920. The 15-inch rangefinder on the spotting top has installed while the main topgallant mast has been lowered.

and the Baltic States). With a Soviet victory becoming apparent, the policy of the British government switched towards maintaining the sovereignty of the Baltic States and maintaining British interests in the region. So it was that the Admiralty ordered Admiral Keyes to take the *Hood* and HMS *Tiger* plus an assortment of destroyers and to sail into the Baltic and to alert the Soviet fleet at Kronstadt of the consequences should it undertake any offensive action. The easing of tensions with the Soviets and negotiations between the Soviets and the Baltic states restricted the Battlecruiser Squadron to a cruise of Scandinavia which had been planned as a cover for the operation.

On the evening of 31 May, as the squadron was nearing Denmark, Tomkinson held a memorial service on the *Hood*'s quarterdeck for all those lost at the Battle of Jutland. On 1 June, the *Hood* and the Squadron arrived in Køge Bugt. On 4 June, the Squadron weighed anchor and sailed to Kalmar, Sweden before moving on to Nynäshamn (Stockholm) on 7 June. While at Nynäshamn, on 10 June, the *Hood* was visited by King Gustav V and Prince Eugen of Sweden. On 13 June, the squadron departed Nynäshamn to undertake a series of exercises before anchoring at Åbenrå, Denmark from 15 to 17 June. Copenhagen was the next stop on the cruise. She was in Copenhagen from 18 to 23 June; on the 19th, the *Hood* was visited by King Christian X of Denmark. The King made another visit to the *Hood* on 20 June, accompanied on this occasion by his wife Queen Alexandrine. The Battlecruiser Squadron departed Copenhagen on 23 June and set a course north for Christiana (modern-day Oslo) where it arrived on 24 June. As the squadron sailed up Oslofjord, there was little doubt that the *Hood* was making a lasting impression on all who saw her, as recalled by Lieutenant-Commander Douglas Fairbairn:

A few miles farther on comes the narrowest part, a strait nearly ten miles long and but half a mile wide, with 600 feet of water under the ship's bottom. With the wooded shore slipping past on either side, the *Hood* pursued her stately way through this narrow channel. At each little village we passed were crowds of cheering Norwegians, some of whom even swam out towards the ship. At every white flagstaff among the trees the Norwegian flag was flying, and dipped in salute as we went by: this continued for the whole tour. It was a wonderful welcome, and to those ashore the mighty *Hood*, the largest warship in the world, winding her way through those land-locked waters must have been a magnificent sight.[6]

On 26 June, the Squadron was visited by King Haakon VII of Norway who returned again on the 27th accompanied by Queen Maud and Crown Prince Olaf. The Scandinavian cruise came to an end on 1 July when the Squadron weighed anchor and departed Christiana for Scapa Flow where it arrived on 3 July.

The *Hood* sailed from Scapa Flow to Invergordon on 16 July before proceeding to Dunbar and then Rosyth at the beginning of August. At Rosyth, on 5 August, the *Hood* provided search parties and armed guards for the boarding of the surrendering Imperial German Naval warships SMS *Helgoland*, SMS *Rügen*, and

The *Hood* at anchor in Scapa Flow. In the background, either the *Repulse* or the *Renown* is visible. Note the planks that are laid across the turret to form the flying-off platform stacked atop 'B' turret. (*Author's collection*)

The *Hood* at anchor in Scapa Flow.

SMS *Westphalen*. Departing Rosyth on 10 August, the *Hood* sailed to Lamlash where her crew won the Battlecruiser Regatta before sailing onto Penzance. On 28 August, the *Hood* was to be found anchored off the Isles of Scilly. She moved to her home port of Devonport on 6 September where she remained until the beginning of October.

From 8 October until 3 December, the *Hood* was to be found at anchor at Portland. Despite being anchored at Portland, she was destined to take part in one of the most poignant events to commemorate the Great War. By the end of the Great War in November 1918, in Britain, some 5.7 million men had joined the armed forces. This amounted to a significant proportion of the pre-war labour force, which at the time of the 1911 census had totalled 12.6 million. During the course of the conflict, the British Empire lost approximately 1 million men.[7] Of this figure, it has been estimated that British deaths totalled somewhere in the region of 750,000. Approximately 3 million Britons out of a population of 42 million lost a close relative during the war. These people constituted the 'primary bereaved'; the 'secondary bereaved' (those who under normal circumstances would have attended the funeral of the dead) encompassed almost the entire British population.[8]

In 1920, the Reverend David Railton, who served as an army Chaplin on the Western Front, wrote to the Dean of Westminster and proposed that an unidentified British soldier should be taken from the battlefields of France and buried with due ceremony in Westminster Abbey to represent the many thousands of dead from the British Empire. This idea was supported by the Dean of Westminster and also by the Prime Minister David Lloyd George.[9] On the evening of 7 November 1920, the body of an unknown warrior of the Great War was selected and transported to London. On 11 November 1920, the coffin was buried in Westminster Abbey in the presence of King George V, other members of the Royal Family, Ministers, and other guests. Before being buried, the coffin of the unknown warrior was drawn through the streets of London on a horse-drawn gun carriage through silent crowds. The *Hood*'s marine detachment was called upon to supply a guard of honour at the burial and lined the Mall with bayonets fixed. While undoubtedly an honour for the men who made up the *Hood*'s marine detachment, the fact that it was a detachment from the *Hood* that was called upon to supply the guard of honour did not go down well among the ranks of the Royal Navy as the *Hood* was regarded as the only vessel of the Grand Fleet to have escaped service in the Great War.[10]

The *Hood*'s time at Portland came to an end on 3 December when she weighed anchor and sailed to Devonport where from 6 December until 6 January 1921, she was taken in hand for a refit and alterations.

6

Seeing Red

The *Hood* was released from dockyard control on 6 January and moved to Cawsand Bay the following day where she remained until 11 January. From Cawsand Bay, the *Hood* first sailed to Portland and then departed British waters for Arousa Bay, Spain. While at Arousa Bay, on 23 January, the *Hood* was visited by King Alfonso XIII of Spain before she weighed anchor and sailed to Vigo. Departing Vigo on 7 February, the *Hood* made for Gibraltar where she anchored until the 23rd before returning to Arousa Bay and then Devonport. In the company of the Battlecruiser Squadron, while on route back to Devonport, on 20 March, those aboard the *Hood* held a memorial service over the position where the submarine *K5* had been lost with all hands on 20 January, 120 miles to the south-west of the Isles of Scilly.

The end of March through to the first half of May 1921 found the *Hood* at Rosyth. On 31 March, Rear Admiral Sir Walter Cowan arrived aboard the *Hood* and began to fly his flag in the ship as the commanding officer of the Battlecruiser Squadron. To stand alongside the new admiral on board, the *Hood* also received a new captain, Captain Geoffrey Mackworth. Cowan arrived aboard the *Hood* as a fifty-year-old quasi-hero of the Baltic, as the man who two years earlier had bottled up the Soviet fleet and had planned its potential destruction at Kronstadt during the Russian Civil War. Cowan was a highly strung individual with a reputation as something of a bully who was irritable and plagued by a quick temper and who held high ideals for enforcing strict discipline and efficiency. The crew of the *Hood* did not like what they heard or saw of their new admiral or their new captain, as William Stone recalled:

When I first joined the *Hood* the Admiral flying his flag from her was 'Titchy' Cowan. Walter Henry Cowan was a terrible chap who never missed a chance of telling off any of the officers or ratings. I remember that he would often report the boat crew boys for not pulling properly. On one such occasion, he had a group of boys sentenced to five days in the cells. Boys could not be given time in the cells so he had the whole group rated to Ordinary Seamen so that they could be jailed. I heard that this was subsequently overruled and that they were rated to boys again but it is a

The *Hood* on the Firth of Forth during the 1920s. Behind the *Hood* stands the Forth Bridge. It is likely that at the time that this photo was taken, she had put in at Rosyth. (*Author's collection*)

A roof has been added to the *Hood*'s raised compass platform and the main gallant topmast has been raised, 1921.

good example of what a hard man he was and how he would always find a way of exercising his will on the men under his command. At divisions on the first Sunday of the month Cowan would stand on a spit-kid on the quarterdeck, and the whole ship's company would march past and salute him.

But when he needed to address the crew he had to stand on a box if anyone were to see him, for he was a very short man. In command with him was Captain Geoffrey Mackworth who was likewise severe and cruel. Cowan's on board mascot was a goat that he had won in a raffle competition. The goat was known to eat cigarette ends, ledgers and assorted ship's equipment.[1]

Bill, as the goat was known, was to be the source of amusement for members of the *Hood*'s crew under Cowan's command. Likely as a form of payback at the Admiral, on at least one occasion, one member of the *Hood*'s crew pushed the goat through the skylight located above the Admiral's cabin so that the goat landed on the Admiral's bed.

Despite their dislike of Cowan and Mackworth, there was little else for the crew to do but to carry on. On 1 April, the *Hood* was taken in hand for docking. Her stay at Rosyth coincided with a series of coal and railway strikes in the area. As a precaution for the protection of essential services ashore owing to the fear of a general strike and riots, the government ordered Cowan to put patrols ashore from the *Hood* to protect vital infrastructure. From 5 until 21 April, three battalions of men comprising marines, seamen, and midshipmen were placed under the command of Squadron Gunnery Officer Commander Lionel Wells. The battalions were deployed to Cowdenbeath where a month earlier there had been a riot at the Kinglassie Colliery. To coincide with the other strikes, a sympathy strike by the Scottish Motor Transport bus drivers was expected, which would have left the patrols with no way to reach the mining areas. This problem was overcome by Cowan who organised instruction in bus driving for the midshipmen. At Cowdenbeath, the shore patrols found the miners in a riotous state, yet they did not need their rifles. Tensions were eased by the seamen challenging the miners to a game of football. A small detachment of men was also sent to patrol the Forth Bridge, which it was feared was at risk from saboteurs.

Cowan had a more pressing issue to deal with, however, when it appeared that the dissatisfaction of the strikers in Scotland was spreading to the *Hood*. During his rounds of the ship, Commander Richard Lane-Pool encountered a passive demonstration where the seamen's mess had been decorated in red bunting. Both Cowan and Mackworth were furious and interpreted the action as a sign of revolution and an inducement to mutiny. Able Seamen Thomas Guthrie and John McKirdy were both court-martialled for mutinous practice but were acquitted. Their acquittal did not satisfy Cowan and Mackworth, who proceeded to charge Stoker John Hall with inciting men to commit an act of mutiny and court-martialled the master-at-arms, Walter Batten, for apparently concealing a mutinous practice. The case against Batten was not proved while Hall was held responsible for the incident and was sentenced to three years of penal servitude.

In the wake of the strikes, Cowan tightened discipline in the Battlecruiser Squadron and issued a memorandum to the commanding officers of HMS *Hood*, *Repulse*, and *Tiger* with the intended aim of 'producing a better and more complete understanding and uniformity of thought, procedure and action among us and increase thereby the efficiency and discipline among ships' companies'.[2]

Out of docking, the *Hood* left Rosyth for Portland and then Devonport. The summer 1921 cruise was cancelled before the ship left Devonport on 13 July to conduct two days' worth of exercises with the Atlantic Fleet. The exercises completed, the *Hood* put in at Weymouth from 15 July until the 22nd when she moved to Portland. The *Hood* departed Portland for Cawsand Bay on 27 July before moving on to Devonport where she arrived on the 28th. Taken in hand for a refit from 28 July until 2 September, when released from dockyard hands, the *Hood* sailed north to Invergordon. The period from 4 September until 29 October would see the *Hood* alternating between Invergordon and Scapa Flow every couple of days with the occasional visit to such places as Shandwick Bay on the Moray Firth (10–11 October) and Tarbet Ness (12–13 October).

While at Scapa Flow from 17 to 29 October, the *Hood* participated in the Combined Fleet Regatta. On 18 October, the *Hood*'s teams succeeded in retaining the Queenstown Cup. However, the following day, they lost the Battlecruiser

(*Christopher Hancock*)

'Cock' to the *Repulse*. On 21 October, the silver cockerel was handed over to the *Repulse* in a funeral style procession. The *Hood*'s marine band led a procession consisting of a party of midshipmen and Bill the goat to the *Repulse*, all the while playing Chopin's 'Funeral March' whereupon the trophy was presented to Captain Dudley Pound. It was not all doom and gloom for the *Hood*, however, for on 24 and 25 October, her teams met with success winning first the Battenberg Cup and then the Hornby Cup.

With the Combined Fleet Regatta at an end, on 29 October, the *Hood* weighed anchor and sailed to the Cromarty Firth before returning to Invergordon on 3 November. The *Hood* would alternate between Invergordon and the Cromarty Firth until 13 November when she set sail for Portland where she arrived on 15 November. Sailing to Plymouth Sound on 3 December, the *Hood* dropped anchor in Devonport from 5 December until 9 January 1922.

The *Hood* sailed to Falmouth Bay on 9 January from where on 17 January she departed to begin a spring cruise to Spain and the Mediterranean. Arousa Bay was the first stop of the *Hood* from 20 to 25 January before she sailed to Gibraltar, arriving on 27 January. On 6 February, the *Hood* weighed anchor and left Gibraltar to participate in Combined Fleet Exercises before sailing on to Pollença Bay where she anchored between 9 and 20 February. Departing Pollença Bay, the *Hood* made a port call at Toulon, France, and then Valencia, Spain before sailing on to Málaga where she arrived on 8 March. While at Málaga, a team from the *Hood* participated in a sailing race with a team from the *Renown* for the Squadron cup. The outcome of the race is unknown. The *Hood* departed Málaga in the company of the *Renown* at 2.45 a.m. on 14 March. As the two ships sailed to Gibraltar they conducted a night gunnery exercise using starshell. The *Hood* would remain at Gibraltar from 15 to 22 March during which time numerous drills were carried out including Marine detachment, landing party, and gunnery drills.

The *Hood* departed Gibraltar on 22 March in the company of HMS *Repulse*. Together, the two battlecruisers sailed to Vigo. While *en route* to Vigo, on 23 and 24 March, the *Hood* and the *Repulse* conducted inclination exercises with the ships of the 1st Battle Squadron, namely HMS *Warspite* and HMS *Valiant*. In addition to the inclination exercises undertaken in the company of the 1st Battle Squadron, the battlecruisers conducted torpedo practices. The *Hood* and the *Repulse* dropped anchor at Vigo on 25 March. During their time in the Spanish port, numerous short cruises and drills were undertaken before they weighed anchor on 8 April and sailed to Plymouth.

While *en route* to Plymouth, the battlecruisers engaged in full power, gunnery and torpedo trials. During a torpedo exercise conducted on 10 April, the *Hood* was struck by two dummy torpedoes but was assessed to have survived their detonations with little damage. Later that day, the two ships dropped anchor in Cawsand Bay before the *Hood* sailed to Plymouth the next day. The *Hood*'s time at Plymouth was to be short for on 14 April, she weighed anchor and sailed north to Rosyth where she dropped anchor on 17 April. On 19 April, she was taken in

The *Hood*'s 15-inch guns during combined fleet exercises. In the background is HMS *Renown* and an unidentified aircraft carrier. (*Beeldbank WO2, NIOD*)

hand for docking and berthed in the No. 2 dock. Crewmen from the north were granted two weeks leave while the ship was in dock. For those not granted leave, a programme of repairing, cleaning, and painting ensued. Released from dockyard control on 8 May, the *Hood* departed Rosyth for Plymouth. During the journey south, sea boat crew training was conducted. Upon the ship's arrival in Devonport on 10 May, leave was given to the entire crew until 31 May.

On 20 and 21 June, she fired salutes and raised cheers for the Prince of Wales, Prince Edward (later Edward VIII), during the Prince's visit to Devonport. Sailing to Weymouth on 22 June, the *Hood* conducted submarine attack exercises before sailing to Swanage Bay on 26 June. On 27 June, the *Hood* returned to Devonport briefly before sailing once more to Swanage Bay. While en route back to Swanage Bay, the *Hood* participated in an inclination exercise with ships of the 1st Battle Squadron. Between 28 and 30 June, the *Hood* sailed from Swanage Bay to Portland and then on to Weymouth during which time 15-inch gun firing trials were conducted; some 5.5-inch firing exercises were planned but these were cancelled.

On 2 July 1922, the *Hood* was in Torbay. While there, on 5 July, she was visited by King George V. It was during the visit of King George V that it was first mentioned that the *Hood* would represent the Royal Navy at the centennial celebrations of Brazilian independence that were to be held that autumn in Rio de Janeiro. Leaving Torbay, the *Hood* sailed to Devonport. While *en route*, on 7 July, she sank the ex-Imperial German Navy light cruiser *Nürnberg* as a target before arriving at Devonport the next day.[3] Soon it was confirmed that Cowan was to take the *Hood* and the *Repulse* to Rio to represent the Royal Navy and that while they were there, a sporting competition for the attending navies was to be held.

From 8 July until 14 August, preparations for the Brazilian cruise were underway at Devonport. Such were the preparations, it quickly became clear that the *Hood* and the *Repulse* were to embark on more than a goodwill cruise. National prestige was at stake, and with that, neither effort nor expense was spared to equip the battlecruisers, with the Fleet being stripped of its finest sportsmen. On 14 August, the *Hood* and the *Repulse* left Devonport for Gibraltar from where they sailed on to São Vicente, Cape Verde. While the *Hood* and the *Repulse* were on their way to Cape Verde, one of the boy sailors aboard the *Hood* was found to be missing. Several thorough searches of the ship turned up no signs of the boy and the subsequent court of inquiry returned the verdict that tragically the boy had been lost at sea. Reg Bragg served aboard the *Hood* at this time with his brother and takes up the story:

> On the *Hood*'s return trip she stopped over the presumed spot where he [the boy sailor] was lost, and a memorial service was held, volleys fired, and wreaths dropped in the water.
>
> A few years later, my brother, who had previously left the *Hood*, went into a pub in Sydney, Australia, and could hardly believe his eyes when he beheld the missing boy. When he greeted him by name, he was told to keep quiet. The story came out that he had jumped ship at Gibraltar, and his brother on a merchant [ship] stowed him away to Sydney where he joined the Australian Navy and lived happily ever after.[4]

On 29 August, the *Hood* crossed the equator for the first time. The event was celebrated in a time-honoured fashion before Neptune's court. W. Connor who sailed with the *Hood* to Rio recorded events:

> As we were due to cross the Equator on this portion of our journey, preparations were made for carrying out the ceremony of 'Crossing the Line'. Various meetings were held by those responsible, though the details were shrouded in mystery, and the novices, of whom we carried a good few, began to get somewhat nervous as the time approached, due primarily to the exaggerated rumours which were fling [*sic*.] about as to the 'punishment' they would receive. Four days after leaving St Vincent we arrived at the Equator, crossing the 'line' at nine p.m. A short time previous Father Neptune, accompanied by Amphitrite and their 'court', assembled on the fore end of the ship, which was shrouded in darkness; the lower deck was cleared, and the guard and band paraded to receive them. Suddenly the look-out on the bridge reported 'Line right ahead, Sir'; the Captain gave the order, 'All hands clear away the "line"'. Engines were stopped; a voice was then heard on the fo'csle hailing the ship, searchlights were switched on, and Neptune and his court were discovered on board in full regalia. After asking the name of the ship, whither bound, the entire court, escorted by the band, marched in stately procession to the quarterdeck, where they were received by the Admiral. Greetings were exchanged and officers

were presented to Father Neptune, who announced to all and sundry that he would return on board the following morning and hold his court, where various honours would be presented and all novices were to be ready to be initiated in the 'Order of the Bath'. Neptune and Amphitrite, the latter leaning on the arm of the Admiral, then departed. Punctually at nine a.m. the next day Neptune and his court again appeared and proceeded to the quarter-deck, where an investure [*sic.*] was held, the Rear-Admiral, Captain, and other officers receiving various decorations, after which Neptune gave orders that all novices, irrespective of rank or rating, who had not previously 'crossed the line' should be at once initiated; for this purpose a huge canvas bath had been erected. The candidates were lined up and were inspected in turn by Neptune's physician and his assistants. After swallowing some extremely vile 'medicine' they were passed to the barbers, who lathered them with soap and flour applied with a whitewash brush, finally being 'shaved' with a large wooden razor. Whilst this portion of the operation was in progress the 'victim' would suddenly find himself canted on to a greasy slide which led to the bath, where some twenty lusty 'Bears' gave him a severe dunking, after which he was received by Neptune and presented with a certificate. This was carried out throughout the whole of the day without interruption; no one escaped the ordeal, even the ship's pet, a somewhat hefty goat, being the final candidate.[5]

The *Hood* and the *Repulse* arrived at Rio on 3 September. Already at Rio were the Brazilian Navy's battleships *São Paulo* and *Minas Gerades*, three elderly

Men gather on the quarterdeck and atop 'Y' during the procession of Neptune and his Court, 30 August 1922. (*Author's collection*)

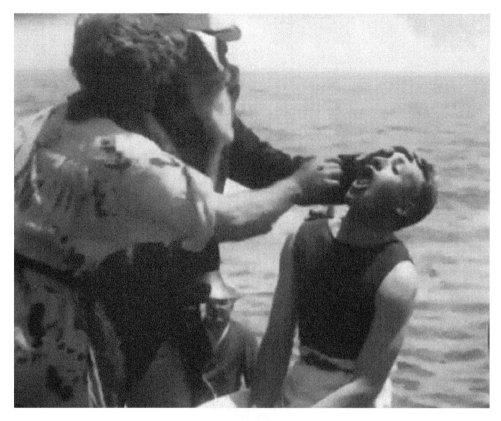

Above: Taken during the crossing the line ceremony, this photograph shows one of *Hood's* crewmen being provided with 'medicine' by Neptune's physician before being passed to the barbers, who lathered them with soap and flour applied with a whitewash brush, finally being 'shaved' with a large wooden razor. (*Author's collection*)

Below: 'The "victim" would suddenly find himself canted on to a greasy slide which led to the bath, where some twenty lusty "Bears" gave him a severe dunking, after which we was [*sic.*] received by Neptune and presented with a certificate'. (*Author's collection*)

cruisers of the Imperial Japanese Navy, and a pair of sloops representing Mexico and Portugal. Two days following the arrival of the *Hood* and the *Repulse*, the American representation arrived at Rio in the shape of the battleships USS *Maryland* and *Nevada*. According to Midshipman Robert Elkins, 'The *Maryland*, which is one of the most modern battleships afloat, looked very small compared to ourselves and *Repulse*. She was also very dirty'.[6] On 7 September, each ship landed a naval battalion for a parade through the city before the commencement of the sporting tournament the following day. On 8 September, it was a day of triumph for the Royal Navy, Robert Elkins recording: 'In every race our competitors walked through, the Japanese and Americans being nowhere this is just the sort of thing that raises British prestige, which has suffered here just lately at the hands of the Yanks'.[7] The first setback for the British competitors came on 10 September. That morning, the Royal Navy lost 0–2 in the football final against the Brazilian Navy. That afternoon, the Brazilians won the skiffs while the US Navy took victory in the Seaman's Cutter with the Royal Navy coming second. Some pride was, however, salvaged with victory in the Midshipman's Cutter. In the athletics events held on the 11th, the *Hood* and the *Repulse*'s sportsmen won nine out of the fifteen events held.

The climax of the sporting events came with the boxing competition held on the evening of the 11th. Some 4,000 British and American personnel crowded into a marque that had been pitched on the outskirts of the city. Eight bouts were scheduled, the outcome of which was to decide the overall winner of the games. Heading into the final bout, the British led the Americans by four wins to three. The British had reason to be confident ahead of the final bout as the last boxer was the Royal Navy's and the British Amateur Champion, Petty Officer Spillar, a Stoker aboard the *Hood*. Midshipman Gerald Cobb recalled events:

> Spillar advanced to touch gloves with his rival—as all boxers in previous bouts had done—when the American immediately struck Spillar with a straight left, followed by a right hook. Curtains for Spillar. Uproar![8]

Quick action by Cowan prevented the uproar developing into a riot as he climbed into the ring and ordered his men to give three cheers for the US Navy. The final bout was declared null and void, giving the British Squadron overall victory. Cowan's American counterpart apologised for the final bout.

The following day, the *Maryland* and the *Nevada* weighed anchor and set sail for New York, cheered on as they sailed past by the *Hood*'s company. That evening, a grand ball was held on the *Hood*'s quarterdeck, which was attended by President Epitácio Pessoa and the cream of Rio society. On 13 September, the squadron was presented with the trophies that it had won for their achievements in the sporting competitions before taking part in the closing act of the centennial celebrations: an illuminated water pageant held in Botafogo Bay in which the *Hood*'s chief painter was cast in the role of Britannia. Raising anchor on 14 September, the *Hood* and the *Repulse* swept out of the anchorage at Rio and into the South Atlantic, destined for Santos (modern-day São Paulo), leaving a flotilla of Brazilian destroyers in their wake.[9] The *Hood* and the *Repulse* dropped anchor at Santos on 15 September. Three days after arriving, battalions from the ships took part in a parade through the city before the ships departed on 20 September.

Leaving Santos, the *Hood* and the *Repulse* sailed to Trinidad where they anchored between 30 September and 10 October before moving on to Barbados. Anchoring for four days at Barbados, the squadron swiftly moved on to St Lucia from where they journeyed onto Las Palmas, the Canary Islands. The squadron spent ten says sailing from St Lucia to Las Palmas, one day of which was spent anchored off Rosseau, Dominica. From 30 October until 2 November, the squadron anchored at Las Palmas before sailing to Gibraltar where it arrived on 4 November. While at Gibraltar, the *Hood*'s crew partook in the Battlecruiser Squadron Regatta, which was held between 15 and 17 November. Leaving Gibraltar on 30 November, the *Hood* returned to her home port of Devonport where she would remain until 6 January 1923, thus allowing her crew to spend Christmas and New Year at home.

Between 1 and 6 January, while at Devonport, the *Hood*'s crew conducted action station exercises before the ship weighed anchor to conduct inclination exercises with HMS *Resolution*. Leaving Devonport on 6 January, the *Hood* sailed to Portland. Four days following her arrival, she left Portland with the Atlantic Fleet for Gibraltar. Between 10 and 15 January, during the journey to Gibraltar, the *Hood* engaged in a series of exercises against the battleships and cruisers of the Atlantic Fleet as well as against submarines. Things did not go according to plan, however, for the *Hood* was 'struck' by torpedoes, which saw her awarded a negative grade in the exercises.

The *Hood* arrived in Gibraltar on 15 January. While in Gibraltar, a number of exercises were undertaken including crew drills plus day and night gunnery exercises. In addition to this, in co-operation with the *Repulse*, torpedo exercises were undertaken. When not on exercises, the crew engaged in a programme of cleaning and painting. On 31 January, Petty Officer Thomas Broad of the *Hood* died as a result of an acute haemorrhage of the pancreas. The day following Broad's death, the *Hood* weighed anchor and sailed to Málaga. While *en route*, submarine exercises in conjunction with the *Repulse* and the *Queen Elizabeth* were staged. Having docked at Málaga, a further programme of cleaning was instigated between boat training and a gunnery programme. On 5 February, the *Hood* was placed at 'Squadron at Home' status to the residents of Málaga. She left Málaga on 6 February in the company of the *Repulse* and sail to Cartagena where the ships saluted numerous dignitaries before moving on to Valencia on 8 February. The *Hood* and the *Repulse* anchored at Valencia until 16 February, during which time the squadron was placed at 'At Home' status to the local residents.

The *Hood* and the *Repulse* sailed for Gibraltar on 16 February and dropped anchor at the Rock the following day. While there, the ship's company took part in a march past and review for Cowan and then for Admiral Sir John de Robeck, the Commander-in-Chief of the Atlantic Fleet. Departing Gibraltar on 24 March, the *Hood* sailed to Arousa Bay where she dropped anchor between 26 and 31 March before sailing to Devonport.

The *Hood* arrived back at Devonport on 3 April and would remain at anchor there until 21 April; she then weighed anchor and sailed to Rosyth where between 23 April and 11 May, she was taken in hand for docking. The *Hood* returned to Devonport on 14 May and was taken in hand for a refit on 15 May. That same day, she was paid off and recommissioned as 'Flagship of the Battlecruiser Squadron'. The paying off of the *Hood* marked the end of Cowan's tenure as the admiral commanding the Battlecruiser Squadron and also saw the departure of Captain Mackworth. Rear-Admiral Frederick Field was Cowan's successor as the commander of the Battlecruiser Squadron.

Born on 18 April 1871, Field joined the Royal Navy in 1884 and had attained the rank of lieutenant by 1893. During the Boxer Rebellion of 1900, Field served aboard HMS *Barfleur*. Wounded during the rebellion, Field was Mentioned in Dispatches. Promoted to commander in 1902, he was promoted to captain in December 1907. During the First World War, Field first commanded the stone frigate HMS *Vernon* before being appointed the commanding officer of the dreadnought HMS *King George V* which he commanded during the Battle of Jutland. Upon leaving the *King George V*, in November 1916, Field served as the Chief of Staff to Admiral Sir Charles Madden, the commanding officer of the 1st Battle Squadron before becoming Director of Torpedoes and Mines at the Admiralty in June 1918. Appointed aide-de-camp to King George V in October 1918, Field was promoted to rear admiral on 11 February 1919. He became the Third Sea Lord and Controller of the Navy in March 1920 and was knighted in the 1923 New Year's Honours.[10]

Field's flag captain, John Knowles Im Thurn, was born in 1881 and joined the Royal Navy in 1895. Promoted to lieutenant in January 1902, Im Thurn was appointed to the torpedo boat depot ship HMS *Vulcan* in August 1902. Im Thurn saw service during the First World War and was appointed to the rank of captain on 30 June 1918. After the war, Im Thurn held staff appointments: Assistant Director of Electrical Torpedo and Mining until 1920 and then director of the signals department until 1921. His next posting was to the light cruiser HMS *Ceres* where he served as the ship's commanding officer before being selected to be Field's flag captain in the *Hood*.

The *Hood*'s refit lasted until 20 June and the following day, she departed Devonport for Portland. At Portland from 21–25 June, the *Hood* visited Bournemouth (25–26 June) before embarking on a cruise to Scandinavia with HMS *Repulse* and the destroyer *Snapdragon*. The first stop on the cruise was Christiania from 29 June to 7 July. While at Christiania, the *Hood* was visited by King Haakon VII of Norway and his wife Queen Maud. Departing Christiania on 7 July, the *Hood*, *Repulse*, and *Snapdragon* sailed to Aalborg Bay, a bay in the Kattegat. The squadron anchored here from 7 July until 16 July when it weighed anchor and sailed to Portland, arriving on 18 July.

The *Hood* firing a salute off Christiana during her Scandinavia cruise. (*Richard Toffolo*)

The *Hood, c.* 1923. (*Christopher Hancock*)

The *Hood* sailed to Torbay where she anchored from 20 to 27 July before sailing to Devonport where she was taken in hand for a refit from 31 July until 31 August. The *Hood* followed this by sailing to Portland where she dropped anchor between 3 and 28 September and then Invergordon (30 September–15 October). She left Invergordon on 15 October and sailed to Rosyth where she was taken in hand for docking between 17 and 30 October. Departing Rosyth on 31 October, the *Hood* sailed to Portsmouth before sailing to Devonport where she anchored from 4 to 27 November ahead of what would be the single greatest cruise of her career.

The Cruise of
the Special Service Squadron

Throughout the interwar years, the Royal Navy (and its perceptions by the public both at home and overseas) was conditioned by four main factors: technological change; operational overstretch; international competition; and economic constraints.

The Empire Cruise of the Special Service Squadron was an attempt to encourage greater commitments to imperial defence by the Dominions and began after the conclusion of the Imperial Conference in November 1923. The purposes of the cruise were concisely laid out in an Admiralty memorandum dated 23 April 1923 by the Director of Naval Operations for the First Sea Lord, Leo Amery. The memorandum stated:

> I am considering the desirability … of sending a really representative Squadron of our most modern ships around the Empire (a) in order to follow up any agreements for co-operation at the Imperial Conference by creating Dominion interest and enthusiasm so that such agreements may really be carried out; (b) to let the local forces in Australia and elsewhere not only see our standard of work etc. but have an opportunity of doing joint exercises etc., and getting in touch generally, as a prelude to some more permanent system of interchange and co-operation; (c) to give our own ships more experience of long distance cruises and of waters practically unvisited by the Navy for nearly 20 years …[1]

In essence, like the world cruise of the United States Navy's Great White Fleet, which lasted from 16 December 1907 to 22 February 1909, the Empire Cruise was to be, in part, a large public relations exercise. Ahead of the cruise, the Admiralty began a large-scale correspondence with newspapers in Britain and overseas. Arrangements were also made for a cinematographer to accompany the cruise aboard HMS *Hood*. The film that was produced ran for 106 minutes and was released to cinemas on Empire Day (24 May) 1925. In addition to this, the Admiralty arranged for an author and journalist to travel aboard the *Hood* in order to produce an account of the cruise that would be suitable for publication. Written by V. Scott O'Connor and entitled *The Empire Cruise*, the book that was produced was 300 pages long and was illustrated with numerous photographs, some of which were in colour.[2] What the Empire Cruise would serve to do was to give notice that Britain and the Royal Navy could not effectively sustain the Empire unassisted and that it was time for the so-called 'partner nations' (namely Australia and Canada) to make a greater contribution to imperial defence in terms of ships, men, and money.

Leo Amery enthusiastically backed the cruise from the initial proposition. To Amery, the cruise would serve to strengthen imperial unity:

> The British Empire is an Oceanic Commonwealth. It has grown by sea-power and seafaring … in the long run an ocean-wide system of defence of naval powers such as those which are coming to the front to-day, cannot be maintained indefinitely by the resources of this small island alone. The naval problem, like all our other problems, can only be solved by the co-operation of all the partner nations in the British Empire.[3]

From the early planning stages of the proposed cruise, it was understood that owing to the success of the Brazilian cruise, the *Hood* would be the centrepiece of this new endeavour. The initial suggestion that was forthcoming was 'for a squadron say of *Hood* and *Repulse* and a squadron of modern light cruisers'.[4] By mid-May 1923, the Admiralty had settled on a provisional list of seven vessels: the *Hood*, *Repulse*, and *Delhi*-class light cruisers *Delhi*, *Dauntless*, *Danae*, *Dragon*, and *Dunedin*. Despite the hopes that the cruise would stimulate a greater contribution to imperial defence by the 'partner nations', some doubts were raised regarding the potential messages that would be conveyed by the inclusion of the *Repulse* and the *Hood* in the squadron. One Admiralty minute, dated 6 June 1923, voiced the concern that 'it is possible that if battle cruisers are sent, it may … discourage rather than stimulate the Dominions from making an increased naval effort'.[5] Attached to the minute was a note written by a Royal Navy officer, Commander C. A. Spooner, who had recently returned from service on the Australian Navy Board. Spooner's note argued:

> It will be beyond the capacity of Australia to acquire or maintain capital ships for many years to come, and their presence might tend to discourage proposals to build lesser ships, which might appear to the public to be of doubtful value in comparison.
> Furthermore a visit of capital ships to Australia might give rise to undue confidence in the power and mobility of the British Fleet, and might tend to stifle an inclination to improve the local navy, which latter is the only form of Empire naval contribution that is wise to advocate.[6]

The suggestion that the Special Service Squadron, as the fleet was to be officially named, consist of only light cruisers was not, however, ever seriously considered. The *Hood* and the *Repulse* were seen by those with a vested interest in the success of the Empire Cruise—the Admiralty, the Treasury, and the Foreign and

Colonial Offices—as essential to the nature of the modern navy as they were big, impressive, and powerful and also showcased British naval might. When he learned of the proposed cruise, the British Ambassador to the United States, Sir Auckland Geddes, wrote to the Admiralty suggesting that the Special Service Squadron call at New York, Newport, and Rhode Island when sailing from the Caribbean to Canada. According to Geddes, 'The effect of the visit of two of His Majesty's Ships of the size of the *Hood* and the *Repulse* would, I am confident, create an excellent impression'.[7] The Admiralty did not share the same view, suggesting instead that 'the presence of our latest battle-cruisers might only serve to stimulate [the United States'] naval ambitions'.[8] The Foreign Office echoed the view of the Admiralty and pointed out that a 'visit to New York of two of the latest British capital ships' at a time when Congress was in the midst of discussing the naval budget for the United States could serve to act as 'propaganda in favour of an increase in naval power ... as intense as ever in the United States', which would encourage America to engage in a naval arms race that Britain could not ignore but ultimately would not be able to win.[9]

Instead, it was decided that the battlecruisers would put in at the United States but that they would be limited to Hawaii and San Francisco, far removed from the centres of American naval and political power.[10]

Between 5 and 26 November 1923, the *Hood* was taken in hand in preparation for the Cruise of the Special Service Squadron. On 27 November, the *Hood*, the *Repulse*, and the 1st Light Cruiser Squadron weighed anchor and departed Devonport, bound for Freetown, Sierra Leone.[11]

While on route to Freetown, the *Hood* carried out a number of exercises including collision quarters, action stations, and sea boat exercises. In addition to

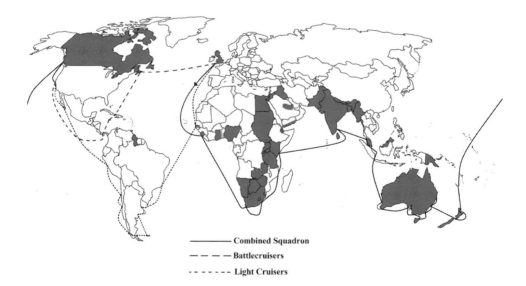

The route of the ships partaking in the Cruise of the Special Service Squadron. (*Author's collection*)

conducting exercises, the crew also engaged in a thorough cleaning and painting of the ship. Averaging a speed of 10 knots, the Squadron arrived off Tenerife, Canary Islands on 3 December. Tropical rig was adopted aboard the *Hood* on 7 December before the Squadron arrived at Freetown the following day. While docked at Freetown, some members of the crew were granted leave while the *Hood* had her stocks and stores replenished. On 11 December, visitors were permitted aboard the *Hood* and the *Repulse*. Lieutenant Charles Benstead commented:

> We saw our ship invaded by Freetown negroes who gaped in open-mouthed astonishment at a ventilating van; by the bearded Boer farmers from the South African veldt; by white-robed Mohammedans from Zanzibar who, at sunset, spread their prayer-mats upon the quarterdeck and reverently knelt to invoke the protection of Allah.[12]

One of those who paid a visit to the *Hood* was the Governor of Sierra Leone, Alexander Ransford Slater, before the squadron weighed anchor and departed for Cape Town, South Africa on 13 December.

The squadron spent nine days sailing from Freetown to Cape Town. During the cruise from Sierra Leone to South Africa, the Squadron carried out a day and night searchlight exercise, action stations exercises, and a number of gunnery exercises. On 15 December, the Special Service Squadron crossed the Equator leading to the traditional 'Crossing the Line' ceremony in which those who had never before crossed the Equator appeared before Neptune and his court. V. Scott O'Connor noted:

> On December 15th we crossed the Line, and 950 men who had never crossed the Equator prepared to face the terrors of the bath! Thrones or chairs were placed upon a dais for Neptune and his Court at the end of the quarterdeck—with eight chairs below them for the Admiral and other distinguished persons. The rest of the deck was crowded with spectators. The Oceanic Court was seen approaching to the strains of music, the drum-major brandishing his staff at the head of the bandsmen whose cheeks were filled out with air, while the drummers beat a rataplan on their drums. The spectators made way; the Royal Marines delivered a salute with their customary smartness—but to-day with grins upon their faces. Neptune ascended his throne. His bears, well suited by their massive frames and hairy forms to inspire novices with terror, lay at his feet.
>
> The Admiral then left his seat and marching up to the dais, saluted and went down upon his knees to receive the ribbon and the Order of the Bath. He then rose, saluted, and returned to his seat. One by one the other recipients of honours went up and returned with smiling faces, like schoolboys at an annual prize-giving. All round us were assembled, in the scantiest of clothing, the neophytes who were this day to be initiated; while those who still wore uniform, the captain of the *Hood* himself, the Admiral's political secretary, and other persons of rank, made a dash for their cabins, to shed their trappings and appear in bathing suits. An enormous bath, some 10 feet

high, had been erected on the port side of the quarter-deck, with a steep ladder for those ascending to their ordeal, on one side, and another for those descending after its completion on the other. Every vantage-point, including the gun turrets and the gangways, was occupied by hilarious onlookers, including hundreds of those who were themselves to be initiated. Upon a wooden platform above the bath were now assembled the Chief Justice in his scarlet robes, the Neptune barber and physician, and other officials. As each neophyte ascended the ladder he was well beaten over the head with an inflated bladder, or baton, by the Neptunic police; seized and placed upon a stool and dosed by the physician with a very disagreeable pill, that to make sure it reached its goal was rammed into his mouth and was followed by a glass of medicine, which willy nilly he had to swallow, while an attendant held his nose! He was then rapidly passed on to another stool, to the ministrations of the court barber, his face lathered and 'shaved' with a wooden razor, until of a sudden the stool, most unexpectedly, tipped over and he found himself descending head-foremost, his feet flying in the air, along a soapy slide into the bath. Swift and sure was his descent into this Avernus, where he was seized by the grimy bears and ducked repeatedly until at last, completely out of breath and spluttering sea-water, he came to the end of his purgatory and was suffered to rise up on his feet, and make for the descending ladder, half-choked, but delighted to find himself free, while from behind him came the splash of his successor's arrival, to shouts of laughter from the assembled spectators.

Meanwhile Neptune still sat upon his throne, administering justice to all backsliders, shammers, conscientious objectors and other recalcitrant. These delinquents, arrested in secret haunts and caverns of the ship, were brought up in custody by the Oceanic police and their offences detailed. One who may have been shamming only to please the company, was produced from a bag carried on a pole, from which he rolled out at His Majesty's Feet, emerging with a smile; another it was reported 'had been found skulking in the Admiral's galley frying a kipper, in defiance of your Majesty's commands'.

'Have them rubbed into him' came the stentorian judgement, 'and especially the kipper!'

After this there were sliced oranges and champagne and similar polite attentions from the Admiral.

'Let those not interested look the other way', roared His Oceanic Majesty, gazing benevolently at the bubbly.

By 1 o'clock in the afternoon the Captain and 950 officers and men had been received into the fold, and as joyous and hearty a ceremony as it is possible to imagine came to an end, lightening people's hearts, making a break in the routine of the voyage, and increasing good-fellowship and comradeship all round.[13]

By the time the squadron arrived off Cape Town, it had sailed 6,057 miles. Upon arriving at South Africa, the ships saluted a number of dignitaries and were promptly visited by the Governor General. The ships were opened to the public on 23 and 24 December, 26 December and from 28 to 31 December. On Christmas Day, over 900 sailors and 300 marines from the *Hood*, accompanied by

Members of the *Hood*'s Royal Marine band arranged beside one of her guns during the cruise of the Special Service Squadron.

many other sailors and marines from the squadron, participated in a ceremonial march through Cape Town. On 26 December, the Squadron Ball was held. While in South Africa, Field called on the country to build up its naval resources. On 2 January, the squadron departed Cape Town.

On 3 January, the squadron made a brief stop at Mossel Bay where sea boat exercises and gunnery trials were carried out. That evening, the squadron set a course for East London, South Africa, where it dropped anchor briefly on 5 January. While at East London, the *Hood* was visited by the port captain. Here, the sea boat crew were again exercised while the remaining majority of the crew engaged in the mending of clothes and cleaning the ship. Durban was the next stop for the squadron on 6 January before dropping anchor at Zanzibar from 12 until 17 January. Opened to visitors, the *Hood* was visited by Sultan Khalifa Bin Harud on 16 January. For the crew, life went on more or less as usual with much cleaning and provisioning taking place. At Zanzibar, the *Hood* conducted a gunnery programme before members of the crew took part in a ceremonial march through the town. Some leave was granted to the crew before the *Hood* and the *Repulse* departed amid much fanfare, which included a personal 'escort' by the Sultan aboard his yacht.

While the *Hood* and the *Repulse* were at Zanzibar, the cruisers *Delhi*, *Dauntless*, and *Dragon* spent time anchored at Mombasa while the *Danae* made a call at Dar es Salaam. The account given by V. Scott O'Connor in his book chronicling the cruise—of the events that occurred while the *Delhi*, *Dauntless*, and *Dragon* were in Kenya—are typical of the sorts of activities that took place at various stops during the tour.

> [Rear Admiral Sir Hubert Brand, Commanding Officer Light Cruiser Squadron] had the great pleasure of receiving a deputation of ex-Naval Officers of the Colony, and was presented by them with a silver cup for the First Light Cruiser Squadron, as a memento of its visit; and paid a visit to Lord Delamere ...
>
> Seventeen officers and a hundred men were entertained in Nairobi. They were welcomed on arrival by the Colonial Secretary and a large number of inhabitants. Headed by the superb band of the King's African Rifles, they marched to their quarters at the New Stanley Hotel. Thirty motor-cars took them for tours through the country. Concerts, public dinners, and a Ngoma given by a thousand natives, were part of the entertainment provided for our men. The officers of the detachment were badly beaten at cricket, golf, and tennis. The cricket of Nairobi was practically up to county form. The men were rather more successful, and at boxing distinguished themselves, winning six out of seven bouts. The last bout was for the Middle-Weights Championship and belt of Kenya. Able-Seaman Hopper of HMS *Delhi* knocked his opponent out in the second round, and received a very handsome cup for his victory.
>
> All these competitions were carried through in the most sporting manner and were enjoyed by all; and when on January 16th the Contingent marched to the station on its departure for Mombasa, again headed by the band of the K.A.R., it was acclaimed with the wildest enthusiasm ...
>
> While these fortunate officers and men were being entertained in the salubrious climate of Nairobi ... the rest of the Squadron were making the best of their lot in the intense and stifling heat of Mombasa. They played football, they played cricket, they went to dances. Disastrously beaten at first at rugger, the arrival of *Dragon* enabled them to put a better team into the field and very nearly to secure victory. Five hundred people visited the ships, including thirty Arab Chieftains, and forty native chiefs from the interior of the country: people in full regalia and of the most picturesque appearance. Some of them who had never before set eyes upon a ship-of-war, had travelled eight hundred miles to pay their visit. *Dauntless* gave a concert, and the Rear-Admiral a dinner on board *Delhi*, followed by a reception, at which a hundred guests were present.[14]

Sailing again as one unit, 26 to 31 January found the Squadron at Trincomalee, Ceylon. Here the ships were again opened up to visitors. The visitors to the *Hood* and the *Repulse* at Trincomalee were on a smaller scale than at their previous stops. Between 31 January and 4 February, the Special Service Squadron sailed for Port Swettenham, Kuala Lumpur, Malaysia. While at Kuala Lumpur, as was usual, the *Hood* received the lion's share of the visitors. In between painting and cleaning the ship, leave was granted to some of the crew. While at anchor, seventeen-gun salutes were fired for the Sultans of Perak, Pahang, and Negri Sembilan. It was while at Kuala Lumpur that the first tragedy struck the *Hood* when on 5 February, Able-Seaman Walter Benger died from malaria. Benger was buried in a cemetery in Kuala Lumpur with a tombstone that was erected for him by the Government of the Federated Malay States. Benger's death was not, however, the first tragedy to be suffered by the squadron. While at Trincomalee shooting parties had been arranged for the officers of the squadron by the Ceylon government. During an excursion to Kandy, the ancient capital of Ceylon, one of the buses that had been laid on to transport the officers overturned while taking a sharp turn. The incident led to the death of one of *Repulse*'s crew, Stoker Petty Officer George Wood, who was pinned under the vehicle.

On 9 February, the squadron weighed anchor and set sail for Singapore where plans were being drawn up for a fortified naval base from which the Royal Navy could maintain and operate a fleet in the event of a war in the Far East. At Singapore, the *Hood* and the *Repulse* were again open to visitors; the *Hood* also delivered a series of salutes. The Commander-in-Chief of the China Station, Admiral Sir Arthur Cavanaugh Leverson received a seventeen-gun salute; the Governor of Straits Settlements and High Commissioner for the Malay States, Sir Laurence Nunns Guillemard also received a seventeen-gun salute; and the General Officer Commanding the troops in the Straits Settlements, General Sir

The *Hood* in Ceylon. (*Author's collection*)

Neil Malcolm, was given a fifteen-gun salute. While at anchor in Singapore, the crew operated the main derrick, exercised the searchlights, tested the lifeboats, cleaned the ship, and were granted leave. The field and machine gun sections of the Royal Marines also participated in a ceremonial march through Singapore while the squadron admirals were invited to a dinner held at Government House on 11 February. With the ship provisioned while in port, on 17 February, the squadron departed for Fremantle, Western Australia. As the squadron sailed for Fremantle, aboard the *Delhi*, Marine Henry Layfield fell down an ammunition hoist and broke his back with no hope of recovery.

While *en route* to Fremantle, the squadron conducted a brief visit to Christmas Island and undertook further exercises. During the journey to Fremantle, the squadron was forced to sail through a patch of rough weather, which brought large waves that crashed against and over the ships.

On 27 February, the *Hood* and the other ships of the squadron arrived at Fremantle. Since leaving Devonport, the squadron had sailed a total of 15,719 miles. On 28 February, a naval brigade from the *Hood* took part in a march through Fremantle and then through Perth before the squadron departed for Albany on 1 March.

The *Hood* entering Fremantle Harbour, 27 February 1924. (*State Library of West Australia, 042155PD*)

The *Hood* sailing into Fremantle Harbour. (*State Library of West Australia, 008834PD*)

The *Hood* entering Fremantle. (*State Library of West Australia, 042156PD*)

Left: HMS *Delhi* and HMS *Hood* enter Fremantle Harbour, 27 February 1924. (*State Library of West Australia, 042154PD*)

Below: The *Hood* in Fremantle Harbour, 27 February 1924. (*State Library of West Australia, 008840PD*)

Crowds gather along the wharf to watch the *Hood* berth at Victoria Quay. (*State Library of West Australia, 111890PD*)

With the assistance of a tug, the *Hood* enters Fremantle harbour. (*State Library of West Australia, 111889PD*)

Left: The *Hood* being
turned into Victoria
Quay, Fremantle.
(*State Library of
Western Australia,
BA533/512*)

Below: Sailors in a
rowing boat cross the
bow of the *Hood* as
she approaches the
wharf. (*State Library
of West Australia,
111888PD*)

Crowds watching the arrival of the *Hood*. (*State Library of West Australia, 112349PD*)

The *Hood* approaching the wharf. (*State Library of West Australia, 111887PD*)

The *Hood* approaching Victoria Quay. (*State Library of West Australia, 008836PD*)

Crowds gather to watch the *Hood* berth alongside in Fremantle. (*State Library of West Australia, 008838PD*)

Sailors line the rails as the *Hood* berths at Victoria Quay. (*State Library of West Australia, 008833PD*)

Vice Admiral Field and Rear Admiral Sir Hubert Brand landing from the *Hood* at 10.15 a.m., 27 February 1924. (*State Library of West Australia, 008830PD*)

Field and Brand on the quayside. (*State Library of West Australia, 008829PD*)

The *Hood* glides into Fremantle, 27 February 1924. (*State Library of West Australia, 008835PD*)

Members of the public stream aboard the *Hood* while she at anchor at in Fremantle. (*State Library of West Australia, 008864PD*)

Field inspecting a guard of honour, 27 February 1924. (*State Library of West Australia, 008839PD*)

Victoria Quay as viewed from the *Hood*. (*State Library of West Australia, 008625PD*)

The *Hood* at Fremantle. (*State Library of West Australia, 042162PD*)

The *Hood* alongside at Fremantle. (*State Library of West Australia, BA1410/2/46*)

The *Hood* alongside Victoria Quay. (*State Library of West Australia, BA1410/2/47*)

Field inspecting a guard of honour at Government House, Perth.
(*State Library of West Australia, 008832PD*)

Sailors line the rails as crowds gather to watch *Hood* depart Victoria Quay.
(*State Library of West Australia, 008623PD*)

Sailors line the deck of the *Hood* as the ship prepares to sail from Fremantle. (*State Library of West Australia, 111923PD*)

The *Hood* preparing to sail, 1 March 1924. (*State Library of West Australia, 111924PD*)

The *Hood* preparing to depart Fremantle for Albany, 1 March 1924.
(*State Library of West Australia, 111925PD*)

The *Hood* off Port Adelaide.
(*PRG 280/1/40/166, Searcy Collection, State Library of South Australia*)

The *Hood* and the *Repulse* off Adelaide.
(*1-2-062598-F, Alexander Turnbull Library, Wellington, New Zealand*)

The *Hood* off Glenelg, Adelaide. (*B41019/297, State Library of South Australia*)

Following anchoring for a few days in Albany, the squadron moved swiftly on to Adelaide where it arrived on 10 March. At Adelaide, the squadron was visited by 69,510 people before departing for Melbourne, Victoria on 15 March. According to Lieutenant Benstead, the population of Melbourne 'lined every foot of deck space, climbed every ladder, adorned every excrescence upon which a man could stand and suspend itself in monkey-fashion where foothold was denied'.[15] Alf Batchelder recalled:

> It was … glorious weather. Every road and pathway was thick and many families were making a day of it, taking out all the children and hampers and bottles of beer. The bay was dotted with sailing boats. Everyone who had anything that would float … was out there on the water … I believe the papers said there were 500,000 people wanting to see the ships … It was a wonderful sight.… The mist out at sea and then a few minutes later the *Hood* herself, with the white cloud seeming to peel away from her as she came into the bright sunlight of Port Philip …[16]

While at Melbourne, Signal Boatswain Alfred Punshon was evacuated ashore on a stretcher through crowds of thousands after suffering a heart attack. V. Scott O'Connor's account of the world cruise noted:

> His heart had failed, though none of us had suspected this when he played the part of Neptune so jovially in the ceremonies of crossing the line. But he took not [*sic*] part in our festivities at Melbourne, and the day we sailed away [25 March] he died. The following day was one of the most perfect imaginable. A memorial service for him took place on the quarter-deck, attended by the Vice-Admiral, the Officers, and all those who were not on duty; for in the Navy men stand by each other. Eleven trumpeters on a gun turret, standing erect in a line against the sky, sounded the Last Post; followed after a brief interval by the Réveillé. The flag fluttered at half mast; and the Padre read the solemn and inspiring words of our burial service. That was the end of poor Punshon; in the words of the Vice-Admiral, 'One of the best and most loyal Warrant Officers he had ever known'.[17]

On 18 March, the Naval Brigade marched through the city before a sporting festival began the following day. On 19 March, the squadron football team took on Victoria at the Melbourne Cricket Club's Albert Ground. Ahead of the game, *The Sporting Globe* reported: 'Soccer is the most popular game with the fleet. There can be no doubt about that. All the officers and men keenly debate the game, notwithstanding that it is solely the ratings that play'.[18] The game finished 2–2. The following day, the Melbourne Cricket Club was the site of a cricket match between the squadron and a team drawn from the Australian Army, Navy, and Air Force. In an unusual display, the Australians gave the men of the Squadron two hours to bat. Despite this, they could only muster 113 runs against the Australian 211. The newspaper *The Argus* remarked: 'It was apparent by their lack of judgement in the field that the visitors were very short of practice, but

The *Hood* on 17 March 1924 while *en route* to Melbourne. The gleaming brass on the ship's guns and the whiteness of the scrubbed deck are clearly evident. (*Author's collection*)

The *Hood* off Melbourne. (*Author's collection*)

Crowds on HMS *Hood* and the *Delhi*, Princess Pier, Melbourne.
(*Ronald Alfred Cheers, Museums Victoria*)

nevertheless they played keenly to the end'.[19] According to Lieutenant Charles
Ransome of the *Repulse*, cricket was 'sadly in need of stimulation as far as the
British Navy is concerned … deck cricket is little practised and the opportunity
to gain proficiency is limited'.[20] Another game of cricket was held on 21 March,
which the British sailors also lost.

On 23 March, a massed band concert was held at the Lord Mayor's Fund for
Metropolitan Hospitals and Charities. In anticipation of large crowds, additional
trains and trams were laid on by the transport authorities. Massed bands from
the *Hood*, *Repulse*, and *Delhi* were all scheduled to perform at the event. It had
been intended that the Navy bands would march to the Cricket Club where the
concert was to be held but the idea was unpractical. In a day of glorious sunshine,

large crowds of eager visitors flocked to Port Melbourne to tour the *Hood* and the other ships. Such was the density of the crowd that mounted police had to clear the way for the bands who were transported to the ground.

During the time that the *Hood* was anchored alongside Princes Pier Port Melbourne, over 200,000 people managed to get aboard the ship. It has been estimated that just as many were turned away.[21] Lieutenant Geoffrey Wells recalled the time that the *Hood*, the *Repulse*, and the cruisers of the Special Service Squadron spent at Melbourne:

> We remained at Melbourne for seven days and enormous crowds besieged us. Numbers unprecedented percolated into every place in the ship. Women fainted on the gangways which almost gave beneath the weight. To get ashore became a feat of no mean skill and elbows. The *Repulse* also suffered. The little boys of the crowd fared best, they would squeeze where their sisters could not and could deal more rapidly with the ladders.[22]

On 25 March, the Squadron weighed anchor and left Melbourne. At 6 a.m. on that dull autumn morning, the officers and men aboard the *Hood* held masses of coloured paper streamers that stretched over to the crowd that had gathered on the pier to see them off. The streamers were a 'frail link with the friends they were leaving behind'.[23] One by one, the streamers snapped as tugs guided the ships away from the pier. With smoke belching from her funnels, the *Hood* made for Mornington for a day of speed tests in Port Philip Bay.

From 27 March until 3 April, the squadron anchored at Hobart, Tasmania. Leaving Hobart on 3 April, the squadron stopped briefly at Twofold Bay, New South Wales on 4 April. The squadron encountered heavy seas on 4 April and picked up a distress signal from the Japanese steamer *Honolulu Maru*, which reported that in the gale its cargo had become loose and had moved on deck, and that as a result of this the ship was in danger of capsizing. The *Dauntless* and the *Dragon* were dispatched to assist the *Honolulu Maru* and stood by her until she was no longer at risk of capsizing. The squadron arrived at Jervis Bay on 5 April. On 8 April, the squadron weighed anchor and set a course for Sydney where it arrived the following day. Half a million people lined Sydney harbour to watch the Special Service Squadron glide into anchor before a parade by the Naval Brigade took place through the city that afternoon. More sporting events were held and entertaining done while the squadron was at Sydney. While there, the squadron received news from London that the naval base at Singapore would not be constructed.

In the meantime, the Australian government had ordered a pair of heavy cruisers from British shipyards and had detached the newly refitted 6-inch gun *Town*-class light cruiser HMAS *Adelaide* to the squadron along with ten midshipmen from the naval college at Jervis Bay.[24] On 14 April, a musical revue of 'The Cheer Oh Girls' was held aboard the *Hood* before the Squadron departed Sydney on 20 April. It was at this point that the *Adelaide* joined the squadron. In

The Special Service Squadron arriving off Hobart.
(*B 41019/242, State Library of South Australia*)

The *Hood* pictured while at Hobart, Tasmania between 27 March and 3 April 1924.
(*Author's collection*)

The *Hood* amidships during the visit of the Special Service Squadron to Hobart. (*B1019/247, State Library of South Australia*)

The *Hood* at anchor in Hobart. (*B 41019/243, State Library of South Australia*)

Left: The *Hood* at anchor at
Hobart. (*B41019/227, State
Library of South Australia*)

Below: The *Hood* alongside
at Hobart. (*B41019/230, State
Library of South Australia*)

Right: The *Hood* alongside
Ocean Pier, Hobart.
(*B41019/232, State Library of
South Australia*)

Below: Cleaning work being
undertaken on the *Hood* while
at Hobart. (*B1019/244, State
Library of South Australia*)

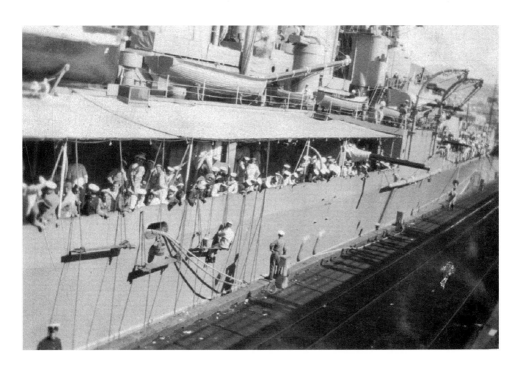

'At Home' status aboard the *Hood* while the ship is at anchor at Hobart.
(*B41019/248, State Library of South Australia*)

A crowd of people gather on Ocean Pier to tour the ships of the Special Service Squadron.
(*B41019/255, State Library of South Australia*)

Visitors boarding the *Hood* at Hobart. (*B41019/253, State Library of South Australia*)

The *Hood* alongside the wharf at Hobart. (*B41019/233, State Library of South Australia*)

The *Hood* off Sydney. (*Christopher Hancock*)

The *Hood* (left) and the *Repulse* (centre) entering Sydney Harbour, 9 April 1924.
(*SRV16083, City of Sydney Archives*)

The *Hood* entering Sydney harbour. (*Author's collection*)

The *Hood* in Sydney Harbour between 9 and 20 April 1924.
(*City of Sydney Archives 092503, Graeme Andrews 'Working Harbour' Collection*)

The *Hood* at anchor while in Sydney Harbour. Note that 'X' turret has been traversed to starboard. (*City of Sydney Archives 092504, Graeme Andrews 'Working Harbour' Collection*)

A close up of the *Hood*'s aft section while she lies at anchor in Sydney Harbour. Note how on the railings the crew have begun hanging letter spelling 'HOOD' but have yet to hang the 'H'. (*City of Sydney Archives 90460, Graeme Andrews 'Working Harbour' Collection*)

Women and children sit on the *Hood*'s deck around the anchor cables while the ship is in Sydney. (*Author's collection*)

addition to HMAS *Adelaide*, the *Hood* was accompanied by another Australian ambassador in the form of Joey the wallaby, a mascot gifted to the ship by the people of Sydney.

Joey the wallaby was not the only animal to grace the *Hood*'s decks. As noted by Andrew Norman, the *Hood* became a 'veritable Noah's Ark' acquiring a number of different animals and mascots during her travels.[25] As previously noted, there was Bill the goat who was unceremoniously pushed through the skylight into Cowan's cabin and on to his bed (see Chapter Six). In Calgary, a black beaver was presented to Admiral Field. The beaver made its home on the boat deck. While in the tropics, some of the ship's company elected to sleep on the deck and received quite a surprise when they woke and found the beaver curled up next to them. Other animals gifted to the *Hood* during the cruise included a ring-tailed possum, a pair of cockatoos, numerous parrots, a squirrel, and a kiwi. Most of these animals would be offloaded to zoos upon the arrival of the squadron in Devonport at the end of the cruise with the exception of Joey who remained aboard the *Hood* until 1926 when he too was donated to a zoo. In 1928, during a spring cruise, the *Hood* acquired a racehorse, a donkey, a pair of flamingos, and a baby seal before Lady Hood presented a bulldog called Angus to the ship. In 1933, Commander O'Conor brought with him to the *Hood* his West Highland Terrier, Judy. The 1930s saw the *Hood* acquire her best-loved mascots: the cats Ginger and Fishcake. Ginger was greatly respected by the crew and would lose a portion of his tail when the ship was carrying out a full-calibre firing exercise. As was usual during such an exercise, the two cats were rounded up and placed in a wash-deck locker out of harm's way. When the exercise was complete, a

Joey the wallaby held by one of the *Hood*'s crewmen while at anchor in Fremantle. Joey was presented to the crew of the *Hood* as a mascot by the Australian Imperial Band Committee, Fremantle. (*State Library of Western Australia, 008831PD*)

One of the *Hood*'s best-loved mascots, Ginger.

sailor lifted the iron lid of the locker, completely unaware of the presence of the cats. Ginger scrambled to get out of the locker. The startled sailor dropped the lid in shock, which slammed down, amputating a portion of Ginger's tail.[26] Both Fishcake and Ginger were aboard the ship when she sank in May 1941.

Ginger and Fishcake were not the last animals to be brought aboard the *Hood*. A cruise to the Canary Isles in 1936 saw the *Hood* return with numerous birds while in June 1939, when he joined the ship, the Reverend Harold Beardmore brought with him his bull terrier, Bill. Bill almost met his maker before he left the ship with Beardmore in February 1941 when he cocked his leg on a length of exposed electrical cabling.

The squadron's next stop was Wellington, New Zealand where it arrived on 24 April. Following arriving at Wellington, HMS *Dunedin* was transferred over to the Royal New Zealand Navy. At Wellington, the usual hospitalities and entertainments that had been extended at all the squadron's previous stops ensued.

> There was a Navy League ball at the Town Hall; excursions in the neighbourhood of the city; concerts and dances for men, and naval sports and athletic competitions. At soccer, rugger, hockey, and golf, the honours lay with Wellington; at cricket, *Hood*, *Repulse* and *Adelaide* won. A two-mile cutter race between the *Hood* and

The *Hood* entering Wellington Harbour, 24 April 1924. (*William Hall Raine, 1/2-100604-G, Alexander Turnbull Library, Wellington, New Zealand*)

[HMNZS] *Chatham* was won by *Chatham*. [For her victory *Chatham* was awarded the Frobisher cup].

Repulse as usual distinguished herself by a children's party, and by a pantomime given by her Officers at the Opera House.

The public were entertained on His Majesty's Ships; at a Squadron 'At Home', at which 900 guests were present; at a ball in *Hood*, at which there were 700 guests; at a Ship's Company 'At Home' in *Repulse*, and at the Vice-Admiral's official dinner in *Hood* to which the Governor-General, the Prime Minister and other distinguished persons were invited. In addition 153,872 visitors were shown over *Hood*, *Repulse* and *Adelaide*, including 12,000 school children.[27]

On 8 May, the *Hood* and the squadron left Wellington. At Vice Admiral Field's request, Earl Jellicoe, now the Governor-General of New Zealand, accompanied the squadron to Auckland and hoisted his flag beside that of Field. By this point, exhaustion was beginning to set in among the crew of the squadron's ships. During the journey to Auckland, Jellicoe volunteered to ease the burden on members of the crew by taking the middle watch from 12 a.m. to 4 a.m. on the bridge.

It is worth noting that during the first six months of the cruise, 151 men deserted the squadron, 141 of whom set up a new life in Australia. Accompanying the squadron to Auckland was the *Chatham*, which would ultimately sail from Auckland on 27 May and make for England.

At Auckland, hundreds of small craft 'escorted' the *Hood* into the harbour while all available vantage points were crammed full of cheering people. At Auckland, Jellicoe left the *Hood* and returned to Government House. While there, the *Hood* was opened to the public. During the five days that she was at anchor, she was visited by 78,240 people. On the first day of the squadron's visit, the crowds that greeted the ships were so large that the ships were temporarily locked down. The squadron left Auckland for Suva, Fiji on 18 May. As the *Hood* sailed for Fiji, Geoffrey Wells noted:

> It is very noticeable on board now passed New Zealand everyone seems to be getting bored with the cruise. I certainly am. Going around the world is alright. In fact being paid to go around and under such circumstances as this is great but one needs a fortnight's holiday at home in the middle of it. Everything moves at such a pace.[28]

By the time the squadron dropped anchor at Suva, it had covered 22,073 miles. At Fiji, spirits were revived with draughts of Kava and by the women of Western Samoa where the *Hood* briefly dropped anchor on 29 May. On 6 June, the squadron arrived at Honolulu, Hawaii. Following leaving Western Samoa, there had been a gradual suspension of alcohol among the ships as they became 'dry' in deference to the prohibition laws of the United States. While at Honolulu, the squadron cricket team was embarrassed when it was beaten at cricket by an American baseball team. Aboard the *Hood*, a dance was held for 1,100 guests, which toasted the King and President Calvin Coolidge in water and which was remembered as one of the finest events of the cruise.

The squadron left Honolulu on 12 June for Victoria, Canada where it anchored from 21 to 25 June before moving on to Vancouver. At Vancouver, Field was to attempt to fulfil his remit of encouraging Canada to maintain a pair of cruisers on the east coast for imperial defence. This suggestion was met with a storm of protest in Ottawa. During the ten days that the *Hood* and the squadron anchored at Vancouver, the ships were opened to the public and a march through the city by the naval brigades was held. Leaving Vancouver, the squadron set a course south for San Francisco.

Field's ships were enthusiastically welcomed to San Francisco. The arrival of the Special Service Squadron marked the first time in forty years that a British squadron had dropped anchor in American waters. The squadron was placed in 'At Home' status for Britons living in the area while Vice-Admiral Field was presented with the key to the city. The visit of Field's ships also served to strengthen relations between Britain and America with Major James Rolph telling Field:

> Your presence with us today will, we trust, make a pact between the British-speaking races even closer. We take pride in your magnificent ships, which we feel will never be used except in the defence of world peace. We surrender our city unto you. We capitulate.[29]

While at San Francisco, it became apparent that the efforts of the squadron to adhere to America's prohibition laws outstripped those of their hosts. Geoffrey Wells recalled one such incident:

> 'I guess you guys will have a drink' said one of our hosts producing, as the conjurer does the rabbit, a bottle of whiskey which he passed to the bar attendant who therewith dispensed whiskey and sodas. We received sympathy for our stocks on board being locked up and it became apparent that the only dry community in the district was the British ships. There were some that did not believe that we had no bottles in our cabins. Our reason for not having any was that it was not allowed. This absolutely baffled the American mind![30]

The squadron left San Francisco on 11 July. Having departed San Francisco, the squadron split; the First Light Cruiser Squadron sailed for Callao, the first stop on a tour of South America while the *Hood*, *Repulse*, and *Adelaide* made for Balboa, Panama. When the battlecruisers and the *Adelaide* arrived at Panama, the stores of the ships were replenished and mail was brought aboard before the ships began the transit of the Panama Canal on 24 July. Passing through the Panama Canal, the *Hood* became the largest vessel to traverse the passage and had only thirty inches of clearance on either side. Exiting the Gatún locks, the *Hood* exited the Panama Canal and emerged into the Caribbean. The cost of her passage through the canal totalled $22,399.50 (£5,000), a figure worked out at $0.50 per ton plus towing fees. In today's money, the cost to the British government for the *Hood*'s transit through the Panama Canal would be approximately £286,384.

Left: This photograph taken while alongside in Wellington during the Empire Cruise provides a detailed illustration of the area around the *Hood*'s conning tower, bridge, and foremast. (*PAColl-6304-13, Alexander Turnbull Library, Wellington, New Zealand*)

Below: Taken from the area of the bow, looking aft, this image, taken while anchored in Wellington, shows the *Hood*'s main armament in all its imposing glory with the guns of 'A' turret elevated slightly to starboard and 'B' turret in the forward position. (*James Hutchings Kinnear, 1-2-015263-F, Alexander Turnbull Library, Wellington, New Zealand*)

The *Hood* alongside in Wellington. (*1/2-062599-F, Alexander Turnbull Library, Wellington, New Zealand*)

The *Hood* in Wellington harbour. Note the sailors milling around her decks. (*PAColl-6304-11, Alexander Turnbull Library, Wellington, New Zealand*)

The *Hood* at anchor in Wellington harbour.
(*PAColl-6304-12, Alexander Turnbull Library, Wellington, New Zealand*)

The *Hood* at Auckland. (*Author's collection*)

HMS *Repulse* alongside at Auckland. (*Author's collection*)

The *Hood* seen from the *Repulse* during the Cruise of the Special Service Squadron.

The *Hood* sailing in American waters around the time of her visit to Honolulu. (*NH 60404, US Naval History and Heritage Command*)

The *Hood* in American waters. (*NH 60421, US Naval History and Heritage Command*)

Above: The *Hood* docked at Honolulu, Hawaii on 11 June 1924.
(*NH 58635, US Naval History and Heritage Command*)

Below: The *Hood* off Honolulu, 12 June 1924.
(*NH 60409, US Naval History and Heritage Command*)

Crowds gather at Brockon Point to watch the arrival of the Special Service Squadron in Vancouver. (*City of Vancouver Archives CVA 99-1210, Stuart Thomson*)

The *Hood* entering Vancouver Harbour. (*City of Vancouver Archives, Bo N88.4, W. J. Moore*)

The *Hood* sailing into Vancouver Harbour. (*City of Vancouver Archives, CVA 289-003.053*)

The *Hood* sailing into Vancouver Harbour.
(*City of Vancouver Archives, CVA 99-1204, Stuart Thomson*)

Stern quarter view of the *Hood* as she enters Vancouver Harbour.
(*City of Vancouver Archives, CVA 99-1205, Stuart Thomson*)

Entering Vancouver. (*City of Vancouver Archives, CVA 447-2304, Walter Edwin Frost*)

(City of Vancouver Archives, CVA 447-2304.1, Walter Edwin Frost)

(City of Vancouver Archives, CVA 447-2304.2, Walter Edwin Frost)

(City of Vancouver Archives, CVA 447-2304.3, Walter Edwin Frost)

(City of Vancouver Archives, CVA 447-2304.4, Walter Edwin Frost)

Mayor W. R. Owen welcomes and presents an illuminated address to Admiral Field, Captain Im Thurn (the *Hood*) and Captain Henry Parker (the *Repulse*) to Vancouver. (*City of Vancouver Archives, Port P728.2*)

Mayor Owen welcomes Field, Im Thurn, and Parker to Vancouver. (*City of Vancouver Archives, Port P728.1*)

Mayor Owen presenting Admiral Field with a bison's head.
(*City of Vancouver Archives, CVA 99-1212, Stuart Thomson*)

Signalmen aboard the *Hood* showing children a semaphore signal device.
(*City of Vancouver Archives, CVA 99-1203, Stuart Thomson*)

Visitors to the *Hood* mill around the foredeck while the ship was anchored in Vancouver. (*City of Vancouver Archives*, CVA 289-003.062)

A crowd of visitors swamp the *Hood*'s forecastle. (*City of Vancouver Archives*, CVA 289-003.059)

Taken while the *Hood* was in Vancouver, this image shows one of the *Hood*'s sailors with Joey the wallaby on deck. (*Stuart Thomson, CVA 99-1213 City of Vancouver Archives*)

Officers and crew from the *Hood* and the *Repulse* parading down Hastings Street, Vancouver. (*City of Vancouver Archives, Bo P540*)

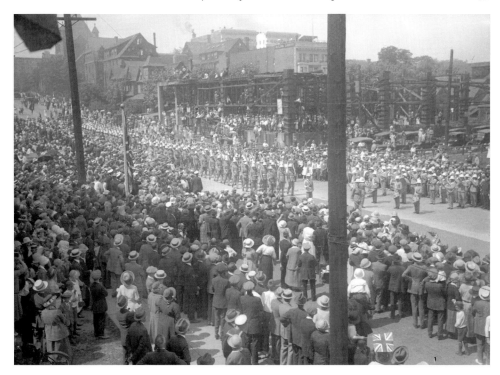

Shore parties from the *Hood*, the *Repulse*, and HMAS *Adelaide* parade on Burrard Street, Vancouver. (*City of Vancouver Archives, CVA 99-1201, Stuart Thomson*)

The *Hood* at anchor in Vancouver Harbour. (*City of Vancouver Archives, CVA 152-9.09*)

One of the *Hood* boats in Vancouver harbour carrying visitors.
(*City of Vancouver Archives, CVA 152-9.09*)

At anchor in Vancouver. Note the visitors on her decks.
(*City of Vancouver Archives, CVA 447-10 Walter Edwin Frost*)

From 26 to 30 July, the *Hood* and the *Repulse* anchored at Kingston, Jamaica before sailing north to Halifax, Nova Scotia. Leaving Halifax on 15 August, four days later, the *Hood*, *Repulse*, and *Adelaide* dropped anchor in Quebec, Canada where Field had to deal with questions relating to comments that he had made while in Vancouver relating to calls for Canada to maintain a pair of cruisers on each coast. On 2 September, the *Hood*, *Repulse*, and *Adelaide* left Quebec and set a course for Topsail Bay, Newfoundland. At Topsail Bay on 15 September, the crew of the *Hood* posed over the forward turrets and forecastle for a crew photograph. This was followed on 19 September by a 'Miss World' competition hosted aboard the *Hood*.

On 21 September, the ships left Newfoundland for Devonport. Off Lizard Point, the *Hood*, *Repulse*, and *Adelaide* rendezvoused with the First Light Cruiser Squadron before sailing into Devonport, thus completing the world cruise of the Special Service Squadron.

The world cruise was a crucial episode in establishing the reputation of HMS *Hood*. In ten months, the Special Service Squadron had sailed 38,152 miles around the globe, hosted around 2 million visitors and had dropped anchor in forty-three locations; during the course of the cruise, the *Hood* was visited by 752,049 people.[31] Nothing else in the *Hood*'s career would equal the Cruise of the Special Service Squadron, but it set the tone for many events that would follow. In all, the cruise was a successful public relations exercise which served as a subtle reminder to friend and foe alike that Britannia ruled the waves.

The *Hood* in the Panama Canal Zone, 24 July 1924.
(*NH 60452, US Naval History and Heritage Command*)

Above: The *Hood* entering the Pedro Miguel Lock of the Panama Canal. (*Richard Toffolo*)

Left: The *Hood* in the Pedro Miguel Lock of the Panama Canal.

The *Hood* in the Panama Canal. (*Author's collection*)

Above: The *Hood* entering the Gatún lock.

Left: The *Hood* descending the Gatún locks of the Panama Canal.

The bow of *Hood* is awash as she sails through Caribbean waters between July and August 1924. HMS *Repulse* is on the horizon. (*Author's collection*)

The *Hood* in front of the Château Frontenac, Quebec. (*P428, S3, SS1, D7, P134/Fonds L'Action catholique / Croiseur de bataille 'HMS Hood' à la hauteur du Château Frontenac/Photographe non identifié, Bibliothèque et Archives nationales du Québec*)

The *Hood* on the St Lawrence River passing in front of the Citadelle of Quebec and Château Frontenac. (*P428, S3, SS1, D7, P132/Fonds L'Action catholique/Croiseur de bataille 'HMS Hood' à la hauteur de la Citadelle/Photo C. P. R., Bibliothèque et Archives nationales du Québec*)

The *Hood* at anchor on the St Lawrence River. (*P428, S3, SS1, D7, P133/Fonds L'Action catholique/Croiseur de bataille 'HMS Hood' à la hauteur du Château Frontenac/Photo C. P. R., Bibliothèque et Archives nationales du Québec*)

The *Hood* lying at anchor in the centre of the St Lawrence River, Quebec during her visit to the city between 19 August and 2 September 1924. (*P428, S3, SS1, D7, P37/Fonds L'Action catholique/Croiseur de bataille 'HMS Hood' sur le fleuve Saint-Laurent / Photo C. P. R., 1924*)

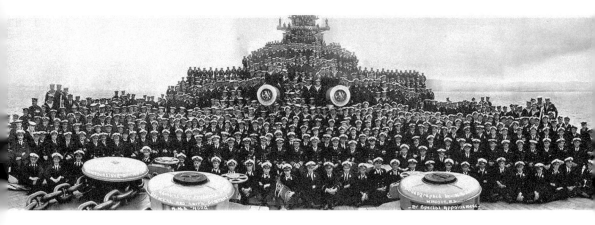

While in Topsail Bay, the entire the crew congregated on the forecastle and atop the forward turrets for a crew photograph, 15 September 1924. Note Joey the wallaby in the front row. (*HMS Hood Association*)

8

Routine Work

Having arrived back at Devonport on 28 September, the *Hood* was taken in hand for a partial refit until 5 November when she sailed to Rosyth. At Rosyth, she was taken in hand for docking until 22 November before returning to Devonport. Arriving back at Devonport, she was again taken in hand for docking from 25 November.

On 10 January 1925, the *Hood*'s refit was complete. Four days later, she departed Devonport for Portland, from where she sailed to Lisbon, Portugal on 19 January. Anchoring at Lisbon from 23 to 30 January, the *Hood* participated in the Vasco da Gama celebrations held in the city. The celebrations saw the *Hood*'s Naval Brigade participate in a march through the city. Departing Lisbon, the *Hood* sailed to Gibraltar where she anchored until 23 February before docking in Palma de Mallorca. Weighing anchor at Palma on 2 March, the *Hood* sailed to Almería before returning to Gibraltar, dropping anchor on 6 March. On 14 March, the *Hood* arrived once more at Palma from where she departed three days later to undertake exercises. The *Hood* returned to Palma from 18 to 21 March before sailing to Gibraltar (22–29 March) and then Devonport where she arrived on 1 April.

From 3 April until 7 May, the *Hood* was taken in hand for alterations. On 30 April, Admiral Field bid farewell to the *Hood* when he hauled down his flag to take up a new position as Deputy Chief of the Naval Staff. Field's replacement as Admiral Commanding the Battlecruiser Squadron was Rear-Admiral Sir Cyril Fuller, the Third Sea Lord and Admiralty Controller. Fuller had quickly risen through the ranks of the Royal Navy, being promoted to lieutenant at the age of nineteen, commander at twenty-nine, and captain at thirty-six. The *Hood* also received a new commanding officer in Captain Harold Reinold. Reinhold had seen service during the First World War as the commanding officer of the monitor HMS *Prince Rupert* off the Belgian coast during which time he was Mentioned in Dispatches twice. In 1917, Reinhold was appointed as the King's Harbour Master, Plymouth. Promoted to captain that same year, Reinhold would hold this position until he was appointed captain of HMS *Ceres* in the Mediterranean immediately after the war. The period from 1922 until his appointment as flag captain of the

The *Hood* at Devonport in January 1924 while in hand for docking.

Hood saw Reinhold return to Britain, where he was drafted to the Royal Navy's navigation school.

On 8 May, the *Hood* weighed anchor and sailed to Invergordon where she dropped anchor from 11 to 31 May before sailing to Rosyth. Departing Rosyth on 22 June the *Hood* visited Portree, Isle of Skye (23 June–1 July), Portrush, Northern Ireland (1–6 July), Greenock (6–10 July), and Lamlash, Isle of Arran (10–17 July). While at Lamlash on 15 July, the *Hood* participated in the Battlecruiser Squadron Regatta before sailing to Portland. From Portland, the *Hood* sailed to Devonport where she was taken in hand for repairs. With the repair work complete, on 1 September, the *Hood* returned to Portland before sailing to Invergordon where she anchored from 17 September until 19 October when she weighed anchor and sailed to Rosyth where she arrived on 20 October. She would remain at Rosyth until 21 November following being taken in hand for docking and repairs between 4 and 20 November. The *Hood* would end 1925 at Devonport. Arriving back at Devonport on 23 November, three days later, she was taken in hand for a refit which lasted until 6 January 1926.

With the refit completed on 6 January, the *Hood* was paid off before being recommissioned on 7 January for further service as the Flagship of the Battlecruiser Squadron. The year 1926 began with a spring cruise to Spain and the Mediterranean. The cruise began on 12 January when the *Hood* sailed for Arousa Bay where she anchored for six days from 15 January. From Arousa Bay, the *Hood* sailed to Gibraltar and then on to Palmas Bay. Departing Palmas Bay on 3 March, the *Hood* anchored at Palma between 5 and 9 March before returning to Gibraltar. Departing Gibraltar on 18 March, she returned to Arousa Bay from 20 to 27 March before sailing back to Devonport.

The *Hood* at Portrush before sailing to Greenock. (*Author's collection*)

Back at Devonport, on 29 April, the *Hood* was taken in hand for a minor refit and for alterations to be made. On 3 May, she departed Devonport for Greenock to lend assistance during the General Strike. The *Hood* lay quietly off Greenock and departed for trials off the Isle of Arran on 31 May before returning to Greenock on 4 June. The *Hood* remained off Greenock until 24 June when she sailed to Rosyth and from there to Shoeburyness, Essex. Departing Shoeburyness on 7 July, she dropped anchor in Torbay (8–15 July) before sailing to Portsmouth where on 21 July until 30 August she was taken in hand for docking.

Out of docking, the *Hood*'s first journey was to Spithead. On 4 September, the *Hood* dropped anchor off Scarborough and then continued north to Invergordon. From 9 September until 24 October, the *Hood* remained at Invergordon, then sailed for Portland where she arrived on 28 October. At Portland, the *Hood* participated in a series of tactical exercises staged by the Atlantic Fleet just off the coast for the benefit of delegates of the Imperial Conference. She sailed from Portland for Devonport on 17 November where she was taken in hand for a refit between 22 November and 24 December.

The year 1927 began in a very much similar manner to 1926 when the *Hood* weighed anchor and departed Devonport for Arousa Bay as the first stop on a Cruise to Spain and the Mediterranean. Arriving back at Devonport on 28 March, because she was available, between 5 and 30 April, the *Hood* was taken in hand for repairs. At the beginning of May, the *Hood* sailed to Invergordon where on 21 May, Fuller hauled down his flag and left the ship along with Reinhold. Fuller's replacement as the Admiral Commanding the Battlecruiser Squadron was Rear-Admiral Frederic Dreyer.

The *Hood* underway off Portsmouth in 1926. A Fairy Flycatcher can be seen atop 'B' turret, which has been trained to starboard to allow the aircraft to take off into the wind.

Born in January 1878, Dreyer joined the Royal Navy in 1891, joining HMS *Britannia*. Upon leaving HMS *Britannia*, Dreyer first served on the ironclad HMS *Anson* and then the pre-dreadnought battleship HMS *Barfleur*. Attaining the rank of lieutenant in 1898, Dreyer was posted to the Royal Navy gunnery school, HMS *Excellent* in 1899 in a move that would shape the rest of his career. By 1901, Dreyer had qualified as a gunnery lieutenant. Such was Dreyer's grasp and insight into the subject of gunnery that his first appointment was to the Gunnery School at Sheerness. Two years later, Dreyer joined the battleship HMS *Exmouth*, the flagship of the Home Fleet. Dreyer served aboard the *Exmouth* until 1907 when at the insistence of Lord Fisher, he was transferred to the then newly commissioned HMS *Dreadnought* to assist with her gunnery trials. This posting was followed by a posting in late 1907 to the Naval Ordnance Department.

In 1909, Commander Dreyer was appointed as the executive officer of HMS *Vanguard* before gaining his first command in 1913 when he was posted to HMS *Amphion*. Later that year, Dreyer was promoted to captain and was appointed as flag captain to Sir Robert Arbuthnot, the commanding officer of the 2nd Battle Squadron aboard HMS *Orion*. In 1915, Dreyer was appointed to HMS *Iron Duke* where he became the flag captain to Admiral Jellicoe. When Jellicoe was posted to the Admiralty in March 1917, Dreyer followed the admiral to the Admiralty and took up a posting as the Director of Naval Ordnance. In 1918, Dreyer was selected to be Jellicoe's Chief of Staff on a cruise of the empire, which was undertaken in a similar manner to the *Hood*'s cruise as part of the Special Service Squadron. April 1922 found Dreyer in command of HMS *Repulse* where he gained his first close contact with HMS *Hood*. Promoted to flag rank in December 1923, he returned to the Admiralty in 1924 as the Assistant Chief of the Naval Staff before taking up his posting in the *Hood* in May 1927.

Flying Dreyer's flag, the *Hood*'s first journey was to Gareloch were she dropped anchor between 8 and 15 June before sailing to Helensburgh. The end of June 1927 found the *Hood* at Newcastle, County Down before sailing to Portland (1–7 July) and then Portsmouth. At Portsmouth, between 13 and 19 July, the *Hood* was taken in hand for docking. With August spent at anchor in Portsmouth, the beginning of September found the *Hood en route* to Invergordon where she arrived on 2 September. The *Hood* would remain at Invergordon throughout September and throughout much of October, departing the anchorage on the 26th to sail to South Queensferry.

At South Queensferry until 2 November, the *Hood* made for Portland, dropping anchor there from 4 to 7 November. Thereafter, she sailed to Devonport where she arrived during the course of 7 November. Between 10 November and 29 December, she was taken in hand for a refit and was ready once more for service on 4 January 1928.

The *Hood* began 1928 at Devonport before weighing anchor on 4 January to sail to Portland. On 10 January, the *Hood* began her Spanish Cruise when she departed Portland for Vigo. At Vigo from 13 to 23 January, the *Hood* sailed on to Gibraltar where she arrived on 25 January. The *Hood* would remain at Gibraltar until 7 March, her time anchored at the Rock proving uneventful. The next stop for the *Hood* was Málaga where she dropped anchor on 7 March. Two days later, the ship was visited by Victoria Eugenie of Battenberg, the Queen of Spain and wife of King Alfonso XIII, and their son Infante Jaime, Duke of Segovia. On 10 March, the *Hood* weighed anchor and returned to Gibraltar where she arrived the same day. On 13 March, the *Hood* again returned to Málaga, which she again left the following day in order to conduct a series of exercises before arriving at Gibraltar once again on 16 March. The *Hood* would remain at Gibraltar until 22 March when she left for the Mediterranean and sailed to Portland.

Arriving at Portland on 28 March, the *Hood* weighed anchor to participate in a series of tactical exercises staged by the Atlantic Fleet off Portland in honour of King Amanullah of Afghanistan on 3 April. Having completed the exercises off Portland, the *Hood* sailed to Devonport where she dropped anchor on 4 April. On 9 April, because she was available, she was taken in hand for repairs, which would last until 28 April. Two days after completing the repairs, the *Hood* left Devonport and sailed north to Invergordon. The *Hood* arrived at Invergordon on 4 May and would remain at anchor there until 4 June when she raised steam and sailed to Scapa Flow. Leaving the anchorage of Scapa Flow four days later, the *Hood* sailed to South Queensferry before returning once more to Invergordon. On 12 June, she left Invergordon for Loch Kishorn where she anchored from 13 to 18 June.

The *Hood* soon moved on to Ballachulish and then on to Portsmouth where she arrived on 27 June. While at Portsmouth, on 3 July, the *Hood* was taken in hand for a refit, which was completed on 31 July. On 2 August, the

Photographed from the *Hood*, this photograph shows HMS *Renown* and another unidentified vessel engaged in 15-inch firing exercises off Portland sometime during the 1920s. It is likely that this photo was taken on 3 April 1928 when the Atlantic Fleet undertook a series of tactical exercises in honour of King Amanullah of Afghanistan. (*NH 57181, US Naval History and Heritage Command*)

Hood left Portsmouth for Devonport where she remained at anchor from 3 August until 5 September. Between 7 and 31 August, she was taken in hand for alterations. While undergoing alterations, on 27 August, she was paid off before being recommissioned the following day for further service as Flagship of the Battlecruiser Squadron.

On 5 September 1928, the *Hood* departed Devonport for Invergordon where she anchored alongside other ships of the Battlecruiser Squadron and Home Fleet. On 29 September, while at Invergordon, Admiral of the Fleet Jellicoe joined the *Hood* ahead of the autumn gunnery cruise which lasted until 4 October. While undertaking the exercises with Jellicoe aboard in the North Sea, the *Hood* caused quite a stir. While sailing at full speed, plumes of water were forced through the ship's hawsepipes and into the air. The *Hood*'s siren became jammed, the ear-splitting sound of which reverberated out across the North Sea. In naval language, a prolonged blast of a siren is a distress signal. The *Hood*'s jammed siren caused must consternation among the other ships partaking in the gunnery exercises. Panic ensued aboard the *Hood* while engineers attempted to fix the problem. Eventually, the siren was silenced but another problem arose. The ship's bearings began to run hot, which forced a reduction of speed. Despite the issues, the *Hood* succeeded in returning to Invergordon with the remainder of the fleet.[1] The *Hood* would remain at Invergordon until 23 October when she raised anchor and set sail for South Queensferry where she anchored between 24 and 31 October.

The *Hood*'s next port call was Portland from 2 to 14 November. Departing Portland on 14 November, the *Hood* returned to Devonport where on 16 November until 1 January 1929, she was taken in hand for repairs.

The *Hood* departed Devonport for Portland on 9 January. On 12 January, she departed Portland to conduct exercises before sailing on to Falmouth. The *Hood* anchored at Falmouth from 12 to 15 January when she weighed anchor and set a course for Arousa Bay. Anchoring at Arousa Bay on 18 January, four days later, she sailed to Gibraltar where she spent the period from 25 January to 26 February. Leaving Gibraltar on 26 February, the *Hood* made port calls at Barcelona, Palma, and Port de Pollença before returning to Gibraltar on 26 March.

On 2 April, the *Hood* departed Gibraltar for Portsmouth. Arriving at Portsmouth four days later, the flag of Vice Admiral Dreyer was transferred to HMS *Repulse*. That same day, the *Hood* departed Portsmouth for Devonport where she arrived on 7 April. The *Hood* would remain at Devonport until 1 May during which time she was taken in hand for repairs. On 1 May, she departed Devonport for Portsmouth. While at Portsmouth, on 17 May, the ship was paid off into dockyard control while her crew were transferred to the battlecruiser HMS *Tiger* to continue service with the Battlecruiser Squadron. With the *Hood* paid off into dockyard control Lieutenant-Commander French passed the *Hood* into the charge of Lieutenant-Commander W. M. Phipps-Hornby. The *Hood* would be under the charge of Phipps-Hornby for the next two years as she underwent an extensive refit.

The primary alterations made to the *Hood* during this refit included the addition of two Mark VIII pop-pom anti-aircraft guns that were fitted on each side of the boat deck, which was also enlarged. An aircraft catapult was also placed on the roof of X turret. A mock-up of the catapult was constructed on the roof of 'X' turret but was subsequently removed because it was considered more practical to fit a catapult and a crane to recover an aircraft on the extreme end of the quarterdeck. With this modification, the *Hood* was equipped with a Fairey III seaplane. Costing £687,074 (approximately £45,387,921 in today's money), the refit was completed in early 1931 with the *Hood* commissioned for trials at Portsmouth as a tender to HMS *Victory* on 10 March.

Opposite above: Looking aft, 'X' turret is at the limit of its firing arc while the *Hood* is on manoeuvres off Portland with HMS *Repulse* astern, 8 November 1926. The right-hand gun of 'X' turret is at its maximum elevation of 30 degrees. Of note is the tall structure on the left, which is the wireless trunking from the second wireless office located on the lower deck. (*NH 57184, US Naval History and Heritage Command*)

Opposite below: The *Hood* entering Portsmouth harbour during the 1920s.

The mock-up of the catapult and aircraft constructed on the roof of 'X' turret. This was subsequently removed because it was considered more practical to fit a catapult and a crane to recover an aircraft on the extreme end of the quarterdeck. (*Author's collection*)

A Fairey IIIF on the quarterdeck of the *Hood* following the completion of her refit in 1931. (*Author's collection*)

9

The Invergordon Mutiny

In 1931, Britain was in the throes of an economic crisis brought about as a result of the Great Depression. At this point, a time of high inflation and with a devalued currency, the British government had amassed a budget deficit of around £170,000,000. In response to this, the government appointed the Committee of National Expenditure under Sir George May, a former Secretary of the Prudential Assurance Company, the task of reducing government finances. In July 1931, the Committee of National Expenditure warned Ramsay MacDonald's Labour Government that it would face an even greater deficit by April 1932 unless it took far-reaching steps to balance its budget.[1]

The Committee of National Expenditure recommended a series of tax increases and that a drastic reduction in public expenditure be made, which included pay cuts for teachers, the police and the armed forces. The Committee also strongly urged that a 20 per cent reduction be made in benefits for the unemployed whose ranks had swelled to approximately 2.5 million. Faced with a major financial crisis, the MacDonald government decided to heed the advice of the Committee and decided on a course of drastic measures necessary to restore foreign confidence in Britain's finances. Despite this, the Cabinet was sharply divided on the issue of cutting benefits for the unemployed. With around half of the Cabinet prepared to resign rather than accept a reduction of 10 per cent in unemployment benefits, MacDonald made the decision to go to Buckingham Palace and tenure the resignation of his Labour government. That same day, 24 August 1931, saw the formation of a new National Government which was headed by MacDonald and was composed of a handful of his Labour ministers as well as leading members of both the Conservative and Liberal parties. The path was now clear to large scale cuts in public expenditure.

For the Royal Navy, the timing could not have been worse. Leading members of the Board of the Admiralty, including the First and Second Sea Lords, the Deputy Chief of the Naval Staff and the Permanent Secretary had either been taken ill or were away on extended periods of leave during August with the result that the Admiralty, at a critical time, was without any firm leadership. With a lack of firm leadership, the Admiralty did little to thwart the proposal from the Committee of National Expenditure that the 1925 pay scales be invoked throughout the Navy. On 8 August, the Admiralty informed the Cabinet's Economic Committee that cutting pay to the 1925 pay scale would be 'regarded by the whole Navy as a breach of faith'. A Cabinet memorandum, circulated by the First Lord of the Admiralty, A. V. Alexander, disagreed with the Admiralty's assessment, claiming that the measure would be accepted as a necessity. Alexander's memorandum stated:

> I think the personnel of the Navy as a whole would loyally accept the sacrifices which it had been decided were necessary in the public interest ... if equivalent reductions were made throughout the public service and in the unemployment pay.[2]

With the formation of the National Government on 24 August 1931, Alexander was succeeded as First Lord of the Admiralty by Sir Austin Chamberlain who saw no reason not to cut naval pay. It was against this backdrop that the Board of the Admiralty reassembled on 3 September and ratified the decision already reached by the government to apply the 1925 pay rates universally.

Before being recommissioned into the navy, something which was expected to occur in May 1931, there was still work to be done aboard the *Hood*. The time spent in the dockyard undergoing the refit had left the ship in a deplorable state. As Lieutenant-Commander Eric W. Longley-Cook, who was appointed to the *Hood* as the ship's first lieutenant and gunnery officer recalled:

> I was thrilled when I was appointed to her, but then came the shock of finding her in such a state. Fortunately the *Valiant* was just completing a refit and her captain, B. G. Washington, took one look at her and told the admiral's superintendent [that] he refused to accept the *Valiant* in this state and that he would tell their Lordships. There was a quick reaction by Portsmouth Dockyard to clear the *Valiant* and also the *Hood*. For the next four months trainloads filled with dirt and scrap left daily from alongside us.[3]

The *Hood*'s refit resulted in additional changes to those asides from her configuration. Devonport no longer had the facilities to repair her bulk so her home port became Portsmouth. On 10 March, the *Hood* commissioned for trials at Portsmouth as tender to HMS *Victory*. On 27 April, Captain Julian F. C. Patterson assumed command of the *Hood* before she once again took up the role as Flagship of the Battlecruiser Squadron on 12 May with a full crew of Portsmouth ratings.

On 16 June, the *Hood* left Portsmouth for Portland. At Portland from 17 June until 10 July, the *Hood* worked up along the south coast. On 26 June, the *Hood*'s new Fairy IIIF floatplane was lost on take-off at Weymouth. A few seconds after lifting off from the surface, the aircraft lost speed when 2 feet above the sea, the port wing caught the surface of the water, causing the aircraft to cartwheel. Breaking up as it cartwheeled, the crew were thrown clear to be rescued by one

A dirty run-down *Hood* sailing from Portsmouth on 16 June 1931. Rear-Admiral Tomkinson did not like what he saw when the *Hood* arrived at Torbay. (*NH 60419, US Naval History and Heritage Command*)

Taken from another angle, this image shows a run-down *Hood* sailing from Portsmouth on 16 June 1931. (*NH 60418, US Naval History and Heritage Command*)

of the *Hood*'s boats. The aircraft, meanwhile, finally came to a rest and sank in thirty seconds. The next day, divers would salvage the plane. On 12 July, the *Hood* was at Torbay where the flag of Rear Admiral Wilfred Tomkinson was transferred from the *Renown*. In transferring his flag to the *Hood*, Tomkinson gained the distinction of being the only individual to have commanded the *Hood* both as captain and then as an admiral. Tomkinson did not like what he saw when the *Hood* arrived at Torbay on 11 July, as recalled by Eric Longley-Cook:

> We sailed early one fine morning to take station astern of the Battle Cruiser Squadron. I was on the bridge and wondered what the Admiral's signal would be. 'Glad to see you back'? 'Welcome back to the BCS'? No. A flag signal 'Manoeuvre badly executed'; from tails up to tails nearly down. Next morning, Sunday 08.00 in Torbay, we hoisted the flag of ACQ. At 09.00 he arrived on board, walked round divisions, then 'clear lower deck, everyone aft'. From the after capstan the Admiral addressed us. Summarily he said 'I was the first captain of this ship and until you reach something like the standard in which I left her, I shall not be satisfied.' Now, we had worked very hard indeed to get her from dockyard condition, so tails went down even lower. So on we went, not entirely happy.[4]

Returning to Portsmouth on 21 July, from 27 July until 7 September, as she was available, the *Hood* was taken in hand for repairs. Despite undergoing repairs, between 1 and 5 August, the *Hood* took part in Navy Week. Beginning in the late 1920s, Navy Weeks were a response to the dire economic situation faced by Britain during the interwar period. In the pre-welfare state Britain of the late 1920s, real hardship among ex-sailors and the many widows and orphans of those from the navy who had been killed during the Great War existed. Following the Great War and with the signing of the Washington Naval Treaty, the Royal Navy had been reduced. The reduced size of the navy restricted the money raised by serving officers and men who had their own families to support. Therefore, a fundraising show for the public was convened aimed at filling the gap. The first Navy Week was held at Devonport and ships including the *Rodney*, *Iron Duke*, *Lion*, *Glorious*, and *Devonshire* were on display to the public. More than 67,000 attended the first Navy Week and such was its success that it was decided to make the event an annual occurrence.

The repair work on the *Hood* was completed on 7 September and the following day, she sailed north to Invergordon where she arrived on 11 September. As the *Hood* sailed to Invergordon, she was to join the bulk of the Atlantic Fleet in conducting a series of exercises in the North Sea. As the *Hood* sailed north, the decision had already been taken to cut the pay of ratings back to the 1925 scale. On Monday 7 September, Admiral Sir Michael Hodges, the Commander-in-Chief of the Atlantic Fleet, was suddenly hospitalised with the result that Rear-Admiral Tomkinson became the senior ranking officer of the Atlantic Fleet. It is worth briefly noting here that even before Hodges' hospitalisation on 7 September, on 3 September, an Admiralty cypher had been prepared for Tomkinson outlining

Above: The *Hood* while working up along the south coast, July 1931. (*Author's collection*)

Right: The *Hood* viewed from the stern in July 1931. A supply vessel and one of the ship's 50-foot steam pinnacles are alongside, visible on the left of the image. (*Author's collection*)

A crowd of visitors boarding the *Hood* during Navy Week 1931. When this photo was taken, the *Hood* had not long emerged from her refit. A prominent addition to the superstructure as a result of the refit was the Mk I high-angle director.

The *Hood* at anchor in 1931. It is likely that this photograph was taken shortly before the Invergordon Mutiny. (*Chris Hancock*)

the proposed pay cuts. Debate surrounds whether or not Tomkinson saw this cypher before 13 September. Either Tomkinson never saw the cypher or he failed to take it in. Whatever the case, Tomkinson gave no indication of having seen the cypher before an Admiralty Fleet Order was issued on 12 September detailing the same.[5]

On 10 September, while the Atlantic Fleet was still at sea, the Chancellor of the Exchequer, Philip Snowden, delivered an emergency budget to Parliament in which he publicly announced the pruning of government expenditure. Despite the bulletin from the BBC that same day announcing the government's measures, it was not until the Atlantic Fleet dropped anchor at Invergordon on 11 September and the day's papers came aboard that the 70 per cent of sailors on the 1919 pay scale learned that their basic pay was to be reduced by 25 per cent.

Ratings were shocked by the proposed cuts. The imposition of the 1925 pay rates throughout the service meant that 94 per cent of chief and petty officers along with 72 per cent of all other ratings would be affected by a basic pay cut of 25 per cent. The cuts translated into a 10 per cent pay cut for officers and senior ratings in line with the 10 per cent cuts across the board for public sector workers. For junior ratings, a 'new rate' of pay was introduced for entrants from 1925 onwards. At the same time, ratings below the rank of petty officer who had joined the navy before 1925 were to have their pay cut to the same level of those who entered the service after 1925, which amounted to a 25 per cent cut. The impact of the cuts would be less severe than implied as almost all ratings had their incomes supplemented by specialist bonuses and allowances, nevertheless, attention was focused on the high reduction in basic pay. To the men affected, it appeared that the lower deck was being disproportionally hit by the government's pay cuts. For example, whereas the basic pay of many able seamen would be cut from four to three shillings a day (a cut of 25 per cent), an Admiral of the Fleet would only see a 17 per cent reduction in his basic pay under the government proposal. The universal application of the 1925 pay scales threatened to cause real distress for many of Britain's naval families. One officer noted:

> [It was] not an exaggeration to say that, in many cases, it is not hardship that they are facing but the ruin of their carefully and thriftily built-up homes. These men literally budget their commitments in pence. What little margin they have disappears entirely under the new scale.[6]

Anger was generated by the severity of the proposed cuts and by the conviction that the Admiralty had broken binding promises not to replace the 1919 pay scales. The feeling of betrayal harboured by the ratings was further exacerbated by the government's proposals to reduce naval pensions, something that would and could have little immediate impact on the state of the government's finances. The reductions were scheduled to come into effect from 1 October, leaving those affected with little time to get their finances in order. So it was that the reductions, the manner in which they became known, the impact that they would have on the men's families and the speed with which the cuts were to take effect all combined to lay the foundations for the Invergordon Mutiny.

The seat of the mutiny movement lay in the battleships *Rodney* and *Valiant*, the cruiser *Norfolk*, and the minelayer *Adventure*. Lieutenant-Commander Ross of the *Rodney* recalled men visiting him in private to discuss the proposed cuts: 'They all had the same story to tell: disaster faced them, they were up to their limits in Hire Purchase payments and margins. Some even expressed sympathy for the financial dilemma in which I must also be placed'.[7] On the lower decks of HMS *Rodney*, there was a feeling of foreboding that was described by one sailor as a climate of suspicion:

> When you was [*sic.*] on board ship the atmosphere didn't seem to be right. It was tense and everyone was looking at each other, like you was spying on each other. You could cut the air with a knife. It was that thick.[8]

The mutiny owed much of its support to the leading seamen, able seamen, stokers, and marines on the 1919 pay scales who represented the groups worst affected by the proposed cuts. It is worth briefly noting the practical difficulties of coordinating a mutiny in numerous vessels. Owing to the number of vessels involved, any central organisation was prevented, meaning that the participation of individual ships would come to rest on the morale, convictions, and moods of their crews.

With Tomkinson and his staff oblivious to the gathering unrest on the mess decks of the ships of the Atlantic Fleet as rumours of the cuts abounded before it became widespread common knowledge, the *Hood* passed quietly into harbour routine at Invergordon on 11 September. Most of those not on watch duty spent the afternoon of 12 September at the Invergordon Highland Games where the ship's marine band formed one of the attractions. During the evening of 12 September, a bundle containing the sixteen-page Admiralty Fleet Order 2339/31 outlining the cuts arrived on board the *Hood*. As the bundle came aboard, the naval canteen ashore was buzzing with men anxiously discussing the cuts, the details of which had been broadcast by the BBC. At this meeting, it was agreed that a larger gathering should congregate the following day. In the wake of this decision, canvassing for action to be taken over the cuts began in and among the ships of the Atlantic Fleet.

Early on 13 September, the worst fears of the lower decks were confirmed and brought with it the first indications that trouble was afoot within the ranks of the fleet. Shortly before midday aboard the *Hood*, Lieutenant-Commander Harry Pursey, one of the handful of officers in the Royal Navy at the time to have won promotion from the lower deck, was approached by a member of the lower deck. Presenting Pursey with one of the Sunday papers, the headline of which outlined the cuts, the member of the lower deck informed Pursey that 'The lads won't stand for this!'

Pursey took the paper and passed it on to Commander Cecil McCrum to whom he offered a stark warning: 'If these cuts are not reduced there will be trouble …

If there is trouble, it will be on Tuesday—at eight o'clock.... Four capital ships due to sail ... It's tailor-made for the job'.[9] McCrum dismissed the suggestion and assured Pursey that everything would be alright and that the *Hood*, the *Valiant*, the *Nelson*, and the *Rodney* would all sail as planned on Tuesday 15 September. With discontent throughout the fleet at the proposed cuts, leaders and plans began to emerge.

At noon on 13 September, Captain Patterson received intelligence of the planned canteen meeting from his opposite number in HMS *Warspite*, Captain St Aubyn Baldwin Wake. It would appear that Tomkinson was not privy to this information and that no preventative action was taken with leave being granted at 1 p.m. A number of men headed ashore to watch the naval cup final game played between the football teams of the *Hood* and the *Norfolk*, which the *Hood*'s team ultimately won 2–0, but despite this, the number of men who poured ashore was unprecedented. Patterson and McCrum noted nothing untoward during a visit ashore but the men knew differently and soon gravitated away from the football pitch to the large canteen that overlooked the anchorage.

The gathering in the canteen began as a sombre occasion but quickly gathered steam as the afternoon transitioned into evening. Many men, most of whom were a little worse for wear, climbed atop tables to deliver speeches and opinions of the cuts. One of those who climbed atop a table that evening was twenty-four-year-old Able Seaman Len Wincott of HMS *Norfolk*. Wincott was a natural orator who urged those who had gathered in the canteen to remain aboard their ships but to implement a programme of passive resistance when the order came to put to sea. His words had an electrifying effect on the crowd of over 600 sailors. One man who heard Wincott's speech was Rear-Admiral Edward Astley-Rushton, the commanding officer of the 2nd Cruiser Squadron. Rear-Admiral Astley-Rushton overheard Wincott when he was in full flow and immediately informed the shore patrol, which was manned that evening by men from HMS *Warspite*. The *Warspite*'s shore patrol promptly requested reinforcements from the *Hood* who soon arrived, but not before an increasingly rowdy gathering emerged from the canteen and proceeded to return to their ships.

As the men emerged from the canteen, HMS *Nelson* arrived into the anchorage. Aboard the *Nelson* were the Admiralty cyphers, which warned of the cuts and which had supposedly been in Tomkinson's hands the previous week. Astley-Rushton boarded the *Hood* during the course of the evening to discuss events ashore with Tomkinson, who dismissed the events as being of no consequence. Given the circumstances, it was possibly expected that the men would be disgruntled at the proposals and would 'blow off steam'.

With no sign that the canteen meeting had taken a mutinous turn, on the morning of 14 September, Tomkinson informed the Admiralty that there had been a 'slight disturbance' ashore in the canteen, which was 'caused by one or two ratings endeavouring to address those present on the subject of pay'. Tomkinson went on to signal that there was 'no importance to the incident from a general disciplinary point of view'.[10]

The companies of each of the ships had settled down upon their return to their respective vessels and routines aboard the ships began as normal the following morning. Aboard the *Hood*, Commander McCrum could sense the volatile atmosphere aboard the battlecruiser and limited work to a little general drill. At 10 a.m., Tomkinson sent a signal to all of his captains ordering them to explain the contents of the Admiralty cypher outlining the cuts to their men. Tomkinson's signal was only received in five of the twelve ships at anchor. Aboard the *Hood*, the atmosphere was further stoked by copies of the *Daily Worker* that had arrived on board that morning. Patterson recommended that aggrieved men bring their hardship cases to the attention of their respective divisional officers. It was a recommendation that was met with calls of 'We're all hardship cases'. Patterson also recommended that the men refrain from illegal action and channel their grievances through him, something which did little to lighten the mood. The daily routine aboard the *Hood* continued as normal until leave was granted at 4.30 p.m. despite indications throughout every ship that another meeting was planned to occur in the canteen that evening.

The shore patrol that evening was drawn from men from HMS *Valiant* and was commanded by Lieutenant Robert Elkins. At the canteen, speeches of a general inflammatory nature were delivered. At 6.15 p.m., as Able Seaman Bond of the *Rodney* was delivering a speech, Elkins and the shore patrol arrived at the canteen. Elkins was met with a hostile reception, struck by a beer glass and bundled outside before the doors to the building were locked. Elkins managed to get himself readmitted to the meeting, which subsequently broke to reassemble on a nearby football pitch. Elkins called for a reinforcement patrol from the *Hood* before following the crowd to a spot where they had gathered to hear men speak from the roof of a wooden hut. Among the speakers was a marine from the *Hood* whose medals denoted him as a veteran of the Great War.

At 7.30 p.m., the meeting on the football pitch adjourned to reconvene in the canteen. It may be noted that a significant number of men took this opportunity to return to their ships. Those that remained headed to the canteen where the *Hood*'s shore patrol soon arrived under the command of Lieutenant-Commander L. G. E. Robinson. Robinson and the patrol marched into the canteen intent on closing it down for the evening. Robinson climbed on top of the bar and attempted to make himself heard:

> For some minutes I was shouted down, but the majority of the men were shouting 'Give him a fair hearing'—'Let's hear what he's got to say', and eventually I had silence. I told the men they were going the wrong way about things and would only bring discredit on themselves and the Navy, that they should bring up and complaints in the Service manner and that I would permit no more speeches.[11]

Robinson's speech brought an end to the meeting that evening but swayed only the minority of those who heard the speech. As the men headed back to the jetty, they did so with the knowledge that they had taken a decision to prevent the Atlantic Fleet from putting to sea.

At the jetty, the men embarked for their ships in a rowdy manner. Shouts of 'Don't forget—six o'clock tomorrow' drifted across the anchorage as searchlights from the ships swept over the jetty. Those boarding the *Hood*'s launch, the *Horizon*, began to shout stanzas from the Red Banner, something that was an offence punishable by court-martial. The rowdiness of the men returning to their ships interrupted a dinner party being held by Tomkinson in the *Hood* for his fleet commanders. The *Horizon* was ordered to lay off the *Hood* until the men were silent. The singing and shouting were a clear indication to all in the fleet that something had been settled ashore. It was only now that the commanding officers of the Atlantic Fleet finally realised the seriousness of the situation. As recalled by Captain Fischer Watson of HMS *Nelson*, following dining with Tomkinson aboard the *Hood*, it was evident that 'the men were out for a serious demonstration'.

> When we left at about 10.30 *Rodney*'s ship's company were cheering and making a continual noise one the forecastle. *Hood*'s had also given some signs of their intentions, which were that the ships of the Atlantic Fleet should NOT proceed to sea next day, as a public demonstration of their protest against the cuts of pay. On my return to the ship, the commander met me with the information that there had been a meeting on the forecastle but otherwise quiet. He had heard that all the men did not intend to turn to at 0600 next morning.[12]

At 9 p.m., Elkins finally managed to leave the pier to report the activities ashore to Tomkinson. By the time that Elkins arrived aboard the *Hood*, a crowd of approximately 100 men had gathered and were cheering a rating who was inciting them to refuse work the following day. Elkins was welcomed aboard the *Hood* by Lieutenant-Commander J. S. Gabbett who informed him that there had already been trouble on board. When Elkins spoke to Tomkinson, the Admiral was informed of events but did not think that the situation was as bad as it sounded.

Commander McCrum ordered the master-at-arms to clear the forecastle where a group of men had gathered to spend the night to keep watch and provide a warning if any attempts were made to weigh anchor.

At 6 a.m. on 15 September, the crew of the *Hood* turned out as per the normal routine but all eyes were focused on the *Rodney* and the *Valiant* on which the mutiny depended. Aboard the *Hood*, the fact that the crew had turned out encouraged the ship's officers to believe that the ship would be spared what all believed to be about to occur. By 7 a.m., it became apparent that neither the *Rodney* nor the *Valiant* was being prepared for sea. With that, the forecastles of the eight main protagonist vessels, including that of the *Hood*, filled with cheering sailors. At 7.45 a.m., McCrum climbed atop one of the ship's capstans and implored the men to return to work. His request was declined. In the ship's cable-locker flat, Lieutenant-Commander J. F. W. Mudford, the ship's torpedo officer, attempted to unshackle the bridles. Mudford was met by quiet resistance which was repeated across the ships of the Atlantic Fleet:

With Petty Officers and a few available hands from the cable party I went on to the forecastle to unshackle the first bridle. No marines were present in the cable-locker flat so that both the naval pipes and cable lockers had to be uncovered by my small party. The demonstrators were standing over both bridles and the hawsepipe cover, which was still in place. I went amongst them to view the cables and was immediately hemmed about by the crowd who stood a yard or two away from me. One man shouted 'What's the use of trying to take the ship to sea like this?' I said 'What about it! If I give the order to heave in, are you going to stop me?' They replied 'Yes, Sir, we shall have to'. I felt it would be unwise to use force without instructions to do so from higher authority, and the futility of giving a direct order to so large a number of men, when I knew I could not possibly enforce that order, was too obvious.[13]

Colours were hoisted at 8 a.m. and at 8.30 a.m., approximately 30 per cent of the *Hood*'s crew turned out for work. Shouts drifted across the anchorage from the men aboard the *Rodney*, which settled the matter of work. A large meeting was convened in the fore topman's mess located on the upper deck amidships in which it was agreed that the ship would not be allowed to sail. At the meeting, it was also made clear that it was not to be a mutiny in the truest sense of the word, but a strike. Violence was to be avoided at all costs. As a party of men on the forecastle rove a heavy wire hawse through the cables and around the capstan to prevent the anchor from being slipped, Tomkinson cancelled the planned exercises and signalled the Admiralty of the transpiring events. Something that came as a surprise to the *Hood*'s officers was the way in which the ship slipped into harbour routine once the crew realised that the ship was not going to put to sea. Against a backdrop of sporadic cheering between ships, aboard the *Hood*, normal work and divisional drill continued, causing considerable resentment aboard the *Rodney*. Nevertheless, despite it being clear that the ship would not be putting to sea, a party of men kept watch from the forecastle prepared to give warning of any attempt to prepare the ship for sea.

With the ships not putting to sea, rehearsals for a concert party began while on the *Rodney* one of the mess deck pianos was hoisted atop one of the gun turrets whereupon a stoker kept the men entertained by playing the latest music hall hits.

While communication between the ships consisted of the use of flags, the waving of caps, Aldis lamps, and body language (such as the crossing of forearms to convey the message of a crew being united in their strike), the ship's boats were in constant use throughout by both the mutineers and officers. While discipline on board HMS *Valiant* deteriorated to such an extent that the *Hood* had to provide a boat for use by her captain, Tomkinson was saved by the loyalty of the *Hood*'s telegraphists who allowed him to maintain steady contact with the Admiralty.

While it is likely that some officers within the fleet would have preferred Tomkinson to have taken a firmer line with the mutineers, many officers were completely at a loss at what to do. Orders were passed by Tomkinson to begin investigating hardship cases. At midday, Tomkinson let it be known that he was dispatching Rear-Admiral Reginald Coluin to London to confer with the Board

Telegraphists on board the *Hood*. (*Author's collection*)

of the Admiralty. With this news, the atmosphere aboard the *Hood* lightened somewhat as many waited to hear what the Admiralty had to say.

The first indication of the Admiralty's response was seen on the morning of 16 September when the morning papers arrived aboard the ships and it was seen that the Admiralty was referring to the mutiny as unrest among some of the lower ratings, something which sparked anger. Some work began aboard the *Hood*, which was regarded with discontent and disgust by those aboard the *Rodney*, which was at a standstill. From the late morning, the *Hood* teetered on the brink of open mutiny when rumours abounded that the ship was to be interned at Scapa Flow or placed under close arrest at Portsmouth.

> The normal work of the ship proceeded throughout the forenoon, though the atmosphere was somewhat strained. It unfortunately happened that the turn of the tide coincided with 'Stand Easy' in the forenoon, with the result that the two ships [*Hood* and *Rodney*] were swung parallel with one another. A mutual demonstration of cheering between the men assembled on *Rodney*'s forecastle and the men who had gone forward for a smoke during 'Stand Easy' in *Hood* took place.... During the dinner hour one or two leading seamen reported to the Commander that the feeling on the mess decks was growing strongly in favour of stopping work, and that the life of those against it was being made difficult. It became evident from various sources that the men would probably not 'Turn To' after dinner, and just before the routine time for falling in the hands of the Senior Engineer reported to the Commander that the Stokers appeared not to be coming down below. In order to avoid an open demonstration, the hands were piped to 'Make and Mend Clothes'. This took them

somewhat by surprise and resulted in [men] proceeding down below to sleep instead of cheering on the forecastle.[14]

As the afternoon progressed, it would appear that Tomkinson was meeting with some success in conveying the gravity of the situation and the resulting consequences to the Admiralty for at 3.10 p.m., he received a signal that stated the following:

> The Board of the Admiralty is fully alive to the fact that amongst certain classes of ratings special hardships will result from the reduction in pay ordered by H. M. Government. It is therefore directed that the ships of the Atlantic Fleet are to proceed to their home ports forthwith to enable personal investigation by C.-in-C.s and representatives of Admiralty with view to necessary alleviation being made. Any further refusals to carry out orders will be dealt with under the Naval Discipline Act.[15]

News of the signal wound its way down to and around the lower decks where it received a mixed response, causing a rupture. Some viewed the signal with relief and an attempt by the Admiralty to end the mutiny. Others viewed the order to return to home ports as an additional opportunity for leave while those from the north of England and Scotland regarded the order as something of a trap. At 4.45 p.m., Captain Patterson cleared the lower deck and climbed on top of 'A' turret to address the ship's company. Watched on by Tomkinson from the bridge, Patterson informed the ship's company of the Admiralty's order and stated that he could neither confirm nor deny the rumours that were doing the rounds. The Admiralty signal caused debate throughout the fleet.

As the men debated the Admiralty's order, the debate boiled down to what the other ships of the fleet would do. No vessel wanted to leave Invergordon and sail to its home port lest its reputation be tarnished among the other ships of the fleet, yet at the same time none of the ships wanted to remain alone at Invergordon and incur the wrath of the Admiralty. It became very much a case of 'if other ship don't go, we won't go; if other ships go, we will go'.

At 5 p.m., the full engine room watch turned out to light the boilers. Despite a party of men preventing the cable party from doing its job, at 8 p.m., the men of the *Hood* were preparing for sea. Despite the men, by and large, taking up their stations, Tomkinson was still unsure of whether or not the other ships of his command would leave the anchorage. Having signalled this to the Admiralty, orders were received permitting ships to sail independently as opposed to by squadron, an action that served to extinguish the last embers of resistance. By 11.30 p.m., the last ships of the Atlantic Fleet had cleared Invergordon.

Shortly after 6.30 a.m. on 19 September, the *Hood* dropped anchor at Portsmouth. Leave was granted until the evening of the 21st. Ashore, the bars filled with sailors, communist agitators and secret service agents. As soon as the *Hood* was alongside Tomkinson disembarked and began to make his way to the Admiralty in London.

As he made his way to the Admiralty, mail was taken on board the *Hood*. One of the letters taken on board was a letter from Admiral Field:

> My Dear Tomkinson, I congratulate you on the very able way you handled a most difficult situation ... well done! All the board [of the Admiralty] consider you handled the job with great ability and tact.[16]

On the evening of 21 September, while hardship statements were being taken, an announcement came from the government that the cuts to pay would be reduced to a maximum of 10 per cent. On 1 October, the entire navy was placed on the 1919 pay scales less 11 per cent. While the lower decks could claim a victory of sorts, the damage was done.

News of the mutiny was followed by a run on the pound with the result that Britain was forced off the Gold Standard. At the same time, the Admiralty was setting about getting its house in order through punitive action. On 6 October, Admiral Sir John Kelly succeeded Hodges as Commander-in-Chief of the Atlantic Fleet. Kelly was a dispassionate admiral who spoke the language that sailors understood. He was appointed to this new position with a special brief to conduct his own investigations with a view to restoring discipline. Despite the amnesty that the First Lord of the Admiralty Austin Chamberlain had promised to Parliament after the fleet had sailed from Invergordon, Kelly was determined that the ringleaders of the mutiny be rooted out and expelled from the Navy. Within days of his appointment as Commander-in-Chief of the Atlantic Fleet, Kelly was making rounds of the Fleet.

The *Hood* left Portsmouth on 8 October with the Atlantic Fleet and sailed north to Rosyth. By that time, 120 men had been confined to barracks; of these men, ten were from the *Hood*. The *Hood* spent October and the first half of November between Rosyth and Invergordon before sailing back to Portsmouth where she would finish up the year. At Rosyth, Kelly began to put the fleet through a series of rigorous exercises. A. F. Paterson, an able seaman aboard the *Hood* at the time, recalled:

> One evolution meant *Hood*'s marine band lowering a boat, putting their instruments in it and pulling it over to the flagship [HMS *Nelson*] to play a popular tune. The bandmaster led them in to 'Anybody Here Seen Kelly?' The c-in-c was not amused.[17]

On 27 October 1931, Ramsay MacDonald was returned to power as Prime Minister at the head of the National Government. No sooner had the National Government been returned to power then the first men caught up in the mutiny were discharged. On 2 November, a signal arrived in from the Admiralty for the Commander-in-Chief of Portsmouth informing him that the Board of the Admiralty had approved the discharge of twenty-six men who had been classified as 'Services no longer required'. Following listing the names of the men and from which ship they came from, the signal stated:

They are to be regarded as eligible for unemployment benefit and plain clothes gratuity, and should be given a free railway ticket to their homes, in accordance with Article 1664, King's Regulations and Admiralty Instructions. Steps should be taken, so far as may be possible, to ensure that men whose homes are not at Devonport or in the neighbourhood do not remain in the port. The men's addresses after discharge should be reported.

No reasons for their discharge should be given to the men. An official statement will be published when the discharges have been affected and for that purpose you should report by telegram when the discharges have been carried out. Discharge should be effected as soon as possible on the same day and in any case before Atlantic Fleet ships return to Devonport.[18]

It may be noted that none of these twenty-six men came from the *Hood*. By the time the clear-out was complete, almost 400 men had been discharged. Only three of those accused of involvement from the *Hood* escaped discharge.

On 19 November, the *Hood* returned to Portsmouth where Kelly reported to the Admiralty that the fleet was at a high level of efficiency. Despite this, Tomkinson recommended that the *Hood* be paid off and recommissioned with a different crew but his request was rejected. Instead Christmas leave was granted immediately. Tomkinson departed the *Hood* on leave believing that he had ridden out the storm. However, that was not to be the case. Their Lordships at the Admiralty were studying Kelly's highly controversial report and had not dismissed him from their thoughts. His future would be discussed from New Year through most of January. All the while, Tomkinson was oblivious to proceedings.

10

Redemption

From 27 November 1931 until 5 January 1932, while at Portsmouth and available, the *Hood* was taken in hand for repairs. On 6 January, the Battlecruiser Squadron, headed by the *Hood* and comprising HMS *Repulse*, and the cruisers *Delhi*, *Dorsetshire*, and *Norfolk*, departed Portsmouth for a spring cruise to the Caribbean. The first stop on the cruise was made from 12 to 13 January when the squadron anchored at Faial in the Azores. Bad weather dogged the journey to the Azores. It was during this part cruise that the additional weight added to the *Hood* during her 1929–31 refit showed itself to have drastically affected the freeboard of the quarterdeck to such an extent that the aircraft catapult and handling crane were deemed unworkable at sea owing to the quarterdeck being awash. So swamped was the *Hood*'s quarterdeck and the aircraft apparatus that S. V. Goodall recorded that the 'the *Hood*'s catapult is a washout literally'.[1] Weighing anchor, the Squadron set a course for Carlisle Bay, Barbados which was reached on 21 January. The squadron would anchor there until 5 February when it departed Barbados for St Vincent. Following a week at St Vincent, 12 February saw the squadron drop anchor at Grenada. Port of Spain, Trinidad was the Battlecruiser Squadron's next destination and it was here that the squadron anchored from 16 to 25 February.

It was while at anchor at Port of Spain on 16 February that Tomkinson read a transcript of a BBC broadcast that had been picked up by the *Hood*'s communications department. The broadcast transcript revealed that Tomkinson had been replaced as Admiral Commanding the Battlecruiser Squadron by Rear-Admiral Sir William James. Tomkinson had received no prior warning that he was to be relieved of his command. From the transcript, he was unable to ascertain when he was to be replaced. One thing that he could deduce, however, was that he was about to become the scapegoat for the mutiny at Invergordon. For two days, Tomkinson was in a state of limbo, of not knowing whether or not the report was correct or a mistake. On 19 February, he received two letters from the Admiralty dated 2 February and marked 'Personal and Secret'. The first letter informed Tomkinson that on 28 January he had been promoted to vice-admiral but also informed him that his tenure as the admiral commanding

The *Hood* seen in the period 1931–31. (*Jamie Grierson*)

The *Hood* in European waters during 1931–32. HMS *Repulse* can be seen behind the *Hood*. It is likely that this image was taken at some time between 6 and 13 January 1932. (*NH 60792, US Naval History and Heritage Command*)

The *Hood*'s quarterdeck awash. Taken some time after the *Hood*'s aircraft, catapult, and handling crane had been removed, this image serves as an illustration of how much of a 'washout' the *Hood* quarterdeck could become. (*Douglas Sizer Photo Collection, HMS Hood Association*)

the Battlecruiser Squadron would only last for another six months. The second letter informed Tomkinson that his peacetime career in the Royal Navy was as good as over as a result of the Invergordon Mutiny. The letter stated:

> After making every allowance for the difficult and unusual circumstances in which you were placed, Their Lordships are unable to relieve you of responsibility for a serious error of judgement in omitting to take any decided action on the 13th and 14th September, when dis-satisfaction had begun to show itself amongst the men. If the situation had been well handled on those two days, instead of being allowed to drift, Their Lordships consider it improbable that this outbreak would have occurred.[2]

That same day, Captain Patterson was informed that he too was to be relieved of his command at the same time as Tomkinson. The blow to Patterson was, however, lightened somewhat for while he was to be relieved as commanding officer of the *Hood*, the commanding officers of the *Valiant*, *Rodney*, *Nelson*, *Norfolk*, *York*, and *Adventure* were all also to be relieved of their commands as a result of Invergordon.

Leaving Trinidad on 25 February, the squadron set a course for Faial where it arrived on 4 March before arriving back at Portsmouth on 13 March. Having returned to Portsmouth, 31 March saw the *Hood* taken in hand for repairs.

Returned from dockyard control on 10 May, four days later, the *Hood* departed Portsmouth for Invergordon before sailing on 28 May to Scapa Flow. The *Hood* left Scapa Flow on 4 June and made a succession of port calls at Rothesay, Bangor and Guernsey before putting in at Weymouth on 7 July. Sometime between her arrival on the 7th and her departure on 14 July, the *Hood* participated in a series of tactical exercises staged by the Atlantic Fleet for the leaders of the Dominions. She was also visited by King George V during this period. Calls at Portland (14–15 July) and Sandown (15–21 July) followed before she returned to Portsmouth on 21 July.

On 25 July, the *Hood* was taken in hand for repairs before she participated in Navy Week from 30 July to 6 August. On 15 August, the *Hood* received a new commanding officer in Captain Thomas H. Binney. That same day, Rear-Admiral William James hoisted his flag in the *Hood* as the Admiral Commanding the Battlecruiser Squadron. Five days later, the *Hood* was recommissioned as flagship of the Battlecruiser Squadron.

Born in December 1881, James had but one handicap, he was the grandson of the painter John Everett Millais who had left James a legacy by making him the model for his painting *Bubbles*: a blonde curly haired tot seated gazing at the soap bubbles he has just blown. Electing to pursue a career in the Navy, following his service on the training ship HMS *Britannia*, James was promoted in 1901 to sub-lieutenant before attaining the rank of lieutenant the following year, and commander in 1913. During the First World War, James served as the executive officer aboard HMS *Queen Mary* and left the battlecruiser the day before she sailed towards her downfall at the Battle of Jutland. James's next posting was to be flag-commander to Vice Admiral Sturdee, the commanding officer of the 4th Battle Squadron. Later in the war, James assisted William Reginald Hall, the Director of Naval Intelligence and was eventually promoted to deputy director. Following the cessation of hostilities with Germany, James served in the China Station as the commander of HMS *Curlew* before being appointed the Deputy Director of the Royal Naval College, Greenwich in 1923. In 1926, James returned to sea as the flag captain of HMS *Royal Sovereign* before going on to be Naval Assistant to the First Sea Lord in 1927, Chief of Staff to the Commander-in-Chief Atlantic Fleet in 1929, and Chief of Staff to the Commander-in-Chief Mediterranean Fleet in 1930.

Born on 9 December 1883, Binney, having joined the Royal Navy, was in the first instance sent to HMS *Britannia*. During the First World War, he served as a gunnery officer aboard the battleship HMS *Queen Elizabeth* before ending 1918 on the staff of the Commander-in-Chief of the Grand Fleet, Admiral Beatty. Promoted to captain in 1922, from 1923 to 1925, Binney served as Flag Captain to Rear-Admiral Ernle Chatfield, the commander of the 3rd Light Cruiser Squadron aboard HMS *Cardiff*. Leaving the *Cardiff* in 1925 Binney was appointed Deputy Director of the Plans Division at the Admiralty until 1927. From 1928 until 1930, Binney served once more as flag captain to Chatfield who was appointed as Commander-in-Chief of the Atlantic Fleet and flew his flag in

The *Hood* lies at anchor at Invergordon in May 1932. Eight months earlier, her crew had been in mutiny.

The *Hood* sailing into Portsmouth around 1932. Note the aircraft catapult on the quarterdeck. (*Jamie Grierson*)

Admiral Sir William James.

HMS *Nelson*. Just prior to being appointed to the *Hood*, Binney had spent the 1931–32 period as the Director of the Royal Navy's Tactical School. In addition to the above, Binney had been James' executive officer in the cruiser HMS *Hawkins* and was to prove an inspired choice as captain of the *Hood*. Together, James and Binney set about restoring the vitality of the ship and dispelling the gloomy atmosphere that had existed on board since Invergordon almost a year earlier.

Having been recommissioned, the *Hood* departed Portsmouth for Southend. It was while at Southend that James set about restoring the happiness of the ship and laid the foundations of the tone that would exist for the remainder of the *Hood*'s career, as recalled by the ship's then First Lieutenant, Lieutenant-Commander Eric Longley-Cook:

> We sailed to Southend and again on a Sunday afternoon 'clear lower deck, everyone aft'. He [James] addressed us. How differently! 'I am proud to have joined you' and for the first time in my eighteen years at sea I was told what the peacetime job of the Royal Navy was. To train for war in order to keep the peace. To 'show the flag'. In home waters to show the British public what they were paying for and abroad to be good ambassadors for Great Britain. From then on it was 'tails up'.[3]

Departing Southend on 7 September, the *Hood* sailed north to Hartlepool where she dropped anchor off the mouth of the River Tees from 8–14 September. At Hartlepool, children's parties were held aboard while hundreds of miners who had been made redundant as a result of the depression were invited aboard to have tea with the crew. In addition to these activities, the *Hood*'s crew played the town at water polo.

It was while she was anchored off Hartlepool that nine-year-old Albert Edward Pryke 'Ted' Briggs first saw the *Hood*. Young and impressionable, he immediately fell in love with the mighty battlecruiser as she stood off the mouth of the River Tees, swinging gently at anchor, proud and belligerent, her grey paint almost bleached white in the sun, accentuating her clipper-like bows that flared extravagantly, leading to the menacing 15-inch guns as the brass on her decks glistened making her an awesome sight to behold. As he stood on the beach at nearby Redcar, Briggs could hear the occasional bugle call blare out and a boatswain's whistle shrill across the sea. Picket boats and motor launches swarmed around the *Hood* while local fishermen charged 5 shillings (25 pence) a time to row people around the ship. He ran home to ask his mother for the money but she refused. Ted's father had died three months before he was born when he fell from scaffolding. With a thirteen-year-old daughter to raise, clothe, and feed also, Ted's mother could not spare the five shillings.[4]

> I stood on the beach for some considerable time, drinking in the beauty, grace and immaculate strength of her. 'Beauty' and 'grace' seem rather ludicrous words to describe a vessel of such size, particularly one whose primary function was for

destruction. But I can honestly say I never could, nor indeed can even today, think of more suitable words to describe her.[5]

Not to be defeated, having been told by his mother that she could not spare the money, Ted returned to the beach to offer the fishermen his services as an oarsman in rowing people around the ship. They laughed him away. As he could not get any closer to the *Hood* than Redcar beach, Ted decided that he would get closer to the ship through joining the Royal Navy. The day after seeing the *Hood* from Redcar, he went to a Royal Navy recruiting office but was turned away for being too young and as told to return when he was fifteen.

Departing Hartlepool, the *Hood* sailed to Rosyth where she anchored from 15 September until 10 October before sailing to Invergordon where she anchored until 20 October. The *Hood* returned to Rosyth from 21 October to 15 November whereupon she sailed south to Portsmouth, arriving two days later. The *Hood* would spend the Christmas and New Year period in dockyard hands when she was taken in hand for repairs from 7 December until 9 January.

On 11 January, the *Hood* departed Portsmouth for Arousa Bay where she dropped anchor from 13 to 21 January before sailing to Gibraltar. From Gibraltar, on 26 January, the *Hood* sailed to Algiers where she anchored from 28 January to 7 February before returning to the Rock. On 9 March, the *Hood* weighed anchor and set sail for Tangiers for a five-day visit before returning once more to Gibraltar on 14 March. On 21 March, she left Gibraltar for Arousa Bay and then Portsmouth where she arrived on 28 March. The *Hood* would remain at

The Home Fleet at anchor at Gibraltar, 26 January 1933. From left to right, the ships at anchor are HMS *Lucia*, *Nelson*, *Rodney*, *Warspite*, and *Valiant*. Between the *Nelson* and the *Rodney*, the *Hood* may be seen. HMS *Renown* is on the left in the Bay of Gibraltar. (*Beeldbank WO2, NIOD*)

Portsmouth until 9 May when she weighed anchor and made the journey to Invergordon (12 May–3 June) and Scapa Flow (3–10 June).

Oban, Scotland was the *Hood*'s next stop from 11 to 14 June before she returned to Portsmouth. Having arrived back at Portsmouth on 16 June, four days later on the 20th, she was taken in hand for a refit that lasted until 4 September. While in dockyard hands, on 30 August, the *Hood* was paid off before being recommissioned for further service as flagship of the Battlecruiser Squadron. That same day, Captain Francis T. B. Tower assumed command of the ship.

Born in December 1895, Tower had joined the Royal Navy in 1902 before being educated at HMS *Britannia*. Following seeing service during the First World War, Tower was promoted to captain in 1923. Tower joined the *Hood* fresh from the position of Director of Naval Ordnance, a position he had occupied since 1931.

When the *Hood* was recommissioned under Captain Tower, she recommissioned with a new executive officer who would transform the ship: Commander Rory Chambers O'Conor. O'Conor was born into an Anglo-Irish family in Buenos Aires in 1898. Entering the Royal Navy College at Osborne in 1911, O'Conor spent much of the Great War in the gunroom of the pre-dreadnought battleship HMS *Prince of Wales*, seeing action during the Dardanelles campaign. As a formidable sportsman, O'Conor represented the Royal Navy at Rugby between 1920 and 1924, and captained the United Services team during the 1921–22 season. In 1919, O'Conor was promoted to lieutenant and received a posting to the Royal Yacht *Victoria and Albert*. Despite this, it was aboard the battleship *Barham* where he served as a divisional officer between 1921 and 1922 that he first came to prominence.[6] As a specialist in gunnery, O'Conor would spend the ten years following leaving HMS *Barham* between the Royal Navy Gunnery School at Portsmouth, the stone frigate HMS *Excellent*, and various other shore and sea-going commands, including appointments to the battleships *Royal Sovereign* and *Resolution* and the cruiser *Emerald*. Promoted to commander in 1931, it was while on the staff of HMS *Excellent* that O'Conor learned that he had been selected for appointment to the *Hood* as the ship's executive officer.

O'Conor was part of a generation of young officers who were determined to restore the prestige of the Royal Navy and believed that the greatest way to create a happy and successful ship lay in a genuine interest for the welfare of the ship's crew.

The arrival of O'Conor provided an early indication of how shipboard life for the remainder of the commission was to be tuned. With him, O'Conor brought the notion that every man who gave his best could expect fairness, respect, and consideration from his superiors; that hard work would be rewarded and that the interests of the ship should be at the forefront of the mind. O'Conor went to great lengths to memorise the names of the *Hood*'s crew of 1,300, although he would tacitly admit that he could hold no more than 600 in his head at any one time. Despite this, the impression came to be that O'Conor came to know the name of every man aboard the *Hood*.[7]

O'Conor held a great pride in the *Hood* and implored the crew to do the same. In part, this pride was to be shown through sporting achievements. As such, O'Conor was determined that the *Hood* would excel in all fleet sporting competitions. This pride also extended to the ship's appearance. So it was that O'Conor placed a great stress on smartness, cleanliness, and paintwork.

> It is sometimes lightly assumed that the ship's appearance is the concern only of a small hierarchy which includes the Commander, the Chief Boatswain's Mate, the Captains of the Tops and Side, and perhaps a few others. No ship ever kept clean except by the co-operation of all hands, and this needs hammering in, with emphasis on the way in which every individual can help.... Everyone must be jealous of the ship's appearance and must make his contribution, and above all, he must avoid making unnecessary work for others who are striving to keep the ship as she should look.[8]

With this, O'Conor would take the *Hood* to the pinnacle of her appearance.

On 8 September, the *Hood* sailed into Rosyth, where on 10 September until the 26th, James temporarily transferred his flag to HMS *Renown*. On 24 September, the *Hood* weighed anchor and sailed to Invergordon where she anchored until 11 October before sailing to Banff, Aberdeenshire. The *Hood* visited North Berwick between 16 and 24 October before putting in briefly at Rosyth before going on to conduct exercises. With the exercises complete, on 26 October, she returned to Portsmouth. At Portsmouth from 13 November, on 1 December, while available, the *Hood* was taken in hand for repairs. Released from dockyard control on 6 January, the *Hood* left Portsmouth on 12 January and sailed to Arousa Bay, the first stop on her Spring Cruise to Spain and the Mediterranean.

The *Hood* dropped anchor at Arousa Bay from 16 to 20 January before anchoring at Madeira from 22 to 29 January. On 31 January, the *Hood* sailed to Gibraltar where she remained until 6 March when she put to sea for Largos Bay and to participate in spring exercises with the Atlantic and Mediterranean Fleets. The *Hood* returned to anchor at Gibraltar on 16 March and departed for Portsmouth seven days later. She arrived back at Portsmouth on 27 March and would remain there until 11 May. During this period, from 12 April to 4 May, the ship was taken in hand for docking and repairs. Departing Portsmouth on 11 May, the *Hood* sailed to Portland until 1 June when she sailed to Plymouth. A visit to Scapa Flow followed before on 16 June, she sailed to Loch Eriboll. It was while at Loch Eriboll that the 'the *Hood* stones' were laid. Throughout most of the twentieth century, Loch Eriboll was a Royal Navy anchorage. During the 1920s and 1930s, when their ships anchored in Loch Eriboll, some crew members would climb the hillside to the west of the loch above Laid and Portnancon and leave their ship's name in large white stone letters. The *Hood*'s crew were no exception. Today, the stones lie among the names of ships past and present, including the *Valiant*, *Whirlwind*, *Blake*, *Sutherland*, and *Bulwark*.

The *Hood* departed Loch Eriboll on 25 June for Rosyth and then Torbay. Returning to Portsmouth on 24 July, on 1 August, she was taken in hand for repairs until 5 September. While undergoing repairs, the *Hood* participated in Portsmouth Navy Week and saw a new admiral hoist his flag.

Above: A party of men cleaning one of the *Hood*'s 15-inch guns. This photo was taken on 11 November 1933 while the *Hood* was *en route* to Portsmouth.
(*Beeldbank WO2, NIOD*)

Right: While the *Hood* was at Portsmouth, 6,500 children from Coventry were taken by train to Portsmouth to visit the fleet. A group of schoolgirls can be seen aboard the *Hood*. In the background in HMS *Iron Duke*.
(*Beeldbank WO2, NIOD*)

Above left: A signaller at work aboard the *Hood* during exercises with the Atlantic and Mediterranean Fleets in March 1934. (*Beeldbank WO2, NIOD*)

Above right: Gibraltar, 14 March 1934. In the foreground are the 15-inch guns of 'X' and 'Y' turret of the *Hood*. The ship behind the *Hood* is HMS *Renown*. (*Beeldbank WO2, NIOD*)

The *Hood* alongside in 1934. (*Author's collection*)

11

On a Collision Course

On 14 August 1934, James left the *Hood* to become the Deputy Chief of Naval Staff under Admiral Ernle Chatfield. James' successor aboard the *Hood* was Rear-Admiral Sidney Bailey. Captain Tower was to remain in command of the *Hood* under Bailey, who found the battlecruiser seemingly at the peak of its efficiency when he arrived aboard.

Born in August 1882, Bailey joined the Royal Navy in 1896 and first saw action during the Boxer Rebellion, participating in Admiral Edward Seymour's expedition to relieve Peking in 1900. For his service during the expedition, Bailey was Mentioned in Dispatches and promoted to lieutenant. The year 1915 saw Bailey join HMS *Lion*, the flagship of Vice-Admiral David Beatty as a fleet gunnery officer. Bailey's joining the *Lion* began what would be an ongoing association with Chatfield, who was at the time Beatty's flag captain. As part of Beatty's staff, Bailey saw action during the Battle of Jutland. When, in late 1916, Admiral Jellicoe was promoted to First Sea Lord and Beatty was appointed Commander-in-Chief of the Grand Fleet, he took both Chatfield and Bailey with him. Bailey's initial posting was to HMS *Iron Duke* before he was transferred to the new fleet flagship HMS *Queen Elizabeth*. In 1918, Bailey was promoted to captain and was appointed the commanding officer of HMS *Renown*. Promoted to rear-admiral in 1931, Bailey served as Chief of Staff to Chatfield in 1932, who by this time had attained the rank of admiral and held the post of Commander-in-Chief, Mediterranean. By the time that he joined the *Hood*, Bailey was regarded as one of the leading experts in the Royal Navy on gunnery. It is also worth noting that Bailey enjoyed the support of Chatfield, who had risen to the position of First Sea Lord, as well as being held in high regard by both Admiral Dreyer and Admiral James, both of whom were formed Flag Officers of the *Hood*.

Under Bailey, the *Hood* cruised peacefully through home waters for the remainder of 1934, making calls at Hull, Rosyth, Invergordon, Portland, and Portsmouth. The year 1935 saw the *Hood* embark on fleet spring exercises; however, the exercises would bring to an end the sea-going careers of both Bailey and Tower. January 1935 was to see the *Hood*, in the company of the battlecruiser *Renown*, which was commanded by Captain Henry Sawbridge, and the ships of the Second Destroyer Flotilla sail to Gibraltar. The cruise got off to a tragic start on 19 January when in the anchorage of Arousa Bay Commander O'Conor ordered a shipboard search for Boy Jim Brown. Brown was a seventeen-year-old from Portsmouth who had joined the *Hood* nine days earlier on 10 January. Brown had not been seen since he climbed out of his hammock when the Boys were called to at 5 a.m. The search turned up no signs of Brown, which led to the conclusion that he must have been lost overboard. This presumption proved correct when his body was found washed ashore at Villagarcia.

While the Battlecruiser Squadron was at anchor in Arousa Bay, the *Hood*'s wardroom entertained officers from *Renown*. In the wardroom, Commander E. V. Lees, the Squadron navigating officer, and Lieutenant-Commander G. M. S. Stitt, the navigator aboard the *Renown*, discussed an incident that had occurred earlier in the month when the *Renown* had collided with the heavy cruiser *Frobisher* off Sheerness. This was not the first collision incident involving the *Renown*. Indeed, in early 1934, the *Renown* suffered superficial damage when she collided with a Finnish fishing vessel while sailing in thick fog. Talk between the two navigating officers soon turned to the impending squadron exercises. During their discussion, Lees informed Stitt that at the end of the manoeuvres, the *Hood* would make a 180-degree turn when the ships were a mile apart in order to enable the *Renown* to take up formation astern. Stitt later reported this conversation to Captain Sawbridge, who duly noted how the two battlecruisers would take up formation.

The day before the exercises began Rear-Admiral Bailey issued the following signal to the squadron:

> On Wednesday, January 23, the Battle Cruiser Squadron will pass through position two miles 148 Degrees from Slavery Island Light. On passing this point *Hood* is to steer 192 degrees and *Renown* 254 degrees at 12 knots. At 10.50 ships are to turn 223 degrees when inclination exercises will be carried out. On completion *Hood* and *Renown* are to steer 254 degrees and 192 degrees respectively to close. Course after rejoining will be 180 degrees, speed 12 knots.[1]

Wednesday 23 January dawned clear with a light sea, which was ideal for the manoeuvring of capital ships. The vessels of the Second Destroyer Flotilla were the first to slip anchor independently and were soon followed out of the anchorage by the Second Submarine Flotilla, which was to test the anti-submarine defences of the battlecruisers. The Second Submarine Flotilla was tracked by the *Renown* and the *Hood*, which sailed on parallel courses of 223 degrees at 18 knots in preparation for beginning the inclination exercises. At the time, the two battlecruisers were somewhere between ten and twelve miles apart. At 11.35 a.m., Bailey signalled that the manoeuvres were complete prompting the helm of the *Hood* to be put over to 254 degrees at 12 knots while on the *Renown*, the helm altered course to 192 degrees to comply with Bailey's signal from the previous day. The intention was for the *Renown* to glide smoothly astern of the flagship as she turned the Squadron on to a new course of 180 degrees in line ahead.

From the *Hood*'s bridge, Bailey and Tower watched the *Renown*'s approach without concern. The staff operations officer, Commander A. C. Allen, thought the manoeuvre to be so commonplace that he need not bother to stand and watch, so he elected to go to the charthouse instead. Aboard the *Renown*, Captain Sawbridge and Lieutenant-Commander Stitt stood on the bridge waiting for the *Hood* to execute the turn to 180 degrees that would enable them to glide in behind. The minutes ticked by with both battlecruisers holding their course.

After forty minutes, the *Hood* and the *Renown* were 1,400 yards apart. Bailey considered at this point that the *Renown* was so slow in carrying out the manoeuvre that would see her fall into position astern of the flagship. The thought ran through his mind: 'Surely she can't expect the flagship to make way for her'. Still, the *Renown* continued on. Showing no signs of anxiety, Bailey ordered a signal to be made by flag: 'Form single line ahead in sequence of fleet numbers on course 254 degrees. Guide of Squadron to proceed at 12 knots'. It took little over a minute for the flags to be hoisted and to be observed by those aboard the *Renown*. Aboard the *Hood*, Bailey was still convinced that there was time for Sawbridge to alter course. As Bailey was ordering the flag signal to be hoisted, on the bridge of the *Renown*, Stitt told Sawbridge: 'She ought to turn now, Sir'. The range between the two vessels continued to dwindle. With 1,200 yards between the two ships, Sawbridge cried out: 'I don't like this. Stop both [engines]; wheel to starboard 35 degrees'. As the two ships continued to glide on, Sawbridge ordered: 'Full speed astern both'. This order was followed by three short blasts of the *Renown*'s siren to alert the admiral's bridge on the *Hood* that they were on a collision course. The fate of both ships now rested in the hands of Captain Tower. Bailey had wisely decided that he would only confuse the situation if he issued orders alongside his flag captain. A flurry of orders was given to the helm and the engine room.

The *Hood*'s stern swung in towards the *Renown*, which was still approaching despite the engines being put into reverse. To correct the swing, Tower issued the order, 'Starboard 25, hard to starboard, full speed ahead'. Shouts rang out across the *Hood* to close all the watertight doors and to clear the starboard side. Ned Johns, who was a yeoman of the signals recalled, 'There was a jam on the boat-deck at the passageway by the funnels, caused by ratings who knew they shouldn't be there and the nosey who wanted to see what was happening on the starboard side. The crowd cleared as soon as someone shouted "Bugger off! The bloody *Renown*'s coming inboard!"'[2] At 12.21 p.m., the ships collided.

When the collision occurred, the *Hood*'s stern was swinging rapidly away from the *Renown*. However, the stern did not swing quickly enough. The *Renown*'s bow ran along the *Hood*'s A-bracket amidships before bouncing off and being caught in the starboard propeller. In the *Hood*'s engine room, the telegraph signalled 'Stop both' before receiving the signals 'Half speed, astern both, full speed astern both', and then finally 'Stop both'. L. P. Stirk of the *Renown* recalled the impact of the two ships colliding:

I was a member of the Bosun's Party and had just settled myself down in our 'caboush' after dinner, intending to have a short siesta, when a resounding crash and thud made sleep a non-starter. As is usual in an efficient ship there was no panic whatsoever, hands went to their collection stations as if they were taking part in an exercise in the full knowledge that this was the real thing. Many and humorous were the matelots' comments at the time, one of which from the Bosun's Party was—'All the bloody ocean between us and that great lumbering so-an-so has to get in our way'. Other comments were too lurid for me to repeat![3]

In the aftermath of the collision, men streamed up from the mess decks to contemplate what had occurred as *Renown* extracted herself. There were no casualties on either ship; the *Hood* resolutely withstood the ramming, the bulk of the impact being taken by the armoured sides. An examination of the *Hood*'s quarterdeck showed that at the point of collision, an indentation 18 inches in depth had been made, yards of railings had been ripped off and bent, and a portion of O'Conor's prized deck had been turned into matchwood while some planks had buckled. The damage to the *Renown*, as reported by Sawbridge to Bailey an hour after the collision, was more extensive than that sustained by the *Hood*. As assessed by Sawbridge, the damage consisted of: 'Hole in stem, about three feet square, seven feet from just above the waterline upwards. Below water, stem and ram are displaced about 2 feet to starboard and there are at least two large fractures. Side plating is badly buckled and distorted in the vicinity. Ship is dry abaft number ten bulkhead, which is being shored up'.[4] As the *Hood* and the *Renown* collided, other vessels were waiting to open the submarine exercises. Bailey abandoned them and ordered the *Renown* to make for Gibraltar. She was followed two days later, on 25 January, by the *Hood*. By the time the *Hood* arrived back in Gibraltar, O'Conor had worked tirelessly to cover the damage to his beloved ship. A strip of painted canvas was hung over the side to cover the dent in the ship's side while the damaged deck was covered with a layer of yellow ochre. As the *Hood* entered harbour, polite gun salutes were exchanged with the *Renown* but a feud that would worry the First Sea Lord was directly around the corner.

Reports of the collision were studied by the Admiralty and it soon became clear that there was collusion between Bailey and Tower on the one side and Sawbridge and his officers on the other. Faced with this, the Admiralty decided that Bailey, Tower and Sawbridge should all face a court-martial. The three officers were summoned to the court-martial held in Nelson's cabin aboard HMS *Victory* in Portsmouth at the end of February. To an extent, it was fair for the Admiralty to make all three officers face a court-martial trial; however, at the same time, the decision to make Bailey undergo court-martial proceedings was controversial as it was the first time that an admiral had been court-martialled since the First World War.

The deputy judge advocate was Rear Admiral C. G. Ramsey while the President of the Court was Vice-Admiral Edward Astley-Rushton. Vice-Admiral J. A. G.

Taken from *Hood*, this image shows the *Renown* moments after colliding with the *Hood* on 23 January 1935. (*Author's collection*)

The *Hood* enters Portsmouth on 4 February 1935 to undergo repairs following the collision with the *Renown*. (*Author's collection*)

Troup, a tactical expert was appointed to the position of prosecutor while a group of five admirals and three captains all wearing full dress uniform, dark blue frock coats with gold epaulettes, cocked hats, and swords were to judge Bailey, Tower, and Sawbridge.

Bailey was the first to be tried after the court began with the age-old naval symbolism of court-martial flag and gun. Bailey surrendered his sheathed sword which was placed on the table before Astley-Rushton with the blade pointing towards the defendant. Troup alleged that Bailey was to blame for the collision stating, 'Having ordered *Hood* to steer 254 degrees and *Renown* to close on her on a course of 192 degrees, he failed to take action to prevent the development of a situation in which the risk of collision between the two ships arose'. Bailey, who was defended by his predecessor in the *Hood* Vice-Admiral James, replied, 'My impression at this time was that *Renown* was carrying out the manoeuvre badly; in fact that she was making a bad shot. I have been captain of her myself, and I know she is a handy ship'.[5] Bailey went on to state: 'Since the accident I have naturally gone over in my mind whether some other form of signal would have been more appropriate to my purpose, but I cannot think of one unless I had been prepared to give orders for the movements of *Renown*—in fact to command the ship myself'.

Following a recess, the court reached a verdict. Bailey was returned to face the court by a Naval provost-marshal to hear his fate. Bailey saw immediately that his sword had been reversed and that the hilt was now positioned towards him, a sure sign of acquittal. The decision to acquit Bailey was now confirmed by the judge advocate: 'The court finds that the charge against the accused is not proved. The findings are signed by all the officers of the court'. Astley-Rushton then lifted Bailey's sword from the table and strode across the courtroom, handing the sword back to Bailey with the word 'Congratulations'.[6]

Next to face the court was Captain Sawbridge. Sawbridge, defended by his friend Captain R. B. T. Miles, relied on three factors for his defence:

1. Bailey's signal before the exercise stipulated a course for closing, something which had not been ordered previously;
2. The *Renown's* navigator, Lieutenant-Commander Stitt had been summoned by Commander Lees, the squadron navigating officer to discuss the manoeuvre, and because of this discussion Sawbridge regarded the appraisal of the situation as emanating from Bailey and expected that the *Hood* would turn away when *Renown* rejoined in formation;
3. The *Hood* was the overtaking ship and, as such, should have obeyed the law of the road and given way to the *Renown*.[7]

At the beginning of proceedings against Sawbridge, his report of the incident, written two days after the collision, was read out to the court:

I fully realised it was the Admiral's intention to turn both ships to 180 degrees at the proper time to bring them into line on that course. *Hood* was kept continuously under observation, and at 12.18 I decided that although she had ample room and time to carry out the manoeuvre I would take the precaution of turning away.[8]

Sawbridge told the court that at 12.19 p.m., he ordered 'Half speed, astern both', before immediately countering this with 'Full speed astern'. The *Hood* then hoisted and hauled down the signal to execute line ahead. 'Thus, even as late as 12.20 *Hood* could have taken avoiding action by turning outwards, but apparently she did not do so'.[9] Throughout Sawbridge's trial, officers from the *Hood* and the *Renown* gave conflicting times of when differing signals were made. Sawbridge emphasised, however, that when he stopped engines, he ordered everyone on the bridge to make a note of the time. Among those called to give evidence for the defence was Stitt, who told the court that when Sawbridge elected to hold course as the *Hood* appeared to be late in turning, he agreed with the captain's decision. 'I was convinced then, and still am, that *Renown* was ordered to steer that course for one reason only, and that was that when the ships got within a mile of each other *Hood* would turn to 180 and *Renown* would be able to form astern'.[10]

Bailey was also called to give evidence at the trial of Sawbridge. The question was put to Bailey by Troup, 'Would you expect your flagship to avoid *Renown* or *Renown* to avoid the flagship?' to which Bailey replied, 'The flagship being the guide, I should certainly not expect her to have to alter course'. On the subject of course alterations, Sawbridge produced a chart on which the positions of manoeuvres undertaken by the *Renown* were inaccurately plotted in an attempt to bolster his case. Troup countered Sawbridge's and the defence's arguments by stressing that Bailey's original signal had ordered a course of 180 degrees 'after rejoining' and not before. Bailey, in his trial, had insisted that in his view the ships of a unit had not rejoined until they were on station. Troup went on to argue that if Sawbridge had made bold use of the engines at starboard astern and port ahead to turn the ship, then this would have been a more preferable action that stopping the engines and turning the helm to starboard.

The court took an hour and twenty minutes to consider its verdict. When he was led back into the courtroom by the Naval provost-marshal, Sawbridge could see that his sword lay with its tip still pointing towards him. In silence, the judge advocate rose and delivered his statement: 'The sentence of the court, having found the charge against Captain Sawbridge proved, is that he shall be dismissed from His Majesty's Ship *Renown*'. Sawbridge bowed his head to the president who announced the dissolving of the court. The effect of the decision of the court was that Sawbridge was placed on half pay from midnight. Furthermore, as an officer on half pay, he was not permitted to give evidence in the court proceedings against Captain Tower. Finally, he was given a temporary posting to HMS *Victory*.[11]

The trial of Captain Tower followed the same procedures as those borne out in the trials of Bailey and Sawbridge. Defended by Commander O'Conor, Tower told the court that on the day of the collision, he expected that the *Renown* would fall into his wake before stating that approximately two minutes before the collision occurred, he realised that the *Renown* was continuing on her course and tried in vain to turn the *Hood* to avoid a collision. 'I began to get uneasy when the ships were about 6 cables apart. At that time I expected *Renown* to get in astern of *Hood*'. Captain Miles put the question to Tower, 'Why did you not take action to obey the "Rule of the Road"?' to which Tower replied:

> I might have taken action in the literal interpretation of the 'Rule of the Road' when the two ships were separated by 2 or 3 miles. That would have involved using the starboard helm. That I did not consider seriously for I knew it could not possibly have been defended. Later, keeping in mind the whole of the approach, I had no doubt, and had every reason to believe, that *Renown* would fall astern of me. I consider it was my duty to guide the Fleet to continue my course and speed to the last possible moment.[12]

Tower had another defender in Bailey who gave evidence and again stressed his belief that he anticipated that the *Renown* would make the necessary turn. Having exonerated Bailey on 26 February, at Tower's court-martial on 28 February, the court could do little other than deliver the verdict of not guilty.[13]

Aboard the *Renown*, there was much grief. One member of her crew, L. P. Stirk, remembered: 'We on *Renown* followed the courts martial proceeding and when the news filtered through the ship that our captain had been found guilty everything went deadly quiet and despondency settled over us'.[14] Rear-Admiral James, who defended Bailey, later stated: 'After the courts-martial would have been just the moment for the Admiral to have gone aboard *Renown* … and shown a big, generous spirit',[15] rather, the whole incident was naturally resented by those aboard *Renown* who felt themselves the aggrieved party and as the ones having to carry the court-martial.

A week after the not guilty verdicts, Bailey and Tower, aboard a repaired *Hood*, slipped anchor and left Portsmouth to join the other ships of the Home Fleet at Malta. Despite the jubilation of Bailey and Tower, the findings of the courts still had to be confirmed by the Admiralty. Although dismissed from his ship and given an appointment aboard HMS *Victory*, Sawbridge continued to live aboard the *Renown*. Sawbridge told his officers in the wake of the court-martial proceedings, 'My conscious [*sic*.] is clear. I reckon that I have saved the country about £10,000,000 and 1,000 lives'.[16]

On 28 February, the findings of the courts and a Board of Enquiry that had been convened at Gibraltar immediately following the collision were forwarded to the Secretary of the Admiralty. The report that was forwarded stated:

> Sir,
> In accordance with the directions contained in your memorandum … we have the honour to report that we have held a full and careful investigation into the circumstances attending the collision between H.M. Ships the *Hood* and *Renown* which occurred on Wednesday, 23rd January 1935, and we are unanimously of the opinion:-

Above: Dockyard workers gaze at the *Hood*'s damaged propeller in a Portsmouth dry dock following the collision with the *Renown*. (*Author's collection*)

Right: The *Hood* in dry dock at Portsmouth while undergoing repairs following the collision with the *Renown*. (*Author's collection*)

(i) That the Captain of H.M.S. *Renown* was responsible for placing his ship in a dangerous position with respect to H.M.S. the *Hood* at about 1217 having regard to the respective courses and speeds of the two ships at the time.

(ii) That the Captain of H.M.S. *Renown* had not sufficient ground on which to assume that the Admiral would alter the course of the squadron to 180° at any definite time.

(iii) That after a collision became likely the Captain of H.M.S. *Renown* did not take the correct action to avoid it, or alternatively, took the action which he did take too late to avert a collision.

(iv) That the Captain of H.M.S. *Renown* should not have expected H.M.S. the *Hood* to alter course to port and that the Regulations for Preventing Collisions at Sea could not be expected to apply to H.M.S. the *Hood* in these circumstances, and that the captain of the latter ship acted as was best in the circumstances of the moment. ...

2. There being a divergence of opinion between one member of the court and the remainder on a material point as disclosed by the evidence, the following additional and separate expressions of opinion are submitted in accordance with King's Regulations and Admiralty Instructions, Article 488, Paragraph 11:-

(a) We are further of the opinion that when a dangerous situation was developing, the Rear Admiral Commanding Battle Cruiser Squadron, hoisted the signal for single line in sufficient time to avoid such danger.

(b) I am further of the opinion that, in the absence of any definite instructions the Rear Admiral Commanding, Battle Cruiser Squadron's message timed 1351/22/1/35 as to H.M.S. *Renown*'s ultimate station and including H.M.S. the *Hood*'s course and speed should have been made in the early stages of closing, it being inadvisable to direct to heavy ships to close one as another without further definite instructions.

(c) Also that the signal to form single line ahead on a course of 254° should have been hoisted earlier when it was observed that H.M.S. *Renown* was approaching on such a forward bearing.[17]

When the court-martial minutes were pursued at the Admiralty for confirmation, reason began to prevail. On 18 March, while in the Mediterranean, Bailey and Tower received confirmation that the Admiralty dissented from the court-martial findings, taking the view that all three officers were partly at fault for the collision and that Sawbridge would not be dismissed from command of his ship and placed on half pay. The statement from the Admiralty read:

Rear-Admiral Bailey adopted an unusual procedure in directing the *Hood* and *Renown* to steer definite courses to close. Since he had given that order, responsibility for the manoeuvre rested on him and it was incumbent on him at the proper moment to make a further signal to reform his squadron. His not doing so left in doubt his final intention. The signal for the *Hood* and *Renown* to form single line ahead was made too late. For these reasons Their Lordships are unable to absolve Rear-Admiral Bailey from all blame.

Their Lordships agree to the findings of the court-martial held for the trial of Captain Sawbridge, but they have decided to reduce the sentence to a severe reprimand. Captain Sawbridge will therefore resume command of *Renown*. Their Lordships consider that Captain Tower should have taken avoiding action earlier and to that extent they are unable to acquit him of all blame.[18]

The Admiralty had clearly decided not to make one scapegoat for the collision. Partly, the Admiralty's decision owed something to the anomalies that emerged during the trials. Captain Pridham, a member of the court that tried Captain Sawbridge and who would later go on to take command of the *Hood*, revealed many years later the inaccurately plotted chart that was produced by Sawbridge showing the supposed movements of that *Renown* relative to the *Hood* was produced behind closed doors and was not therefore entered into the court's minutes. In addition to this, Pridham also revealed that Bailey instructed Admiral James not to make any statement that might serve to embarrass Sawbridge. None of this was, however, known to those aboard the *Renown* or the *Hood*. For years, following the collision, animosity and hostility would build up whenever the two ships were in port together.

'Far More Afraid of a Battlecruiser than a Battleship'

On 15 May, the *Hood* docked at Southend for a week-long visit before heading north to Scapa Flow. In June 1935, a staple of the Royal Navy's sporting calendar occurred when the Home Fleet Regatta was held in Rosyth. In the regatta, the *Hood*'s thirty-five boats achieved eighteen victories, six second places, and five third places, winning nine trophies. No ship had ever monopolised the regatta to this extent. With a record points total, the *Hood* regained the 'cock' from HMS *Nelson*. Congratulations poured into the *Hood* from all across the fleet with the exception of HMS *Renown*, the company of which still harboured intense animosity towards the *Hood* and her crew following the collision. The exultant reply from the *Hood* to those who congratulated her was 'cock-a-doodle-do'.[1] The year 1935 would see further sporting achievement for the *Hood* when she again won the Palmer Trophy for bayonet fighting (a trophy that she would ultimately hold from 1934 to 1936) and the Arbuthnot Trophy for cross-country running.

No event aboard the *Hood* was more savoured, however, than the Silver Jubilee Fleet Review of King George V held at Spithead on 16 July. This event was the first major fleet review undertaken since 1914. On 12 July, the ships of the Home Fleet assembled at Spithead in the company of the vessels of the Mediterranean Fleet. They were joined three days later by ships of the Reserve Fleet, which was specially commissioned for the occasion. Over 150 warships were arranged into nine columns before being joined by over thirty merchant and fishing vessels, which were present at a fleet review for the first time at the express invitation of King George V and the Admiralty. At the centre of the fleet lay the *Hood*, dressed from bow to stern in flags that had been selected by the chief yeoman of the signals. With his pride in keeping the *Hood* looking immaculate, O'Conor, who, as Bruce Taylor has described, had turned the battlecruiser into 'a vision of scrubbed wood, polished metal and gleaming paintwork', saw to it that the bathroom ejectors that spewed effluent over the starboard side of the ship were shut off for the duration of the review. At 2 p.m. on 16 July, the Royal Yacht *Victoria and Albert* set off from the South Railway Jetty at Portsmouth with the King aboard, ready to take the salute of the fleet. As the Royal Yacht sailed from the jetty, every capital ship and cruiser present at the review opened fire in a synchronised twenty-one-gun salute. The *Victoria and Albert* secured in front of the battleship *Queen Elizabeth* where the Board of the Admiralty and Flag Officers paid their complements before the Royal Yacht began to sail elegantly between the columns of warships, each of which was manned, the crews drawn up along the railings to cheer the King as he passed. Following the review, the Fleet Air Arm delivered an aerial salute that brought the first part of the review to a close. That evening from 10 p.m. until midnight, the entire fleet was illuminated in a mass of coloured lights and decorative schemes.[2]

On 17 July, the *Hood* weighed anchor and led HMS *Renown* as well as the battleships *Barham* and *Valiant* out of the anchorage to conduct a concentration fire exercise off the Isle of Wight against a target towed by the cruiser *Curacoa*. From the *Victoria and Albert*, King George V watched the exercise which was conducted successfully. At the conclusion of the exercise, the Royal Yacht led the ships back into the anchorage where the signal 'Splice the Mainbrace' was hoisted, entitling every man who desired it to an additional tot of rum that evening to drink to the King's health. Later that day, in Portsmouth, those aboard the *Hood* prepared the ship for her participation in Navy Week (3–10 August). The Jubilee Fleet Review at Spithead and Navy Week at Portsmouth were to be some of the last great acts of showmanship put on by those aboard the *Hood*. The following months would see a drift into a state of war readiness with the coming of the Abyssinian crisis.

Following Navy Week, while at Portsmouth, the *Hood* was taken in hand for repairs. The repair works were completed on 28 August and two days later, the *Hood* departed Portsmouth for Portland to conduct a series of exercises.

The Abyssinian crisis had its origins in the Walwal Incident in which a skirmish occurred between a garrison of Somalis pressed into Italian service and a force

The *Hood*, decorated from bow to stern in flags, at the Silver Jubilee Fleet Review of King George V. (*Jamie Grierson*)

The *Hood* pictured at Spithead during the Silver Jubilee Fleet review of King George VI, 16 July 1935. (*Author's collection*)

The *Hood* pictured during the Silver Jubilee Fleet Review of King George V. (*Author's collection*)

Right: As the Royal
Yacht sails elegantly
between the
columns of ships,
members of the
Hood's crew gather
along the railings
to cheer the King.
(*Beeldbank WO2,
NIOD*)

Below: As the
Royal Yacht
passes, the *Hood*
fires a salute to
King George V.
(*Beeldbank WO2,
NIOD*)

Bank holiday crowds aboard the *Hood* during Navy Week, 4 August 1935. (*Beeldbank WO2, NIOD*)

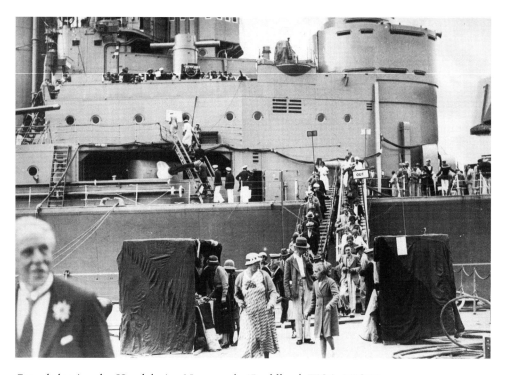

Crowds leaving the *Hood* during Navy week. (*Beeldbank WO2, NIOD*)

of armed Abyssinians between 5 and 7 December 1934. According to Italy, their Somalian forces were attacked by the Abyssinians armed with rifles and machine guns while the Abyssinians claimed that Italian troops, supported by three aircraft and two tanks attacked them.[3] Whatever occurred, the incident resulted in the deaths of around 107 Abyssinians and fifty Italians and Somalis. Preferring to keep Italy on side as an ally against Germany, Britain and France did not take strong steps to discourage the build-up of Italian forces on the border of Eritrea and Abyssinia. Efforts to deter possible Italian aggression against Abyssinia through 1935 were largely left to the League of Nations.

In September 1935, Italy threatened to invade Abyssinia. In response to the Italian threat, the British government began to play for time. During secret talks with the French government, it was decided that if economic sanctions were to be placed on Italy by the League of Nations then they should be placed cautiously. With tensions heightening, the government decided to hedge its bets on a game of blind brinkmanship with Mussolini. On 14 September, the *Hood* was ordered to leave Portland for Gibraltar. Upon arriving at Gibraltar, she was to be the Royal Navy's bluff ship, to be sent wherever it was likely that trouble was arising. Despite being fifteen years old, the *Hood* remained a powerful symbol of British domination of the seas. Having been in service for such a length of time, questions had still not been raised in public about her inadequate armour protection.

The move from Portland to Gibraltar got off to something of a bad start when a disgruntled stoker who was angry that the ship was being transferred away from home ports used a fistful of razor blades to sabotage one of the ship's turbines.[4] Despite this setback, the *Hood* arrived at Gibraltar on 17 September accompanied by HMS *Renown*, three cruisers, and six destroyers. This sudden move of key elements of the Home Fleet incensed Mussolini. So incensed was Mussolini that on 20 September, the British Ambassador to Italy, Sir Eric Drummond visited the Italian dictator and reassured him that the movement of ships from Britain to Gibraltar was not to be interpreted as an aggressive move but was to be viewed instead as a consequence of the anti-British stance in the Italian press.[5]

As commander of the Battlecruiser Squadron flying his flag in the *Hood*, Bailey's task while at Gibraltar was to use his hastily assembled force of ships to bottle up the Strait of Gibraltar. This would prove to be something of an easy task, and by and large, the ship's companies settled into lethargy. Aboard the *Hood*, Commander O'Conor was determined that the time that the *Hood* spent operating from Gibraltar would not be a time of boredom for the crew.

In an effort to combat the attractions of bars and brothels ashore, O'Conor had catamarans placed between the ship and the Mole which could be used as a lido for sunbathing and swimming. With the aid of paint and church pews, the coal shed on the South Mole was converted into a cinema. All the while, the appearance of the ship was maintained. So smart was the exterior of the battlecruiser that some Gibraltarians thought that she looked more like a yacht than a warship. Below deck, away from the eyes of Gibraltar's inhabitants, things were not as smart. The ship's dentist, Surgeon Commander William Wolton, recalled: 'Air conditioning

The *Hood* at Portland. (*Author's collection*)

The *Hood* at anchor at Portland in September 1935 prior to sailing to Gibraltar.
(*Author's collection*)

The *Hood* (left) and the *Renown* (right) at Gibraltar. (*Author's collection*)

was very poor. There were several deaths from tuberculosis. At Gibraltar a rating sat up in his hammock, coughed up a lot of blood and was dead in a few minutes.'[6]

Tuberculosis as an issue aboard the *Hood* had first been brought to the attention of the Admiralty after a midshipman and an able seaman had been invalidated off the ship with the condition in 1932. Concerns for the disease were, however, brushed aside by the Admiralty, which noted that £5,000 had been spent during the 1929–1931 refit improving habitability and that the number of cases aboard the *Hood* compared favourably with the number of cases among the other ships of the Home Fleet and the civilian population. By the mid–late 1930s, the *Hood* had earned the reputation as being 'the TB ship' with the result that the Admiralty could no longer ignore the disease which, in the case of the Royal Navy, had double the mortality rate than among civilians and was just as prevalent as it had been thirty years previous. When he was drafted to the *Hood* in June 1937, Vice-Admiral Andrew Cunningham had been chairing a committee looking into the issues of ventilation and habitability afloat.[7] Commander O'Conor was all too aware of how bad conditions could be below deck and decreed that the ship would follow a 'holiday routine'. In essence, this meant that all work ended at 8 a.m. with the exception of the duty watch meaning that the remainder of the day was free for the crew to do more or less as they pleased. This spoiling of the crew was a talking point around the Rock.

A second talking point surrounded the activities of Captain Tower and would grow into a scandal that reached the attention of Admiral Sir Roger Backhouse, Commander-in-Chief of the Home Fleet, and the First Sea Lord, Lord Chatfield.

Since the collision between the *Hood* and the *Renown*, the relationship between Bailey and Tower had been under scrutiny. Backhouse arrived at Gibraltar during the period that the *Hood* was at anchor there. When he arrived, Backhouse claimed that the Rock was abuzz with the rumour that there was trouble between Bailey and Tower which stemmed from a reported mistress kept by the *Hood*'s captain at the Rock Hotel. This rumour and the reported tension between Bailey and Tower were passed on by Backhouse to Chatfield. Chatfield decided to investigate the matter further and turned to Admiral James for a report on his former captain. James informed Chatfield that gossip was rife at Gibraltar and that it was quite possible that a friendship may well have been magnified into something more and that an injustice was being done to both Tower and the resident of the Rock Hotel. All the while, Backhouse continued his own investigation and reported to Chatfield:

> As regards the lady at the Rock Hotel—that is correct, but there is no evidence that the conduct was scandalous. He [Tower] spent much time in her company, but he slept in his ship. Bailey would not ask her on board and I believe she was not asked either to Government House, when it was known about her. I gather that Tower has a wife and three children, but that he does not go home.[8]

Backhouse questioned Bailey as to why he did not discuss the matter with Tower in an effort to prevent the rumours to which Bailey replied that he wished to avoid an argument at the end of Tower's time as captain and because of the trouble that had surrounded the collision with the *Renown*.

As rumours wound their way around Gibraltar, the crisis over Abyssinia deteriorated and the British government relied more on the *Hood* as a bargaining chip. Italy invaded Abyssinia on 3 October, which prompted economic and military sanctions to be placed on Italy by the League of Nations four days later. In the event, the trade embargos were not implemented until 18 October and the military sanctions never came to fruition. With the naval balance of power still in Britain's favour, at the end of October, the suggestion was forthcoming from Mussolini that if Britain was willing to withdraw both the *Hood* and the *Renown* from Gibraltar then he would be willing to withdraw one division from Libya and have it ordered back to Italy. The British Cabinet was prepared to listen. With an assurance from France to provide naval support if war broke out, on 13 January 1936, the *Hood* departed Gibraltar for Portsmouth. Before she left Gibraltar for Portsmouth, between September and December 1935, the *Hood* was visited by Emperor Haile Selassie of Ethiopia.

By January 1936, Tower had been the *Hood*'s captain for five months longer than was usual. The rumours of his activities at the Rock Hotel and the court-martial events following the *Renown* collision combined to convince the Admiralty that he was no longer fit for a sea-going commission. The *Hood* arrived at Portsmouth on 16 January and was taken in hand for docking on 21 January. Tower was promoted to rear admiral and summarily left the *Hood*. To the amazement of Backhouse, Tower departed the *Hood* with a perfect confidential report of all nines from Bailey. Almost a year after leaving the *Hood*, Tower was appointed

This image shows the *Hood* framed in lights while at Gibraltar on 6 November 1935. She was framed in light to celebrate the wedding of Prince Henry, Duke of Gloucester. (*HMS Hood Association*)

director of Naval Equipment. He would remain in this position until the outbreak of war when he was promoted to vice-admiral and appointed Deputy Controller of the Navy. Knighted in 1942, Tower would remain Deputy Controller of the Navy until the end of the war when he retired. Tower's replacement as captain of the *Hood* was Captain Arthur F. Pridham who assumed command on 1 February during the period in which the *Hood* was in hand for docking.

Born on 3 June 1886, Arthur Francis Pridham had joined the Royal Navy in 1901 and had saw service during the First World War as the gunnery officer aboard HMS *Weymouth*, *Shannon*, and *Marlborough*, where he saw service in the North Atlantic, Mediterranean, and Adriatic Sea. Promoted to captain in 1926, Pridham had attended the Imperial Defence College in 1927 before going on to command the destroyer HMS *Curlew*, the cruisers *Calliope* and *Concord*, and the shore establishment HMS *Excellent*. He was dispatched to take command of the *Hood* by Backhouse, who was now based in Gibraltar, with the following brief: 'I want you to get the *Hood* out of cotton wool. Take your time, but as soon as you think you have got the feel of your ship, I want you to bring the *Hood* in here after dark and in foul weather. My ships will most certainly have to do such things in time of war'.[9] In essence, Pridham was to oversee the transformation of the *Hood* from the showpiece of the Royal Navy to a ship ready for war. The arrival of Captain Pridham aboard the *Hood* brought a very different style of leadership when compared to that of Tower. Pridham was a more hands-on captain who immediately found much to criticise in his new ship and in the style of her executive officer. The first thing that struck Pridham was that the *Hood* was far below the required standard of cleanliness. Pridham would later recall:

> It took me some time before I could believe my eyes. Between decks she was the dirtiest ship I had ever seen. I could find no sign that the good 'ship husbandry' was within the knowledge or competence of her officers.... The messdecks were disgusting and swarming with cockroaches. These dirty pests are easily eradicated— if you know how; the Commander [O'Conor] did not. One of my first orders to him was that I expected to find the mess decks free from cockroaches in six weeks' time; and I told him how to set about it.[10]

According to *Hood* historian Bruce Taylor, '[t]he evidence is that the *Hood* was still infested months later, as she could hardly fail to be in the Mediterranean' where she spent considerable time.[11] Pridham also found the layers of paint with which O'Conor had coated and recoated every surface on the *Hood* as another point of criticism.

> It was by no means difficult to point out to the commander that under all the paint he had plastered on the Quarterdeck were layers of dirt. I had one spot chipped down to bare metal and found a quarter of an inch of layers of paint and dirt on top of rust, indicating two departures from first principles: don't try to cover rust by painting over it, and don't paint over dirt.[12]

From that moment, Pridham initiated a paint removal drive to chip away the countless layers of paint before having the surfaces cleaned and repainted. It is worth noting that the paint removal drive initiated by Pridham had not been completed by the time the *Hood* sank in May 1941. Simply put, the *Hood* was loaded down with too many layers of O'Conor's paint. The *Hood* was also, in Pridham's view, deficient in basic seamanship. The shortcomings found by Pridham without doubt owed something to the many months that she had spent at anchor in Gibraltar.

By early 1936, developments in Germany, the continuing crisis over Abyssinia and the Japanese invasion of Manchuria had begun to ring the bells of a potential global war. A potential war against Germany, Italy, and Japan had yet to fully impress itself on the Royal Navy and the *Hood*, but preparations for war under Pridham began to be made. William Handing, a warrant engineer aboard the *Hood* between 1936 and 1937, recalled:

> The Warrant Shipwright persuaded the Boatswain to convince the Commander to operate again the bower cable holder, which was not used because it spoilt the

paintwork. It took two days and a fire around the spindle before the shipwrights freed it. The Torpedo Gunner was also given permission to work the above-water [torpedo] tubes. This entailed spoiling the side paintwork and it took almost a week to get the doors open.[13]

Inspecting the *Hood* with a fine-tooth comb, Pridham was astonished to discover that many of the 700 hull compartments aboard the ship had not been entered since she had been built. Examinations and checks of all were instigated. Pridham found further issues when he took the *Hood* to sea.

I was shocked to see evidence of ignorance of elementary details of lowering and hoisting boats at sea. The Commander expected me to stop the ship's way before he gave the order to slip. I had never dreamt of such slovenliness. The boats were hoisted lazily at a slow walk; I ordered them to be lowered and hoisted again.[14]

Pridham also turned his attention to the *Hood*'s gunnery. Once he had brought the gunnery up to an acceptable standard of efficiency, he resolved that the ship would thereafter conduct her practice shoots in conditions that were likely to be encountered in battle. This meant at speed, at night, and in foul weather. Before beginning such exercises, Pridham faced technical and administrative obstacles. Those facing him ahead of a practice shoot in 1938 are detailed below and are similar to the difficulties he faced in 1936:

A restriction to gunnery training which caused me some concern was the economy drive which, amongst other things, demanded a minimum expenditure of oil fuel. The consequence of this was that all exercises and firings were to be carried out at not more than about half the speed the ship could reach on full power. I was most anxious that all our firings should be done at the speed at which the ship would be fought, namely full speed, and often in bad weather. This combination could be a full test of the ship's efficiency with her fire control equipment and procedure. The two foremost turrets might well be, with the gun control tower [i.e. armoured director], enveloped in heavy spray obscuring their rangefinders. I knew that at speeds around 21 knots, vibration was so extensive that the High Angle Control Position [located on the aft searchlight platform] was unable to function, although at higher speeds the vibration was far less. I wanted to obtain evidence, supported by a naval constructor, to back up my recommendation for some structural alterations to this position.

On receiving orders for my next full-calibre firing, I proposed to carry it out at full speed and in bad weather. This was not approved on account of the extra expenditure of fuel oil. In point of fact, the extra fuel needed, if I only used full speed during the firing would not amount to more than about 20 tons, possibly £50 worth! In my opinion an insignificant price to pay for testing the ship's gunnery under conditions which would be encountered in battle. I had already been smarting at having been given detailed orders, which should have been decided in consultation with me, the captain of the ship, or left to my discretion, so I studied ways of obtaining my entirely reasonable objective. While discussing the question with my Engineering Commander [C. P. Berthon] he assured me that with only twenty of our twenty-four boilers alight, about normal for entering harbour in bad weather, he would be able to work up to 28½ or 29 knots and hold it for fifteen or twenty minutes. That was good enough; ten minutes would be sufficient, probably.

The firing proved to be just the test I had hoped for. It was blowing a full gale with a nasty short sea, so that when heading into it the ship was washed down with heavy spray fore and aft. Only from the Fore bridge and Fire Control Position aloft could the target be seen. I had ordered the target-towing ship to steer down wind at utmost speed during the *Hood*'s firing, while I took the ship to a position from which she would approach the target up wind and so experience the full force of the gale. It proved to be a real 'test firing'. In my report I came out in the open by stating that experience of firing practice at 29 knots had proved most valuable was not told subsequently to give 'My reasons in writing' for exceeding the speed authorised in the C in C's [Admiral Sir Dudley Pound] orders! I had invited the Naval Constructor on the C in C's staff [Commander W. J. A. Davies] to be on board during the firing, and had asked him to note the condition of vibration, at various speeds, in the High-Angle Control Position. His report led to approval of my recommendation that the structure of this position should be stiffened.[15]

'The firing proved to be just the test I had hoped for. It was blowing a full gale with a nasty short sea, so that when heading into it the ship was washed down with heavy spray fore and aft.' A heavy sea breaks over the forecastle and the front turrets as the *Hood* engages in a firing exercise.

As Pridham went over the *Hood* in minute detail, in the Mediterranean, Admiral Sir William Wordsworth Fisher, the Commander-in-Chief of the Mediterranean Fleet, who was requesting reinforcements, requested that the *Hood* should be sent to join him at Malta before sailing on to Alexandria where she could be used to deter Mussolini from any moves directed against the Suez Canal. A sick Chatfield considered Fisher's request and instructed Admiral James to approach the Foreign Office for approval. At the Foreign Office, appeasement as opposed to deterrence was the order of the day. James later described his visit to the Foreign Office:

> When I stated the object to [Sir Anthony] Eden, [the Foreign Secretary] he rang for Sir Robert Vansittart (Permanent Secretary). They told me frankly that Mussolini was in an excited state and the strengthening of the fleet at Alexandria by the *Hood* might tip the balance over to war, which was the last thing they wanted. I must have been nearly an hour with them developing every argument I could muster and in the end they agreed to the movement.[16]

Eden also sought the opinions of Lancelot Oliphant, the Assistant Under Secretary of State who was handling the Abyssinian crisis and the tensions with Mussolini. 'I believe that Mussolini is far more afraid of a battlecruiser than a battleship', Oliphant told Eden.[17] Oliphant's view was not, however, in line with that of Stanley Baldwin's military advisors. So it was that Eden and Vansittart's agreement to send the *Hood* to Malta and Alexandria was countermanded.

On 21 February, the *Hood* left Portsmouth for Portland from where she sailed to Arousa Bay and then on to Gibraltar where she arrived on 7 March to continue her watch over the Strait. The same day that the *Hood* arrived back at Gibraltar, Adolf Hitler denounced the Treaty of Locarno and ordered German soldiers to reoccupy the demilitarised zone of the Rhineland. With an increasing number of crises, Chatfield boasted to the Cabinet that within seven days he could move the Home Fleet from Gibraltar and the Mediterranean Fleet from Alexandria so that both fleets could be in the North Sea to meet any threats posed by Germany. At the time, however, the Royal Navy possessed only one cruiser, seventeen destroyers and a handful of submarines in home waters. The *Hood* and the *Renown* were the only vessels possessed by Chatfield which could be hastily deployed to the North Sea within the seven-day time frame to combat the threat posed by the *Kriegsmarine*'s *Deutschland*-class cruisers, more commonly referred to as pocket battleships.

Since the collision in early 1935 with the *Renown*, the *Hood* had not been handled boldly. She was given a wide berth by other vessels and seldom moved in a harbour without the assistance of between six and eight tugs. Aware of his orders from Backhouse to take the *Hood* out of cotton wool, Pridham was determined to cease using tugs to guide the *Hood* in and out of harbour. Indeed, Pridham described the *Hood* as 'handling wonderfully well, so long as one used engine power and treated her roughly as soon as she showed the slightest sign of taking the bit beneath her teeth'.[18] When Pridham informed O'Conor of his

The *Hood* departing Portsmouth for Portland, 21 February 1936. (*Beeldbank WO2, NIOD*)

At anchor in Portland. From left to right, the capital ships are the *Hood*, *Nelson*, and *Iron Duke*.

intention to take the *Hood* from her berth alongside without the assistance of tugs, O'Conor showed and voiced an opinion of doubt which immediately led to a lecture on seamanship from Pridham.

Pridham commenced the manoeuvre by giving the ship a slight move ahead before checking her way and pushing her off the wall by going astern on the starboard propeller. The *Hood* responded and began to leave the berth completely under control. Pridham still had to bring the *Hood* in, however. Previously, the *Hood* had been eased into a position along the South Mole 6 feet from the wall whereupon she was hauled in using long hawsers. This took time and was described by Pridham as looking untidy. The first opportunity that Pridham possessed to satisfy Backhouse's request that the *Hood* be brought alongside in poor weather occurred during a north-westerly gale. For two hours, Pridham decided against attempting to moor between the aircraft carrier *Furious* and the battleship *Nelson*, electing instead to anchor outside the harbour. Eventually, pride prevailed. After raising steam, the *Hood* made her approach. As she neared the *Nelson*, the *Hood* canted sharply to port and then starboard, before suddenly pointing at a 45-degree angle towards the mole with the ship closing rapidly on the mole, Pridham ordered full speed astern. The *Hood* came to a rest 30 feet from the wall. Delicately using the engines, Pridham finally brought the *Hood* in astern of the *Nelson* where he could see Backhouse watching from the quarterdeck. A dejected Pridham turned to Admiral Bailey and apologised for what he claimed was a poor performance. 'Don't be silly. Haven't you seen the C-in-C's signal?' Bailey countered. Glancing at the signalman's pad, Pridham read the signal 'Manoeuvre well executed'.

On 5 May 1936, Italian troops entered Addis Ababa, which just about brought the Abyssinian war to an end. At the same time, sanctions against Italy began to lessen and the demands placed on the Home Fleet began to disintegrate. Despite her outward appearance, the *Hood* was not in a fighting state as the result of a defect in one of her turbines which damaged some of her rotor blades. Temporary fixes were exacted at Gibraltar with a full repair delayed until her return to Portsmouth. On 4 July, the League of Nations lifted all sanctions against Italy and the *Hood* was ordered to sail to Portsmouth for a refit and to recommission. At the same time, Bailey was informed by the Admiralty that he would no longer be considered for a seagoing commission, but that he would be placed on full pay until he was given another appointment. The original plan drawn up by the Admiralty was for Bailey to transfer his flag from the *Hood* to the *Renown*. Bailey was aware, however, that the officers in the *Renown* disliked him as a result of the collision and the subsequent court-martial hearings, and that their animosity towards him had not abated since Captain Sawbridge had left the battlecruiser to be replaced by his court-martial defender Captain R. B. T. Miles. Bailey pleaded with Backhouse to remain aboard the *Hood* and stated that he would go on half pay for several months in preference to joining the *Renown*. Following deliberations between Backhouse and Chatfield, Bailey was allowed to remain aboard the *Hood* and returned in her to Portsmouth in July where she was paid off.

A sailor at work cleaning the aircraft carrier HMS *Courageous*. Behind the *Courageous*, the *Hood* lies majestically at anchor. (*Beeldbank WO2, NIOD*)

The *Hood* at Portsmouth, *c.* 1935. (*Author's collection*)

Taken from aboard HMS *Furious*, this photograph shows the *Hood* at anchor prior to summer exercises with the Home Fleet. (*Beeldbank WO2, NIOD*)

Bailey retired voluntarily following returning to Portsmouth but had his career reactivated six months later when he took a senior officers war course. In July 1937, Bailey, then a vice-admiral, commanded the Royal Naval College, Greenwich and received a knighthood at the conclusion of a two-year appointment. Recalled to a desk job at the Admiralty following the outbreak of war, Bailey died in March 1942 after failing to make a full recovery from an appendicitis operation.

The Spanish Civil War

While the *Hood* was an iconic ship that captivated individuals like Ted Briggs, she did not captivate everyone. Noel Pugh, who in 1936 was a civilian who served with the Royal Naval Wireless Auxiliary Reserve and who served in this capacity between 1932 and 1939, recalled seeing the *Hood* in the flesh during a visit to Portsmouth:

> I hoped [that] I never got drafted to her because I didn't like her. Well for one thing, being in dockyard hands she was very dirty, and for another thing; we were taken from the lorry into the bowels of the ship where they were trying to get a VHF set working … We went through this manhole into a cabin where this VHF thing was and one of the Reservists said to the Petty Officer in charge of showing us around, 'What would happen if the *Hood* was in action?' 'Oh, well', he [the Petty Officer] said, 'the manhole cover would be clamped down'. The Reservist said, 'You mean the operator wouldn't get out!' No. It was as simple as that. The *Hood* gave us a rather poor impression.[1]

On 8 September 1936, the *Hood* was recommissioned into the Mediterranean Fleet with Pridham reappointed as flag captain. At this time, international developments were increasingly making it look likely that war would break out in Europe. Having begun with the onset of the Abyssinian crisis, the *Hood* was often at the forefront of Britain's diplomatic efforts in the late 1930s, a fact which was not lost on Pridham who wrote: 'It is true that whenever international relations become strained the question was asked "Where is the *Hood*"?'[2] This fact was also not lost on the men of the lower decks who christened the *Hood* 'The Seven Bs: Britain's Biggest Bullshitting Bastard Built By Brown'.

While the *Hood* was in hand for repairs, on 17 July 1936, the Spanish Civil War had broken out. The Spanish Civil War would provide the background against which the ambitions and concerns of every power in Europe would be played out. Almost from the outset, the Royal Navy became involved in a humanitarian effort connected with the war which required the transfer of a number of destroyers to French ports and the appointment of a Senior Naval Officer Northern Spain. The outbreak of the Spanish Civil War served to inspire the Admiralty to attach the *Repulse* and the *Hood* to the Mediterranean Fleet. On 22 July, Vice-Admiral Geoffrey Blake had been appointed Admiral Commanding Battlecruiser Squadron and had hoisted his flag in the *Hood*.

In September, prior to her sailing for Malta red, white, and blue stripes were painted atop 'B' turret to identify the *Hood* as a neutral ship involved in non-intervention patrols. On 19 July, in the early days of the coup that sparked the civil war, the Republican government had sought military aid from Britain and France. The Spanish government's requests came up against British hostility and French reluctance. On 8 August, France closed its border with Spain as the Western democracies proposed a non-intervention treaty that debarred both State and private enterprise in signatory countries from delivering war materials to Spain. Germany and Italy were signatories of the treaty of non-intervention although both would supply the Nationalist rebels with support and equipment. The commission got off to a poor start when the *Hood* attempted to leave for Malta. The ship's new navigator, Commander E. D. Brooks piloted her over a shallow off Spithead. Gravel was sucked into the ship's condensers with the result that, to Pridham's consternation, she was forced to return to Portsmouth for the condensers to be cleaned. In the meantime, Blake's flag was temporarily transferred to the battleship *Barham*. Finally, on 10 October, the *Hood* sailed from Portsmouth for Gibraltar before moving on to Malta where she arrived on 24 October. During the journey to Malta, Pridham pushed the crew as far as he dared and it quickly became obvious that more time and work was needed before Blake could rehoist his flag. Gunnery trails were carried out, the results of which were abysmal. What struck Pridham was that many of the ship's new crewmen appeared scared and frightened by the firing of the main battery guns. During the first full-calibre night-firing exercise conducted following her recommissioning, Pridham came across young seamen who were supposed to be manning the ship's 5.5-inch guns but who were so scared by the blast and roar of the main battery guns that they sought shelter away from their posts. When the exercise was concluded, Pridham rounded the young sailors up and bluntly told them: 'You're not fit for me to take into action against even an Eyetie ship'.[3]

The *Hood* spent the period from 24 October to 2 December at Malta working up. It was while at Malta that Pridham received detailed plans of an extensive rebuilding programme for the *Hood* estimated to cost £4.5 million. The plans were for a complete reconstruction of the upper deck in the area from 'B' turret to 'X' turret. The BL 5.5-inch guns were to be removed and replaced by QF 4-inch Mk XVI dual purpose guns. Additional 'pom-pom' anti-aircraft guns were to be installed and the underwater torpedo tubes were to be removed. In addition to this, new turbine machinery was to be fitted with high-pressure boilers. A hanger deck was planned and additional armour of 12 inches was to be fitted over the upper deck and the armour over the magazines and machinery was to be increased to 5 inches. Also included in the plan was a proposal to remove the bridge and the admiral's bridge. The bridge had been a source of complaint from every captain. If he wanted to look aft, the captain was forced to venture out on to one of the

The *Hood* entering Malta during the Spanish Civil War. Note the red, white, and blue stripes atop 'B' turret denoting her neutrality and involvement in the non-intervention patrols. (*Author's collection*)

platforms on the side of the position which took him away from the voice pipes. The admiral's bridge was inadequate, with vision blocked by the armoured hood of the rangefinder above the conning tower.

There were two main drawbacks to the reconstruction plans. The first drawback was that the magazines would remain sited above the shell rooms. Second, while experts had expressed doubt over how much longer the *Hood*'s machinery would last, the reconstruction was not scheduled to begin until March 1942.[4] It is likely that the refit would have seen the *Hood* transformed to look something like a cross between the *Renown*-class battlecruisers and the *King George V*-class battleships.

On 28 November 1936, Pridham considered the *Hood* ready to accommodate Blake and his staff. Four days later, the *Hood*, flying Blake's flag once more, sailed to Gibraltar, where in the company of the *Repulse* she relieved the battleship *Valiant* and the cruiser *Sussex*. For the next five months, Gibraltar would become the *Hood*'s second home away from Malta. On 11 December, the *Hood* left Gibraltar for Tangier. It was while at Tangier on 12 December that from the quarterdeck the proclamation of abdication of King Edward VIII and the ascension of King George VI was read. The increasing outside interest in the civil war in Spain was obvious to Blake for also at anchor in Tangier were two Italian warships including the cruiser *Aquila*, and a number of German ships including the cruisers *Nürnberg* and *Königsberg* and the Type 24 gunboat *Iltis*. In addition to this, when the *Hood* returned to Gibraltar for Christmas, she was followed into harbour by the German pocket battleship *Admiral Graf Spee*.

The *Hood* off to starboard of the *Repulse*. The exact date of this photo is unknown but the stripes on the *Hood*'s 'B' turret date this as being taken during the Spanish Civil War. (*Richard Toffolo*)

The *Hood* weighing anchor in Malta, *c.* 1937.
(*Sea Power Centre Australia, Royal Australian Navy*)

The *Hood* departing Malta, *c.* 1937. (*Richard Toffolo*)

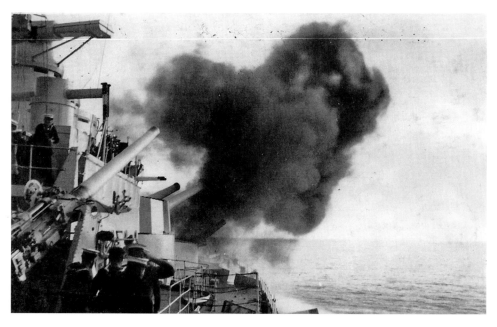

The *Hood* engaged in a firing exercise, *c.* 1937.
(*Leonard Eaves Photograph Collection, HMS Hood Association*)

Early January 1937 saw the *Hood* sailing between Gibraltar and Tangier before she left for Malta on 16 January. On 21 January, the *Hood* weighed anchor at Malta and sailed to Plateía Island, Greece. She departed Plateía Island on 1 February to sail back to Malta and to conduct a series of exercises between Malta and Gibraltar. During this period, two incidents occurred. While the *Hood* was conducting exercises, hydraulic tests were carried out on her forward turrets. Towards the end of an exercise, the knee of a gunner's mate accidentally knocked a hydraulic switch in 'B' turret. A 15-inch shell was in the cage. The knocking of the switch allowed the shell to be rammed into the gun where it crushed the arm of electrician Able Seaman Fred Hard. Hard's arm was broken, while muscle tissue and arteries were severed. Conscious, Hard managed to climb down the twenty-five-foot ladder into the turret barbette before proceeding through the mess decks to the sickbay. In the sickbay, medical personnel hastily applied a tourniquet before Hard passed out owing to a lack of blood. An emergency operation was carried out on the arm but after three days gangrene began to set in. Pridham decided to leave the fleet exercises and set a course for Malta at 28 knots. It was anticipated that at Malta's Bighi hospital, Hard would have his arm amputated. The physician aboard the *Hood* administered Prontosil, which was a relatively new drug at the time. The Prontosil arrested the gangrene's development. At Malta, Hard was taken off the *Hood* by a tug before being transferred to Bighi hospital where the surgeon, Commander Keating, decided to try and save the arm. Following three months of operations and observation, Hard's arm was saved and he was discharged whereupon he joined HMS *Queen Elizabeth* before rejoining the *Hood* when the two ships anchored at Spithead.[5]

The second incident was more tragic and occurred when the *Hood* was berthing at Gibraltar's South Mole. A sudden strong gust of wind blew the stern of the ship away from the Mole. One of the hawsers snapped and whipped across the deck where it struck Ordinary Seaman D. D. Smith in the head, fractured the leg of J. E. Kelly and seriously injured Marine Corporal W. J. Hayward. Smith would die from the head injuries he sustained in this accident.[6] Despite these setbacks, the *Hood* continued to conduct exercises between Malta and Gibraltar before on 23 March, when at Malta, she was taken in hand to have her propellers changed.

Despite the increasing involvement of Italy and Germany on the one hand and the Soviet Union on the other in the Spanish Civil War, the British Government continued to insist on a policy of non-intervention. The patrol bluffs of the Royal Navy off northern and southern Spain were now, however, often being called. By the beginning of April 1937, General Franco's Nationalist forces had been stopped in their drive on Madrid and had decided to turn their attention to the Republican enclaves in the north and the Basque forces holding Vizcaya with the ultimate aim of capturing Bilbao. On 6 April, the Nationalists announced a blockade of all Republican-held ports on the Cantabrian coast.[7] Franco had realised early on that one sure way to make Bilbao capitulate was to prevent the supply of food to the city by sea, which was the only real option left open to supply the town. During previous months Franco's Nationalists had only been able to affect a legal

The *Hood* seen from HMS *Nelson*, *c.* 1937. Note the *Nelson*'s 16-inch guns at the top of the image. (*Beeldbank WO2, NIOD*)

Ships on exercises. At the head of the formation in the image is HMS *Renown*. In the centre is the *Hood* with the battleship *Valiant* (foreground) bringing up the rear of the formation. (*Author's collection*)

The *Hood* rolling in the Mediterranean sometime during 1937. (*Jamie Grierson*)

The *Hood* sailing through the Mediterranean in 1937. Note the non-intervention stripes on 'B' turret and that 'A' turret has been traversed to port. (*Jamie Grierson*)

blockade of war materials; however, now Franco warned British merchantmen who were running supplies into Bilbao that signals from his warships must be obeyed.[8]

In Britain, Bilbao was proving a contentious issue. Merchant ships were delivering supplies to the Spanish port and the British government had to consider whether and how to protect these merchantmen against the Nationalist blockade. It was an issue of extreme importance; the British merchant fleet was the largest in the world. Many merchant ships had been put back to use following the Great Depression and a large number of foreign vessels were being re-registered under the British flag. It was vital therefore that British merchant shipping was protected. The task of protecting the British merchant fleet, it was decided, should fall to the Royal Navy. It may be noted that some embarrassment was caused to the British government when it was realised that despite the stated policy of non-intervention, a significant amount of war material was being delivered to the Basques in ships flying the Red Ensign alongside food stocks and other essential supplies.

The policy decided upon by the British government was that no Spanish vessel should be allowed to stop a British merchant ship 'on the high seas'. This did not apply, however, to the strip of sea three miles off the coast defined as 'territorial waters'. Here it was the strongest party that commanded authority. Around Bilbao, the strongest party was the Basque government. The Basque government kept the sea around Bilbao clear of mines and had powerful artillery positions situated along the coast to keep Nationalist warships away.[9]

The first incident arose on 6 April when the merchant ship SS *Thorpehall*, which was loaded with food destined for Bilbao, signalled that, 10 miles off the Spanish coast, she had been intercepted and fired on by the Nationalist trawler *Galerna*. The destroyer HMS *Brazen* under the command of Captain R. M. T. Taylor soon arrived on the scene and signalled to the *Galerna* to 'cease interference'. Shortly afterwards, the *Galerna* was still blocking the advance of the *Thorpehall* when the Nationalist cruiser *Almirante Cervera* approached prompting Taylor to order his crew to action stations. Taylor signalled that the *Thorpehall* was loaded only with food but the Nationalist vessels remained intent on preventing her passage. A three-hour stand-off ensued with the Nationalist vessels lying between the *Thorpehall* and Bilbao while the crew of *Brazen* stood by at action stations. Other vessels began to nose in during this time. The *Admiral Graf Spee* was followed by HMS *Blande* aboard which was Commander C. Carson, the senior officer of the British flotilla. Appreciating the tenseness of the situation, *Kapitän zur See* Conrad Patzig decided to extract the *Graf Spee* from the situation and sailed away. Tensions were further heightened by the arrival of a third British destroyer, HMS *Beagle*. Suddenly, the *Almirante Cervera* began to steam towards the *Thorpehall* whereupon Carson ordered his destroyers to interpose themselves between the Nationalist cruiser and the merchantman. The *Thorpehall* was effectively screened and, under the cover of the British destroyers, succeeded in reaching the 3-mile limit.

While he had kept his nerve, Carson reported to Backhouse that the Nationalist-reported blockade of Bilbao appeared to be a reality and that his small flotilla of destroyers would not be able to protect merchant shipping against Nationalist forces amounting to a battleship, two cruisers, a destroyer, and an armed trawler. Carson also served to bolster the Nationalist blockade by advising all merchant ships bound for Bilbao to put in at the small French harbour of St Jean de Luz, which lay just across the border from Bilbao.

While not supporting the so-called blockade busters (as the merchantmen were referred to in the British press), the British government recognised that national prestige was at stake. Sir Samuel Hoare, the First Sea Lord, was severely alarmed by the reports from Carson of superior Spanish naval forces. The battleship to which Carson referred to was the *España*, a coal-burning battleship commissioned in 1921 as the *Alfonso XIII* but renamed in 1931, equipped with eight 12-inch guns. Anthony Eden made it quite clear that blockades were not acceptable. Public opinion in Britain showed outrage that the most powerful navy in the world should not be allowed to protect its merchant shipping against Franco. Eden's view prevailed during the cabinet meeting of Wednesday, 7 April 1937, and the Admiralty was obliged to reinforce the British forces in the Bay of Biscay. The view of the blockade of Bilbao by Nationalist forces held by the Royal Navy led to furious scenes in the House of Commons. Four Nationalist warships were keeping watch over 200 miles of coastline while Basque shore batteries controlled an area beyond the 3-mile limit. The British government was in something of a limbo over Bilbao. Non-intervention meant that the government was reluctant to commit British forces, even in a humanitarian role. At the same time, there was, according to Sir Samuel Hoare, a threat to British warships from mines in the Nervión; what Hoare forgot to mention was that his source regarding this information was the Nationalist navy.

At a special ministerial meeting held on 10 April, the government decided that the *Hood* should be sent from Gibraltar to the Bay of Biscay to lift the blockade of Bilbao. Eden insisted that it should be made clear to the Nationalist forces that, should they fire upon a British ship, then they would be sunk. It was felt that the presence of the *Hood* would be enough to avoid further confrontation.[10]

At 2.48 p.m. on 10 April, an 'Immediate' signal was sent to Blake ordering him to take over as Senior Officer, Northern Spain and to take the *Hood* to the Bay of Biscay as soon as possible. It was a Saturday afternoon and a large proportion of the crew had been granted shore leave. Commander Orr-Ewing formed special shore patrols and embarked on a tour of all of the bars, cafes, and other haunts of sailors at Gibraltar to round up the leave-goers and ordered them to return to the ship immediately. While the crew was rounded up, the *Hood* was refuelled and had her provisions restocked. At 8.45 p.m., she cleared Gibraltar and was soon making 27 knots, maintaining radio silence.

In an effort to mislead Nationalist informers ashore as to where the *Hood* was sailing, Pridham at first sailed eastwards into the Mediterranean before backtracking through the Strait of Gibraltar and out into the Atlantic. The

Government's orders to Blake to take the *Hood* to the Bay of Biscay were secret but that evening, as the crew listened to the radio, they heard via a BBC news bulletin that they were on their way north to escort a merchant ship loaded with potatoes from St Jean de Luz to Bilbao. Lieutenant-Commander William Harding stated:

> *Hood*'s movements had been kept under wraps all day, and many people were upset at this disclosure on the news. We put the leak down to John Reith, the director of the BBC. He had been Blake's guest in *Hood* and left at Gibraltar, where we believed he phoned the news to the BBC.[11]

The following day, the British Cabinet convened to discuss a threat from Franco that he would use force to enforce the blockade. Following the Cabinet meeting, the British government issued a statement:

> His Majesty's Government cannot recognise or concede belligerent rights and they cannot tolerate any interference with British shipping at sea. They are, however, warning British shipping that in view of conditions at present prevailing in the neighbourhood of Bilbao, they should not, for practical reasons, and in view of risks, against which at present [it may be] impossible to protect them, go into that area, so long as these conditions prevail.[12]

On 12 April, the *Hood* dropped anchor off St Jean de Luz, where Blake received a signal from the Admiralty stating: 'If a British ship proceeding to Bilbao, in spite of Government advice, calls on you for protection in a particular case, you should render protection on the high seas'.[13] Owing to the size of the harbour at St Jean de Luz, the *Hood* anchored 4 miles off the coast. Crowds descended on the area to gaze at the majestic battlecruiser anchored off the coast. Early on the morning of 13 April, a violent south-westerly gale accompanied by rain squalls forced Pridham to raise anchor and sail out of sight of land and prompted Blake to request permission from the Admiralty to withdraw from the area owing to the lack of a base unless the use of force was necessary. The *Hood* departed for La Pallice but Blake had observed enough to convince himself that, despite what Carson had told the Admiralty, the blockade of Bilbao was a myth. When he informed the Admiralty that he was yet to see a Nationalist warship and that the Navy had insufficient forces to shield all the British merchant ships looking to sail to Bilbao, the Admiralty were inclined not to believe Blake and asked for further details.

As the Admiralty groped for intelligence, the eyes of the world turned to St Jean de Luz where it appeared that a convoy of six merchant ships escorted by four destroyers were preparing to make a run for Bilbao. On 15 April, the *Hood* was to be found anchored at La Rochelle. During the course of the afternoon, Blake and three members of his staff landed and journeyed the 175 miles to St Jean de Luz where they discussed the blockade with Commander Carson whose flotilla was scheduled to shortly be relieved by five destroyers under the command of Captain V. H. Dankwerts. Blake and his party also visited Hendaye where they met with the British Ambassador, Sir Henry Chilton, who warned Blake that Nationalist officers were likely to open fire on merchant ships inside territorial waters. Blake and Chilton discussed the matter well into the evening before, the following day, Blake signalled the Admiralty that he believed there to be a strong indication that merchant ships would be intercepted and fired upon inside the 3-mile limit and requested clarification on the action to be taken in such a scenario. The Admiralty's reply told Blake to 'intervene if a ship had been fired on, once it had submitted'.[14] That same day Captain Dankwerts arrived at St Jean de Luz with the destroyers *Faulkner*, *Fury*, *Firedrake*, *Forester*, and *Fortune*. Almost immediately, Dankwerts heard a rumour that the merchantman *Seven Seas Spray* was leaving St Jean de Luz at 10 p.m. to run the gauntlet of the blockade. Blake was informed and the *Hood* left La Rochelle to take up station off Bilbao for the night. At the anticipated time, the *Seven Seas Spray* weighed anchor.

The merchant ship was spotted by those aboard HMS *Faulkner* at 6.30 a.m. To the challenge from the *Faulkner* 'Where Bound?', the captain of the *Seven Seas Spray*, W. H. Roberts, made no attempt to conceal his destination. Luck was on the side of the merchantman. No interception was forthcoming from the Nationalist warships and the *Seven Seas Spray* slipped into Bilbao at 9 a.m.

Arriving back at St Jean de Luz that afternoon, Blake received a further signal from the Admiralty requesting information on the Bilbao situation. Blake still believed that if a merchant ship was escorted up to the territorial limit then it would be virtually guaranteed to complete its mission owing to the insurance provided by the Basque shore artillery. Blake did, however, caution that there was a risk that a Nationalist warship outside the 3-mile limit might fire on a British merchant ship inside territorial waters but reaffirmed his view that providing the Royal Navy was deployed in significant enough numbers Nationalist vessels would not prey on merchant vessels. In addition to this, Blake informed the Admiralty that he proposed to test the resolve of the Nationalists by providing an escort to a group of three merchantmen which proposed to enter Bilbao on 23 April. Blake's justification was that the Government and the Admiralty would suffer an embarrassment if an incident occurred outside the territorial limit and adequate protection was not on hand. Blake dramatically ended his signal with the words 'HMS *Hood* will be there'.[15]

So it was that on 23 April the merchant ships *MacGregor*, *Hamsterley*, and *Stanbrook* prepared to enter Bilbao. The *Hood* had left her anchorage at 11 p.m. on 22 April. As dawn broke on 23 April, not a hammock was occupied aboard the *Hood* as every crewman stood watching and waiting for the appearance of the merchant ships. A light mist covered the convoy as it sailed to within five miles of Bilbao. It was at this time, at 5.45 a.m., that the Nationalists made an appearance. Both Blake and Pridham had their binoculars trained on the *MacGregor*, which was sailing around half a mile ahead of the other merchant ships when the armed trawler *Galerna* chugged out of the mist. The *Galerna* signalled for the *MacGregor* to stop. The *MacGregor*'s commander did as he was ordered. He also signalled an SOS to HMS *Firedrake*. Picking up the signal, Blake signalled the *Firedrake* at 6.39 a.m. to 'Follow in and report immediately any action by insurgents when merchant vessel outside territorial waters'. As the *Firedrake* sailed in, the *Almirante Cervera*, which had been standing off, appeared and cleared for action. The commanding officer of the *Almirante Cevera*, Captain Manuel de Navio don Moreu, signalled to the *Firedrake* at 6.45 a.m.: 'Please tell steamers not to enter Bilbao'. In unison signals were sent by Blake and the *Firedrake*'s captain, Lieutenant-Commander J. M. Rodgers, informing the Nationalists to cease interference. For forty-five minutes, a stand-off ensued in which signals were flashed back and forth. For the British there was difficulty in reading the Nationalist signals as they were in Spanish, but, despite this, Blake gathered that the *Almirante Cevera* was claiming jurisdiction of territorial waters extending to 6 miles as opposed to three.

At 7.17 a.m., the Nationalists lost patience. The *Galerna* fired a shell that tore across the *MacGregor*'s bow after the merchant ship attempted to sail on having been told by Blake that they could proceed to Bilbao if they so wished. With the merchant ships still 2 miles outside the territorial limit, Rodgers ordered the guns of the *Firedrake* to be trained on the *Galerna*. This marked the first occasion in which a Royal Navy vessel had ranged on a Nationalist ship. In response, the *Almirante Cevera* sailed slowly by the *Firedrake*, showing that her eight 6-inch guns were cleared and ready for action. In response to this move, the *Hood* began to slowly close. Captain Moreu sent a stream of light signals to the *Hood* stating his right to prevent the ships from entering Bilbao and stated that the Royal Navy had no right to interfere. Blake reiterated that he did not recognise the 6-mile limit claimed by the Nationalists. This back and forth continued for twenty minutes during which time the three merchant ships managed to inch closer to Bilbao harbour. At 7.56 a.m., within range of the Galea Point Battery, the Basques opened fire on the *Galerna*. The shells fell short but it was enough to drive off the armed trawler. Thirty minutes later, as the merchant ships approached the harbour entrance Blake received a signal from Commander I. Black of the *Fortune*, which had sailed in to assist the *Firedrake*, which stated that the *Almirante Cevera* had her guns trained on the merchant ships. In response, Blake ordered the *Hood*'s main battery to be traversed to Green 30 in a broadside to the Nationalist cruiser but 20 degrees off target. The Admiral's command was misunderstood and the *Hood*'s eight 15-inch guns were found to be pointing directly at the *Almirante Cevera*. The ploy worked as the *Cevera* held its fire, and as the merchant ships entered Bilbao, sailed away her guns trained fore and aft. In the harbour, the merchant ships were greeted by hysterically cheering crowds.

That evening, Blake made a personal report to ambassador Chilton detailing events, a watered-down account of which was passed on to the press. Three days later Blake and the *Hood* were relieved by the arrival of Rear-Admiral C. G. Ramsey and the battleships *Royal Oak* and *Resolution*.

On 26 April, the *Hood* weighed anchor and set sail for Portsmouth to take part in the Coronation Review of King George VI. The *Hood* was the first ship of the

Mediterranean Fleet to arrive for the review and gained the distinction of being the first capital ship to approach Portsmouth through the Solent as opposed to the normal route through Spithead. During her days off, Spain side-parties had painted the *Hood* in a light Mediterranean grey enamel. The paint highlighted the *Hood*'s graceful symmetrical lines as she glistened in the sunlight. Such was the *Hood*'s appearance that the commander of the USS *New York* signalled to the *Hood* 'You sure do look swell'.[16]

Unlike the Fleet Review for the Silver Jubilee of King George V two years earlier, the Coronation Review of 1937 was attended by no fewer than eighteen foreign warships including the American battleship USS *New York*, the French battleship *Dunkerque*, the German pocket battleship *Admiral Graf Spee*, and the Japanese heavy cruiser *Ashigara*. Held on 20 May, the review took the same form as previous fleet reviews with the Royal Yacht *Victoria and Albert* sailing among the lines of warships as their crews manned the rails and cheered on as the King sailed past. At anchor each evening, the *Hood* and the other ships dazzled as they were illuminated by numerous lights. The occasion was famously described in a BBC broadcast by Lieutenant-Commander Thomas Woodrooffe from on board HMS *Nelson*. In a drunken rambling that lasted for almost four minutes before he was faded out, Woodroofe began his broadcast with the lines: 'At the present moment, the whole fleet is lit up. When I say "lit up", I mean lit up by fairy lamps. We've forgotten the whole Royal Review. We've forgotten the Royal Review, the whole thing is lit up by fairy lamps. It's fantastic, it isn't the fleet at all. It's just, it's fairyland, the whole fleet is in fairyland'.

On 1 June, the *Hood* departed Portsmouth for Gibraltar. By this point, Republican resistance in the Basque country was almost at an end, meaning there was no longer a pressing need to safeguard British shipping off northern Spain. In the Mediterranean, however, it was a different story, thanks in large part to the more proactive role of Mussolini's Italy in assisting the Nationalist forces. Arriving at Gibraltar on 5 June, Blake was appointed senior officer, Western Basin.

Before all this, however, it is worth revisiting May 1937 briefly. On 29 May, while the *Hood* was at Portsmouth, the German pocket battleship *Deutschland* lay off the island of Ibiza. On 29 May, a pair of Soviet Tupolev SB bomber attached to the Republican Air Force raided Nationalist airbases and the port of Ibiza. The *Deutschland*, anchored off Ibiza, was allegedly misidentified by the crew of the bombers as being the Nationalist cruiser *Canarias*. The Soviet pilots released their bombs on the *Deutschland* sparking large fires and killing thirty-one German sailors and wounding a further seventy-four. The *Deutschland* quickly weighed anchor and left Ibiza. Rendezvousing with the pocket battleship *Admiral Scheer* to take on additional doctors, *Deutschland* proceeded to Gibraltar. By the time the *Deutschland* arrived at Gibraltar, the *Hood* had returned from Portsmouth. The *Hood*'s crew watched as the wounded *Deutschland* was manoeuvred carefully into the harbour. Many of the wounded German sailors were hospitalised in Gibraltar while the dead were buried with full military honours. Each of the German sailors received a cap tally from the *Hood* while £5 was donated to the *Deutschland* from

The *Hood* at Spithead ahead of the Coronation Review. (*Richard Toffolo*)

The *Hood* (background), HMS *Resolution* (centre), and the German pocket battleship *Admiral Graf Spee* (forefront) anchored at Portsmouth ahead the Coronation Fleet Review of King George VI held on 20 May 1937. The light Mediterranean grey enamel highlighted the graceful symmetrical lines of the *Hood*, which contrasts against the Home Fleet grey of HMS *Resolution*. (*Author's collection*)

The *Hood* (right) and the heavy cruiser HMS *London* (left) at the Coronation review of King George VI. (*Higginson Photo Collection/HMS Hood Association*)

The *Hood* dressed in flags at Spithead for the Coronation Review. The Japanese cruiser *Ashigara* is on the left. (*Steve Welsh, HMS Hood Association*)

The *Hood* at the Coronation Review. HMS *Repulse* can be seen on the right. (*Higginson Photo Collection/HMS Hood Association*)

The American battleship USS *New York* at the Coronation Review of King George VI. The *New York* was the sole representative of the US Navy at the review and had carried President Roosevelt's personal representative for the review, Admiral Hugh Rodman, across the Atlantic. Of note is how the *New York* is flying the Stars and Stripes from her aft flagpole and the Royal Navy's White Ensign from her aft tripod mast.

The Japanese cruiser *Ashigara* during at the Coronation Fleet review. (*Author's collection*)

The fleet dazzles in light at the Coronation Review. The *Hood* can be seen silhouetted in the centre of the image. (*Author's collection*)

The *Hood* at anchor in 1937.
(*Author's collection*)

the *Hood*'s canteen funds in a gesture of sympathy. No sooner had the *Deutschland* moored alongside the *Hood* then Blake was received aboard by *Kapitän zur See* Wennecker. In boarding the *Deutschland*, Blake became the first British flag officer to set foot aboard a commissioned ship of the German Navy since 1912. Following a tour of the ship, tea and cakes were served before Blake was paid the honour of being rowed back to the *Hood* by a ten-man oar cutter crewed entirely by German officers. The following day, Blake extended an invitation to Wennecker and the entire off-duty watch of the *Deutschland* to dine in the *Hood*.

Ultimately, Blake would not enjoy his appointment in the Mediterranean long for on 20 June, he was admitted to Bighi hospital in Valetta after suffering an embolism following his accustomed early morning pulling in a skiff. Five days after being admitted to Bighi hospital, he was forced to strike his flag to be replaced by Vice-Admiral Andrew Browne Cunningham, who was known affectionately to his men as ABC. During the Second World War, Cunningham would cement his reputation in history during battles in the Mediterranean and would go on to succeed Admiral Sir Dudley Pound as First Sea Lord. On 15 July, while the *Hood* was in Malta's Grand Harbour, Cunningham arrived on board to begin his tenure as Admiral Commanding Battlecruiser Squadron.

One of Cunningham's first decisions aboard the *Hood* was to take the ship to sea for gunnery trials. The exercise almost ended in tragedy when the minelayer

Protector towing a target found herself on the receiving end of the *Hood*'s 15-inch shells. Fred Coombs who was stationed in 'B' turret later recalled the incident:

> We normally did a shoot while heading on the same course as the target but this time Cutts [Cunningham] had us heading into the sea and on the opposite course to make things harder. In 'B' turret we had loaded both guns, but in salvoes only fired the left gun, waiting for a range correction before firing the right gun. This time all four shells landed round the *Protector* and instead of a range correction we got a 'Cease fire' and did not fire the right gun. That finished the shoot. According to the ship's signalmen on the bridge we received a signal from the *Protector* reporting that the ship's cat had shit eight of its nine lives, but if Cutts Cunningham saw it he was not amused. He was too busy making sure that heads rolled, which suited us as we were too far down the ladder for it to reach us. The buzz went round that 15 degrees left throw-off had been set on the sights but that, when the run had been altered to the following course, some idiot had ordered 15 degrees left throw-off which had only set them straight. But whatever it was we had enough trouble in unloading the right-hand gun.[17]

From 26 July until around 20 August, the *Hood* was taken in hand for repairs. On 27 July, a wedding was held aboard the *Hood* when Commander James Gould of the *River*-class submarine HMS *Thames* married Miss Anne Pridham, the eldest daughter of Captain Pridham. On 24 August, the *Hood* departed Malta from Argostóli, Greece. On 30 August, the *Hood* departed Argostóli for Split, Yugoslavia, where she would anchor from 1 September until the 8th before returning once again to Malta. The *Hood* would remain at Malta until 30 September during which time she was taken into the Admiralty Floating Dock at Parlatorio, Grand Harbour.

In September 1937, the war against merchant shipping and warships undertaken by submarines and aircraft of Italy led to France and Britain convening a conference in the Swiss town of Nyon. The conference was boycotted by both Italy and Germany, both of whom had withdrawn their forces from the naval patrols conducted by the non-intervention Committee in June following losing men to air attacks undertaken by Republican forces. At the conference, the British and French delegates agreed that declared routes for merchant shipping should be introduced and that these routes should be patrolled by ships and aircraft with orders to meet force with force. So it was that out of Malta, the *Hood* was directed to the Western Basin of the Mediterranean where she would spend her time between Arzew, Algeria; Gibraltar; Tangier; and Palma. Admiral Cunningham commented:

> We made Palma our headquarters, with periodical visits to Valencia and Barcelona to visit the British consuls and the British minister, and to allay the fears of the latter. Almost every day we spent at Palma squadrons of S.79's roared overhead to bomb Valencia or Barcelona, though when we lay off these ports the bombers never came, so the inhabitants were glad of our arrival.[18]

The wedding party of Commander James Gould and Anne Pridham aboard the *Hood* on 27 July 1937. (*HMS Hood Association*)

One of the *Hood*'s 5.5-inch guns being removed while at Malta, 1937. The ship in the background is HMS *Renown*. (*Douglas Sizer Photo Collection, HMS Hood Association*)

The *Hood* off Split, Yugoslavia between 1 and 8 September 1937. (*Richard Toffolo*)

The patrols conducted by the *Hood* were not, however, without incident. On a number of occasions, the *Hood* was buzzed by aircraft of the *Regia Aeronautica* with Cunningham ordering the *Hood*'s guns to be manned and trained against the offending aircraft. On 4 November, the *Hood* departed Palma for Malta where she arrived two days later. Christmas and New Year were spent at Malta with the *Hood* being taken in hand for docking and a refit between 8 November and 16 December.

The *Hood* began 1938 by sailing to Palma on 5 January and then on to Barcelona. By and large, January was spent sailing between Palma, Barcelona, and Valencia with occasional stops in Marseilles. Things could have been different, however. On 3 January, Chatfield met the head of the US Navy Delegation in London, Rear-Admiral Royal E. Ingersoll, to discuss the size and composition of the force Britain would send to the Far East if war broke out with Japan.[19] The meeting came three weeks after the United States had been brought to the brink of war with Japan after Japanese aircraft had bombed the gunboat USS *Panay* on the Yangtze River. Chatfield proposed that the Royal Navy would send a large fleet eastward, which would include the *Hood*. It is likely, however, that if the *Hood* was sent east to engage in hostilities against the Japanese that she would not have fared well against Japanese aircraft given the disasters that befell the Allied navies between December 1941 and the end of the battle for Java in early 1942.

On 11 February, the *Hood* was taken in hand for docking in Malta before departing Malta for Gibraltar on 3 March. Exercises were conducted out of

The *Hood* in Spanish waters, *c.* 1937. (*Author's collection*)

The *Hood* entering Grand Harbour shortly before undergoing the refit that saw her armoured torpedo director station replaced with a pop-pom bandstand. (*HMS Hood Association*)

The aft pom-pom 'Auntie' is hoisted atop its newly installed bandstand during the *Hood*'s refit in Malta between 8 November and 26 December. (*Jim Higginson/HMS Hood Association*)

Gibraltar from 7 to 11 March before the ship sailed on to Palma at the end of the month. By this point in the Spanish Civil War, the steady Nationalist advance along the Valencian coast had made the evacuation of British nationals and refugees an urgent priority for the Royal Navy. So it was that in April, the *Hood* began to embark parties of refugees from Valencia and Barcelona before sailing on to Marseilles. The *Hood* was kept busy in April 1938. Her exertions called for the occasional rest-cure, the first of which was taken at the end of April when she sailed to Golfe-Juan on the Côte d'Azur. The unique charms of the French Riviera were not lost on the ship's liberty men, many of whom were still to be found in bars and cafes on the morning of 2 May when the *Hood* was scheduled to weigh anchor. When shore parties finally did get the last of the liberty men on board, it was so the ship could sail to Corsica for a day of punitive drill while Cunningham and his staff went fishing in the mountains overlooking St Florent.

In April, one month after the German *Anschluss* of Austria, Britain signed a rapprochement with Italy. Related to this, it was decided in London that a squadron of Italian warships should be invited to Malta to reignite the cordiality that had previously existed between the Royal Navy and the *Regia Marina*. It was also decided that the *Hood*'s quarterdeck would lend itself best for such an occasion, a decision that was accepted grudgingly by Cunningham.

On the evening before the Italian arrival, there were some complications to be overcome concerning 'Y' turret, which were recalled by Louis Le Bailly:

Ships of the Mediterranean (light grey) and Atlantic Fleets (dark grey) at Gibraltar in 1938. The *Hood* is moored at the detached mole. HMS *Nelson* or *Rodney* lies at anchor astern of the *Hood*. Two *County*-class cruisers are in the harbour with a number of destroyers and an unidentified battleship. Outside the harbour, the *Repulse* and the *Renown* may be seen along the aircraft carrier HMS *Glorious*. (*Neville Chipulina*)

The *Hood* on the Côte d'Azur in April 1938. (*Author's collection*)

On the day before the arrival of the Italian Squadron the *Hood*'s Gunnery Officer had arranged that Y 15-inch turret, which had been under repair, should be trained under power from its foremost bearing to starboard to its foremost bearing to port. All went well until the pair of guns were pointing directly at the harbour entrance, through which the Italian ships would enter the next morning. And at that point the turret well and truly jammed. Whilst this obviously hostile gesture was privately approved of by the admiral, it was felt that diplomatic niceties required the turret to be in its regular fore and aft position. Indeed, if it was not so trained, then it would remain impossible either for the main canvas awning or the ceremonial red and while awning to spread for the vast cocktail party to be given in honour of the Italians. Commander E. Berthon, as the ship's technical expert, though not himself responsible for the turret machinery, was called in to advise the poor Warrant Ordnance Officer who operated under the authority of the Gunnery Officer. After a detailed examination of the roller path, Berthon gave it as his view that the correct method of curing the situation would be to remove, individually, the grossly corroded rollers from the equally corroded roller path, clean off both and then replace the rollers. Such an operation would probably occupy at least a week. But of course hours were available. Thus the only remedy seemed to be the old naval one of 'BF and BI' or Brute Force and Bloody Ignorance—although in this case the word 'ignorance' could be omitted. It was a remarkable feat. With the help of two hydraulic engines coupled to the hydraulic ring main, a block and tackle with luff upon luff led from the after capstan to the muzzle end of one 15" gun and a similar arrangement from the other muzzle, to the ship's tug-of-war team, the turret was finally brought to the fore and aft position. But the price was quite heavy. The after capstan was pulled out of line and the quarterdeck slightly buckled.[20]

In the event, the events passed off without incident.

In May 1938, Pridham ended two successful years as captain of the *Hood*. During his time as the *Hood*'s commanding officer, Pridham had achieved a marked improvement in discipline, seamanship, and fighting efficiency with the help of Commander O'Conor's replacement, Commander David Orr-Ewing. Pridham had excelled in leading by example and through providing focus, an example of which is provided in the *Hood*'s sporting achievements. Commander O'Conor had been determined to see the *Hood* excel in every sporting competition while Pridham had, as captain, focused on sailing as the essential part of good seamanship with the result that in 1938, the *Hood* won all five Mediterranean Fleet sailing cups including the Combined Fleet Sailing Regatta. Before he left the *Hood* on 20 May to be replaced by Captain Harold Walker, Pridham reminisced about his time aboard the battlecruiser:

I told Orr-Ewing about Sir Roger Backhouse's demand when I first joined the ship— to get the *Hood* out of cotton wool—and remarked that together we had succeeded in doing so and a bit more, for we could each be proud of our service in the *Hood* for the rest of our lives. We had made her not only a ship of faultless appearance but also of her ship's company a truly efficient fighting machine—our main purpose.[21]

It is unfortunate that with the clouds of war becoming ever denser, and with naval drafting, refits, and recommissioning, this level of efficiency could not be maintained.

On 24 May, the *Hood* entered a floating dock in Malta for repairs and a minor refit. Visited by King George VI on 5 June, the *Hood* departed Malta for exercises off Corfu on 28 June. In August, the *Hood* was once again active in transporting refugees from Barcelona and Valencia to Marseilles. On 9 August, after having embarked a group of 100 refugees at Caldetas, the *Hood* was called upon to rescue the crew of the SS *Lake Lugano* after she had been bombed at Palamós.

While the patrols around Spain continued, it came as something as a relief to the Admiralty when victory for the Nationalists over the Republicans promised an easing of the burden on its ships and men. In February 1938, Cunningham had been appointed Deputy Chief of the Naval Staff at the Admiralty, but it was not until 22 August that he finally struck his flag. Cunningham would leave the *Hood* with a lasting memento in the form of his coxswain, Leading Seaman Percy Walts (who during the Second World War would accompany Cunningham through all of his subsequent battles and appointments). Cunningham's replacement as Admiral Commanding Battlecruiser Squadron was Vice-Admiral Geoffrey Layton.

Before Cunningham struck his flag, there was a further incident involving the *Hood*'s gunnery which occurred on 30 July. While sailing for Crete, a 5.5-inch shoot was arranged against the dreadnought-era battleship HMS *Centurion*. The

In May 1938, after two successful years as the commanding officer of the *Hood*, Pridham left the ship. This photo shows Pridham leaving the *Hood*, rowed to the shore in one of the *Hood*'s whalers. Pridham is sitting in the stern of the whaler wearing a suit and bowler hat.

Centurion was the navy's remote-controlled target ship and was being controlled from the destroyer HMS *Shikari*. Aboard the *Shikari* was the Commander-in-Chief of the Mediterranean Fleet Admiral Dudley Pound who had hoisted his flag in the destroyer to watch the exercise. Aboard the *Hood*, confusion in identifying the target resulted in a double salvo being directed at the *Shikari*. Able Seaman Len Williams witnessed the incident:

> I was on deck watching the firing, and looking at the direction in which our guns were pointing, it was obvious that it was not going to be *Centurion* who was going to receive our bricks. Why this simple observation was not also noticed by the gunnery people heaven only knows, but it was a very long time before they lived it down. History does not record what the C-in-C might have said![22]

Pound responded to the incident with a furious string of signals and a Board of Enquiry.

Despite the burden on the Admiralty gently easing with regards to the Spanish situation with the promise of victory by one party over the other, the international situation continued to spiral towards war. On 12 September, Hitler spoke at Nuremberg. During the course of his speech, he attacked the government of Czechoslovakia over the Sudetenland, which set in motion a series of events that would result in the Munich agreement. The *Hood* had arrived at Gibraltar on 10 September, two days before Hitler delivered his speech. On 20 September, while leaving harbour she grounded. Only minor damage was caused to the ship but the grounding came at an awkward moment for the Royal Navy, which, at the height of the crisis over the Sudetenland, mobilised for war on 28 September. The *Hood* was no exception. On 28 September, she slipped out of Gibraltar in the company of the 3rd Destroyer Flotilla in order to provide an escort to the liner RMS *Aquitania*, which had been requisitioned for use as a troopship. The *Hood* had been detailed to provide escort to the *Aquitania* as it was feared that the pocket battleship *Deutschland*, which was then at Tangier, might attempt an interception. The atmosphere aboard the *Hood* was fever pitch as everyone prepared for war. Reverend Edgar Rea noted:

> When our men were feverishly fusing shells in preparation for battle, and things were at their critical worst, [Admiral Layton] handed me an unsealed envelope with the remark: 'You may find these useful one of these days'. Inside, I found the famous prayers composed respectively by Nelson and Drake before engaging the enemy. Soon afterwards, we started to raise steam. All leave was stopped and men already ashore were recalled by siren blasts. Towards evening we sailed and ordinary mortals like myself were left to guess both our destination and the nature of our mission. In view of all the circumstances most of us were convinced that a formal declaration of war was not far off.[23]

The Munich Agreement saw the *Hood* return to Gibraltar on 1 October where she was joined the following day by the *Deutschland*. It may be noted that despite the bitterness over Germany's actions regarding Austria and the Sudetenland,

Above: The *Hood* in Malta in late 1938. In the foreground is the destroyer HMS *Zulu*. (*Christopher Hancock*)

Left: Some 15-inch ammunition being hoisted aboard the *Hood* in September 1938 while at Gibraltar.

these events did not dampen the spirits between the crews of the *Hood* and the *Deutschland*. The *Deutschland* had arrived at Gibraltar to disinter and repatriate her dead from the action of 29 May 1937. Despite this, the opportunity was taken by the crews of both ships to renew acquaintances and to drink beer. In addition to this, the football teams of the two ships played one another. Fraternisation was permitted between the sailors of the two ships but there was to be no official entertaining aboard the *Hood*. Captain Walker had lost an arm during the Zeebrugge raid of April 1918 while Rear-Admiral Layton despised the Germans as a result of having been taken prisoner and forced to spend the final months of the Great War in captivity.

While the *Hood* was at anchor at Gibraltar during this period, Robert Tilburn arrived on board. Tilburn, the son of a policeman from Leeds, fell in love with the idea of life in the Royal Navy at the age of ten when he was on holiday with relatives in Portsmouth during which time he attended Navy Week and toured several ships. His father took considerable persuading, but finally relented and when he was aged sixteen, he was permitted to enter the navy as a boy seaman.

On 17 October, the *Hood* weighed anchor and departed Gibraltar for Gandia. From Gandia, the *Hood* sailed on to Palma before spending the period between 22 October and 7 November sailing between Gandia, Palma, and Marseilles. On 7 November, the *Hood* departed Marseilles for Malta where she arrived on 9 November. On 10 November, she was taken in hand for docking and repairs. The *Hood* was laid up in dock until 12 December while the repairs were exacted, including repairs to the roller path of 'Y' turret and the quarterdeck. The *Hood* would remain at Malta over the Christmas period. On New Year's Day 1939, the ship's company assembled on the forecastle for a photograph taken by R. Ellis of Valletta. Eight days later, Layton transferred his flag to HMS *Barham* before the *Hood* set sail for Gibraltar where she arrived on 13 January before moving on to Portsmouth, arriving there on 18 January. The *Hood*'s arrival at Portsmouth ended her involvement in the Spanish Civil War which by 1939 was in its closing stages and would come to a recognised conclusion on 1 April.

At no other point in her career was the *Hood* as prepared for war and as efficient as she was during the period of the Spanish Civil War from 1937 to 1938. It may be noted that during this period also, and through 1939, that owing to almost continuous service, the *Hood* was beginning to tire and show signs of strain. Between 1937 and the end of 1938, the *Hood* was taken in hand for docking and for repair work on three occasions. Dr Eric Grove commented:

> *Hood* had become a middle-aged lady by the late 1930s. Her wrinkles were beginning to show under the shining coats of battleship-grey make-up. Yet there were ever older ladies in the fleet more in need of major face lifts than her: the other two much more thinly armoured battlecruiser *Renown* and *Repulse*, for example, and the more lightly protected, fast battleships of the 'Queen Elizabeth' class. The Lords of the Admiralty were absolutely right in their priorities to put *Hood* last in the queue for rebuilding. She was one of the best all-round ships they had as she was.[24]

The football team from the *Hood* at Tangier just before playing a match against a team from the German pocket battleship *Admiral Graf Spee*. (*Chris Hancock*)

The *Hood*'s crew assemble for a photograph on the forecastle on 1 January 1939 while at anchor in Malta (*HMS Hood Association*)

14

The Gathering Storm

At Portsmouth from 18 January, the *Hood* was taken in hand for a refit on the 23rd, which included the replacement of some of her armament, repairs to her turbines, and repairs to her outer bottom. Such was the extent of the refit that it would not be fully complete until 12 August. In light of the deteriorating international situation, it was decided that most of the key ratings would be retained aboard the ship when she was undergoing the refit. Among those kept on board were the vast majority of the Engineering Department personnel. Only 500 members of the *Hood*'s crew were drafted to Portsmouth naval barracks.

While she was undergoing the refit, on 30 January, Captain Walker was transferred to HMS *Barham* where he would become the Flag Captain to Layton, the Admiral Commanding the 1st Battle Squadron. With Walker's transfer to HMS *Barham*, the *Hood* passed into the temporary command of Commander William Davis. Davis would retain command of the *Hood* until Captain Irvine Glennie assumed command on 3 May.

Born on 22 July 1892 in Scotland, Glennie was educated as an officer cadet at the Royal Naval College, Osborne and then at the Royal Naval College, Dartmouth before joining the Royal Navy in 1905. Between 1910 and 1914, Glennie saw service in home waters as well as at the China Station. During the First World War, Glennie saw service aboard destroyers in the Grand Fleet. Joining the staff of the Royal Naval College, Dartmouth from 1922 to 1924, Glennie received his first command in 1925 when appointed to a destroyer. Between 1930 and 1932, Glennie served at the Admiralty before returning to sea to command destroyers. Promoted to Captain in 1933, in 1935 he attended the Imperial Defence College. In 1936, he was appointed the flag captain of the cruiser HMS *Achilles*, part of the Royal Navy's New Zealand Squadron and Chief of Staff to the Commander-in-Chief New Zealand Squadron. In 1938, Glennie himself became Commander-in-Chief of the New Zealand Squadron and would hold this command until he was appointed to the *Hood*.

On 1 June 1939, the flag of Rear-Admiral William J. Whitworth, the Admiral Commanding the Battlecruiser Squadron, was hoisted aboard the *Hood* before she was again commissioned as flagship of the Battlecruiser Squadron the following day. The mobilisation of personnel that followed the *Hood*'s recommissioning in

At anchor, 1938. (*Christopher Hancock*)

June served to begin the dilution of her complement first with reservists and then with 'Hostilities-Only' ratings. Through June and July 1939, the *Hood* was worked up and undertook a number of sea trials, including full power trials off the Isle of Wight. A snapshot of this period of the *Hood*'s career was provided by Commander Robert T. Grogan, who filmed footage aboard the *Hood* using a 16-mm cine-camera. Grogan filmed the *Hood* in June and July 1939 off the south coast; in the summer of 1940, while the ship was in the Mediterranean; and in the autumn of 1940, when the *Hood* was at Rosyth. The intended result was to be a film to be entitled The *War from HMS Hood* with the footage set against a musical score. The footage taken by Grogan offers a glimpse into life aboard the *Hood* and at the preparations that were underway aboard the ship as war with Germany rapidly approached. Commander Grogan would ultimately go down with the *Hood* in May 1941. By the time that the *Hood* had completed her engine and compass trials off the Isle of Wight, her crew had increased to approximately 1,400, which was approximately 15 per cent higher than her ordinary peacetime levels.

Having enlisted in the Royal Navy as a boy seaman on 3 March 1938 (a mere two days after his fifteenth birthday), Ted Briggs was sent to the shore establishment HMS *Ganges* located in Shotley, Suffolk where he was given a strict but fair introduction to life in the Royal Navy. Electing to specialise in visual signalling (which constituted being able to send signals by signal lamp, flag, flag Morse, and semaphore), by the summer of 1939, he was ready for his first posting. On 29 June 1939, he was posted to HMS *Hood*:

> Much to my surprise and much to my delight, I was sent to the *Hood*. It was entirely different from training. You were treated as one of the ship's company and, although

The *Hood* in June 1939. (*Author's collection*)

the discipline was still there, it was more relaxed. As boys we had our own mess deck and you were kept segregated as much as possible within the confines of the ship. The older personnel treated you with rather amused tolerance. I joined her in June just as the *Hood* had finished her refit in Portsmouth. It was a very crowded ship ... the main problem was sleeping billets. There were not enough sling billets [for hammocks] and so you slept where you could on the mess deck tables or on the deck.[1]

On 13 August, in the company of HMS *Courageous*, the *Hood* sailed to Scapa Flow where she arrived on 14 August. On the 16th, she sailed to Rosyth where she briefly dropped anchor before returning to Scapa Flow. With war just over the horizon, from 17 August until 20 August, the *Hood* sailed between Scapa Flow, Rosyth, and Invergordon against the passage of German surface raiders into the Atlantic. For the men aboard the *Hood*, this was a period of ceaseless drills, exercises, and manoeuvres as the ship worked up to war readiness. On 24 August, the *Hood* sailed to Scapa Flow where she dropped anchor on 25 August. At Scapa Flow, the strength of the Royal Navy's Home Fleet gathered in preparation for war. Aboard the *Hood*, a ship that had spent her career being cleaned and repainted as a gleaming showpiece of the navy, a transformation was taking place.

Unit by unit the biggest fleet I have ever seen gathered at Scapa. Battleships, cruisers, carriers, destroyers came and went ... No longer were there great wide open spaces below decks: the full wartime complement of just over fourteen hundred were embarked. At night hammocks were slung in every passageway, in every nook and cranny. Sleeping space was guarded jealously, and once a claim had been staked, it was rarely relaxed ... Black-out curtains were rigged, and 'darken ship' was piped at sunset. Polishing was down to the minimum, and apart from the working parts of the guns, equipment that sparkled was dulled by gallons of grey paint. The once white decks began to take on a greyish tint, and most of the other woodwork was toned down. All the hangings and 'niceties'—including the many mess pianos—were landed. The *Hood* was never to know peace again.[2]

The *Hood* passing Southsea, 10 August 1939. On the right in the background is the
Isle of Wight. (*Denis Domsby, HMS Hood Association*)

The *Hood* departing Scapa Flow in August 1939. Note the crewmen lining the rails.
(*Author's collection*)

15

'Commence Hostilities Against Germany'

On 31 August 1939, the Royal Navy mobilised for war. As part of this mobilisation the *Hood* and the other ships of the Battlecruiser Squadron—HMS *Renown* and HMS *Repulse*—accompanied by three destroyers, departed Scapa Flow to undertake a patrol between Iceland and the Faeroe Islands.

On 1 September 1939, Germany invaded Poland. At 4 a.m., the *Hood*'s crew went to action stations while German troops, tanks and other vehicles were filing across the German–Polish border. As details of the German invasion became clear, the British Cabinet, working in conjunction with the Foreign Office, spent most of 1 September drafting an ultimatum to Hitler demanding the withdrawal of German forces from Polish soil. The ultimatum, which was handed by the British Ambassador to Germany, Sir Neville Henderson, to the German Foreign Minister, Joachim von Ribbentrop, demanded a withdrawal of German forces by 3 September. There was no response from the German government to either of the British or French ultimatums. Hitler still maintained his conviction that the British and French would lose their nerve and would back down, and that German forces would be allowed to continue their advance through Poland. Against this backdrop, Sir Neville Henderson carried out his instructions to the letter. Hitler's conviction, reinforced heavily by von Ribbentrop's assurances that the British would back down and would not go to war over Poland, was shattered, and the Führer was left clearly stunned.[1] On the morning of 3 September, Henderson delivered a text to the German government. After the text had been read out to Hitler, there followed a long silence. Finally, Hitler turned to von Ribbentrop and, breaking the silence, angrily demanded 'What now?' Von Ribbentrop had constantly assured Hitler that Britain would not go to war over Poland and was now left without an answer.

In London at 11.15 a.m., from 10 Downing Street, Neville Chamberlain broadcast to the British people, and to an appalled world, that since 11 a.m., Britain was once again at war with Germany.

Ted Briggs recalled the moment on 3 September when war was declared on Germany:

We were actually at sea when the declaration of war was made. The captain broadcast that we were at war and as flagship of the ships at sea we made the general signal to the fleet to commence hostilities against Germany. One of the jobs I had was making that signal by semaphore from the director of the *Hood*.[2]

Briggs would go on to recall the moment in more detail:

The flag 'E' was hoisted as a preliminary for a general semaphore message, and Chief Yeoman George Thomas ordered: 'Briggs, get a pair of hand-flags and get up to the fifteen-inch director and show up 46'. It was with a strange sort of pride and yet a sinking feeling in my belly that I spelt out to the fleet: 'Commence hostilities against Germany'. Over the tannoy to all parts of the ship came Prime Minister Chamberlain's almost somnolent, low-key announcement that Britain's ultimatum to Germany to withdraw from the invasion of Poland had expired.[3]

The news that Britain was at war with Germany was received with mixed reactions below decks as recalled by Lieutenant Stanley Geary:

A prominent member of the crew thus-described the scene, 'I remember passing along the Mess Deck and everyone was crowded round the loudspeakers, waiting for the news which told us we were at war. There was much talk as to how long it would last, and one heard such phrases as 'we shall have them whacked by Christmas' and 'what battlewagons have the Jerries got?'.[4]

On 6 September, the *Hood* was back at Scapa Flow. Between 6 and 8 September, the *Hood*'s crew undertook anti-aircraft drills, washed the decks, conducted 4-inch gunnery practices, and mended clothing before putting to sea once more in the company of the *Renown*, the cruisers *Edinburgh* and *Belfast*, and four destroyers to take up a patrol line between Iceland and the Faeroe Islands. While on patrol, on 11 September, the Commander-in-Chief of the Home Fleet, Admiral Sir Charles Forbes, sent a signal to Rear-Admiral Whitworth ordering him to return to Scapa Flow with the entire Battlecruiser Squadron. The *Hood* was to be found at anchor in Scapa Flow the following day. While at Scapa Flow, gunnery and spotting drills were undertaken, the ship was washed, and a cinema rigged before she weighed anchor; in the company of the *Rodney* and four destroyers, she set a course for Loch Ewe.

The *Hood* and the *Rodney* arrived at Loch Ewe on 15 September and would remain there until 20 September, where the *Hood*'s crew were granted recreation time. In addition to this, the ship's company undertook a cleaning routine. On 17 September, the First Lord of the Admiralty, Winston Churchill, accompanied by Admiral Forbes, visited the ship. Departing Loch Ewe on 20 September, the *Hood* returned to Scapa Flow before putting to sea to provide cover for a raid in the Skagerrak. She returned to anchor at Scapa Flow on 23 September.

On 20 September 1939, the submarine HMS *Spearfish*, under the command of Lieutenant J. H. Eaden, left Dundee, Scotland to embark on her second war

The *Hood* silhouetted beneath a 15-inch gun of HMS *Renown*, 1939.

The *Hood* at Scapa Flow, 1939. (*Author's collection*)

patrol off the coast of Denmark. On 24 September, while off Horns Reef, the *Spearfish* was depth charged by German warships. Damaged, the *Spearfish* managed to evade the German vessels that were intent on sinking her and during the early morning hours of 25 September managed to transmit a signal requesting assistance. That same day, in the company of the battleships *Nelson* and *Rodney*, HMS *Repulse*, the aircraft carrier *Ark Royal*, the ships of the 18th Cruiser Squadron, and destroyers, the *Hood* left Scapa Flow to provide distant cover for the rescue of the *Spearfish*.

While at sea on 26 September, the battle group was sighted by aircraft from the Luftwaffe's *Kampfgeschwader* 26 and *Kampfgeschwader* 30. In the air attacks that followed, the *Hood* was struck by a 550-lb (250 kg) bomb. Many sources state that the aircraft was a Junkers Ju 88, while Ted Briggs cited the aircraft as being a Heinkel He-111. Owing to the fact that *Kampfgeschwader* 26 operated He-111s and *Kampfgeschwader* 30 Ju 88s at the time, it is difficult to pin the aircraft type down. The bomb served to damage the ship's condensers, caused flooding to the port bulge amidships, sprung some rivets, and caused shrapnel damage. The episode was recalled by Ted Briggs:

The first real action we saw was shortly after the commencement [of hostilities] when the submarine *Spearfish* was damaged and the Home Fleet went to sea to escort her back in the hope of tempting the German fleet to come out. The German fleet didn't come out, but the German air force did and the carrier *Ark Royal* and *Hood* were singled out for attacks. *Ark Royal* consistently had many near misses. They got a very near miss on *Hood* which peppered the port side with shrapnel. I was on the flag deck and actually watched the Heinkel that dived on us. I saw this black object leave the aircraft, and it didn't register with me what was happening until it exploded just at the side of us and I realised we might easily have been hit.[5]

The following day, the *Spearfish* was escorted into the Firth of Forth whereupon she docked at Rosyth, bringing to an end her second war patrol. The *Hood*, meanwhile, returned to Scapa Flow.

The *Hood* remained at Scapa Flow until 1 October when she sailed to Loch Ewe accompanied by HMS *Nelson* before returning once more to the Flow four days later. While at Scapa Flow, the *Hood* was paid a brief visit by King George VI before she weighed anchor on 8 October accompanied by HMS *Repulse*, the cruisers *Sheffield* and *Aurora*, and four destroyers to intercept a German squadron comprised of the battleship *Gneisenau*, the cruiser *Köln*, and nine destroyers that were reported to be sailing off Obrestad Lighthouse, Norway. The German squadron eluded the British force prompting a return to anchor. Further patrols followed for the *Hood*: 16 October saw her providing cover to armed merchant cruisers of the Northern Patrol in the company of the battleships *Rodney* and *Nelson*, the aircraft carrier *Furious*, the cruisers *Aurora* and *Belfast*, and nine destroyers; 23 October saw her on patrol in the Norwegian sea with the *Rodney* and the *Nelson* to search for the merchant ship *City of Flint* off the Lofoten

Taken from the flight deck of HMS *Furious*, this image shows the *Nelson*, *Rodney*, and *Hood* underway. The original image caption states that the ships are passing into Invergordon; however, it is more likely that this photograph was taken on 5 October 1940 and that the ships are departing Loch Ewe *en route* to Scapa Flow. (*Beeldbank WO2, NIOD*)

Islands, which had been intercepted and seized by the German pocket battleship *Deutschland*. In addition to this, the *Hood* also provided cover to an iron ore convoy sailing from Narvik to the Firth of Forth. While on patrol, on 30 October, the group (comprising the *Hood*, *Nelson*, and *Rodney* as well as escorting destroyers) was subjected to an unsuccessful attack by *U-56*.

U-boats posed a particular threat to capital ships like the *Hood*, *Nelson*, and *Rodney*. Len Nichol, a Marine gunner aboard HMS *Rodney*, recalled a submarine scare when his ship was sailing in the company of the *Hood*:

> *Rodney* sailed with her a couple of times in the North Sea in the early part of the war. One time I spotted a broom handle in the water and somebody thought it was a periscope. The whole fleet dispersed at different angles. I watched *Hood* pull away at full speed and it was a terrific sight to watch. She certainly left us far behind that particular morning.[6]

On 31 October, the *Hood* docked at Greenock where she was again visited by Winston Churchill. During the course of Churchill's visit to the ship, Commander Grogan caught a moment with the First Lord and told him that the situation with the *Hood*'s condensers as a result of the damage suffered on 26 September along with her unremitting service through home waters could be ignored no longer—that the ship's speed was down to a maximum of 27 knots and other problems were being exacerbated by almost continuous service. The beginning of

November was a busy period for the ship. Departing Greenock on 2 November with HMS *Nelson* and other vessels of the Home Fleet to cover an operation of the Northern Patrol to the west of the Hebrides and in the Norwegian Sea, 4 November saw the *Hood* making dispositions to intercept the German vessel SS *New York*. Two days later the *Hood* was to be found providing cover to the convoy ON-1, the first outbound Scandinavian convoy of the war. She briefly docked at Rosyth on 9 November before weighing anchor later that same day to sail to Plymouth escorted by the destroyers *Fearless*, *Intrepid*, and *Ivanhoe*. Arriving at Plymouth on 11 November, two days later, she was taken in hand for repairs at Devonport. While at Devonport, the ship's boilers were to be cleaned and a week's leave granted to the crew. On 20 November, shortly after the second watch of leave goers had gone ashore, they were recalled. News had been received that the merchant cruiser HMS *Rawalpindi* had been sunk. Her refit uncompleted, on 25 November, the *Hood* put to sea to search for the *Deutschland* which it was presumed had sunk the *Rawalpindi*. In reality, the slayer of the *Rawalpindi* was not the *Deutschland* but the *Scharnhorst* and the *Gneisenau*. To make up the numbers aboard the *Hood*, 150 men from Devonport Barracks had been drafted aboard shortly before she weighed anchor.

The *Hood* sailed north to hunt for the German surface raider(s) and took up a patrol line to the south of Iceland. The *Hood* and her escorting destroyers combined forces with ships of the French Navy: the battleship *Dunkerque*, the light cruisers *Georges Leygues* and *Montcalm*, and two destroyers. This combined force operated under the command of Vice-Admiral Marcel Gensoul before the *Hood* and her destroyers put in at Greenock on 2 December.

The *Hood* was soon once again on patrol to the north of the Faeroes. While on patrol, from 5 to 8 December, she provided distant cover to a Norwegian convoy. On 9 December, the *Hood* was ordered back to Greenock where she arrived two days later. On 13 December, she departed Greenock in the company of the battleships *Warspite* and *Barham* and seven destroyers to intercept a group of German vessels comprised of the cruisers *Köln*, *Leipzig*, and *Nürnberg* plus five destroyers which were reported to be in the North Sea. Having put to sea to intercept the German warships, the British battle group was rerouted to provide cover to convoy TC-1, the first Canadian troop convoy. To the north of Ireland on 16 December, the British squadron linked up with TC-1, which was escorted into Greenock the following day. On 23 December, the *Hood* provided support to HMS *Edinburgh* and *Glasgow* in escorting convoy DHN-6, which was loaded with arms for Finland. Back at anchor on 24 December, the *Hood* embarked on another patrol on 27 December, undertaking a patrol from the area to the west of the Hebrides to the north of the Shetlands.

New Year 1940 found the *Hood* at sea providing escort to another convoy before anchoring at Greenock on 5 January until the 15th. Weighing anchor on 15 January, the *Hood* accompanied HMS *Warspite* and the ships of the 8th Destroyer Flotilla on a patrol around the Shetland–Faeroes gap. Following undertaking gunnery trials on 22 January, the *Hood* returned to anchor on 24 January until

Taken from the French battleship *Dunkerque*, this photo shows the *Hood* operating in heavy seas to the south of Iceland. Apparently, this photo was made available to members of the *Hood*'s company at the suggestion of Vice-Admiral Gensoul as a gesture of goodwill between the two ships. (*Richard Toffolo*)

Here, the *Hood* can be seen sailing in heavy sea with her main battery trained to port. Owing to the absence of the UP launched atop 'B' turret, it is possible to date this photo as being taken prior to April 1940. It is likely that this photograph was taken on 22 January 1940 when the *Hood* undertook gunnery trials. (*Richard Toffolo*)

9 February when, again in the company of HMS *Warspite*, she proceeded to the area to the west of the Hebrides to provide cover to a convoy from Scandinavia. On 16 February, the *Hood*, the *Warspite*, and their destroyer escorts headed east towards Norway in order to provide support to a small group of destroyers under the command of Captain Philip Vian, which intercepted and boarded the German merchant ship *Altmark*. The *Altmark* had supplied the pocket battleship *Admiral Graf Spee* during her sortie through the South Atlantic in 1939 before she was cornered by a force of British cruisers off South America and scuttled in Montevideo harbour. When boarded by Vian's force, the *Altmark* was carrying a number of British merchantmen prisoners who had been taken off their vessels by the crew of the *Graf Spee* before their ships were sunk. Intercepted in Norwegian waters, the *Altmark* incident is often cited as one of the reasons behind the German decision to invade Denmark and Norway.

From 18 to 19 February, the *Hood* anchored at Greenock. In February 1940, while at Greenock, amidst her constant and fruitless war patrols, the *Hood* became the first ship in the Royal Navy to be fitted with a degaussing coil around her hull. The coil served to neutralise the magnetic field around the ship and thus proved an effective counter to German magnetic mines. The coil, formed from 100 feet of 2-inch copper cable was manhandled into position before being stapled to the ship's side during the course of several days and nights of work. The degaussing coil would not remain a secret for long, however. The liner RMS *Queen Elizabeth* had been fitted with a similar coil ahead of her maiden voyage across the Atlantic to New York. When the *Queen Elizabeth* arrived in New York on 7 March, the mysterious band around the hull was unmasked by the American press. The coil required deperming when the *Hood* entered dry dock in order to remove the accumulated magnetism of the ship. The deperming process was recalled by Leading Seaman Len Williams:

> We had to 'deperm' the hull and structure whilst she was in dry dock. This was done to remove the magnetism which had been put into the ship by our degaussing generators. In order to remove this magnetic effect, thick heavy cables were put around the ship in an opposite direction to the run of the degaussing circuit, i.e. the cables were run under the keel and up over the deck and bridge structure; and continued along the whole length of the ship until we were lying in the spiral of heavy cables. A heavy electric current was then passed through the circuit for a few seconds, this de-magnetising the ship. It was heavy, backbreaking work, hauling the cables across the bottom of the dock, and up the sides of the ship, and it took us a week to complete the job, and all for a few seconds' flash of current.[7]

By the beginning of 1940, the *Hood*'s speed was down to 26.5 knots and her long overdue refit could not be overlooked any longer. On 21 February, as the *Hood* was at sea, covering convoy DN-14 to the north-east of the Shetlands, the Admiralty was making preparations for the *Hood* to undergo her refit in Malta:

The *Hood* in 1940. (*Christopher Hancock*)

Taken at some point between 25 August and 18 December 1940, this image shows the *Hood* at Scapa Flow with her degaussing coil clearly visible along the forecastle deck. (*Michael Mason, HMS Hood Association*)

The *Hood* at speed, *c*. 1940. (*Author's collection*)

The *Hood* in a heavy sea, *c*. 1940.

Owing to congestion in home yards it will be necessary to carry out retubing of condensers of the *Hood* at Malta where she can be taken in hand about 3 March. Maximum time required for this work is 45 days. the *Hood* should be sailed for Malta after *Renown* has finished giving leave.[8]

In the event, this order was rescinded and the *Hood* soldiered on with countless patrols and escort details. With relations with Italy deteriorating, on 29 March, the decision was taken not to refit the *Hood* at Malta; instead she was to be taken in hand in Devonport. Arriving on 2 April, she was finally taken in hand two days later. On 12 April, with relations with Italy rapidly deteriorating and with Mussolini becoming increasingly belligerent, Churchill wrote to the Third Sea Lord Controller of the Navy, Vice-Admiral Bruce Fraser, 'The most intense efforts should be concentrated upon the *Hood*, as we may need all our strength to meet an Italian threat or attack. Pray let me have a time-table showing when she will be ready for sea.'[9] The following day, Churchill was informed that what he believed would be a thirty-five-day refit would, in fact, take much longer. Needless to say, he was not best pleased, writing to Forbes and Fraser:

This is a very different story to what was told [to] me when it was proposed to repair this ship at Malta. I was assured that the whole operation would take thirty-five days, and that the ship would never be at more than thirty-five days' notice, and that only for a short time. When I asked the other day how long it would take to bring the *Hood* back into service I was told fourteen days. I take it therefore she has been above twenty days under repair at present, to which must now be added seventeen days more in April and thirty-one in May—total sixty-eight days—or double what I was told before this vital ship was laid up in this critical period. Pray give me an explanation of this extraordinary change. Moreover, after these sixty-eight days there are to be fourteen days repairing her reserve feed tanks—total therefore eighty-two days, or three months at the most critical period in the war.

The engineer in charge of the *Hood* assured me when I was last at Scapa that they had found out the way to nurse her defective condenser tubes so as to get twenty-seven knots, and that there was no reason why she could not remain in commission and carry on for six months.

I much regret not to have been more accurately informed, in view of the Italian attitude.[10]

It would appear that when it came to his 'vital ship' Churchill had leaned too heavily on the assurances of Commander Grogan from October 1939 as opposed to the very different state presented during his visit of 8-9 March. The *Hood*'s refit kept her out of action for a total of seventy-four days, during which time the German occupation of Denmark and Norway had begun, France had been invaded and Churchill had become Prime Minister. During the course of her refit, the *Hood*'s condensers were retubed, her remaining 5.5-inch guns were replaced with three dual purpose 4-inch guns, and five Unrotated Projectile launchers were

Captain Glennie and the *Hood* crew are mustered on the forecastle in what is believed to be the last full-crew photograph taken of the *Hood*. While many of the men captured in this picture would be posted away from the ship over the next year, it should be noted that a significant proportion of the men in this image were probably aboard the ship on 24 May 1941. (*HMS Hood Association*)

fitted. As the refit was underway, fourteen days of leave was granted to the crew, taken a watch at a time.

On 9 April, German forces occupied Denmark and landed in Norway at Narvik, Trondheim, Bergen, Kristiansand, and Egersund. With the German position in Norway precarious, the War Cabinet was resolved to dispatch troops to Norway to combat the German landings. Among the plans formulated was a series of landings at Namsos and Åndalsnes. The landing at Åndalsnes was given the codename Operation Primrose. In order to help man this expedition the government turned to the Royal Navy. So it was that on the morning of 13 April, while in hand for repairs, orders entitled 'Primrose' began to arrive aboard the *Hood*. Within a few hours, the ship's old 3.7-inch howitzer had been landed and a force of 250 officers and men under the command of Lieutenant-Commander C. A. Audrey had been convened. Royal Marines comprised two-thirds of the 250-man expeditionary force from the *Hood*. At midnight, they boarded a train to Rosyth with an assortment of weapons and stores where they boarded the sloop *Black Swan* alongside contingents of men from HMS *Barham* and the *Nelson*.

The *Hood*'s men landed at Åndalsnes on 17 April. On 19 April, the *Hood*'s howitzer detachment numbering nineteen men assisted in the capture of forty-five German *Fallschirmjäger*, helmets from whom ended up on the ship's mess decks. Another contingent of men from the *Hood* were sent to Ålesund where they assisted in setting up a number of 4-inch gun battery positions while the ship's marines defended the improvised airfield on Lake Lesjaskog. The Germans soon learned that the area around Åndalsnes was under British occupation with the result that from 20 April, the men came under almost constant Luftwaffe bombardment. As the days wore on, the Allied offensive began to stagnate with the result that evacuation became inevitable. On 29 April, the *Hood*'s howitzer detachment was evacuated aboard the sloop *Fleetwood*. They were followed the following day by the main body of the *Hood*'s detachment who were evacuated aboard the cruiser HMS *Galatea*. On 1 May, the last remaining members of the *Hood*'s detachment were evacuated from Norway. Three weeks after leaving the *Hood*, they arrived back at Plymouth. Operation Primrose cost the *Hood* four men, all of whom were taken prisoner, and the howitzer, which was thrown over the side of a cliff to deny its use to the Germans.[11]

On 27 May, the *Hood* departed Plymouth and sailed to Liverpool accompanied by the destroyers *Escort*, *Wolverine*, and *Witch*. Arriving on 28 May, the *Hood* anchored at Liverpool until 12 June. At Liverpool, the ship was taken in hand for additional refitting and repairs in the Gladstone Dock. While in hand for repairs in the Gladstone dock, leave was granted to the crew. In addition to this anti-aircraft, small calibre and main armament drills were all carried out. For many members of the ship's company this period in dock was uncomfortable as a wave of stomach illnesses swept across the ship. With no working bathroom facilities on board, the crew were forced to make for the dockside facilities. On 11 June, a boarding party from the *Hood* captured the Italian merchant vessel SS *Erica*. Two days earlier, Mussolini had stood on the balcony of the Palazzo Venezia to inform the Italian people that from midnight, Italy would be at war with both France and Great Britain. For the *Hood*, a new chapter in the war was beginning.

16

Mers el-Kébir

The *Hood* departed Liverpool on 12 June in the company of three Canadian destroyers to rendezvous with what has been called 'the greatest troop convoy of the war', US-3. Comprised of the *Queen Mary, Empress of Britain, Empress of Canada, Aquitania, Andes,* and *Mauretania,* US-3 embarked some 26,000 Australian and New Zealand troops who, while too late to play a part in the battle of France, were destined to play a pivotal role in the war in the desert. The *Hood* and the destroyers rendezvoused with US-3 and the convoy's escorts, the aircraft carrier *Argus,* and the cruisers *Cumberland, Dorsetshire,* and *Shropshire* in the Bay of Biscay on 14 June and escorted the convoy safely into the Clyde two days later.

The *Hood* remained at Greenock until 18 June, but it quickly became apparent that something was afoot on the evening of 17 June when liberty men were returned and Captain Glennie broadcast to the ship's company. Unlike in other addresses to the ship's company, Glennie did not provide the crew with any indication of where they were bound; rather, he told the crew to prepare for sea and for steam to be raised. At 2.30 a.m. on 18 June, special sea duty men were ordered to their stations. Two hours later, the *Hood* thundered through the submarine boom from the Cloch lighthouse to Dunoon escorted by the *Frazer, St Laurent, Wanderer, Skeena,* and *Restigouche.* With the *Hood* and the destroyers sailing a south-westerly course, thoughts immediately turned to the expected German invasion of Britain, and that the *Hood* would be involved in the defence of Southern England—how wrong those thoughts were. During the afternoon of 18 June, the *Hood* joined HMS *Ark Royal* in the Bay of Biscay. It was then that Glennie announced to the ship's company that in the company of the *Ark Royal* and their destroyer screen, they were to head to Gibraltar where they were to form a new fleet in the Mediterranean called Force 'H'. Force 'H' was first constituted as a hunting group during the Royal Navy's hunt for the German pocket battleship *Admiral Graf Spee.* The news came as something of a surprise to the men aboard the *Hood* as no preparations for operations in the Mediterranean had been made. None of the crew had been issued with their white uniforms typically worn when in the Mediterranean and tropical climates; rather, they possessed clothing consisting of balaclavas and thick, woollen garments.

The liner *Empress of Britain*, part of convoy US-3 carrying 26,000 Australian and New Zealand troops arrives at Greenock, with the *Hood* visible in the background, 14 June 1940.

It was at 6.36 p.m. on 22 June 1940 near Compiègne, France, that officials of the Third Reich and the French Third Republic signed an armistice bringing an end to the Battle of France, which established a German occupation zone in Northern and Western France that encompassed the ports on France's Atlantic Coast and the English Channel. The remainder was to be 'freely' governed by the French. The new government of France under Marshal Philippe Pétain established itself in the town of Vichy, leading to the new French state to take the name of Vichy France.

Following the fall of France and the signing of the armistice between France and Germany, the British War Cabinet was apprehensive about the possibility of Germany acquiring the ships of the French Navy through the Vichy government. The combination of the French Navy (the *Marine Nationale*) and the *Kriegsmarine* would serve to tip the balance of power at sea into the favour of the Axis powers, threatening British Atlantic trade and communications with the remainder of the British Empire. That the armistice terms had a paragraph stating that the German government 'solemnly and firmly declared that it had no intention of making demands regarding the French fleet during the peace negotiations', and that a similar term existed in the terms of the French armistice with Italy, the British War Cabinet felt that this could not guarantee the neutralisation of the French fleet. On 24 June, the Commander-in-Chief of the French fleet, Admiral François Darlan, assured Churchill that the French fleet would under no circumstances fall into German hands. Churchill was not convinced and ordered that a demand be made to the *Marine Nationale* to either sail to British ports and join the Royal Navy or face neutralisation in some way to ensure that it did not fall into German hands.[1] To Churchill, the fate of the French fleet carried with it the hinge of the world naval balance. 'Were it to fall into German or Italian hands the Mediterranean would become an Axis lake and the already doubtfully secure British command of the Atlantic would be undermined'.[2]

In a speech made in the House of Commons, Churchill told of how the French armistice with Germany was a betrayal of the Allied agreement, which forbade each country from surrendering to Germany without first notifying its allies. This apparent betrayal by the French government, coupled with the Nazi history of not respecting previous agreements, led Churchill to spell out the practical consequences of Article 8 of the Franco-German armistice terms before the House of Commons on 25 June:

> We must look to our own salvation and effectual defence, upon which not only British but French, European, and world-wide fortunes depend. The safety of Great Britain and the British Empire is powerfully, though not decisively, affected by what happens to the French Fleet … It was, therefore, 'with grief and amazement'—to quote the words of the Government statement which we issued on Sunday—that I read Article 8 of the Armistice terms.
>
> This Article, to which the French Government have subscribed, says that the French Fleet, excepting that part left free for the safeguarding of French interests in the Colonial Empire, shall be collected in ports to be specified and there demobilised and disarmed under German or Italian control. From this text it is clear that the French war vessels under this Armistice pass into German and Italian control while fully armed. We note, of course, in the same Article the solemn declaration of the German Government that they have no intention of using them for their own purposes during the war. What is the value of that? Ask half a dozen countries what is the value of such a solemn assurance. Furthermore, the same Article 8 of the Armistice excepts from the operation of such assurances and solemn declarations those units necessary for coast surveillance and minesweeping. Under this provision it would be possible for the German Government to reserve, ostensibly for coast surveillance, any existing units of the French Fleet. Finally, the Armistice can at any time be voided on any pretext of non-observance, and the terms of Armistice explicitly provide for further German claims when any peace between Germany and France comes to be signed. Such, in very brief epitome, are the salient points in this lamentable and also memorable episode, of which, no doubt, a much fuller account will be given by history.[3]

During the days and months between the French declaration of war on 3 September 1939 and the signing of the armistice, the French fleet had seen little fighting and was largely intact. Approximately 40 per cent of the fleet was at anchor in Toulon, while a further 40 per cent was at anchor in harbours in French North Africa. The remaining 20 per cent of the French fleet was to be found in British ports, Alexandria harbour, and in the French West Indies.

Although Churchill was fearful of the ships of the French fleet being put into action, either through the application of pressure to the Vichy government or by Axis forces forcibly seizing the vessels, Axis leaders did not, in fact, intend to employ a combined Franco–German–Italian force. While Mussolini and officers within the ranks of the *Kriegsmarine* encouraged the seizure of the French fleet, Hitler feared that the French fleet would join the Royal Navy and would be used against Germany and her U-boats in the Atlantic if any attempt were made to seize the ships. It is somewhat ironic that both Churchill and Hitler viewed the French fleet as a potential threat. Vichy French leaders, including Pétain had, for their part, used the mere existence of the fleet, and the threat of its defection, as leverage against Germany to keep their forces out of the unoccupied zone of France and the North African colonies. Under the armistice agreements the French had the right to man their own naval vessels and Darlan had, prior to the surrender of France, ordered the Atlantic bases to be destroyed and the fleet to sail to Toulon. In addition to this, Darlan had ordered his Admirals to scuttle their ships should German forces attempt to seize them.[4]

So it was that the British were faced with the situation of having the French Atlantic ports in German hands at a time when the Royal Navy needed to protect the convoys carrying supplies coming from across the Atlantic against German surface raiders and U-boats, keep the *Kriegsmarine* out of the Mediterranean, restrict the activities of the Italian navy within those waters, and blockade the Vichy ports.

On 25 June, Force 'H' was dispatched on what has been described as a 'panic mission'. With the entry of Italy into the war on the side of Germany, the Admiralty began to take steps to fill the void that was created by the collapse of French power in the western Mediterranean. So it was that Force 'H' was transformed into an independent command that was to operate throughout the Mediterranean from Gibraltar and became directly responsible to the Admiralty in London. Force 'H' occupied an odd place within the Royal Navy's chain of command. Normal practice at the time was to have naval stations and fleets across the globe whose commanders reported to a Flag Officer, who in turn reported to the First Sea Lord. In the case of Force 'H', however, based at Gibraltar, there was already a flag officer: the Flag Officer Commanding North Atlantic. So it was that the commander of Force 'H' reported directly to the First Sea Lord. Force 'H' was placed under the command of Vice-Admiral James Somerville.

On the face of it, Somerville was a strange choice for the Admiralty. From a respectable family, part of the Somerset squirearchy, Somerville had attended Dartmouth Naval College in 1897 at the age of fifteen. Somerville saw action in the Dardanelles during the Gallipoli campaign of the First World War and subsequently developed an interest in radiotelegraphy and signals. In 1936, he was appointed rear admiral (destroyers) in the Mediterranean Fleet and had a number of run-ins with the Italian Navy during the Spanish Civil War as Italian submarines frequently targeted British ships. In 1939, Somerville's career came to an abrupt end when he was diagnosed with tuberculosis and was placed on the

Navy's retired list. When war broke out in September 1939, he was recalled to duty by the Admiralty and was placed in the Signals Division where he became responsible for the development of ship-borne radar. Somerville's return to active service became permanent in May 1940 when he became assistant to Vice-Admiral Bertram Ramsay, who oversaw the evacuation of the British Expeditionary Force and other Allied forces from Dunkirk.[5]

On 15 June, the French Admiralty had placed the 15-inch gun battleship *Richelieu* under the command of Admiral Jean de Laborde, the Commander-in-Chief of the French Navy at Brest, with orders for her to be sailed to the River Clyde. Designed to counter the Italian *Littorio*-class battleships, the *Richelieu* was the first 35,000-ton French battleship. Armed with eight 15-inch guns, the *Richelieu* was the first modern battleship constructed under the 1922 Washington Naval Treaty. On 18 June, new orders were received ordering the battleship, in the wake of German advances, to leave Brest, not for the River Clyde, but for Dakar. Leaving Brest escorted by the *Fougueux* and the *Frondeur*, the *Richelieu* reached Dakar on 23 June.

At this time, the highest administrative authority in French West Africa, Gouverneur Général de l'A.O.F., Léon Cayla, and the flag officer of the French Navy West Africa, Rear Admiral Plançon, as well as the town authorities in Dakar, were inclined to continue the war against Germany alongside the British. When the *Richelieu* arrived in Dakar, the British aircraft carrier HMS *Hermes* was moored in the inner harbour. Aware of the Franco–German armistice and Admiral Darlan's instructions that his ships remain under the French flag otherwise they were to be scuttled or sailed to the United States, Captain Paul Jean Marzin became determined to escape what he viewed as a British trap. Against the advice of Gouverneur Général Cayla, who considered this to be an act of desertion, Marzin decided to sail for Casablanca on 25 June.[6]

Fearing that the *Richelieu* would return to France following learning of the battleship's departure from Dakar, the Admiralty dispatched the *Hood* and the *Ark Royal* from Gibraltar to intercept the *Richelieu* off the Canary Islands, before escorting her to Gibraltar. Aboard the British ships, no one knew what action to take should Captain Marzin refuse to comply. Britain's policy of dealing with the French fleet had yet to be decided.[7] Fearing that the *Richelieu* would join the British, the French Admiralty summoned Marzin to return to Dakar. Reversing course and shadowed by the heavy cruiser HMS *Dorsetshire*, the *Richelieu* arrived back at Dakar on 27 June. At 10 p.m on 25 June, the *Hood* and the *Ark Royal* were ordered back to Gibraltar. The *Hood* and the *Ark Royal* put to sea again a few days later following news that the *Richelieu* was again preparing to sail and was going to make a run for Toulon. For sixteen hours, the British ships raced towards Dakar but the emergency fizzled out and proved to be a false alarm as the *Richelieu* never left Dakar harbour.[8]

With no clear solution to the problem of the French Navy, on 24 June, the British War Cabinet met in four extraordinary sessions. No final course of action was agreed upon at the sessions, however, the consensus among those present was that something must be done to gain control of the French ships or to permanently put them out of action. On 25 June, Vice Admiral Dudley North was sent to Oran to meet the French naval commander there in order to gauge his views on the situation with regards to the French fleet. During the course of the meeting, the French Admiral flatly refused to hand his ships over to the British under any circumstances. With the threat of a German invasion of Britain looming large, one of Churchill's overriding concerns was to concentrate the maximum possible naval strength in home waters to counter the German threat. Therefore, it was imperative that the uncertainty surrounding the French fleet be resolved as soon as possible in order to release the British warships shadowing their French counterparts for operations elsewhere. Churchill was also keen to entice the United States for assistance in providing material and, hopefully, to enter the war against Germany. However, prominent world opinion was against Britain at the time with many believing that she would soon collapse under the Nazi onslaught. Churchill knew that he had to demonstrate to the world, and in particular to those in the United States that the British people, with their backs to the wall, still had the determination to carry on fighting. Although there had been occasional squawks from Lord Halifax about the danger of being too hostile to the Vichy government, Churchill had no real difficulty in carrying the support of the War Cabinet for this very hard line.[9]

So it was on 27 June that the War Cabinet met to plan a decisive action. With 3 July set as the deadline, the decision was taken to neutralise the French fleet. So began a period of six days over which the plans to neutralise the French fleet, under the codename Operation Catapult, were formulated. In planning the operation, the planners felt that there was little to be feared with regards to the French ships that had taken refuge in British ports. It was decided that these ships, which included a number of old French dreadnoughts and several destroyers, plus the cruiser submarine *Surcouf*, which was at the time the largest submarine ever constructed, could be seized at Britain's convenience. Likewise, the planners felt that there was no immediate concern regarding the *Richelieu* which was covered by an adequate number of Royal Navy warships. Nor was there any immediate concern over her sister ship, the *Jean Bart*, which was under construction and had sailed from Saint Nazaire to Casablanca without her main armament, nor the majority of her secondary armament fitted. In addition to these ships, three old French battleships and a light cruiser were to be found at anchor in Alexandria and could easily be neutralised by Admiral Andrew Cunningham and his Mediterranean Fleet stationed there.

The major concern for the British planners was what to do with the French ships at or near Oran. Here the situation was different. Oran harbour was home to a modest force of seven destroyers, four submarines, and a handful of torpedo boats. Further along the coast lay the port of Mers el-Kébir, which lay under the protection of powerful shore batteries that sat atop cliffs. Anchored here was the strongest concentration of French warships in the world. The ships at anchor at Mers el-Kébir formed the French Atlantic Fleet, the *Force de Raid* and had moved to the North African port from Brest in early June. At Mers el-Kébir lay anchored two of the French Navy's finest ships—the *Dunkerque* and the *Strasbourg*—built with the express purpose of being superior to the *Deutschland*-class pocket battleships. Like the *Scharnhorst* and the *Gneisenau* (which were built in response to the *Dunkerque*-class), the *Dunkerque* and the *Strasbourg* have been alternatively classified as fast battleships and as battlecruisers. At 706 feet long and with a displacement of approximately 35,500 tons, the *Dunkerque*-class were armed with eight 13-inch guns, between 8 and 11 inches of armour, and were capable of over 30 knots. The *Dunkerque*-class were formidable ships. Also at Mers el-Kébir were the battleships *Bretagne* and *Provence*, each capable of 20 knots and armed with 13.4-inch guns, a seaplane carrier, and six destroyers.[10]

During the course of 27 June, the War Cabinet discussed the best way to eliminate the threat posed by the vessels at Mers el-Kébir. Churchill's main concern was that the ships be contained within the harbour and then neutralised. As a means of accomplishing this, it was decided to have Force 'H' sail from Gibraltar and drop anchor off Mers el-Kébir and to offer Admiral Marcel Gensoul, the commanding officer of the French Fleet there four options: join the Royal Navy in continuing the war against Germany and Italy; sail to a British port with skeleton crews whereupon they would be interned for the duration; sail to the West Indies or the United States and remain there for the duration of the war; or scuttle the ships in Mers el-Kébir harbour. If Gensoul refused all four options, the Royal Navy would sink the French fleet.[11]

Having made a decision, the next few days saw the build-up of Force 'H'. First to arrive was the light cruiser HMS *Enterprise* followed by four destroyers of the Thirteenth Destroyer Flotilla and finally HMS *Valiant*, a 15-inch gun battleship and veteran of the Battle of Jutland.[12] At 2.25 a.m. on 1 July, Somerville received orders from the Admiralty simply reading 'Be prepared for "Catapult" July 3'.

The French battleship *Dunkerque* in 1937. (*Author's collection*)

One of Somerville's officers was Captain Cedric Holland, the commanding officer of HMS *Ark Royal*. Before the war, Holland had been the naval *attaché* in the British Embassy in Paris and had a very good knowledge of both the policies and personalities of the French government, and more importantly, the French Navy. Holland, like Somerville and the other officers in Force 'H', strongly opposed the use of force. They proposed instead that a show of force should be given and the French ships sunk only after their crews had been evacuated. At the same time, the view of Somerville and his officers at Gibraltar was that the French Admirals would be bound to see that they had no alternative and would therefore give in to the British demands.[13] So it was that during the course of the afternoon of 1 July that Somerville telegraphed the Admiralty:

> After a talk with Holland and others Vice-Admiral 'Force H' is impressed with their views that the use of force should be avoided at all costs. Holland considers offensive action on our part would alienate all French wherever they are.[14]

At 6.20 p.m., a reply was received from the Admiralty: 'Firm intention of H.M.G. [His Majesty's Government] that if French will not accept any of your alternatives they are to be destroyed'.[15] This message was followed at 1.08 a.m. on 2 July by a carefully conceived transcript of the communication that was to be communicated to Admiral Gensoul reaching Somerville.

> It is impossible for us, your comrades up to now, to allow your fine ships to fall into the power of the German or Italian enemy. We are determined to fight on to the end, and if we win, as we think we shall, we shall never forget that France was our Ally, that our interests are the same as hers, and that our common enemy is Germany, Should we conquer, we solemnly declare that we shall restore the greatness and territory of France. For this purpose, we must make sure that the best ships of the French Navy are not used against us by the common foe. In these circumstances His Majesty's Government have instructed me to demand that the French Fleet now at Mers-el-Kébir and Oran shall act in accordance with one of the following alternatives:
>
> (a) Sail with us and continue to fight for victory against the Germans and Italians.
>
> (b) Sail with reduced crews under our control to a British port. The reduced crews will be repatriated at the earliest moment.
>
> If either of these courses is adopted by you, we will restore your ships to France at the conclusion of the war or pay full compensation, if they are damaged meanwhile.
>
> (c) Alternatively, if you feel bound to stipulate that your ships should not be used against the Germans or Italians unless these break the Armistice, then sail them with us with reduced crews to some French port in the West Indies—Martinique, for instance—where they can be demilitarised to our satisfaction, or perhaps be entrusted to the United States and remain safe until the end of the war, the crews being repatriated.
>
> If you refuse these fair offers, I must, with profound regret, require you to sink your ships within six hours.

Finally, failing the above, I have the orders of His Majesty's Government to use whatever force might be necessary to prevent your ships from falling into German or Italian hands.[16]

Stiffened by units of Admiral Dudley North's North Atlantic Command, Force 'H' set sail from Gibraltar on 2 July.[17] There can be no doubt that the task entrusted to Somerville was, and remains to this day, one of the most unenviable tasks ever assigned to a British commander, something echoed by Churchill who requested the Admiralty dispatch a message to Somerville during the evening of 2 July:

> You are charged with one of the most disagreeable and difficult tasks that a British Admiral has even been faced with, but we have complete confidence in you and rely in you to carry it out relentlessly.[18]

Operation Catapult was launched, as planned, on 3 July 1940. During the early morning hours of 3 July, Royal Navy warships blockaded both Portsmouth and Plymouth harbours where French warships that had sailed to Britain were anchored. Ultimatums were delivered calling on the French to rejoin the fight against Germany, sail their ships out of the reach of the Germans, or scuttle their ships. At the same time, the ships were boarded by armed groups of sailors and by soldiers. By and large, the commanding officers of the French ships agreed to join the British in continuing the fight against Germany. However, one serious incident did occur in Plymouth aboard the submarine Surcouf. When boarding the French submarine two Royal Navy officers, Commander Dennis Sprague and Lieutenant Griffiths were fatally wounded alongside Yves Daniel, a French warrant officer. At the same time, a British seaman, L. S. Webb, was shot dead by the Surcouf's doctor.[19]

At Alexandria during the course of 3 July, following protracted negotiations, Admiral Cunningham succeeded in reaching an agreement with Admiral René-Émile Godfroy. Godfroy agreed to discharge the fuel oil from his ships and to render the guns of his ships useless through the removal of important parts of the gun mechanisms. At Mers el-Kébir, however, events took a different turn. By early morning, Force 'H' stood off Mers el-Kébir. The exact time Force 'H' arrived is open to deliberation as a number of conflicting sources exist; however, it would appear to be around 8.10 a.m.[20]

At around 6.30 a.m., Somerville had dispatched the destroyer HMS *Foxhound* from the main body of the Squadron with orders to sail ahead and to enter Mers el-Kébir harbour. Aboard the *Foxhound* was Captain Holland of the *Ark Royal* who was to attempt negotiations with Gensoul. Holland had been ordered to meet with Gensoul personally and to explain the British terms to him. Not wishing to confer with Holland, at 8.10 a.m., Gensoul sent Flag Lieutenant Antoine Dufray in a launch to confer with Holland. Holland informed Dufray that the matter that he had been sent to discuss was of such importance that he must speak with Gensoul directly. Dufray, meanwhile, simply informed Holland that the French Admiral did not wish to see the British Captain.

For his part, surveying the scene before him, Gensoul grasped the significance of Force 'H' lying off the coast and became indignant at what he felt was likely to be British diplomacy at gunpoint. As such, Gensoul, at 8.47 a.m., ordered that the *Foxhound* immediately leave the harbour. Holland was a devoted Francophile and, as such, was dejected about France's defeat at the hands of Germany. Meanwhile, Gensoul regarded himself as pro-British. However, as a proud naval commander, Gensoul had expected to negotiate personally with Somerville, or at least an officer of flag rank, and thus regarded Holland's presence as negotiator, as something of a snub.[21] Knowing the repercussions if negotiations failed, Holland attempted once again to meet personally with Gensoul. In a feint, the *Foxhound* began to leave the harbour. As the destroyer did so, Holland boarded a fast launch and sped towards Gensoul's flagship, the *Dunkerque*. Before he could reach the *Dunkerque*, Holland was intercepted by Dufray who again explained that Gensoul would not grant him an audience. In an act of desperation, Holland handed Durfay a briefcase containing the text of the British terms before returning to the *Foxhound*, which had again dropped anchor in the harbour. The British plan had been to communicate the terms of the text orally but Gensoul's stubbornness had precluded that option. Aware that Force 'H' had been set the deadline of resolving the situation by sunset, Holland felt it imperative to deliver the terms by any means possible.

The British terms were passed on to Gensoul who upon reading them became incensed. At 9.45 a.m., he sent a signal to the French Admiralty in Toulon informing them that a British squadron was standing off Oran and that he had been issued with an ultimatum to sink his ships within six hours, before communicating his intention to reply to force with force.[22]

While awaiting a reply from Gensoul, from aboard the *Foxhound*, Holland reported observing that the French ships were beginning to have their awnings unfurled and were beginning to raise steam. This was a report that was backed up by a reconnaissance aircraft from the *Ark Royal* and indicated that the French vessels were preparing to leave harbour and put to sea. With these reports passed on to the Admiralty, the First Sea Lord, Sir Dudley Pound, ordered Somerville to sow the harbour entrance with mines in order to prevent the French ships from leaving. This was followed at 10 a.m. with a message from Gensoul stating that in light of what amounted to a veritable ultimatum, the French fleet would resist any British attempt to gain control of the ships. Gensoul further informed Somerville that the first shot fired by the British against the French Fleet at Mers el-Kébir would have the effect of turning the entire French navy against Britain. Undeterred, and with Gensoul refusing the British terms, Somerville informed the Admiralty in London that he would open fire against the French Fleet at 1.30 p.m. Still convinced that a peaceful solution could be achieved, Holland implored the Admiralty for more time to negotiate. Delay after delay followed with an eventual deadline of 4.30 p.m. being set.[23]

At 1 p.m., a flight of Swordfish aircraft took off from the *Ark Royal* to lay a series of mines, blockading the French in the harbour and placing further pressure on Gensoul.[24] In the meantime, the constant delays during the course of the afternoon, as Holland attempted to negotiate, appeared, at first, to pay off. At 4.15 p.m., Gensoul relented and agreed to parley with Holland. While this, at first, appeared to be an encouraging development, the mood soon dampened as Gensoul informed Holland that so long as Germany and Italy abided by the terms of the armistice and allowed the French fleet to remain in French metropolitan ports with French crews, then he too would remain. To Holland, it appeared at times that an agreement was in sight, but it was becoming increasingly clear to the British that Gensoul was merely stalling for time.

In the meantime, the signal that Gensoul had sent to the French Admiralty at 9.45 a.m. had finally arrived in Toulon. Darlan was absent from the Admiralty building and could not be located. In his absence, Admiral Le Luc, the French Chief of Staff, issued a response in Darlan's name informing Gensoul to stand firm and ordered all French naval and air forces in the Western Mediterranean to prepare for battle and head for Oran with the utmost haste.

In Britain, the order issued by Admiral Le Luc in Darlan's name was intercepted by the Admiralty and was transmitted to Somerville before Gensoul could inform the British of the orders that he had received. During the course of the afternoon, Churchill sat in the Cabinet Rooms in frequent contact with both the First Lord of the Admiralty and the First Sea Lord. Becoming increasingly impatient, Churchill, conscious that French reinforcements were perhaps making their way to Oran, ordered that Somerville settle matters at once.

Under orders from London, Somerville sent a signal to Gensoul that was received at 5.15 p.m. stating that unless one of the British proposals was accepted by 5.30 p.m., it would be necessary for the Royal Navy to sink the ships of the French fleet. This message put an end to all further discussions and negotiations. So it was that at 5.25 p.m., a sombre Holland departed the *Dunkerque* and proceeded to leave the harbour.[25] Before the *Foxhound* had left the harbour, Force 'H' opened fire, beginning the first Anglo-French naval engagements since the Battles of the Nile (1789) and Trafalgar (1805).

Aboard HMS *Hood*, Boy Signalman Ted Briggs hoisted the order for instant action to the starboard signal yard, followed by the order to open fire:

> The response was immediate. Just as I turned around to watch, the guns of the *Resolution* and *Valiant* roared in murderous hair-trigger reaction. Then came the ting-ting of our firing bell. Seconds later my ears felt as if they had been sandwiched between two manhole covers. The concussion of *Hood*'s eight fifteen-inch guns, screaming in horrendous harmony, shook the flag deck violently.[26]

It was very much a one-sided affair. According to French Admiral Gabriel Auphan, the British fire was very heavy, very accurate and of a short duration. One of the first salvos struck the battleship *Bretagne* which blew up, while the destroyer *Mogador* lost her stern to a direct hit, which left her a smouldering wreck in the harbour waters that turned black with oil and bodies.[27] A British report composed after the attack records the carnage that ensued:

The first salvo fell short, the second hit the breakwater, sending large fragments of concrete flying into the air, which probably caused casualties to personnel on the upper decks of the battleships. The third salvo fell among the ships, and the battleship *Bretagne* blew up, column of orange flame of leaping into the sky followed by an immense column of smoke several hundred feet high. Another smaller explosions indicated that a destroyer had blown up. By this time the harbour were [*sic.*] shrouded in smoke from explosions and fires; direct spotting was almost impossible and air spotting was most difficult. The French shore batteries and the battle cruisers *Dunkerque* and *Strasbourg* opened fire about a minute after the first British salvo. The shore batteries were promptly engaged by the *Arethusa*, the older guns of the *Enterprise* being out ranged. Heavy projectiles were … falling near the British battleships as the enemy fire, at first very short, began to improve in accuracy. The observers in the *Foxhound*'s motor boat recorded several direct hits on the French ships, another explosion with a sheet of orange flame from a battleship and a direct hit on a large destroyer as she was leaving the harbour. None of the French projectiles hit, though a number of them … fell close to and in some cases straddled the British ships.

Some splinters caused minor superficial damage in the *Hood* and injured one officer and a rating.[28]

The *Dunkerque* received several hits but managed to fire approximately forty rounds at the *Hood* before being put out of action by the British bombardment. Sustaining heavy damage, the *Provence* was forced to run aground. Before the smoke cleared, the bulk of the French Fleet at Mers el-Kébir was either ablaze or at the bottom of the sea, while 1,297 French sailors had been killed.

At 6.04 p.m., nine minutes after opening fire, Somerville issued the order to cease fire. This allowed some French sailors to abandon their ships to avoid further losses of life. A few minutes later, Force 'H' came under increasingly accurate fire from the shore battery at Fort Santon, which obliged the *Hood* to return withering fire while the other ships of the squadron sailed out of range.

This might have been the end of the affair had a report not reached the flag officer of Force 'H', which was immediately passed on to Somerville stating that a *Dunkerque*-class ship was leaving the harbour and setting a course east. The report was initially dismissed by Somerville but by 6.30 p.m., it became apparent that the *Strasbourg* had somehow survived the bombardment unscathed and had successfully negotiated the minefield that had been laid by the Swordfish from the *Ark Royal*. Believing that the *Strasbourg* was heading for Toulon, Somerville order the *Hood*'s course changed in order to give chase. At the same time, aircraft from the *Ark Royal* worked up to launch an attack.

At 6.43 p.m., the cruisers and destroyers were ordered to the van leaving the *Ark Royal* and the battleships to follow on unscreened. The *Hood* and a number of destroyers worked up to full speed and pressed on after the *Strasbourg*. Giving chase at 28 knots, the *Hood*'s turbines were stripped. Meanwhile, Swordfish from

The French battleship *Provence* (foreground) under fire as the *Strasbourg* (centre) makes for the harbour entrance. In the background, the battleship *Bretagne* can be seen burning furiously.

The destroyer *Mogador* running aground having been struck by a British 15-inch shell.

the *Ark Royal*, approaching from the north and, diving on the battleship from 4,000 feet, launched their attacks. The *Strasbourg* responded with an intense barrage of anti-aircraft fire. Releasing their bombs, one bomb was believed to have hit the French battleship, but in reality, the *Strasbourg* was unscathed. Having made their attack, the Swordfish returned to the *Ark Royal*.

Between 7.33 and 7.45 p.m., a French destroyer, the Rigauld de Genouilly, was sighted sailing inshore and was engaged by the Enterprise and the Arethusa. The Hood and the Valiant fired several salvos at the destroyer, which reversed course and returned to Oran, having sustained three hits. The Hood and the other ships were, however, forced to take evasive action to avoid a volley of torpedoes fired by the French destroyer.

The chase continued until approximately 8.20 p.m. when it was calculated that a French force of heavy and light cruisers had put to sea from Algiers and would likely rendezvous with the Strasbourg at 9 p.m. Furthermore, with the light failing, any engagement would likely occur at night, which Somerville considered unjustified. With his destroyers having had no recent experience of shadowing an enemy at night, and knowing that the French force would be numerically superior, Somerville summarised the situation:

1. The prospects of locating the Strasbourg at night was small.
2. Force 'H' will be at a disadvantage, being silhouetted against the afterglow.
3. The speed of advance was too high to allow the destroyers to spread.
4. For the fuel endurance of the 'V' and 'W' class destroyers only permitted a three-hour chase.
5. Unless the Hood was in a position to support the advanced forces, the latter were numerically much inferior. This support could not be assured under night action conditions.
6. The possible loss of British ships was unjustified as against the possibility of French ships being allowed to fall into enemy hands.
7. The Valiant and the Resolution were unscreened.

So it was that the Admiralty was informed that Force 'H' was breaking off the chase. At 8.25 p.m., Force 'H' altered course westward.[29] A second Swordfish strike was made against the Strasbourg with torpedoes at 8.55 p.m., which reported two hits. Nevertheless, the speed of the French battleship remained unimpaired and she reached Toulon the following day.

Following the attack on the French Fleet at Mers el-Kébir, Somerville wrote about the experience in a letter to his wife:

We all feel thoroughly dirty and ashamed that the first time we should been in action was an affair like this ... I feel sure that I shall be blamed for bungling the job and I think I did. But to you I don't mind confessing I was half-hearted and you can't win an action that way.[30]

The German propaganda machine made enormous capital out of the British destruction and seizure of the French ships, in particular out of the bombardment by Force 'H' of the French Fleet at Mers el-Kébir with the Nazi propagandist William Joyce, more commonly known and referred to as Lord Haw-Haw, referring to Force 'H' as 'Somerville's assassins'. There was grim amusement to be had from the German broadcasts, but also anger—anger at the Germans for precipitating the disaster, but also anger at Gensoul for not continuing the war alongside the Royal Navy.[31] There can be little doubt, however, that the effect of the British attacks with regards to Anglo-French relations, was wholly negative. On 3 July, the French chargé d'affaires formally protested the British action and for a while it appeared as if the Vichy government had been provoked to the point of declaring war on Great Britain. Upon hearing of the attack on Mers el-Kébir, Darlan issued a series of orders to all French warships to engage the British wherever they were encountered. On 8 July, the Vichy government officially severed all diplomatic ties with London.[32]

In the space of a few hours on 3 July 1940, the world's fourth-largest naval power lost some 84 per cent of its battleship force and was reduced, by and large, for the time being, to a token force of light craft and submarines. In the act, while sacrificing French goodwill, the Royal Navy had successfully eliminated the danger of an augmented Axis Fleet and had reaffirmed its naval supremacy. Furthermore, and perhaps most important of all, Operation Catapult served to alter world opinion as Churchill had hoped. It became apparent that Britain would pursue the war at all costs and against all odds. In the United States, President Roosevelt lauded Churchill's action and welcomed it as a service to American defence. Moreover, Churchill's decision to eradicate the threat posed by a potential takeover of the French Fleet served to eradicate the doubts of many American officials of Britain's ability to repel a German invasion. For Britain, this new-found confidence in her ability to pursue the war translated into material benefits as President Roosevelt increased pressure on Congress to provide further support to Britain through Lend-Lease and destroyers for bases arrangements.

For the *Hood*, her business at Mers el-Kébir was not over. On 5 July, accompanied by the *Ark Royal*, *Valiant*, *Enterprise*, and ten destroyers, she returned to Mers el-Kébir to implement Operation Lever, an airstrike against the *Dunkerque* following a French broadcast that stated 'The damage to the *Dunkerque* is minimal and the ship will soon be repaired'. Torpedoed, the *Dunkerque* would not be repaired sufficiently to leave Mers el-Kébir until 1942.

The *Hood* would continue on as flagship of Force 'H' for over a month following the neutralising of the French fleet at Mers el-Kébir. In the wake of the attack on Mers el-Kébir, Somerville sought to take the war in the Mediterranean to the Italians. On 8 July, Force 'H' left Gibraltar and set a course for Cagliari, Sardinia. Somerville intended Force 'H' to launch a diversionary attack by bombarding Cagliari as cover for the passage of two convoys sailing between

Taken from on board HSM *Ark Royal*, this picture shows Force 'H' under attack by Italian SM.79 bombers on 9 July 1940. The nearest ship is HMS *Valiant*. The bow and foretop of HMS *Resolution* can be seen behind the *Valiant*. On the right is the *Hood*. The cruiser on the left beyond the bows of the *Valiant* and the *Resolution* is HMS *Arethusa*. (*Author's collection*)

Taken from the *Ark Royal*, this image shows the *Hood* disappearing behind columns of water as bombs detonate as the ship becomes a target of Italian SM.79 bombers. (*Richard Toffolo*)

Malta and Alexandria. At around 4 p.m. on 9 July, Force 'H' came under heavy air attack from Italian SM.79 bombers. Fortunately for Somerville, no serious damage was inflicted on his ships by the Italians. Despite this, shortly after dusk, he decided that the risk of damage to his ships from enemy aircraft was not worth the objective and promptly cancelled the operation, recalling the squadron to Gibraltar.

Workhorse

On 27 July, while at Gibraltar, the Unrotated Projectile launcher located atop 'B' turret accidentally discharged twenty projectiles over the harbour. The projectiles caused no fatalities but badly burned three ratings. On 31 July, the *Hood* put to see with Force 'H' to carry out Operation Hurry, a diversionary raid on the Italian airfield at Cagliari, Sardinia, which was an operation conceived to cover the transport of twelve Hawker Hurricanes to Malta aboard the aircraft carrier *Argus*. On 1 August, Force 'H' was subjected to a high-level attack by a flight of Italian SM.79 bombers. Fortunately for the men of Force 'H', the Italian attack was unsuccessful and no damage was inflicted. The following day, escorted by the *Hood*, the *Ark Royal* launched the diversionary air raid against Cagliari airfield. To the south-west of Sardinia, HMS *Argus* launched the twelve Hurricanes that flew to Malta to assist in fending off the aerial onslaught that the Axis powers were undertaking against the Island and its defences. With the diversionary raid on Cagliari complete, Force 'H' returned to Gibraltar where it arrived on 4 August.

On 4 August 1940, in the company of the battleship *Valiant*, the *Ark Royal*, the cruisers *Enterprise* and *Arethusa* and the destroyers *Escapade*, *Faulkner*, *Foresight*, *Forester*, and *Foxhound* (bolstered two days later by the destroyers *Bedouin*, *Punjabi*, and *Tartar*), the *Hood* set sail for Scapa Flow. On 10 August, the ship's company watched with regret as Somerville hauled down his flag to be replaced by that of Vice-Admiral William J. Whitworth, the Admiral Commanding Battlecruiser Squadron. Though no one was to know it at the time, the Mediterranean sun, which had beamed down on the *Hood*'s decks for almost twenty-five years, had shone its last and was never to grace the ship again.

On 16 August, the *Hood* departed Scapa Flow with the destroyer *Vimiera* for Rosyth where between 17 and 24 August she was taken in hand so that the left hand 15-inch gun of 'A' turret could be replaced. This repair work completed, the *Hood* returned to Scapa Flow, dropping anchor on 25 August.

Throughout the summer months of 1940, in the skies above southern England, the Royal Air Force had been engaged in a life or death struggle with the Luftwaffe. As the Luftwaffe attempted to destroy the RAF to gain air superiority ahead of an invasion of the British Isles, the British population and the remainder

Taken from aboard the destroyer HMS *Javelin*, the *Hood* is seen passing through boom defences in the Firth of Forth. It is likely that this image was taken in August 1940 when the *Hood* sailed to Rosyth. (*Richard Toffolo*)

of the British Army that had been evacuated from the beaches of Dunkirk and elsewhere on the French coast began to prepare to fight a German landing. On 7 September, intelligence sources in Britain suggested that a German invasion was imminent prompting army and Home Guard units to mobilise. With warning levels increasing across the British Isles, on 13 September, the *Hood*, accompanied by the *Nelson*, *Rodney*, *Naiad*, *Cairo*, *Bonaventure*, and a handful of destroyers sailed from Scapa Flow to Rosyth as a pre-emptive move to help defend against a German invasion. Despite the warnings, the invasion would not come, although it would not be until October 1940 that the warning levels were decreased. This mixed force remained at Rosyth as a squadron until 28 September when the *Hood* departed Rosyth in the company of HMS *Naiad* to intercept a German cruiser and a convoy that was reported to be sailing off Stavanger. On 29 September, the *Hood* sailed into Scapa Flow where she would remain for the next couple of weeks.

In mid-October, the *Hood* put to sea in the company of the destroyers *Eskimo*, *Somali*, *Mashona*, *Punjabi* and *Matabele* to cover an anti-shipping operation around Tromsø by Force 'D', a task force comprising the cruisers *Berwick* and *Norfolk* and the aircraft carrier *Furious*. Arriving back at Scapa Flow on 19 October, the *Hood* returned to sea four days later accompanied by the *Repulse*, the cruisers *Dido* and *Phoebe*, and the destroyers *Punjabi*, *Somali*, and *Matabele*,

Right: A posed-for image taken in autumn 1940. The men gathered on the forecastle are apparently being instructed in the fusing of 4-inch shells. Note the UP launcher atop 'B' turret that a censor has attempted somewhat unsuccessfully to remove from the image.

Below: The *Hood* viewed between two of the 16-inch guns of HMS *Rodney* while the two ships were at Scapa Flow in the autumn of 1940. HMS *Renown* and the *Repulse* are astern of the *Hood*. (*Richard Toffolo*)

Taken from the quarterdeck in October 1940 while at Scapa Flow, the *Hood* is in her final colour scheme of Home Fleet medium grey. (*Author's collection*)

Men repainting one of the *Hood*'s funnels. (*Author's collection*)

making for Obrestad to investigate reported movements that were being made by the *Kriegsmarine*. The squadron returned to Scapa Flow the following day, having failed to locate any *Kriegsmarine* vessels.

From 28 to 31 October, the *Hood* was at sea as part of a hunting group consisting of HMS *Repulse*, the *Furious*, and a group of six destroyers searching for a German raider in the North Atlantic that had been reported by the merchant ship SS *Mahout*. It is likely that the German surface raider which eluded the Royal Navy hunting group was the pocket battleship *Admiral Scheer* for on 5 November, the *Admiral Scheer* stumbled upon convoy HX-84. Five ships were sunk and several others damaged before the convoy scattered. As the convoy attempted to scatter the armed merchant cruiser HMS *Jervis Bay* attempted to engage the *Admiral Scheer* but was quickly overwhelmed and sunk. Despite this, the sacrifice of the *Jervis Bay* combined with failing light allowed the other ships of HX-84 to successfully escape. In response to reports that HX-84 was under attack, the Home Fleet put to sea. The *Hood* put to sea alongside HMS *Repulse* and the ships of the 15th Cruiser Squadron comprising HMS *Dido*, *Bonaventure*, and *Naiad* as well as a group of destroyers to cover the approaches to Brest and Lorient against the *Admiral Scheer* putting in on the Atlantic coast of France. On 9 November, the *Hood* was forced to abandon her patrol area and made for Scapa Flow accompanied by the *Phoebe*, the *Naiad*, the *Eskimo*, and the *Sikh* in order to refuel. The Home Fleet ultimately failed to locate the *Admiral Scheer* in the vastness of the Atlantic and she managed to sail into the South Atlantic before reappearing in the Indian Ocean in December.

The *Hood* anchored at Scapa Flow between 11 and 23 November when she departed the anchorage and rendezvoused with the ships of the 1st Minelaying Squadron and HMS *Aurora* before sailing to an area off Reykjanes, Iceland. Shortly thereafter, she returned to anchor at Scapa Flow.

At the beginning of December 1940, Admiral Sir John Tovey succeeded Admiral Sir Charles Forbes as the Commander-in-Chief of the Home Fleet. On 4 December, Tovey visited the *Hood*. Seven days later, he returned to the *Hood* whereupon he undertook an inspection of the ship. It was also in early December that it was learned by those aboard the *Hood* that they would be spending the ship's second wartime Christmas without leave. Among the ship's stokers, the mood of discontent bordered on mutiny. One of the *Hood*'s crew, Bill Crawford, recorded the discontent of the stokers in his diary:

> Tuesday 10 December: There sure is unrest as regards leave. The captain spoke to us about it today, he said nothing could be done.
> Wednesday 11 December: There is open talk about mutiny, especially among the stokers, who have already had one bit of trouble.
> Thursday 12 December: Things came to a head today. The stokers practically mutinied, locking up officers and saying they wouldn't work. The captain asked them all to come up into the battery, he told them he could do nothing about leave and asked all the ship's company to stand firm.

The *Hood* returning to Scapa Flow during Autumn 1940.

The *Hood*, *c.* 1940.

Friday 13 December: Things have kind of eased off today. The captain told us yesterday that he was doing all he could but he did not think we would get leave till next year. He said all he could, also say he knew some things but he was only a captain and if he was to tell us it might cause unnecessary trouble.[1]

On 18 December, she departed Scapa Flow to conduct tactical exercises in the company of HMS *Repulse, Nelson, Nigeria, Manchester, Edinburgh, Arora,* and a number of destroyers to the south-west of the Faeroe Islands. The *Hood* returned to Scapa Flow on 20 December but departed again on Christmas Eve to conduct a patrol in the Iceland-Faeroes gap against a breakout attempt by the German cruiser *Admiral Hipper.* Ted Briggs noted:

At about 14.00 on Christmas Eve at Scapa, just as the messes were preparing for the parties the next day, special sea duty men were piped to their stations. From the flag deck I could see that five other ships—the cruiser *Edinburgh* and the destroyers *Cossack, Echo, Electra,* and *Escapade*—had already weighed anchor and were thrusting out of the Flow. The *Hood* followed, and soon came the announcement over the broadcast system that our Christmas would be spent patrolling the Iceland-Faeroes passage for the purpose of trying to intercept the cruiser *Hipper,* which was being chased by the *Berwick.*[2]

Despite being at sea, the crew made the best they could out of the situation. Carols echoed from the mess decks, tots of rum were freely exchanged and turkey and plum pudding served. Captain Glennie performed a series of rounds and below deck discipline was somewhat relaxed. For those on duty, however, it was very much business as usual.

On 26 December, the crew were cheered to learn that they would be returning to Scapa Flow, the *Admiral Hipper* having eluded the British net. New Year was celebrated at Scapa Flow before the *Hood* was detailed for another patrol on 2 January 1941 as an escort to a minelaying force to the north of the Faeroe Islands. For three days, the *Hood* was battered by the weather in an uneventful patrol before returning once more to Scapa Flow. The *Hood* again departed Scapa Flow on 11 January in the company of the *Repulse, Birmingham, Edinburgh, Bedouin, Eclipse, Escapade, Eskimo, Tatar,* and *Somali* to provide cover to two large convoys against German surface raiders. For days prior to the *Hood's* embarkation on this latest war patrol, rumours had been doing the rounds aboard the ship that she was to put in at Rosyth for an extensive refit and that a long period of leave would be granted to everyone. This news was confirmed on 10 January when the boatswain party struck the pole masts on the fore and main masts, a sure sign that the ship was to pass under the Forth Bridge. On 13 January, on route to Rosyth, the *Hood* was off Dunnet Point Light escorted by the destroyers *Electra, Echo,* and *Keppel* when her port paravane caught a mine mooring. The mooring was swiftly cut and a destroyer detailed to detonate the drifting mine with rifle fire. During the afternoon of 13 January, the *Hood* secured at her berth in the Firth of Forth.

On 16 January, the *Hood* edged into the Royal Navy's dockyard at Rosyth to receive what was to prove to be her final refit. The ship was drained of oil and had its ammunition and stores landed before being taken under tow by a number of tugs and guided through the outer lock of the dockyard from the Firth of Forth into the flooded dry dock. The *Hood* was hauled bow-first into No. 1 dock, one of the few dry docks capable of handling a ship of her length. As the dock was emptied of water, the hull came to rest on carefully laid timber baulks. Of note, in the fitting-out basin at Rosyth while the *Hood* was being refitted was the Navy's newest *King George V*-class battleship HMS *Prince of Wales*.

No sooner had the *Hood* entered the dry dock and had been secured in place than an army of caulkers, shipwrights and welders marched aboard to begin replacing fittings and equipment as well as to carry out repairs on the ship's tired hull. Deck planking was renewed as pneumatic caulking tools were pressed into service to work on overlapping plates to stop the leaks that had served to make life unbearable on the lower decks. Particular attention was paid to the deck seams on and around the forecastle through which water poured relentlessly into the ship when at sea. An inspection of the hull was carried out before it was scraped clean. With the hull scraped clean, a team of female dockyard workers, pressed into service to fulfil roles crucial to the war effort thus freeing up men for the armed forces, set to work with brushes perched atop lengthy poles to begin applying coats of red lead paint. While under peacetime conditions, an inspection of the hull would have shown it to be encrusted with a layer of marine growth; on

HMS *Prince of Wales*. (80-G-190724, US Naval History and Heritage Command)

this occasion, the inspection of the hull showed it to be largely stripped of paint owing to the severity of her wartime service with the result that the fresh paint was applied directly on to bare metal.[3]

At Rosyth, a team of engineers from John Brown and Co. had been gathered, which dismantled the *Hood*'s Brown-Curtis geared turbines and inspected them for damaged nozzles and misaligned wheels and bearings. During the reassembly of the turbines, the blades of the starboard inner turbine which had been stripped during the pursuit of the *Strasbourg* following the bombarding of the French fleet at Mers el-Kébir were replaced. The main work at Rosyth centred around the installation of a Type 284 gunnery radar set on the spotting top and the installation of Type 279M air-warning radar equipment on the main mast. Such was the secrecy surrounding radar that those responsible for welding the platform on which the equipment was to be fitted were told that they were fitting a platform that would become a crow's nest for a lookout. The installation of the Type 284 radar required the removal of the fore topmast and for new yards to be hung on both the main mast and spotting top.

While the *Hood* was undergoing this refit, in early January, seventeen-year-old Midshipman William Dundas joined the *Hood*'s company. Set on a career in the Royal Navy, Dundas had enrolled in Britannia Royal Naval College in May 1937 and had passed out in December 1940. On 17 January, the *Hood* was visited by Prime Minister Winston Churchill and just less than a month later received a new captain. Captain Irvine Glennie was promoted to rear-admiral and was succeeded on 15 February as captain of the *Hood* by Captain Ralph Kerr. Kerr had joined the Royal Navy in May 1904 and saw service during the First World War, mostly aboard the battleship HMS *Benbow*, the flagship of Admiral Sir Doveton Sturdee. Kerr saw action at the Battle of Jutland and in 1918 was given command of the destroyer *Cossack*. Promoted to commander in June 1927, Kerr was given command of the destroyer *Windsor* before moving to HMS *Thruster*. Promoted to captain in June 1935, Kerr was appointed Flotilla Leader, 21st Destroyer Flotilla in September of that year. In May 1936, Kerr stepped down from this position to become Senior Officer, Reserve Fleet aboard HMS *Caledon*. In November 1936, having moved to HMS *Colombo*, as well as holding the position of Senior Officer, Reserve Fleet, Kerr became Chief Staff Officer to the Rear-Admiral of the 10th Cruiser Squadron, a position he held until July 1937. Between 1937 and 1939, Kerr commanded the 2nd Destroyer Flotilla and then the 15th Destroyer Flotilla where he served under Vice-Admiral John Tovey. On 30 August 1939, Kerr took command of the shore establishment HMS *Cochrane* at Rosyth. He would spend the remainder of his time before being appointed to the *Hood* at Rosyth with the Rosyth Destroyer Force and on the staff of the Commander-in-Chief Rosyth.

Two days after Captain Kerr took command of the *Hood*, a fire broke out in the warrant officers' galley. On 6 March, with sleet beginning to blow in the wind, King George VI arrived aboard the *Hood*. The King was piped on to the quarterdeck where he was greeted by Admiral Whitworth and Captain Kerr before being shown below. While aboard, King George VI inspected the *Hood*'s divisions before the crew mustered on the deck to be addressed by the monarch.

King George VI aboard the *Hood* on 6 March 1941 while she was undergoing her final refit at Rosyth. The King is greeting an officer who is most likely Captain Ralph Kerr. (*Chris Judd/HMS Hood Association*)

Having spent time in the dockyard basin to round off her refit, the *Hood* was towed out of the dockyard on 17 March and anchored in the midstream above the Forth Bridge. Following the refit, Kerr's new command had to be worked up but these plans were dashed when news was received that two German surface raiders, the *Scharnhorst* and *Gneisenau*, under the command of Admiral Günther Lütjens had broken out into the Atlantic. During the afternoon of 18 March, the *Hood* passed under the Forth Bridge for the final time and joined the hunt for the German raiders. Little did anyone know, the *Hood* would never again anchor at Rosyth or transit the Forth. On 19 March, the *Hood* joined the battleships *Nelson* and *Queen Elizabeth*, the cruiser *London*, and the destroyers *Arrow*, *Electra*, *Echo*, *Inglefield*, *Eskimo*, and *Eclipse* to search for the *Gneisenau* and the *Scharnhorst*. The following day, the *Hood* joined the *King George V*, the flagship of Admiral John Tovey, to patrol the Iceland–Faeroes gap against the German raiders. On 21 March, the *Scharnhorst* located a convoy in the mid-Atlantic and sank seven merchant ships totalling 27,277 tons.[4] One of the ships in the convoy succeeded in transmitting a distress signal that was picked up by the Home Fleet and provided information on the whereabouts of the German raiders. As HMS *Rodney* appeared on the horizon, Lütjens broke off the attack and made for the cover of a rain squall. The *Hood* was ordered to sail south at maximum speed to try and intercept *Scharnhorst*. It was a futile effort: the *Hood* was too far north to intercept the *Gneisenau* and the *Scharnhorst*, which used their 31-knot speed to keep ahead of the Home Fleet and reached the sanctuary of Brest on 22 March.

Low on fuel, in the company of HMS *Queen Elizabeth* and four destroyers, the *Hood* returned to Scapa Flow.

On 28 March, with the destroyers *Electra*, *Escapade*, and *Tartar*, the *Hood* put to sea to act as an ocean escort to convoy HX-117, which had departed Halifax the day before for Liverpool. Shortly after noon, the *Hood* was diverted south and made for the Bay of Biscay with the cruisers *Nigeria* and *Fiji* to relieve Force 'H' as a blockading force against the *Scharnhorst* and the *Gneisenau* at Brest. On 1 April, the *Hood*, the *Nigeria*, and the *Fiji* reversed course and began to sail a northerly course against a potential German breakout. Three days later, on 4 April, the *Hood* was relieved by HMS *King George V* and the cruiser *London*. Having been relieved, the *Hood* made for Scapa Flow with the *Electra*, *Escapade*, and *Tartar* in tow. Arriving back at Scapa Flow on 6 April, the *Hood* was hastily refuelled before putting to sea and making for the Bay of Biscay once more, accompanied by the *Zulu*, *Arrow*, and *Maori*. The *Hood* would remain on patrol in the Bay of Biscay against a breakout by the *Gneisenau* and the *Scharnhorst* until 13 April when she returned to Scapa Flow with HMS *Kenya*, *Cossack*, *Arrow*, *Zulu*, and *Maori*.

At Scapa Flow from 14 April, the *Hood* again put to sea with the *Kenya* and three destroyers to resume the patrol off Brest on 18 April. The next day, however, the *Hood* and her consorts were given new orders: to alter course towards the Norwegian Sea. A new threat had arisen in the form of the *Kriegsmarine*'s newest battleship: the *Bismarck*.

18

The *Bismarck*

Laid down at the Blohm & Voss shipyard in Hamburg on 1 July 1936 and launched on 14 February 1939, the *Bismarck* was the first of two *Bismarck*-class battleships constructed for the German *Kriegsmarine*. The *Bismarck* was the fourth warship built for the German navy to bear the name of the 'Iron Chancellor' Otto von Bismarck. Design work had begun on the ship in 1932 with German naval architects drawing on experiences gained during the First World War, which were adapted to suit new technologies.[1]

Armed with eight 15-inch guns, the *Bismarck* boasted an overall length of 821.8 feet (250.5 metres) and a displacement of 50,300 tons at full load. Capable of 28 knots, the *Bismarck* was commissioned into the *Kriegsmarine* on 24 August 1940.[2] The *Bismarck*, along with her sister ship the *Tirpitz*, was the largest battleship ever built by Germany.

On 19 April, the *Hood* had been ordered to alter course and to sail into the Norwegian Sea following reports that the *Bismarck* had left Kiel and was sailing north-west accompanied by two *Leipzig*-class cruisers—the *Leipzig* and the *Nürnberg*—plus three destroyers. On 21 April, the *Hood* was diverted to Hvalfjörður, Iceland with the destroyer *Inglefield* so as to be on hand when the *Bismarck* attempted to break out into the Atlantic. Later in the day, it was ultimately learned that the *Bismarck* was conducting sea trials in the Baltic.

The *Hood* would remain at Hvalfjörður until 28 April when she put to sea with the cruisers *Suffolk* and *Norfolk* and the destroyers *Active*, *Achates*, *Anthony*, and *Echo* to provide distant cover for two convoys in the North Atlantic. The *Hood* returned to Hvalfjörður on 3 May before departing Iceland for Scapa Flow the following day.

Having arrived back at Scapa Flow on 6 May, Whitworth struck his flag and departed the *Hood* on 8 May to take up his new position as the Second Sea Lord and Chief of Naval Personnel. The next day, the *Hood* participated in 15-inch and 4-inch gunnery practices before Vice-Admiral Lancelot E. Holland, the new commander of the Battlecruiser Squadron and Second-in-Command of the Home Fleet, arrived aboard and hoisted his flag on 12 May.

The *Bismarck* in 1940 shortly after her completion.
(*NH 110829, US Naval History and Heritage Command*)

The *Bismarck* transiting the Kaiser Wilhelm Canal on 8 March 1941 prior to anchoring at Scheerhafen, Kiel. Her departure from Kiel would prompt the Admiralty to order the *Hood* to Iceland. (*Author's collection*)

The *Hood* anchored off Iceland, 1941. It is possible to date this photo between 21 and 28 April when the *Hood* put in at Hvalfjörður so as to be in a position to intercept the *Bismarck* should she have attempted to break out into the Atlantic. (*HMS Hood Association*)

The *Hood* anchored off Iceland in April 1941. (*Boyd Armstrong, HMS Hood Association*)

Vice-Admiral Lancelot E. Holland.

Holland was born on 13 September 1887 in Middleton Cheney and was raised in the Banbury area. On 15 May 1902, he joined the cadet training ship HMS *Britannia*. Passing out of the *Britannia* in September 1903, he was drafted to the China Station where he served aboard the protected cruiser HMS *Eclipse*. Holland would see service out in the Far East until August 1905, spending the latter half of his time there aboard the armoured cruiser HMS *Hampshire*. Returning to Britain, Holland undertook a brief period of service during the summer of 1908 aboard the Admiralty Survey Ship HMS *Research*. On 14 September 1911, Lieutenant Holland joined the ranks of HMS *Excellent*. There, Holland joined the gunnery school to start the 'long course' that would qualify him as a gunnery lieutenant. Holland subsequently went on to take an advanced gunnery course at the Royal Naval College. Holland would spend the years of the Great War in a teaching role aboard HMS *Excellent*.

After the war, Holland was promoted on 31 December 1919 to the rank of commander and then to captain on 30 June 1926. From May 1929, he served as the flag captain of the 2nd Cruiser Squadron aboard HMS *Hawkins*. This was a position he was to keep until February 1931. From May of that year, Holland headed the British naval mission to Greece. Reaching the rank of Rear-Admiral, Holland saw service as the flag captain aboard the battleship HMS *Revenge* for a year from July 1934.

The year 1937 saw Holland occupy the role of aide-de-camp to King George VI before he was promoted in January 1938 to vice-admiral, receiving command of the 2nd Battle Squadron. August 1939 found Holland as the commander of the 3rd Battle Squadron before becoming the Admiralty representative at the Air Ministry.

From July 1940, Holland saw service in the Mediterranean as the commanding officer of Force 'F'. During the course of this command, Holland led his cruisers during the inconclusive engagement of the Battle of Cape Spartivento on 27 November 1940. By this point in his career, Holland had established himself as something of a gunnery specialist. In early 1941, Holland led his cruiser squadron north to the volcanic island of Jan Mayen to capture the German weather trawler *München*. In early May, the *München* was surprised and boarded by the destroyer HMS *Somali*. Prior to being boarded, the crew of the *München* threw the ship's Enigma machine overboard in a weighted bag. However, the crew neglected to destroy documents relating to the operation of the Enigma machine, nor did they destroy the code books which remained on board, which proved crucial in the breaking of the Enigma code.

Holland was part of a clique of officers that was eventually headed by Sir Dudley Pound which monopolised many of the senior posts in the Royal Navy from the 1930s. On 12 May 1941, Holland was promoted to Vice-Admiral Commanding Battlecruiser Squadron and became the Second-in-Command of the Home Fleet. Command of the Battlecruiser Squadron was to be his last seagoing command before being posted to the Admiralty as Pound's Vice Chief of Naval Staff in late 1941. Holland himself had hopes of one day attaining the position of First Sea Lord.3

On 13 May, the Hood left Scapa Flow to conduct range and inclination exercises with Tovey's flagship HMS King George V in the Pentland Firth. The following day damage control exercises were conducted on board. Thereafter, the Hood would remain at anchor as intelligence suggested that the Bismarck was likely to make a break-out attempt into the Atlantic. Faced with this, the ship's company, like those of the other ships of the Home Fleet, were placed on alert as strategies were planned and discussed.

On 18 May, under the command of Admiral Gunther Lütjens, Bismarck slipped her berth in Gotenhafen Bay to take on additional supplies and a replenishment of fuel before proceeding to sea in the early hours of 19 May accompanied by the heavy cruiser Prinz Eugen. On 20 May, the German Seekampfgruppe began a transit of the Green Belt, Danish waters. While sailing through the Kattegat the German ships were sighted by the Swedish cruiser Gotland. Lütjens was certain that the Gotland would report the presence of his ships. His assumption was to be proved correct for the Gotland passed the sighting on to Stockholm, which in turn informed London.

Dawn on 21 May found the task force off the Norwegian coast. At 8 a.m., they entered the Korsfjord near Bergen. At 11 a.m., the *Bismarck* dropped anchor in Grimstadfjord, an arm of the Korsfjord. While the *Bismarck* was at anchor, the *Prinz Eugen* was a few miles north replenishing her fuel stocks from a tanker in Kalvanes Bay. That afternoon, the Baltic camouflage on both ships was painted over with a standard hull grey in an attempt to make the ships less conspicuous in the North Atlantic. Only the imitation bow waves on the vessels were retained. In the meantime, RAF reconnaissance aircraft were scouring for the German ships. At 1.15 p.m., an RAF Coastal Command Spitfire flown by Flying Officer Michael Suckling flew up Korsfjord at 8,000 feet and winged over Grimstadfjord. Unsighted by the sailors aboard the German vessels and anti-aircraft gunners in the fjord below, Suckling flew over the fjord taking pictures of the activity below. When developed, the photographs would provide the final confirmation that the *Bismarck* and an unidentified heavy cruiser of the *Hipper*-class had left the Baltic and were at anchor in Norway, potentially in preparation for a break out into the Atlantic. While the *Bismarck* and the *Prinz Eugen* were at anchor, British forces were already mobilised to try and prevent them from making a successful breakout. Warships of the Royal Navy were patrolling all the likely routes that could be taken to reach the Atlantic. In the Denmark Strait, under the command of Rear-Admiral Frederic Wake-Walker, the heavy cruisers HMS *Suffolk* and *Norfolk* maintained a vigil against a German transit of the Strait. Unknown to the British, at 8 p.m. on 21 May, the *Bismarck* and the *Prinz Eugen* put to sea with Lütjens setting a course for the Denmark Strait.[4]

At 9 p.m. on 21 May, a seemingly routine signal was addressed to Holland from Admiral Tovey. The signal read: 'Flying your flag in the *Hood* and taking *Prince of Wales*, *Acates*, *Antelope*, *Anthony*, *Echo*, *Icarus* and *Electra* under your orders sail at 0001 on May 22 and proceed with moderate dispatch to Hvalfjord'. Throughout the early evening, there had been an abnormal amount of comings

Above: The reconnaissance photograph taken by Flying Officer Michael Suckling on 21 May 1941 of the *Bismarck* at anchor in Grimstadfjord.

Below: The German battleship *Bismarck*. In this photo, taken on 21 May 1941, the *Bismarck* is seen from the *Prinz Eugen* in Grimstadfjord. Before she departed Norway and set a course for the Denmark Strait, the Baltic camouflage on the side of the ship would be painted over. (NH 69720, US Naval History and Heritage Command)

and goings between the *Hood* and Tovey's flagship *King George V*. These comings and goings were observed by Ted Briggs who noticed the 'ominous, blacker streams of smoke [that] began to emerge from the funnels of the fleet, signifying the usual controlled urgency of wartime preparation for sea'.[5] As light rain began to fall and a thin mist began to descend, Briggs hurried to the cabin of Lieutenant-Commander Hugh Wyldbore-Smith with a confidential signal from Tovey: 'Raise steam with all dispatch and be prepared to leave harbour 0001 on May 22'.

A little before midnight, the *Electra*, *Echo*, *Acates*, *Icarus*, *Antelope*, and *Anthony* slipped their moorings in Gutter Sound and, in line ahead, made their way through the Switha Gate to await the *Hood* and the *Prince of Wales* on the edge of the Pentland Firth. After the last of the destroyers had passed through the Switha Gate, the *Hood* was swung around on her engines before sailing majestically southwards in the Flow towards the Hoxa Gate. In the *Hood*'s wake sailed the newly completed *Prince of Wales*. Suffering teething troubles with some of her 14-inch main battery guns, *Prince of Wales* set sail with a number of civilian contractors and technicians from Vickers-Armstrong aboard. As the *Hood* and the *Prince of Wales* glided through the Hoxa Gate, the destroyers took up station ahead.

As the *Hood*, the *Prince of Wales*, and their destroyer escorts left Scapa Flow and sailed north they passed the aircraft carrier *Victorious*. Patrick Jackson, an officer and pilot with 825 Squadron of the Fleet Air Arm who served aboard *Victorious*, recalled the sight:

> It was a sight [that] I shall always remember. We had been out of Scapa Flow training or giving deck landing training to a few of our new RNVR replacements in the squadron, and on our way back there was a delightful evening; the sun was just going down with broken cloud, and coming towards us down the Pentland Firth at full speed were two wonderful sights—the *Hood* and the *Prince of Wales*. The *Hood* I shall always remember. She was wet and glistening grey with water. The waves on her bow breaking on each side and they went past at high speed. Obviously we knew that something was up. When we got into Scapa, the captain and Lieutenant-Commander Esmonde were called across to the Flagship of Jack Tovey, briefing them that the *Bismarck* was known to be out and was suspected to be coming though [*sic.*] the gap between Iceland ...[6]

Aboard the *Hood*, as the crew breakfasted on 22 May, Commander Cross addressed the ship's company over the tannoy system. Cross, in a calm and carefully controlled voice, revealed that the *Bismarck* and an unidentified heavy cruiser of the *Hipper*-class (it was not known at the time that the ship was the *Prinz Eugen*) had dropped anchor in Norway from where they were expected to break out into the Atlantic. Cross went on to inform the crew that the *Hood* and the *Prince of Wales* with their destroyer escorts were proceeding to Hvalfjörður so as to be in a position to cover the routes into the Atlantic to the north and south of Iceland while Tovey and the Home Fleet remained on standby to set sail as soon as it was known that the German ships had sailed.

The announcement did not cause a stir aboard the *Hood*, the crew had heard many similar addresses since the war had begun. Rather, the feeling among the ship's company was that, like on previous occasions, nothing would happen and that the *Hood* would return to Scapa Flow within a few days. At the same time, there was a belief that the *Hood* was capable of handling any 'jumped-up German pocket battleship'. What the *Hood*'s crewmen did not appreciate was that the *Bismarck* was not a mere jumped-up German pocket battleship, but was, in fact, a vessel superior in every way to the aged the *Hood* and the newly constructed *Prince of Wales*.

During the morning, Holland informed Captain Kerr, Captain Leach of the *Prince of Wales*, and the commanding officers of the destroyers of the gunnery policy that he wanted should they come into contact with the German ships: 'If the enemy is encountered and concentration of fire is required, the policy will be G.I.C. (Individual Ship Control); if ships are spread when enemy is met they are to be prepared to flank mark as described in H.W.C.O.' Range and inclination exercises were carried out aboard the British ships until 1.07 p.m. when they commenced zigzagging as a defence against U-boats which it was thought could be lying in wait. *Prince of Wales* and the *Hood* would continue to zigzag until 6.55 p.m. when they resumed a more direct course for Hvalfjörður.

As the *Hood* and the *Prince of Wales* sailed towards Hvalfjörður with their destroyer escorts during the afternoon on 22 May, Captain Henry St John

Taken from an RAF Coastal Command Hudson, this photograph shows the *Hood en route* to intercept the *Bismarck* during the afternoon of 22 May. (*Barry Roberts, HMS Hood Association*)

Fancourt (the commander of the Royal Naval Air Station at Haston, Orkney) was given permission from RAF Coastal Command to dispatch an American-built Martin Maryland bomber to Norway to reconnoitre the fjords around Bergen for signs that the *Bismarck* was preparing to sail. Piloted by Lieutenant N. N. Goddard with Commander G. A. Rotherham flying as observer, the Maryland soon took off and flew to Bergen. Returning to Orkney, Goddard and Rotherham reported their findings. At 7.39 p.m. that evening, Tovey received a report from Haston: 'Following received from Haston reconnaissance aircraft over Bergen. Battleship and cruiser have left'.[7] Tovey studied the signal on his desk. He was now in possession of the news that the Royal Navy had been awaiting. Tovey now faced a decision of what course of action to take. Had the German vessels actually sailed from Bergen towards the Atlantic or had they sailed to another area of Norway? If the German ships had left Bergen, it was possible that they could be close to breaking out into the Atlantic. If he delayed sailing with the bulk of the Home Fleet, then his ships may not arrive on scene in time to assist in the battle that would ensue as the Royal Navy attempted to prevent the German vessels from breaking out into the Atlantic. On the other hand, if the *Bismarck* and the *Prinz Eugen* were still in and around Norway then he might find himself returning to Scapa Flow owing to a lack of fuel at a critical moment.

At 10.30 p.m., a signal arrived aboard the *Hood* from Tovey in which the Commander-in-Chief of the Home Fleet instructed Holland '*Bismarck* and consort sailed proceed to cover south-west of Iceland'. At 11 p.m., flying his flag in the *King George V*, Tovey put to sea accompanied by the aircraft carrier HMS *Victorious*, five light cruisers, and six destroyers. At the same time, HMS *Repulse* was ordered to put to sea from the River Clyde and to sail a northerly course to join Tovey's battle group.

As the *Hood* altered course in accordance with Tovey's signal, Commander Cross updated the ship's company of the situation. Possibly for the first time in the *Hood*'s career, the nervous feeling of an approaching battle gripped the ship's company. Some felt that they were hungry, yet they did not want to eat. Others yawned nervously and tried to appear unconcerned. Everyone knew it was just an act, yet the possibilities of battle were not seriously discussed.

As he sat in his mess deck that evening playing a game of cards, Ted Briggs sprang into action upon hearing the tannoy blare out 'Flag Lieutenant's messenger report to the SDO [Signal Distribution Office] at the double!' Briggs hastily made his way to the signal distribution office where a signal was thrust into his hand. Briggs hurriedly made his way to the cabin of Lieutenant-Commander Wyldbore-Smith. Wyldbore-Smith already knew of the message's contents, but he still had to see it in writing. The message was short, sharp and concise and served to show that unlike previous occasions when the *Hood* had put to sea to engage elusive German raiders, this was to be no wild goose chase. The message Briggs hand to Wyldbore-Smith simply stated, 'From *Suffolk*—Enemy in Sight!'

At 7.30 p.m. on 21 May, the *Bismarck* and the *Prinz Eugen* began to weigh anchor before sailing at 8 p.m. Admiral Lütjens favoured the Denmark Strait as the route into the Atlantic and decided that his ships would transit the Strait on their way into the Atlantic. It may be noted that the Denmark Strait was the same route that Lütjens had taken while commanding the *Gneisenau* and the *Scharnhorst* on their Atlantic raiding sortie. On 22 May, the weather had begun to deteriorate shielding the German vessels from the prying eyes of Allied aircraft. As they continued towards the Denmark Strait, Lütjens remained under the illusion that the bulk of the Royal Navy's Home Fleet was still at anchor at Scapa Flow rather than sailing north at full speed to intercept him.

At midnight on 23 May, the *Bismarck* and the *Prinz Eugen* executed a south-west turn, which would take them through the Denmark Strait. The speed of the German ships was increased from 24 to 27 knots in an attempt to ensure that the breakout into the Atlantic was achieved before the favourable weather turned. The journey through the Denmark Strait was the most dangerous part of the operation. During the spring months, the navigable channel was only between 30 and 40 miles wide. Lütjens, *Kapitän zur See* Lindemann of the *Bismarck*, and *Kapitän zur See* Helmuth Brinkmann of the *Prinz Eugen* were well aware of this and knew that if the British had discovered their intentions, then patrols would be dispatched to patrol the Strait. If the fog held then they might be fortunate enough to bypass any patrols unnoticed and slip through the Denmark Strait and out into the Atlantic. Unfortunately for the Germans, the weather conditions were changing. By the late afternoon, the fog began to lift and visibility increased to 10 miles. By the afternoon of 23 May, under the command of Vice Admiral Wake-Walker, HMS *Suffolk* and *Norfolk* were on station in the Denmark Strait, the role of the cruisers being to locate the two German ships and to maintain contact with them. There was no question of Wake-Walker engaging the German ships for his cruisers were unquestionably outgunned. The *Norfolk* and the *Suffolk* would patrol down the Strait in a south-east direction and would then reverse their course to the north-west. This patrol would continue until either the German ships were sighted or enough time had elapsed to ensure that they were not making a breakout attempt into the Atlantic via this route.

Both cruisers were fitted with radar equipment; however, that which equipped the *Suffolk* was far superior to that which equipped the *Norfolk*. While the *Norfolk* was equipped with a radar system (which allowed her to see ahead), the *Suffolk* was fitted with multi-directional radar, which had a range of 13 miles. The *Suffolk*'s radar allowed her to sweep all directions with the exception of a blind spot at her stern. It was for this reason that it was decided that the *Suffolk* would patrol the Greenland side of the Strait while the *Norfolk* patrolled from the Icelandic side. The *Suffolk* would keep the pack ice at the limit of her radar, which would allow her room for manoeuvre should the *Bismarck* and the *Prinz Eugen* be sighted. Protection was further enhanced by the foggy conditions. The weather was clear over Greenland and the ice pack; however, a bank of fog was clinging to the Icelandic coast. This fog would provide a blanket of protection into which the British cruisers could slip should the German ships be sighted.

At 6.11 p.m., the radar on the *Bismarck* picked up two objects to starboard. Alarms were sounded causing the crews of the German vessels to rush to their respective action stations. It was soon realised that the objects that had been picked up on radar were far from enemy ships, but icebergs. In the meantime, the Germans had reached the limit of the ice pack, and had set a course that would take them through the Strait. Aboard the *Suffolk*, at 7.22 p.m., while on her south-westerly run of her patrol, Able Seaman Alfred Newell (who was on duty at the starboard lookout position in order to cover the blind spot not covered by radar) was scanning the horizon. As he scanned the horizon, out of the mist at a range of seven miles approached the *Bismarck* and the *Prinz Eugen*. A sighting report was swiftly called out. The reaction aboard the *Suffolk* was swift as the ship heeled over in order to seek the cover of the fog bank. Those aboard the *Suffolk* were encouraged by the fact that neither of the German ships had opened fire. Truth be told, the *Bismarck*'s radar had picked up the British cruiser; however, she was unable to engage the British cruiser as she ran under the cover of the fog. Signals were transmitted from the *Suffolk* stating that contact with the German vessels had been established. The wireless equipment on the *Suffolk* was, however, suffering from damp and the contact report got no further than the *Norfolk*.

HMS *Norfolk*, on her patrol within the safety of the fog, picked up the report from her sister ship. Upon picking up the report, the *Norfolk* steered to take up a position on the edge of the fog bank to assist in the maintaining of contact with the German vessels. At 8.30 p.m., the *Norfolk* strayed too close to the edge of the fog bank resulting in a loss over cover, albeit briefly. The *Norfolk* was sighted

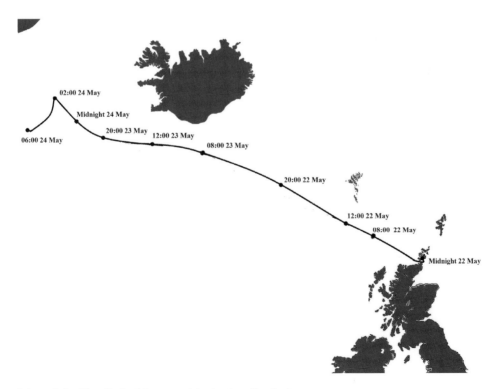

Map of the *Hood*'s final journey. (*Author's collection*)

aboard the *Bismarck*, which opened fire immediately. The *Bismarck* fired five salvos, three of which straddled the British cruiser throwing splinters aboard. Although not hit by a direct impact, the *Norfolk* launched a smokescreen and hastily retired into the fog. This was the first time that the new, mighty German battleship had fired her guns in anger, and it served as a deadly warning to the British of the accuracy of the *Bismarck*'s guns.[8]

The British cruisers took up a position astern of the German ships, with the *Suffolk* off the starboard quarter and the *Norfolk* off the port quarter. Following retreating into the fog, HMS *Norfolk* transmitted a contact report. Both vessels would make further periodic reports on the position of the German ships until more powerful British vessels were in a position to engage.

Aboard the *Bismarck*, there was a problem. The firing of the forward turrets during the one-sided engagement with the *Norfolk* had disabled the forward radar. As a result, the *Bismarck* was blind to what lay ahead of her. The *Prinz Eugen*'s radar was functioning effectively; therefore, Lütjens ordered that the *Prinz Eugen* and the *Bismarck* should exchange positions so that the heavy cruiser with her fully functioning radar could take the lead. The powerful guns of the *Bismarck* at the rear of the battle group would serve to prevent the British from sailing any closer. This change of position would later cause great confusion for the British.[9]

19

'Suddenly,
the *Hood* Split in Two'

By now, the weather was becoming worse. Holland's ships began to bump around in the rough seas as snow flurries began to whip into the ships. Those aboard the destroyers felt the worsening weather the most. The plight of the destroyers became apparent when the senior officer of the destroyer screen, Commander Cecil Wakeford May of HMS *Electra*, sent a signal to Holland stating: 'Do not consider destroyers can maintain present speed without danger'. At 8.55 p.m., Holland replied: 'If you are unable to maintain this speed I will have to go on without you. You should follow at your best speed'.

The determination of the British destroyers was tremendous and for the next half an hour their commanding officers attempted to keep up with the *Hood* and the *Prince of Wales*. Gradually, however, they were forced to accept the inevitable and were forced to reduce speed and drop astern.[1]

As the *Hood* sailed on with the *Prince of Wales* in tow, aboard the battlecruiser Commander Cross delivered an electrifying broadcast to the ship's company in which he stated: 'We are expected to intercept at 02.00 tomorrow morning. We will go to action stations at midnight. In the meantime prepare yourselves and above all change into clean underwear'.[2] The latter part of Cross' message was a measure intended to help reduce the risk of infection in the event of becoming wounded. The last time that this order had been issued to those aboard the *Hood* had been in July 1940, prior to the bombardment of the French Fleet at Mers el-Kébir.

As midnight approached, Ted Briggs changed into clean underwear and socks before putting on his number three tailor suit followed by a lifebelt, waterproof coat, flash hood and gauntlets. A gas mask hung in front of his chest while a tin hat sat snug atop his head. As he waddled around the ship, the young officer's signalman hoped that his several layers of clothing would protect him not just against infection if wounded, but also from the cold and wet, potential flash burns and would offer him a chance of survival if he ended up in the icy water. What unnerved Briggs most of all was not the idea of being blasted into an 'instant oblivion' if on the receiving end of a direct hit, but rather the idea of 'being fearfully wounded or mutilated and screaming out in painful insanity', which he

Believed to be one of the last photographs of the *Hood* as a fighting entity, this photograph was taken from aboard the *Prince of Wales* as the two ships sailed towards the Denmark Strait. (*Sea Power Centre Australia, Royal Australian Navy*)

feared would see him exposed and branded a coward, yet at the same time, he took comfort from the quiet confidence that infused everyone in the ship. While in the process of collecting some signals for the flag lieutenant, Briggs bumped into one of his good friends aboard the ship, Ordinary Signalman Frank Tuxworth. The two young sailors paused briefly for an exchange that served to bolster each other's shield of bravado. Their exchange was cut short by the bugle call over the tannoy system, which summoned everyone to their action stations.

Making his way up to the compass platform, Briggs was somewhat struck by the way in which the floodlights had been replaced by the soft lights around the chart table and the gentle glow of the binnacle. Including Briggs, ten men were to be found on the compass platform. Vice-Admiral Holland dominated the centre of the position sitting in the captain's chair. Captain Kerr stood on Holland's right. A few paces to the right of Captain Kerr stood Commander Edward Gregson, the squadron gunnery officer, the man who would order the signal be issued to the *Prince of Wales* to open fire when the *Bismarck* was intercepted. The flag lieutenant was also to be found on the compass platform, prepared to do the admiral's bidding while Briggs stood prepared to run messages for flags, acknowledge voice pipes, and collect signals. An additional young sailor was also on the compass platform: William Dundas, who served as midshipman of the watch and was to act as a messenger and lookout. The majority of those present on the compass platform were dressed similarly to Briggs, the main difference being that while everyone else wore stout sea boots, Briggs wore shoes. Only

Admiral Holland was dressed differently. Wearing a navy issue greatcoat, Holland was sitting bolt upright in the captain's chair while his fingers tapped nervously on the pair of binoculars that hung around his neck.[3]

At 12.08 a.m. on 24 May, Empire Day, Holland ordered a reduction of speed to 25 knots before altering course due north. In executing this turn to starboard, Holland indicated to all of his officers that he was anxious to close with the German squadron as quickly as possible. In May, the arctic twilight lasts almost all night long, with a five-hour period of comparative darkness. Holland's change of course to due north was based on the assumption that his ships were sailing on a reciprocal course to those of the German squadron. Had Holland maintained his former course and speed he could have expected to engage the *Bismarck* at 2.30 a.m., which would have meant going into action during the darkest period of the arctic night. The change of course was designed to bring the planned interception forward. Providing his course and speed estimates were correct, with the two squadrons closing at a combined rate of approximately 60 knots, it was anticipated that contact would be made at 1.40 a.m. Holland knew that the sun would set at 1.51 a.m., at which point the enemy would be silhouetted against its afterglow. At 12.15 a.m., the final preparations for action were made when the battle ensigns were hoisted. These great White Ensigns, some of the largest in the Royal Navy at 24 feet in length and 12 feet wide were hoisted and instantly began to flutter from the yardarms of the *Hood* and the *Prince of Wales*.[4] No sooner had the battle ensigns been hoisted that a signal was received aboard the *Hood* from the *Suffolk*. The two cruisers had lost contact with the *Bismarck*.

Around the time that the battle ensigns were hoisted aboard Holland's ships, Lütjens ordered the *Bismarck* to reverse course in an attempt to shake off the shadowing the *Suffolk*. Lütjens had not counted on the effectiveness of the radar systems that equipped the British cruisers, which enabled them to track the German ships from afar. When the *Bismarck* reversed course, the *Suffolk* merely withdrew, maintaining the distance between herself and the German battleship. Therefore, the *Bismarck* returned to formation behind the *Prinz Eugen*. The *Suffolk*'s captain, Captain Robert M. Ellis, had been fully justified in ordering the course of the *Suffolk* to be altered so as to stay out of range of *Bismarck*'s guns. However, a problem befell the British. By the time they realised that the *Bismarck* had resumed her original course, and the *Suffolk* had returned to her original bearing, the German battle group had disappeared into a snowstorm. Attempts were made aboard the *Suffolk* to maintain contact with the German ships using radar; however, in the circumstances, maintaining contact proved to be impossible.

Aboard the *Hood*, Holland received the news of the loss of contact in his usual reserved, calm fashion. Holland knew that the worst possible scenario, so far as the British were concerned, was for the *Bismarck* and the *Prinz Eugen* to successfully break out into the Atlantic. To Holland, the best course of action seemed to be to close the distance between his ships and the last known position of the German battle group as quickly as possible. At 2.03 a.m., with the *Suffolk* and the *Norfolk* having failed to re-establish contact with the *Bismarck* and the

Prinz Eugen, Holland ordered a course change to 200 degrees and permitted the crews of his ships to go to relaxed action stations.[5] It was now uncertain whether or not an interception would be forthcoming at all. The uncertainty of whether or not an interception would take place was kept from the *Hood's* crew during this period. All the while, the *Hood* and the *Prince of Wales* ploughed on; spray splattered the glass windows of the *Hood's* compass platform as Holland looked out, sailing the *Hood* in no definite direction.

At 2.47 a.m., the *Suffolk* regained radar contact with the German ships. Her subsequent reports placed the *Prinz Eugen* and the *Bismarck* approximately 35 miles to the north-west of the *Hood* and the *Prince of Wales*. With the regaining of contact, Holland ordered a change of course and speed. At 4.50 a.m., the *Prince of Wales* took guide of the squadron, positioning herself ahead of the *Hood* before the battlecruiser retook the guide at 5.05 a.m. Meanwhile, the *Prinz Eugen* and the *Bismarck* continued to make steady progress through the Denmark Strait. Aboard the *Hood* and the *Prince of Wales*, the crews were ordered to a heightened state of readiness. Everyone expected contact to be made with the German ships, it was just a question of when. As the hours had slipped by, the sky had begun to brighten as dawn neared. The command crews trained their binoculars and strained their eyes to the north where they expected the German vessels to approach from.

Around the time that the *Prince of Wales* took up position as guide of the squadron, the German ships were picked up on radar. From the compass platform, Briggs swapped a few words with his friend, Ordinary Signalman Ronald Bell, who manned the end of the same voice pipe one deck below on the flag deck. What struck Briggs at this moment was the lack of fear in his shipmate's voice. 'Near him would be Tuxworth, helping to handle the halyards and still joking, no doubt. Alongside in charge of the flags I guessed that Yeoman Bill Nevett would be as outwardly calm as ever, despite all the pallor of his face'.[6] Briggs could also imagine Petty Officer Stanley Boardman, a loving family man with a newborn baby at home, clearing for action at his position in charge of the starboard two-pounder Mk VIII pom-pom anti-aircraft gun 'Sally', and Sick Berth Petty Officer George Stannard down in the sickbay sterilising instruments, making sure that bandages were on hand and laying out towels. At 5 a.m., the call rang out throughout the *Hood*: 'Prepare for instant action'. Thoughts quickly turned back to the task in hand.

It was shortly after 5 a.m. when the hydrophone operators aboard the *Prinz Eugen* picked up the sounds of ships way off to port. Aboard the *Bismarck*, *Kapitänleutnant* Burkard von Müllenheim-Rechberg, the ship's fourth artillery officer, was in the aft fire control station when the approaching *Hood* and *Prince of Wales* were first sighted.

> It must have been around 05.45, the rising sun having already lit up the horizon, when the smoke plumes of two ships and then the tips of their masts came into view on our port beam. General quarters was sounded on the *Bismarck*. Through

my director, I watched as the masts in the distance grew higher and higher, reached
their full length, and the silhouettes of the ships below them became visible. I could
hear our first gunnery officer, *Korvettenkapitän* Adalbert Schneider, speaking on the
fire-control telephone. His hour had come, and all our thoughts and good wishes
were with that competent, sensible man ... Now I heard Schneider saying he thought
the approaching ships were heavy cruisers and giving the targeting information on
the lead one; I heard our second gunnery officer, *Korvettenkapitän* Helmut Albrecht,
who was in the forward controlling station, expressing first mildly, then definitely,
doubt that the ships were heavy cruisers and saying that he thought they were battle
cruisers or battleships. Then the turrets were trained, the 38-centimetre guns loaded,
and all we needed was the Fleet Commander's permission to fire.[7]

At the same time, aboard the *Hood* and the *Prince of Wales*, the hydraulic
apparatus that worked the turrets grunted and hissed while the rangefinders
swivelled as 'A' and 'B' turrets rose up into the position to fire.[8] From HMS
Suffolk, Ludovic Porter looked on through a pair of binoculars at the scene that
lay before him:

Against the light horizon were silhouetted the German ships, while away to port,
and barely distinguishable against the low cloud forming their background, were the
Hood and *Prince of Wales*. As they tore along with their guns cocked up in the air
they were a gallant sight, and we watched with the feeling of a producer who has set
his stage and now awaits only the rising of the curtain.[9]

At 5.37 a.m., Holland had ordered an alteration of course 40 degrees to starboard.
This course alteration put the *Prince of Wales* and the *Hood* on a heading of 280
degrees with the *Prinz Eugen* and the *Bismarck* off their starboard bows. Holland
had hoped to emerge ahead of the German ships and to 'cross the T' that would
have allowed him to bring all of the guns of his ships to bear on the enemy who
would have been able only to fire their forward armament. Unfortunately for
Holland, his ships had been on a diverging course as a result of the combination
of the northern diversion during the early hours of the morning and an error in
the position reports from the *Norfolk* and the *Suffolk*.

With his original plan now no longer feasible, Holland planned to close the
range as quickly as possible and to then turn at short range to open A-arcs. By
closing quickly, Holland hoped to reduce the *Hood*'s vulnerability to plunging fire
as at a shorter range the German shells would be fired with a shallower trajectory
and the impact was more likely to be taken by the thicker side armour. Holland
also planned to keep his two ships in close formation for gunnery concentration.
The result of all of this was that the *Hood* and the *Prince of Wales* would
approach the enemy at an acute angle, which served to mask their rear turrets.
Thus Holland would be going into battle with roughly half of his main armament.
To compound matters further, heavy sea spray would pose a problem for the
optical rangefinders of his ships. Lütjens, meanwhile, would be able to engage

with his full main battery complement and the German rangefinders, which were superior to the British types, would suffer less from the effects of wind and spray as the wind was on their disengaged sides.

Holland's decision to approach in this manner has been the subject of much debate in the years following the Battle of the Denmark Strait. Most of those who have sought to criticise Holland and the tactics that he employed have, however, benefitted from hindsight and have often drawn on points that were unknown to Holland at the time. It must not be forgotten that it is problematic to judge historical decisions with hindsight without taking into account the full extent of the information available to the decision makers and the circumstances in which the decision was made. One such work that has been highly critical of Holland was *The Bismarck Episode* by Russell Grenfell.[10] Grenfell's work was written shortly after the war and is damning of both Holland and his tactics. Grenfell's analysis and criticism of Holland are somewhat incomplete owing to the fact that not all of the details of the battle were known at the time of publication. Furthermore, Grenfell fails to acknowledge that Holland appeared to be following contemporary fighting instructions. Grenfell also made the argument that the *Hood* and the *Prince of Wales* had roughly the same armament as the *Bismarck* and that as such, Holland should have stood off and destroyed her. This argument completely ignores the vulnerability of the *Hood* to plunging fire. This book, nevertheless, is an apt starting point for the examining of and formulating counterarguments to criticisms of Holland.

While some works have ridiculed Holland, works such as that by Ludovic Kennedy (*Pursuit*) have sought to vindicate Holland.[11] Indeed, Kennedy points out that Holland ordered a turn to the north that was aimed at bringing about action between the two opposing squadrons, not as a result of losing contact with the *Bismarck* as some have claimed. Indeed, when Holland's handling of the operation that resulted in the Battle of the Denmark Strait is studied and the benefit of hindsight is removed, a very carefully and thoughtfully executed plan remains. On the face of it, it would appear that Holland had made a tactical mistake, and he has received criticism for this. There is more to this approach, however, than meets the eye. Holland's decision for an end-on approach may have had its roots in the Battle of Cape Spartivento. Commanding Force 'F', despite his five ships being loaded with RAF personnel and stores, Holland gave a good account of himself. During the battle, Holland did not concentrate the fire of his ships and operate it as one fighting unit owing to the fact that the crews had received no training and had undertaken no practice in fighting together.[12] In addition to this, Holland regarded the convoy that he was allocated to cover as being more important than engaging the Italian Fleet in battle. During a Board of Enquiry into the escape of the Italian Fleet, Holland was asked why he did not give chase to the Italian Fleet to which he replied that his 'ships were outgunned and he did not think it was a good principle'.[13] Holland's actions appear prudent given his handicapped cruiser squadron; however, the Admiralty's report conclusion disagreed:

The Board of Enquiry suggests ... that the time chosen to give up the chase was slightly early ... The Board of the Admiralty cannot emphasis [*sic.*] enough that in all cases especially when dealing with an enemy who is reluctant to engage in close action, no opportunity must be allowed to pass of attaining, what is in fact, the ultimate objective of the Royal Navy—the destruction of main enemy naval forces when and whenever they are encountered. Only thus can control of the sea communications be properly secured.[14]

From the conclusion of the Admiralty report, it may be deduced that Holland was under pressure to rectify these criticisms of his command from the Admiralty, and that this was on his mind at the Battle of the Denmark Strait. Therefore, it may be said that Holland was following the Admiralty's directives and thus any criticism of Holland should be placed at the Admiralty's door.

Holland was an experienced gunnery and commanding officer. It is very likely that he considered all of the negative factors of his approach that morning, and knew that every action carries an element of risk. It should be remembered that Holland was presented with an opportunity to stop a potentially serious threat to Britain's maritime lifelines and had to seize the initiative and press home the attack with the forces at his disposal.

At 5.52 a.m., the range had decreased to 14.2 miles (22.8 km). The *Hood* and the *Prince of Wales* were now on a course of 300 degrees, having executed a further 20-degree course alteration at 5.49 a.m. At 5.50 a.m., Holland issued the order 'GSB 337 L1', which directed the *Hood* and the *Prince of Wales* to engage the left-hand German ship.

Looking at the enemy ships from aboard the *Prince of Wales* was Lieutenant-Commander Colin McMullen, the ship's gunnery officer. The instruction was received from the *Hood* to 'Engage left hand ship'. In issuing this order, the idea was to have the *Hood* and the *Prince of Wales* concentrate their fire on one ship that would enable a more rapid correction in the fall of shot. Furthermore, the left-hand ship was the lead ship, which convention dictated would be the *Bismarck*. By concentrating fire on the left-hand ship, the idea was to neutralise the *Bismarck*—the more threatening of the two German ships. There was but one problem: Lütjens' decision to have the *Prinz Eugen* lead the squadron with her functioning forward radar had not been noted aboard the *Norfolk* or the *Suffolk*, and this change of position had not been transmitted to Holland aboard the *Hood*. So it was that the *Hood*'s gunners were being instructed to range on the wrong vessel. Aboard the *Prince of Wales*, McMullen suspected that the left-hand ship that he was being ordered to target was not the *Bismarck*. From his perspective, it was an easy mistake to make. Convention dictated that the *Bismarck* should be the lead vessel, and over the horizon emerged two German vessels, one leading the other, with what amounted to virtually the same silhouette, with one funnel and four turrets.

Looking through his more modern and powerful rangefinder, McMullen thought that the left-hand ship, the leading vessel, 'looked definitely smaller ... We immediately realised that the *Hood* had made a mistake'. In response, McMullen ordered that the light signal 'Make IMI' be flashed to the *Hood*. This was a request for the *Hood* to repeat her previous signal and a sign that the elder vessel had perhaps made an error. Believing that a huge error was being made McMullen urged, 'Make IMI, IMI, IMI'.[15] This left Captain Leach of the *Prince of Wales* in something of a predicament. The *Hood* and *Prince of Wales* had been sent to prevent a German breakout into the Atlantic, specifically by the *Bismarck*. His ship had received orders to engage the left-hand ship, but he trusted his gunnery officer. With the seconds quickly ticking down before the order to open fire would be given, and with no corrections coming from the flagship, Leach made a decision. McMullen was ordered to range in on the right-hand ship.

It is not known when exactly the mistake in identification was realised aboard the *Hood*; those serving on board said the order to switch targets came after the ship had fired two salvos while Captain Leach insisted that the order was given before the order was given to open fire. According to the HMS *Hood* Association website, as the distance between Holland and Lütjens' ships decreased, the spotters in the *Hood* realised their mistake; Holland was then informed, and only moments before opening fire, he issued the order 'GOB 1', which directed that fire be switched to the right-hand ship. The order to switch targets was transmitted to the *Prince of Wales*, which was already ranging in on the *Bismarck*. For some unknown reason, however, when the *Hood* did open fire, her gunners were still targeting the *Prinz Eugen*. The reason for the failure of those aboard the *Hood* to switch targets is not known. It may be the case that the gunners simply could not switch targets quick enough, or there may have been communication problems.

Just after 5.52 a.m., Holland issued the order to open fire. From the compass platform, the gunnery officer bellowed 'shoot'. The order was swiftly followed by the ting-ting of the firing gong before the *Hood*'s first salvo belched out with an ear-shattering roar, leaving in their wake a cloud of brown cordite smoke which momentarily hugged the compass platform.[16] As Holland gave the order to open fire, Gregson gave a nod to Chief Yeoman of the Signals George Carn who ordered the raising of Signal Flag 5, which ordered the *Prince of Wales* to open fire when she was ready. A few seconds after the *Hood*, the *Prince of Wales* let loose with her first salvo.

From his position aboard the *Bismarck*, Müllenheim-Rechberg looked on:

> The clock showed 05.53. The range, I figured, was less than 25,000 metres. There were flashes like lightning out there! Still approaching nearly bow-on, the enemy had opened fire. *Donerwetter*! Those flashes couldn't be coming from a cruiser's medium-calibre guns. Certain that we would immediately return the fire, I braced myself for 'permission to fire' and the thunder of our guns that would follow. Nothing happened. We in the after station looked at one another in bewilderment. Why weren't we doing something? The question hung in the air. Schnieder's voice came over the telephone. 'Request permission to fire'. Silence. Schnieder again: 'Enemy has opened fire', 'Enemy's salvos well grouped', and, anew, 'Request permission to

fire'. Still no response. Lütjens was hesitating. The tension-laden seconds turned into minutes. The British ships were turning slightly to port, the lead ship showing an extremely long forecastle and two heavy twin turrets. On the telephone I heard Albrecht shout, 'The *Hood*—it's the *Hood*!' It was an unforgettable moment. There she was, the famous warship, once the largest in the world, that had been the 'terror' of so many of our war games.[17]

The first salvo from the *Hood* landed near the *Prinz Eugen*, but did not hit the heavy cruiser, while the *Prince of Wales*'s opening salvo was observed to come down around 1,500 yards over and aft of the *Bismarck*. This was down to incorrect estimates of the distance to the targets during the initial sightings, and due to a misjudgement in the speed and course of the German ships. When the identification of the British ships became clear, the *Hood* and a *King George V*-class battleship, which it was assumed was Tovey's flagship *King George V*—it was believed that the *Prince of Wales* was still being worked up—and that they were capital ships and not cruisers, Lütjens sent an urgent signal to *Kriegsmarine* headquarters, 'Am in a fight with two heavy units'.

Meanwhile, the *Hood* fired a second salvo at the *Prinz Eugen* which, like the first, missed the target, throwing a few splinters and much water aboard the heavy cruiser. Following firing her second salvo at the *Prinz Eugen*, the guns of the *Hood* were finally traversed around towards the *Bismarck*. At the same time, following firing her first salvo at the *Bismarck*, the *Prince of Wales* began to suffer what would be the first of a number of mechanical problems. No. 1 gun of 'A' turret temporarily broke down, meaning it could no longer fire. Nevertheless, the *Prince of Wales* continued to fire at the *Bismarck*. However, her second, third, and fourth salvos all overshot the *Bismarck* and landed harmlessly in the sea. Following two minutes of British shelling without response, *Kapitän* Lindemann had finally had enough. At 5.55 a.m., Lindemann reportedly turned to Lütjens and stated: 'I will not let my ship get shot from under my arse!' After this exchange, the order was given for the German ships to open fire. The *Bismarck* immediately opened fire and was swiftly followed by the *Prinz Eugen*. Both of the German vessels concentrated their fire on the leading British ship—the *Hood*. The *Bismarck*'s first salvo landed short of the target, coming down in the sea in front and starboard of the British battlecruiser. At 5.56 a.m., the *Prince of Wales*'s fifth salvo landed over *Bismarck* and was swiftly followed by a sixth salvo, which straddled and is likely to have hit the battleship although no hits were observed from aboard the British battleship. In this time, the *Prinz Eugen* fired a further three salvos at the *Hood*. The *Bismarck* fired a second salvo, which landed directly between the two British capital ships. This was followed by a third salvo, which appeared to straddle the *Hood*.

At 5.57 a.m., the *Hood* was struck by a salvo of 8-inch armour piercing shells from the *Prinz Eugen*. The impact rocked the ship from end to end, knocking everyone on the compass platform from their feet. Rising to his feet, Gregson walked almost sedately out to the starboard wing of the compass platform to

Taken from aboard the *Prinz Eugen*, this photo captures the moment 15-inch shells from the *Hood* splashed down near the German heavy cruiser. The *Hood*'s first salvo directed against the *Prinz Eugen* landed harmlessly in the water, while the second salvo crashed down into the sea but threw splinters aboard the German vessel. (*NH 69723, US Naval History and Heritage Command*)

One of the most famous photographs of the *Bismarck* taken as she opened fire on the *Hood*.

The *Bismarck* engaging HMS *Hood* and the *Prince of Wales*. Shells from the *Prince of Wales* can be seen to have fallen short. (*NH 69728, US Naval History and Heritage Command*)

Photographed from the *Prinz Eugen*, the *Bismarck* can be seen firing on the *Hood* and the *Prince of Wales*. (*NH 69722, US Naval History and Heritage Command*)

see what had happened. Almost as if the ship were on manoeuvres, in a calm yet firm tone of voice, he reported, 'We've been hit at the base of the mainmast, Sir, and we're on fire'. A wild cacophony of cries of 'Fire' resounded through the voice pipes and telephones. On the boat deck amidships, a fierce fire blazed, punctured by loud explosions. 'The four-inch ready-use ammunition is exploding,' the torpedo officer reported.[18] Manning one of the 4-inch guns amid the rapidly unfolding horror was Robert Tilburn. Tilburn thought that the Hood had been struck by three shells and heard the gun crews ordered to take shelter inside the ship's superstructure. Along with two other sailors, Tilburn was held back by a gunner's mate and was ordered to douse the exploding ammunition.

Faced with the blaze, which was 'pinkish in colour, with not much smoke', and the exploding ammunition, Tilburn and the other sailors decided they would look to tackle the blaze once the ready-use ammunition had finished exploding. The gunner's mate went to inform the gunnery officer, but at that moment, the recreation space in which the gunners were taking shelter was hit by a German shell, which, according to Tilburn, killed everyone inside—approximately 200 men.[19] Tilburn and the two sailors he was with flung themselves to the deck as anti-aircraft shells began to whizz and explode all around them. The hell that was the boat deck was not visible to Vice-Admiral Holland and Captain Kerr, who kept their binoculars trained firmly on the enemy. As the agonised screams and cries of the wounded and the dying continued to radiate through the voice pipes, Ted Briggs was gripped by fear, the screams he could hear almost turning his blood to ice.[20] As anti-aircraft shells continued to detonate all over the boat deck, Captain Kerr ordered that the 4-inch gun crews should take cover and that the damage control parties should steer clear of the area until the ready-use ammunition had been expended. Keeping away from the area was, in itself, no mean feat as the burning projectiles made a charnel house of the positions above the platform deck, with further screams of the wounded, maimed, and dying continuing to emit through the voice pipes and from the flag deck in a stringent chorus.[21]

It was at this moment, 5.58 a.m., that Holland, believing that he was likely to be out of the danger zone for plunging fire, ordered 'Turn twenty degrees to port together', in an attempt to open A-arcs, bringing 'X' and 'Y' turrets into action. Chief Yeoman Carn passed the order to the flag deck, where surprisingly, among the horror that had ravaged the position, someone appeared to be capable of carrying on with their duties. A blue pennant was run up the yardarm to convey the order to the Prince of Wales. As the Hood turned to port, 'X' turret roared into action, but 'Y' turret remained silent. It was then that the Bismarck's fifth salvo splashed down straddling the Hood. According to Ted Briggs, 'A blinding flash swept around the outside of the compass platform. Again I found myself being lifted off my feet and dumped head first on the deck'.[22]

At least one of the Bismarck's 15-inch shells penetrated the Hood's weakly armoured deck around the area of the main mast. The shell smashed its way through the decks of the battlecruiser where it reached an aft magazine before

Taken in 1940, this image taken from the aft air defence position shows the layout of the boat deck. Centre right in the image, a UP launcher can be seen under cover while three 4-inch guns can clearly be distinguished. Carley floats and numerous boats can be seen also. This particular image also illustrates the arrangement of some of the *Hood*'s searchlights. It was in this area that the ready-use ammunition wreaked havoc from 5.57 a.m.

exploding. The *Hood* was rocked by a violent explosion; a great tower of flame rushed upwards and almost instantaneously, the mighty ship was enveloped from bow to stern in smoke. Large pieces of debris were hurled in the air. Taking shelter on the boat deck, Robert Tilburn felt the explosion. 'It shook the entire ship, blast and shrapnel buffeting the midships position, but the explosion did not seem any worse than the effect of the *Hood* firing a salvo'. Having sought shelter behind the splinter shield of an unrotated projectile launcher, Tilburn was spared immediate death or injury. The sailors that he was with were not so fortunate. One sailor was simply 'blown away' by the force of the explosion while the other 'was disembowelled by a shell splinter which to Tilburn was a vision of horror: "It opened him up like a butcher and all his innards were coming out"'.[23] In the immediate aftermath of the explosion, Tilburn was struck by dead silence. Debris, bodies, and parts of bodies, some of which could clearly be seen to have been those of officers, all started to fall.

From the compass platform, William Dundas had got the impression that the *Bismarck* had fired a shell through the *Hood*'s spotting top, which did not explode but which caused carnage, accounting for the bodies that landed on the upper deck. One body fell by close to the compass platform. Captain Kerr asked Dundas to go and identify who it was who had fallen. Dundas went and looked before reporting back to the captain that he could not tell as the corpse had no face and no hands and that all he could say was that the body was that of a lieutenant.

Having been rocked by the explosion that engulfed her from end to end in smoke, the *Hood* began to list hesitantly to starboard before stopping when the list reached approximately 10 degrees. The call arrived on the compass platform from the helmsman, 'Steering gone, Sir'. Showing no signs of concern, fear, or animation, Kerr simply replied, 'Very good', before immediately issuing the order 'Changeover to emergency steering'.

Burkard von Müllenheim-Rechberg recalled events as they appeared to him from his vantage point aboard the *Bismarck*:

> Convinced that the *Suffolk* and *Norfolk* would leave us in peace for at least a few minutes, I entrusted the temporary surveillance of the horizon astern through the starboard director to one of my petty officers and went to the port director. While I was still turning it toward the *Hood*, I heard a shout, 'She's blowing up!' 'She'—that could only be the *Hood*! The sight I then saw is something I shall never forget. At first the *Hood* was nowhere to be seen; in her place was a colossal pillar of black smoke reaching into the sky. Gradually, at the foot of the pillar, I made out the bow of the battle cruiser projecting upwards at an angle, a sure sign that she had broken in two. Then I saw something I could hardly believe: a flash of orange from her forward guns! Although her fighting days had ended, the *Hood* was firing a last salvo. I felt great respect for those men over there.[24]

Another observer aboard *Bismarck* was an assistant to the navigator *Korvettenkapitän* Wolf Neuendorff:

'Straddling' boomed out of the loudspeaker. I was standing with *Kapitän* Neuendorff in front of the chart on which we were continuously recording our course. We put our instruments down and hurried to the eye-slits in the forward conning tower, looked through, and asked ourselves, what does he mean straddling?

At first we could see nothing but what we saw moments later could not have been conjured up by even the wildest imagination. Suddenly, the *Hood* split in two, and thousands of tons of steel were hurled into the air … the fireball that developed where the *Hood* still was seemed near enough to touch. It was so close that I shut my eyes but curiosity made me open them again a second or two later. It was like being in a hurricane. Every nerve in my body felt the pressure of the explosion.[25]

Aboard the *Prince of Wales*, Able Seaman William Usher witnessed the destruction of the *Hood*:

All amidships seemed to lift up into the air. After that the ship was surrounded by yellow smoke. The smoke seemed to clear away around the foc'sle a little bit and I noticed the ship seemed to be still going ahead. All along the upper deck it seemed to be bubbling up as if it was boiling. That was the foc'sle only, the deck of which seemed to be bubbling like an egg frying. Whilst this was going on the ship seemed to be slewing over to port. The smoke then covered the foc'sle. The next thing I saw was the quarter-deck come up into the air and I saw the screws. After that the quarter-deck disappeared and all I could see then was smoke.[26]

Royal Marine Sergeant Terrence Brooks of *Prince of Wales* noted:

There was an enormous flash which blinded me for a few moments. I took my eye away from the periscope. When I looked through my periscope again I was in time to see a black pall of smoke out of which I distinctly saw a 15-inch gun thrown through the air followed by what appeared to be the roof of a turret. Just before the *Hood* was hit the second time 'Y' turret trained on the foremost bearing starboard side and fired. I immediately depressed my periscope to look into the sea, I don't quite know why. All I could see were objects dropping into the water. When I elevated the periscope again we were slewing round what appeared to me to be part of the forecastle of the *Hood*. The remains of the *Hood* then passed out of my view.[27]

Lieutenant-Commander George Rowell commented:

[T]he fire on the boat deck was spreading forward steadily and appeared to be gaining ground. The fire appeared to me to be similar to a petrol fire. There was a large amount of flame, but very little smoke … I remember thinking that although the fire was spreading it appeared to be confined to above the boat-deck and there was no indication that it was spreading downwards. *Bismarck*'s firing continued to be accurate and salvos fell just short and just over as if she was using some form of zig-zag ladder. The Vice-Admiral hoisted a second signal for another turn of 20 deg. Away but before it could be executed the *Hood* was hit by another salvo. It was clear that she had been hit because of a throwing up of dark coloured debris from just before the mainmast from a position which I am sure in my own mind was close to the centre line on the boat-deck. After perhaps two or three seconds there was an uprush of orange coloured flame from this same position and it was apparent that a very serious explosion had resulted. The flame was followed by a dense column of white smoke which almost had the appearance of steam, and within a few second all that I could see of the *Hood* was her quarter-deck and her fore-top for a moment or two. The fact that the fore-mast was still visible made me hope that she had not gone, but as I remarked to the Captain that her top was still standing it fell backwards towards us and I then saw that the after part of the ship was also plunging forwards. We put the wheel over to starboard to give us a greater clearance from the wreckage and by the time we were abreast of her all that apparently remained were three large sections of the hull which were unrecognisable and themselves slipping into the water.[28]

Chief Petty Officer William Westlake stated:

The *Hood* … became enveloped in smoke and started to heel to port because I saw the black paint of her bottom coming out of the water. The *Hood* was covered in smoke and it was impossible to pick out anything definite of the ship at all. Another salvo hit the waterline of the *Hood*. I saw spurts of smoke coming out of five or six places. After a few seconds the whole ship seemed to blow up in pieces. The bow from between 'A' and 'B' turrets was blown out of the water and then slid directly back. The plating from the ship's side between the foremast and mainmast was blown into the air. There were huge columns of smoke and that was the last I saw of her.[29]

Chief Petty Officer Frederick French noted:

[T]he boat-deck appeared to raise in the middle. Before I saw any more of the boat-deck … cordite fumes came from underneath the ship from aft and about abreast the after funnel. This spread right along the water line to the bows. That stopped me from seeing any more of the boat-deck. The fumes then rose very high and came up to an apex, like the apex of a pyramid, which I should judge to be between 400 and 500 feet … the bows of the *Hood* were broken off abaft number one breakwater and came up to an angle of about 40 deg. And then slid straight back into the water. … From the after end I saw a complete turret with two guns and also a single gun in the air [which] appeared to be coming towards our own ship and then I saw them fall into the water. The fumes were lowering all the time and when the fumes had completely gone off the surface I saw a terrific circle whose perimeter appeared to be all white foam and near the centre was a burning patch of about 30 feet on the surface.[30]

Events were also witnessed from the sky by Flight Lieutenant R. J. Vaughn who was a crewman aboard a Short Sunderland flying boat of 201 Squadron:

SKETCHES BY CAPTAIN J.C. LEACH, M.V.O., ROYAL NAVY,
SHOWING THE APPEARANCE AND POSITION OF THE EXPLOSION
WHICH DESTROYED THE SHIP AS SEEN FROM H.M.S. PRINCE OF
WALES AT A DISTANCE OF 4 CABLES.

Above: Sketch produced by Captain Leach of HMS *Prince of Wales* for the Board of Inquiry in the *Hood*'s loss showing the appearance and position of the explosion as viewed from the *Prince of Wales*.

Right: Sketch produced by Rear-Admiral Wake-Walker showing the stages of the *Hood*'s destruction as viewed by HMS *Norfolk*.

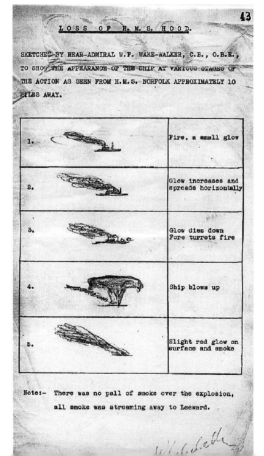

43

LOSS OF H.M.S. HOOD.

SKETCHES BY REAR-ADMIRAL W.F. WAKE-WALKER, C.B., O.B.E.,
TO SHOW THE APPEARANCE OF THE SHIP AT VARIOUS STAGES OF
THE ACTION AS SEEN FROM H.M.S. NORFOLK APPROXIMATELY 10
MILES AWAY.

1.		Fire, a small glow
2.		Glow increases and spreads horizontally
3.		Glow dies down Fore turrets fire
4.		Ship blows up
5.		Slight red glow on surface and smoke

Note:- There was no pall of smoke over the explosion,
all smoke was streaming away to Leeward.

An explosion was noticed on the burning ship of the port column (the *Hood*) and at the same time we came under A.A. fire from the enemy, and were forced to take cloud cover at 2,500ft. On emerging from cloud some five minutes later, the *Hood* had almost completely disappeared and only one part of the bow was showing.[31]

Although the *Hood* had at first angled to starboard, there was no concern on the compass platform as she righted herself. In the captain's chair, Holland looked aft towards the *Prince of Wales* before retraining his binoculars on the *Bismarck*. Having rolled to port to right herself, the *Hood* continued rolling. For Ted Briggs, the sudden cant to port was a horrifying experience that terrorised him.[32] As the *Hood* reached an angle of 45 degrees, everyone on the compass platform realised that this time the ship would not return to the perpendicular. As if in a drill, without a word being muttered, knowing that the ship was finished, everyone began to make their way in single file to the starboard door of the compass platform. It was at this point that some began to break ranks and quietly made their way towards the port door while others attempted to break the reinforced panes of glass on the forepart of the platform. One of those who attempted to break panes of glass to leave the compass platform was Bill Dundas. Doubting that he could make it up the steeply sloping deck, Dundas opted for 'kicking a window on the starboard side until I made a big enough hole to squeeze through'.

In the meantime, Ted Briggs was making his way out of the starboard door of the compass platform:

Photographed from aboard *Prinz Eugen*, this image shows the explosion of HMS *Hood*. Faintly visible to the left of the smoke cloud marking *Hood*, smoke from the gunfire of *Prince of Wales* can be made out. (*NH 69724, US Naval History and Heritage Command*)

I was surprised by my cold yet uncontrolled detachment as I made my way to the door. 'Tiny' Gregson was in front of me with the squadron navigating officer. As I reached the steel-hinged door, Commander Warrand stood aside for me and let me go out first. I looked back over my left shoulder and saw Holland slumped on his chair in total dejection. Beside him the Captain tried to keep his feet as the *Hood*'s deck turned into a slide. I began picking my way down the ladder from the compass platform to the admiral's bridge. Then the sea swirled around my legs and I was walking on the side of the bridge, instead of the ladder. I threw away my tin-hat and gas-mask and managed to slip all my anti-flash gear, but my lifebelt was under my Burberry and I could not get at it to inflate it. There was no one else in sight, although I knew that at least two officers were nearby, as the water engulfed me with a roar.[33]

On the boat deck, taking shelter, Robert Tilburn was struck by human remains which in all likelihood saved his life. 'Bits of bodies were falling over the deck and one hit me on the legs. I thought, "I'm going to be sick", so I got up and went to the ship's side to throw up'.[34] Looking around as he got up, Tilburn noticed that the *Hood* appeared to be going down by the stern and that she had begun to tilt at an alarming angle to port. Turning to see what he believed to be an ammunition locker hurtling towards him, he decided to make a rapid escape. Tilburn leapt on to the half-submerged forecastle and began to discard anything that might weigh him down. Tilburn succeeded in removing his tin helmet, gas mask, and duffel coat before the water swept him over the side. He now set about swimming for his life.

As he swam, Tilburn's belt restricted his breathing. Reaching for the knife that he customarily carried, he cut away his belt. As he did so, the midships section of the ship rolled over on top of him. The main mast came swinging down and caught him across the back of the legs, ensnarling him in the radio wires, which wrapped themselves tightly around his feet. As the pieces of the ship began to descend into the dark depths of the Atlantic, Tilburn was dragged down. Taking a deep breath just as he vanished beneath the surface, Tilburn pulled feverously at the wires around his feet. Still holding his knife, Tilburn reached down and managed to cut the laces of his sea boots which were ripped from his feet. Free of his sea boots, he found himself shooting back towards the surface assisted by air bubbles. As he broke the surface with his lungs gasping for air, Tilburn got one last look at the *Hood*. As he looked, the bow was standing almost vertical in the water before sliding under the surface never to return.[35]

Having squeezed himself out of a compass platform window, Bill Dundas also found himself sucked beneath the surface of the water as everything became dark before finding himself shot to the surface. Dundas's exact experience is vague for he rarely spoke about his experience of the *Hood*'s sinking in public or private life. Ted Briggs, also in the water, knew that he must try and swim away from the ship.

I managed to avoid being knocked out by the steel stanchions, but I was not making any progress. The suction was dragging me down. The pressure on my ears was increasing each second, and panic returned in its worse intensity ... I struggled madly to try to heave myself up to the surface. I got nowhere. Although it seemed like an eternity, I was under water for barely a minute. My lungs were bursting. I knew that I just had to breathe. I opened my lips and gulped in a mouthful of water. My tongue was forced to the back of my throat. I was not going to reach the surface. I was going to die. As I weakened, my resolve left me. What was the use of struggling? ... I had heard it was nice to drown. I stopped trying to swim upwards. The water was a peaceful cradle. I was being rocked to sleep. There was nothing I could do about it—goodnight, mum. No I lay me down ... I was ready to meet God. My blissful acceptance of death ended in a sudden surge beneath me, which shot me to the surface like a decanted cork in a champagne bottle. I wasn't going to die. I wasn't going to die. I trod water as I panted in great gulps of air. I was alive ...

Although my ears were singing from the pressure under water I could hear the hissing sound of a hundred serpents. I turned away and fifty yards away in the sea I could see the bows of the *Hood* vertical in the sea. It was the most frightening aspect of my ordeal and a vision which was to recur terrifyingly in nightmares for the next fifty years. Both gun barrels of B turret were slumped hard over to port and

In this painting by J. C. Schmitz-Westeholt, *Prince of Wales* (foreground) can be seen taking avoiding action from the sinking *Hood*, her bow pointing skyward amongst a great cloud of smoke. (*NH 50741-KN, US Naval History and Heritage Command*)

disappearing fast beneath the waves. My experience of suction seconds before forced me to turn in sheer terror and swim as fast and as far as I could from the last sight of the ship that had formulated by early years.[36]

As the *Hood* exploded, the *Prince of Wales* found herself steering towards the sinking battlecruiser. Captain Leach ordered a violent change of course to starboard to avoid the sinking wreckage. The violent change of course disrupted the gunnery and would serve to make it easier for the Germans to target her. Eight minutes after having opening fire against the *Bismarck* and the *Prinz Eugen*, the *Hood*, for so long the pride of the Royal Navy, had been torn apart by a devastating explosion. Three minutes after the fatal hit had struck the *Hood*, the last traces of the Royal Navy's most famous warship slipped beneath the waves and vanished leaving nothing but a scattering of oil, wreckage, and three survivors out of a crew of 1,418 men.

Survivors

Moments after the *Hood* had been ripped apart by a terrific explosion, aboard HMS *Norfolk*, a horrified Wake-Walker ordered that the Admiralty and Admiral Tovey been informed of events. A gloomy yet simple signal was transmitted that conveyed the shock felt by those who witnessed what had just occurred: '*Hood* has blown up'.

Having avoided the sinking the *Hood*, Captain Leach ordered the *Prince of Wales* back on to her original heading. As she moved back onto her original course, it would appear there was still a chance that the *Hood* could strike a last lethal blow. Moments before being struck by the *Bismarck*'s fifth salvo, the *Hood* had apparently launched torpedoes that, even with the battlecruiser sunk, continued on towards the German ships at 30 knots. Aboard the *Prinz Eugen*, hydrophone operators reportedly heard the sound of three torpedoes in the water. Displaying a cool head under fire, the commanding officer of the *Prinz Eugen, Kapitän zur See* Helmut Brinkmann turned his ship to starboard on three occasions to 'evade' torpedoes at 6.03, 6.06, and 6.14 a.m. Whether the *Hood* fired torpedoes and that Brinkman avoided them is, however, a matter for debate. Based on the charts produced of the battle, there was one point during the engagement in which the *Prinz Eugen* was presented with a slim opportunity to hit the *Prince of Wales* with torpedoes. As events transpired, the *Prinz Eugen*'s torpedo officer decided against attempting to hit the *Prince of Wales* at extreme range with torpedoes. In his work *The Loss of the Bismarck*, Graham Rhys-Jones has stated that 'There is no evidence that the *Hood* fired torpedoes although the possibility cannot, perhaps, be totally discounted'.[1] Rather, Rhys-Jones has speculated that the hydrophone operators aboard the *Prinz Eugen* may have been guilty of panic and a false alarm when hearing torpedoes in the water. Conversely, given that the *Hood* was the only Royal Navy warship in the engagement equipped with an armament of torpedoes, and given that at one point, the *Prinz Eugen* could have struck the *Prince of Wales* with torpedoes, it is possible that the hydrophone operators aboard the *Prinz Eugen* heard torpedoes fired from the *Hood*. The movements made by Brinkmann were, in fact, more in line with him recognising that with the *Bismarck* moving up on the port side of the *Prinz Eugen*, the cruiser was at risk of shells from the *Prince of Wales* falling long. The execution of turns to avoid torpedoes from the *Hood* was more likely a cover story for moves to increase the separation between the *Prinz Eugen* and the *Bismarck* in order to make the cruiser less vulnerable to being hit. Whatever the case may be, if the *Hood* did fire torpedoes at the German ships, they failed to find their mark.

Aboard the *Bismarck*, *Kapitän* Lindemann ordered *Bismarck*'s gunners to shift their fire to HMS *Prince of Wales*. It is worth briefly noting that Lütjens and Lindemann believed the *Prince of Wales* to be Tovey's flagship *King George V* as they had no knowledge that the *Prince of Wales* had been brought to an operational state. Fortunately for the German gunners, the *Prince of Wales* was now in roughly the same position that the *Hood* had been in just before she sank.[2] The untried battleship was now to be on the receiving end of the combined 15-inch and 8-inch fire of the *Bismarck* and the *Prinz Eugen*.

At 6.04 a.m., a salvo fired by the *Prince of Wales* straddled the *Bismarck* and scored a hit, which appeared to cause no damage. At almost the same time, the first salvo fired by the *Bismarck* against this new target found its mark, and straddled the British battleship. One of the *Bismarck*'s shells passed through the bridge before landing in the water. With the exception of Captain Leach, who was left momentarily stunned, and two other personnel, everyone on the bridge was killed. Control was temporarily passed to the aft control position. Both German ships were by now scoring hits with almost every salvo. Some 8-inch shells from the *Prinz Eugen* struck the *Prince of Wales*'s fire-control director, which served the ship's secondary armament. Two more hits were sustained below the waterline, resulting in minor flooding. With the distance to the *Bismarck* now only 7 miles (11.2 km), Captain Leach ordered a hard turn to port to prevent the range from decreasing further. By this point, the *Bismarck* was scoring a number of telling hits. Two 15-inch shells hit the *Prince of Wales*—one struck the battleship amidships next to her funnel and started a major fire while the second struck the waterline, which caused further flooding.

At 6.05 a.m., Captain Leach realised that his ship was being well and truly outfought. The *Prince of Wales*'s radar had been knocked out of action and despite the tireless efforts of the civilian contractors who were aboard, 'X' turret was jammed with a hydraulic leak and her Walrus spotting aircraft had been destroyed. Having seen the demise of the *Hood* moments earlier, and with significant damage sustained to his ship, Leach made the decision to break off action. He issued orders for a change of course to 150 degrees, which would take the *Prince of Wales* south, directly away from the *Bismarck*. As the *Prince of Wales* turned away, the *Bismarck* and the *Prinz Eugen* kept up their fire against the wounded British battleship. Owing to Leach's rapid alteration of course, the German salvos missed their target. At 6.09 a.m., Leach ordered a smokescreen to be produced to obscure the ship from the German gunners. With the *Prince of Wales* obscured by the smokescreen, Lütjens issued the order to cease fire.

The Battle of the Denmark Strait was over. The engagement had lasted seventeen minutes during which time over 1,000 men had lost their lives, the

HMS *Prince of Wales* (left smoke column) alters course to open the range after she was hit by fire from the *Bismarck*. On the right, smoke marks the spot where moments earlier the *Hood* had exploded. (*NH 69725, US Naval History and Heritage Command*)

HMS *Prince of Wales* (the smoke column of the left) under fire from the *Bismarck* and the *Prinz Eugen* with the smoke on the right marking where the *Hood* had sunk. The shell splashes on the right mark where shells from the *Prince of Wales* landed short of the German ships. (*NH 69731, US Naval History and Heritage Command*)

Royal Navy had lost the pride of its fleet, and its most modern battleship had been outfought by its German counterpart.[3] The *Prince of Wales* would link up with Wake-Walker's cruisers and shadow the *Bismarck* as an epic chase across the Atlantic developed, which would culminate in the sinking of the *Bismarck* three days later. The story of the events that occurred in the wake of the Battle of the Denmark Strait have been covered extensively elsewhere, and as such, will not be covered here.

For the survivors of the *Hood*, their ordeal was not yet over. One of the first ships to pick up Wake-Walker's signal about the *Hood*'s loss was the destroyer HMS *Electra*. Wake-Walker's signal was followed by a signal from the *Prince of Wales* confirming the news. A yeoman of the signals who had been infused with excitement minutes earlier when he had reported to Commander Cecil May, the *Electra*'s captain that the *Hood* and the *Prince of Wales* had engaged the *Bismarck* climbed on to the bridge with a look of shock and dejection on his face. Lieutenant Timothy Cain, the destroyer's gunnery officer, asked the yeoman if there was any news. 'From *Prince of Wales*, Sir. *Hood* sunk!' came the reply. Cain was momentarily stunned before he felt his blood boil leading him to explode in anger: 'You can keep your sense of humour to yourself!' The now tearful yeoman responded, 'My God, Sir, but it's true, Sir. It's just come through. I have told the Captain'.[4] Having been informed of the *Hood*'s loss, Commander May instantly began thinking of the survivors in the freezing water who needed rescuing. May was informed by the *Electra*'s navigator that the reported position of the *Hood*'s sinking was 60 miles away to the south. May ordered *Electra* to alter course and make for the site of the *Hood*'s loss. May also ordered the other destroyers under his command to follow suit.

HMS *Electra*. (*Author's collection*)

In the water, Ted Briggs found himself among a morass of debris and oil. Scattered around were a number of Carley floats. Swimming over to one, he managed to pull himself half on to it. Holding on facing down, Briggs finally summoned the strength to look around to where the *Hood* had been. A small patch of oil blazed where the ship had been moments earlier. He could also see the stern of the *Prince of Wales* as she passed by, her gunners still engaged in the deadly duel. Briggs watched on as the battleship was straddled by shells from the *Bismarck* and the *Prinz Eugen*. He did not give her much of a chance of survival.

Briggs' thoughts quickly turned to his own chances of survival. With the sea on fire where the *Hood* had been, Briggs feared that the copious amounts of oil that surrounded the sea in which his float was bobbing might soon be ignited. Fearing this, he began to paddle as far away from the oil slick as he could. He had only been in the water for around three minutes but the freezing temperature was already taking its toll; his fingers, arms, legs, and toes quickly became numb. Paddling away from the oil slick helped his blood to circulate but he soon found himself out of breath. Glancing behind him, Briggs saw that the flames had been extinguished. On the horizon, smoke from the funnels of the *Norfolk* and the *Suffolk* could just about be made out.

It was at this moment that Briggs saw another float around 150 feet away on which there were signs of life. The figure on the raft began to wave. Parallel to this was another float on which was another man flapping his arms. Briggs glanced around for other signs of life but there were none. The three men—Ted Briggs, William Dundas, and Bob Tilburn—all began to paddle towards one another.

The *Hood* had been rocked by two large magazine explosions that broke the ship in half and had extinguished life in many gruesome ways, ensuring that there would be no corpses to show where the battlecruiser had been destroyed. Explosions and firestorms inside the hull dismembered and disembowelled hundreds of men while hundreds more were incinerated. Others were killed by concussion, crushed by heavy machinery and fittings that were ripped from their mounts, or had drowned as the sea poured in. The wreckage sank to the depths, coming to rest on the seabed. As the ship sank, compartments containing air were crushed by the pressure along with anyone left alive in them.

Somehow Dundas managed to sit up on his float. Tilburn and Briggs also attempted to sit up but were unsuccessful, falling off into the water; they eventually had to settle for lying across their respective floats. The three survivors clutched on to the ratlines of each other's floats in an attempt to stay together. Tilburn thought that while it was all very well the three of them joining up in the sea and holding on to one another's floats so as to not drift apart, they were hundreds of miles away from the nearest point of land and there were no signs of any ships, British or German. Seventeen-year-old Dundas, the youngest but most senior of the three survivors now found himself in charge. It was not because of his rank, however, that he found himself in charge, but rather because of the fact that he was relentlessly cheerful. Dundas had recognised that anyone who gave in to the strong desire for sleep that came over them following being exposed to the cold water would slip into a coma and die of hypothermia. So it was that he commenced the three of them singing 'Roll Out the Barrel' to ensure that they stayed awake.

Despite Dundas' efforts, Briggs found the temptation to sleep almost too much to resist. Suddenly, he was aroused by Tilburn shouting that he could see an aircraft. The survivors began to wave their arms, splash the water and shouted 'Help!' but the Sunderland flying boat, from which Flight Lieutenant R. J. Vaughn had witnessed the *Hood's* destruction, flew steadily on, unable to see them in the debris field. Dundas now suggested that they stay awake by sharing the stories of how each of them had survived the *Hood's* destruction. All agreed that they had not heard any loud explosion before the ship sank, which left them puzzled. As they told the stories of their individual escapes, Dundas and Tilburn compared injuries. Dundas was suffering from a sprained ankle that he sustained in his efforts to kick out one of the compass platform windows while Tilburn had managed to cut himself when in the act of cutting away his sea boots. Briggs had, by contrast, escaped without so much as a scratch. Both Briggs and Dundas agreed that they had entered the water on the *Hood's* starboard side. When recounting his story, Briggs recalled that when he broke the surface, he was on the ship's port side and realised that he must have been sucked right under the ship. The swapping of stories, for all its good intentions, was, however, counterproductive for combined with the cold, it served to exhaust them with the result that the ratlines slipped through their fingers and the floats began to drift apart.

Briggs and Tilburn fought to stave off the urge to sleep while Dundas began another chorus of 'Roll Out the Barrel'. Meanwhile, HMS *Electra* had been making steady progress to the site where the *Hood* had sunk. Thinking back to the sinking of the liner SS *Athenia* in September 1939 in which several ships, including the *Electra*, had helped to rescue 981 passengers and crew from the ship after it had been torpedoed by *U-30*, Surgeon Lieutenant Seymour decided to turn the destroyer's main mess deck into a makeshift hospital to supplement the sickbay while officer's bunks were prepared for the many hundreds of men that he expected to treat. As the *Electra* sailed south at top speed, Seymour took a moment to speak with Lieutenant Cain and suggested that some of the younger sailors in the *Electra's* company be sent below in order to avoid seeing some of the more gruesome injuries the wounded were expected to be carrying. Seymour's suggestion was met with a sharp response: 'Bloody nonsense! We'll need everyone we've got to help the poor devils inboard!'[5] Edward Taylor, known to all aboard the destroyer as Jack, recalled events from aboard the destroyer.

> The truth slowly dawned on us as we made ready to pick up hundreds of injured and wounded men from the grey cold sea. We could not turn out our boats as they were smashed, hanging in the davits. Blankets, medical supplies, hot beverages and rum were got ready. Scrambling nets were flung over the ship's side, trailing into the water. Men were lining the side ready with hand lines, eyes straining into the greyness ahead.
>
> It only took what seemed like a matter of minutes when we broke out of a mist patch into the clear. And there it was. The place where the *Hood* had sunk. Wreckage of all descriptions was floating on the surface. Hammocks, broken rafts, boots, clothes,

caps. Of the hundreds of men we expected to see there was no sign. An awestruck moment and a shipmate next to me exclaimed 'Good Lord, she's gone with all hands'.

We nosed our way slowly amongst all the pitiful remains of books, letters, photos, and other personal effects floating by and a shout went up as a man appeared clinging to a piece of flotsam a little further away. Two more were seen—one swimming, the other appeared to be on a small float.[6]

Dundas had suddenly stopped singing and began to cry out: 'There's a destroyer coming along. She's seen us'. Briggs looked up in disbelief. Recognising the pennant number on the side of the ship, H27, he cried out, 'It's the *Electra*!' followed by crazy shouts of '*Electra! Electra! Electra!*' Tilburn and Dundas joined in the shouting and began to furiously wave their arms. As the *Electra* edged slowly forward through the debris field, Dundas once more began to sing 'Roll Out the Barrel' and began to conduct an imaginary orchestra. The first survivor plucked from the water by the *Electra* was Briggs.

Slowly the *Electra* approached my raft, on which I was prostrate. Then a rope sailed into the air in my direction. Although I could not feel my fingers, somehow I managed to cling on to it. A man yelled unnecessarily at me from the scrambling net: 'Don't let go of it'. I even had the heart to retort: 'You bet your bloody life I won't'. Yet I was too exhausted to haul myself in and climb the net. After nearly four hours in the sea my emotions were a mess. Tears of frustration rolled down my oil-caked cheeks again, for rescue was so close and I could not help myself. I need not have worried. Several seamen dropped into the water, and with one hand on the nets they got me alongside and manhandled me up to the bent guard-rail which had been battered by the storm, and into the waist of the *Electra*.[7]

It should be noted that while Briggs says that he had spent nearly four hours in the water, this is a mistake. The time he and the others spent in the water following the *Hood*'s sinking was in the region of two hours. Tilburn found himself hoisted up on to the destroyer's deck and deposited on deck like a sack of potatoes by two sailors who had clambered down the scramble netting to render assistance after he had swam towards the destroyer. Tilburn looked around at a circle of sailors who were staring at him like he was a curiosity from a circus. Shaking and shrugging off water, he snarled: 'And what's up with you—you poverty-stricken crowd? Ain't you got no bloody boats?'

To the crew of the *Electra*, however, it was Dundas' behaviour that they thought the most peculiar. From the bridge, Cain could see Dundas and thought that he had never seen 'a man more nonchalant, or less put out by his circumstances' before noting that he 'made no attempt to precipitate his rescue by trying to swim'.[8] Rather, Dundas sat calmly on his float waiting for someone to rescue him. Men aboard the *Electra* threw lines out to him hoping that he would make an effort to catch them. Dundas could not be provoked to move. Eventually, one of the *Electra*'s crew was lucky enough to land a rope in Dundas' lap. Holding on to the end of the line

Dundas was pulled over to the destroyer before being assisted up a scrambling net. Dundas was welcomed aboard the destroyer by the *Electra*'s first lieutenant. Dundas responded to the first lieutenant's greeting by apologising for losing his cap, which meant that he was unable to offer a salute. Dundas tried to stand but found that his ankle injury prevented him from doing so. Lifted on to a stretcher, he was taken down to the destroyer's sickbay, protesting all the way that he was alright.[9]

The *Electra* was joined in her rescue efforts by the destroyers *Anthony* and *Icarus*. The destroyers stayed on station for a significant amount of time after plucking Dundas, Briggs, and Tilburn from the water looking all the while for survivors, but to no avail. Each man aboard the destroyers had conjured up images of the *Hood* with her large crew, akin to a small army, assembled on her decks. It was when presented with a few pieces of wreckage, floating books, clothes and caps, and no signs of the hundreds of bobbing heads that had been anticipated that the scale of the disaster hit home. The sight that they were presented with was all that remained of 'the Mighty *Hood*' and her crew.

The crews of the *Electra*, *Icarus*, and *Anthony* continued to scan the sea for further signs of life, but all that was found were small pieces of floating debris. A desk drawer bobbed along the *Electra*'s side. Two members of her crew climbed down the scramble netting to retrieve it. Inside the drawer were dozens of personal records relating to the *Hood*'s ratings. It is likely that the drawer came from a desk in the clerical office, located well below decks and that it had been blown into the air when the ship exploded and broke in two. A bitter irony arose for while three members of the *Hood*'s crew had survived, the drawer and the documents and records inside it had escaped the ship unscathed. Low on fuel, the *Electra* and the other destroyers set a course for Reykjavik, Iceland. As they sailed for Iceland, a blanket of dejection settled over the destroyers.

During the journey to Reykjavik, the *Electra*'s crew did their best to cheer up Tilburn, Dundas, and Briggs who were kitted out with new clothes donated by the crew. When the *Electra* berthed at Reykjavik, an ambulance was waiting on the quayside. Helped down the gangway, Briggs, Tilburn, and Dundas were hurried into the ambulance before being driven to the nearby military hospital. At the hospital, they were met by a Chaplin who took their names and addresses so that telegrams informing their families that they were safe could be sent.

The next morning, the three men were smuggled aboard a transport vessel, the *Royal Ulsterman*, which was sailing to Greenock. Given cabins aboard the transport, the three men were told not to reveal their identities, not to discuss the battle with the *Bismarck* or any part of their rescue with anyone on board. The *Royal Ulsterman* docked at Greenock on 29 May. When the ship docked, Dundas, Tilburn, and Briggs were unaware of the stir that had been caused by the sinking of the *Hood*. Herded into a waiting car, they were whisked off to the headquarters of the naval officer in charge where they were kitted out with new uniforms. Given railway warrants, the three men were briefed to take the overnight train to London and to report to the Admiralty upon arrival.

21

Reverberations

The signals announcing that the *Hood* had been sunk were picked up across the North Atlantic and beyond, and sent shockwaves through the Royal Navy and stunned the world. In some instances, naval personnel were aware that a battle was raging in the region of the Denmark Strait before they learned of the outcome and the tragedy of the *Hood*'s loss. Some 250 miles to the south of the Denmark Strait, aboard the steamer *Zouave*, which was sailing in convoy SC-31, firemen had picked up the reverberations of the distant battle as it raged. On the bridge of the *Zouave*, Captain William Cambridge sat completely unaware that at that very moment he was losing his son John in one of the *Hood*'s boiler rooms.[1] In Reykjavik, local residents could hear the reverberations of the battle raging over 200 miles away. At the Admiralty Signals Department located beneath Admiralty Arch, civil service telegraphist Gladys Wilkin was on duty when news about the loss of the *Hood* was received.

> The signals department was situated beneath Admiralty Arch; roughly beneath the left hand pillar looking down the Mall … On the night of 24 May there was a particularly bad air raid on London and a direct hit struck the above mentioned pillar, killing a dispatch rider standing beside his motorcycle at that spot and damaging a portion of the Signals Department below. Now, it just so happened that at that particular time several members of the signals staff were either at rest, supper, off sick, or just not on duty. There was not terribly much 'traffic' that night and I was watching two positions. On one position I received the signal that HMS *Hood* had been sunk; this was marked 'MOST SECRET' and needed to be handed immediately to the Officer in Charge. I was shocked, stunned and unhappy. For another reason also. One of the telegraphists with whom I was particularly friendly at this time was a girl we all called 'Len' because her surname was Leonard … Her fiancé was a member of the crew of the *Hood* and when she came back from supper I was unable to tell her of the signal because of its classification. Naturally, she learned eventually when the lists of casualties began coming in.[2]

Aboard HMS *Rodney*, Lieutenant-Commander Crawford was to be found on the bridge keeping watch when the signal came through that a ship had been sunk.

Crawford later recalled receiving the news. Initially, the name of the ship sunk had not been given:

> Hopes immediately went absolutely sky-high with thinking that it was *Bismarck* sunk. And then a few seconds later it came through, '*Hood* sunk' ... I remember calling the Captain, and he came straight up onto the bridge. For a few seconds there was a great gloom, but then everybody accepted the inevitable ... and hoped that we might possibly get into action, to square the deal.[3]

Also aboard HMS *Rodney* was Lieutenant-Commander Walton, who was one of many aboard the battleship who lost friends in the *Hood*. Like the rest of the *Rodney*'s crew, Walton listened with great sadness to the tannoy broadcast revealing the *Hood*'s loss: 'We had been alongside the *Hood* a week before in Scapa Flow. We'd had a lot of interchange of personnel and suddenly to find the *Hood* was gone really set us back a lot'.[4]

Aboard the destroyer *Cossack*, Captain Philip Vian was commanding the escort to convoy WS-8B sailing to the west of Ireland when he received the '*Hood* sunk signal'. Of receiving the signal, Vian would comment, 'I believe I felt no stronger emotion at any time in the war than at the moment when I read this signal'. Lieutenant Keith Evans aboard the cruiser *Hawkins* lying at Durban, who had served aboard the *Hood* from 1938 to 1939, was one of many of the battlecruiser's former sailors who were unable to control their emotions:

> On that fateful day, after visiting Cape Town and the Seychelles, were coming alongside Mayden Wharf in Durban when on the tannoy of another ship (I think *Dorsetshire*) we heard the announcement 'We regret to announce that in action with the German battleship *Bismarck* in the Denmark Strait off Greenland, HMS *Hood* has been sunk, it is feared with considerable loss of life'. All hands on deck seemed to stop what they were doing for about a minute (in fact more likely to be several seconds). As a former shipmate I could not comprehend that the Mighty *Hood* had gone and am not a bit ashamed to say that I began to cry.[5]

The first lieutenant aboard HMS *Nelson*, Lieutenant-Commander George Blundell, had served as a midshipman aboard the *Hood* between 1922 and 1924. He recalled receiving the news while the *Nelson* was off Freetown:

> The Captain came on to the bridge and said 'The *Hood*'s been sunk by the *Bismarck*'. I thought for a moment [that] he was fooling ... I felt terrible thinking of Tony [Lieutenant-Commander Anthony] Pares ... I can hardly believe that lovely ship is gone nor that one 15-inch shell can do such a horror. All I hope and pray for is that we get the *Bismarck* in revenge. It would be terrible for her to get away. Those poor fellows in the *Hood*—Tony, [Edward] Gregson, dear old [Robert] Grogan, Tubby [Crosse] ... It is a rotten war.[6]

Frank White, who served aboard the *Hood* between 1937 and 1938, recalled learning of the *Hood's* loss through a friend: 'A friend with me on board HMS *Penelope* had just read the notice that had been posted: "*Hood* lost". I felt as though a piece of me had gone down with her'.[7]

David Bone was in charge of a merchant ship set to dock in Gibraltar. He and his crew were first struck by the emptiness of the harbour from warships and learned of events with the arrival of the harbour pilot:

> With the coming of the harbour pilot we were quickly enlightened as to the unusual appearance of the port. Did we not know that the *Bismarck* and the *Prinz Eugen* were at sea and that the Fleet had sailed? We had learned when on passage from Freetown that the great cruiser the *Hood* had been sunk by enemy action at sea on the 24th but the circumstances of her loss had not been mentioned in the brief item included in a news broadcast. For a time, we affected to disbelief it, for it was originally quoted as from [a] German report and had not the *Ark Royal* been sunk on paper by Herr Goebbels so often before? But there had come no denial and sadly we accepted the news that the great ship had been lost. The pilot went about his duties with grave deliberation. I surmise that he would know the *Hood* well for, in her quarter century of supremacy, she had often been based at Gibraltar.[8]

The news of the *Hood's* loss quickly found its way from the Admiralty to Winston Churchill who had embarked on a weekend trip to the Prime Minister's country retreat: Chequers. At Chequers, Churchill was entertaining President Franklin D. Roosevelt's special representative Averell Harriman. Also at Chequers with Churchill and Harriman was Churchill's wife Clementine, his daughter Sarah, her husband Vic Oliver, and his Chief of Staff, Major General Hastings 'Pug' Ismay.[9] Vic Oliver later recalled:

> [Churchill] came down from his study looking inexpressibly grim. We guessed that yet another disaster had occurred, though we knew it was no use to ask him what it was. Mrs Churchill quietly poured him a glass of port, and, thinking it would relieve the tension, suggested I play something on the piano. I was about to start on *Lily on Laguna*, but immediately checked myself, feeling that a popular song would be out of place; so after a few seconds' reflection I decided on Beethoven's 'Appassionata Sonata', but I had played only a few bars when Mr Churchill rose to his feet and thundered 'Stop! Don't play that!'
>
> We were all surprised, for it was the first time he had raised his voice to me. I turned round, puzzled, and asked: 'What's the trouble—don't you like it?'
>
> 'Nobody plays the *Death March* in my house', he said. We all laughed. 'It's not the "*Death March*"', I said. 'It's the "*Appassionata Sonata*"'.
>
> Mr Churchill was notoriously unmusical. He glowered again. 'You can say what you like', he said. 'I know it's the funeral march'.
>
> I turned back to the piano. 'But surely, Sir, you can tell the difference between this...' and I struck a few chords of the 'Appassionata', 'and ...'

Before I had time to finish, Mr Churchill thundered again: 'Stop it! Stop it! I want no "Death March", I tell you!'

Sarah rushed over to the piano and told me to play his favourite song instead. I did so, and the moment passed. Next day it was announced that HMS *Hood* had been sunk with heavy loss of life.[10]

At 9 p.m. on 24 May, the population of Britain at large was made aware of the *Hood*'s loss when the news was broadcast on the radio by the BBC:

British naval forces intercepted early this morning, off the coast of Greenland, German naval forces, including the battleship *Bismarck*. The enemy were attacked, and during the ensuing action HMS *Hood* (Captain R Kerr, CBE, RN), wearing the flag of Vice Admiral L E Holland, CB, received an unlucky hit in a magazine and blew up. The *Bismarck* has received damage, and the pursuit of the enemy continues. It is feared there will be few survivors from HMS *Hood*.[11]

The news, when broadcast to the wider world, was received with shock and great disbelief. Former crew member James Edwards recalled hearing of the loss of the *Hood* via the BBC broadcast:

I was in a pub and had just ordered a pint of beer when the news came over the radio and the pub went totally quiet. I looked at my pint and could no longer face it, so I walked out, leaving it untouched on the bar. I had lost friends and companions, but above all I had lost the beautiful ship which gave me my first real sea-going experience and I felt shattered.[12]

Howard Spence was among the last draft to leave the *Hood* before she set sail to intercept the *Bismarck*.

I arrived home at Portsmouth by 24th May 1941 and heard a radio announcement that HMS Somethingorother had been sunk—we could not catch a name, but I had a presentiment that it was the *Hood*, and this was confirmed the next day. A telegram arrived for my parents and I took it from the telegraph boy: 'Regret your son missing, presumed killed'. A further telegram arrived dated 29th May 1941: 'Your son not on board, regret anxiety caused'.[13]

Before the clock struck midnight as 24 May gave way to the 25th, at the Admiralty, one of the ladies who were entrusted with the task of maintaining the Admiralty's warship index made the final entry on the card of HMS *Hood*: 'At 0635 today blew up and sank in action in the Denmark Strait'.[14] It may be noted that the time recorded on the *Hood*'s card was incorrect as she blew up and sank a little after 6 a.m.

The loss of the *Hood* was widely reported on both sides of the Atlantic in the press: 'Nazis sink the *Hood* near Greenland; 1,300 die in biggest warship'.[15] 'H.M.S.

the *Hood* Blown Up off Greenland: Magazine Explodes in Battle with German Fleet'.[16] 'The *Hood* is sunk: Battle with *Bismarck*'.[17] 'Nazis hit-and-run in great sea battle: the *Hood* blows up after hit from freak shot'.[18] 'H.M.S. the *Hood* sunk: "Blown up, feared few survivors", says Admiralty'.[19] '1,300 dead as the *Hood* sinks in battle'.[20] 'HMS *Hood* sunk with 1,300 in battle off Greenland with Nazis' new *Bismarck*'.[21] 'Germans sink the *Hood*, world's biggest warship, in sea battle: Direct Nazi hit in magazine blows up 42,100 ton craft; 1000 go down with vessel'.[22]

While still a shock, for those who were aware of the *Hood*'s design and the flaws in it, the news of her loss came as no great surprise. This included the Deputy Director of Operations at the Admiralty, Captain William Davis, who had served aboard the *Hood* as the ship's executive officer until September 1940. To him, the loss of the *Hood* came as a shock but was no great surprise.

> The loss of the *Hood* was a tremendous shock to all of us, and especially to me as her last Commander, but I certainly knew of her extreme vulnerability to 15-inch fire with only 3 inches of mild steel armour protection over her magazines ... The *Hood*'s destruction was unlucky, but to me not unexpected for she was not fit to take on modern 15-inch gunfire.[23]

In *The Times*, in the days immediately following the loss of the *Hood*, an article was published that commented on the design of the *Hood* and the supposedly improved armour arrangement in the wake of the Battle of Jutland that was to make her invulnerable to the danger of a shell penetrating one of her magazines. In the article, the writer commented, 'Her loss therefore immediately raises the technical question of whether a miscalculation was made, while probably leaving no evidence to assist in answering it'.[24] Four days following the loss of the *Hood*, *The Times* published a letter by Admiral Lord Chatfield, which has been described by some as 'the most cogent statement ever made on the subject', written in response to the article published a few days earlier:

> In your leading article of today on the destruction of the *Hood* you write that she was the largest and most powerful warship afloat; that she was blown up by a lucky hit, although she had been specifically designed to be invulnerable to that kind of danger. You conclude that this raises the technical question of whether a miscalculation was made in her design. As great concern has resulted from this misfortune it is important that the nation should realise the reason of it.
> 1. The *Hood* was not the most powerful warship afloat. True that she was the largest, but she was constructed 22 years before the *Bismarck*. In those 22 years engineering science and the power weight ratio have changed beyond imagination.
> 2. It cannot be quite truly said 'she was destroyed by a lucky hit'. There are numerous magazines in a capital ship, in addition to the four largest ones, which lie beneath the main turrets. If, therefore, a heavy shell penetrates the armour at the angle of descent given by long ranges, the chance of one of the magazines being ignited is quite considerable.

3. The *Hood* was the most powerful ship of her speed that could be constructed in those days. But after the war the sailor made up his mind, after much experiment, that a very fast ship cannot afford to sacrifices armour to get that speed.
4. So in the *Nelson* class speed was sacrificed to ensure protection against sudden annihilation by shell, torpedo, or bomb.
5. Since the *Nelson* was built, modern engineering has closed the gap between the two factors.

The *Hood* was destroyed because she had to fight a ship 22 years more modern than herself. This was not the fault of the British seamen. It was the direct responsibility of those who opposed the rebuilding of the British Battle Fleet until 1937, two years before the second great war started. It is fair to her gallant crew that this should be written.[25]

Investigating the Loss

Within six days of the loss of the *Hood*, an enquiry into the sinking was ordered by the First Sea Lord Sir Dudley Pound. Pound was concerned by the disturbing nature of the *Hood*'s sinking, expressing in a letter to the Third Sea Lord and Controller of the Navy, Vice-Admiral Bruce Fraser, on 28 May:

> The loss of the *Hood* from internal explosion after a few minutes' action at 23,000 yards is disturbing, as we thought the defects in construction which led to similar losses of three capital ships at Jutland had been eliminated.
>
> As I recollect the mater, after the loss of the capital ships at Jutland we quickly reached the conclusion that it was due to 'flash' passing down the magazines and the sad experience was related to the case of the *Lion* at Dogger Bank, when 'flash' very nearly caused her to blow up ... I cannot recollect the full discussion which led to the conclusion that 'flash' was the cause of our losses at Jutland, nor do I know whether any other possible causes were fully examined.
>
> Now, after a lapse of 25 years, we have the first close action between one of our capital ships and that of the Germans since the Battle of Jutland and the *Hood* has been destroyed in minutes in what appears to the onlooker to be exactly the same manner as the *Queen Mary*, *Indefatigable* and *Invincible*, in spite of the action which was taken subsequent to Jutland to prevent further ships being destroyed as a result of 'flash'.[1]

The central question that the Board of Enquiry was to answer was how it was that the ship that had for so long been the 'Pride of the Royal Navy' had been sunk in such a spectacular fashion with such a catastrophic loss of life.

Headed by Vice-Admiral Sir Geoffrey Blake, the board convened on 30 May 1941 and delivered its findings to the First Sea Lord on 2 June, a mere nine days after the *Hood* had been lost. The findings were contained in a two-page long report signed by S. V. Goodall and were classified 'Secret'. The board's report stated:

> This report contains the findings of the Court, but not the evidence on which those findings are based. Hence, some of the points raised in the following remarks may

have been dealt with in the evidence and the Court's conclusions reached after full consideration of such points ... It is clear ... that a 15-inch shell fired from *Bismarck* at the range and inclination of the fatal fifth salvo could, if lucky and possessing sufficient delay, reach the after magazines. If this shell struck 'somewhere near the mainmast' the delay would have had to be very long for the shell to reach the forward bulkhead of the upper 4-inch magazine. If this magazine, which contained only 467 rounds of fixed ammunition, had exploded, it is not certain that the remaining magazines would have blown up. A still more lucky shot striking the ship farther aft could actually burst in the group of 4-inch magazines; in that case these magazines and the adjacent 15-inch magazines immediately abaft would blow up, and the ship would rapidly sink stern first.

DNC, however, considers it premature to conclude that because the ship <u>could</u> be blown up in this way that was in fact what happened. The reason for this remark is that 'the result of the fifth salvo was a large explosion, the centre of which appeared to be at the base of the mainmast.' It is extremely difficult to associate this observed fact with the explosion of the 4-inch magazines, the forward bulkhead of which is 64 feet abaft the centre of the mainmast and the after bulkhead about 115 feet. If the 4-inch magazines caused 'X' magazine to blow up, a fortiori, 'X' magazine would have caused 'Y' magazine to blow up. The after bulkhead of 'Y' magazine is about 180 feet abaft the centre of the mainmast, so it is even more difficult to reconcile the observed position of the explosion with the blowing up of all the magazines aft.... The after group of 4-inch H.A. magazines comprises 6 separate watertight compartments. Over then are 7 hatches and trunks through which the explosion of the magazine contents would vent. The flame, &c., would then have appeared at the after end of the superstructure and forward of 'X' turret. The roof of 'X' and 'Y' magazines is the lower deck, two decks below the weather deck. If the large quantity of cordite in these magazines blew up, the pressure would be so great that the superstructure above would be entirely destroyed and the flame from the explosion would have been seen around 'X' and 'Y' turrets. Is there any possible reason why the products of combustion from these magazines should have passed through the after engine-room and up round the mainmast over the centre engine room? No reason is indicated in the report, neither can one be imagined.

The question naturally arises, if the explosion at the base of the mainmast was not due to the after magazines, was there any other large quantity of explosives in that neighbourhood which could have caused the observed effect? The answer to that question is, 'Yes, on the upper deck abreast the mainmast there was a total quantity of about 4,000 lb of T.N.T.' If one or more shells from the fifth salvo detonated sufficiently close to one of the eight torpedo-heads confined in strong boxes on the upper deck, and if one or more of these warheads detonated, the result would be an explosion where it was actually observed.... The detonation of a torpedo-head in the open air is fairly damaging, but in a confined box in a ship would be far more devastating. In fact, such a detonation in the position of these tubes in the *Hood* would probably break the ship's back and result in rapid foundering ... The foregoing alternative explanation of the occurrence appears plausible and it is considered the finding of the Court should not be accepted as final until further facts are elicited ... It is important that the doubts concerning the loss of this ship should be cleared up if possible at a very early date, as although action is being taken to implement the lessons of both explanations, it is impossible to do this quickly for all our old capital ships if the true explanation is as found by the Court. Moreover, it will never be possible to give these ships such protection to their magazines as to ensure certainty that modern shells and bombs under all circumstances that may exist in modern actions cannot reach their magazines.[2]

When the report of the Board of Enquiry is read, it is apparent that the investigation that was conducted and the findings were rather incomplete. In short, the Board had concluded that one or more shells from the *Bismarck* had struck the *Hood* in the vicinity of the mainmast and had reached the 4-inch magazines, which detonated and in turn brought about the detonation of the 15-inch magazine.

It is worth noting that no minutes were left by the Board, no technical advice was sought, and limited interviews were conducted. Indeed, of the *Hood*'s three survivors, only Dundas had been called to present evidence. While endorsed, the findings of the board were heavily criticised with the result that a second Board of Enquiry was convened.

The second Board was convened under Rear-Admiral Harold Walker, one of the *Hood*'s last peacetime captains. The second board began by taking evidence from 176 individuals who witnessed the sinking from HMS *Norfolk*, the *Suffolk*, and the *Prince of Wales*. Technical experts were consulted and former officers were called to provide evidence and give testimonies. The Board was first convened on 12 August aboard HMS *Devonshire* and continued the following day aboard HMS *Suffolk*. The final sessions of the Board were held at Dorland House, London, between 27 August and 5 September. It was during these sessions that testimony was taken from Ted Briggs and Robert Tilburn. Dundas was not able to attend on this occasion. Evidence gained from survivors of the *Bismarck* was also taken into consideration.[3]

During its sessions, the Board went to great lengths to attempt to establish whether or not the fire that erupted on the Boat Deck or the ship's torpedoes had any bearing on her loss. At the second Board of Enquiry, it was suggested by expert witnesses that what was observed was a violent, but not instantaneous explosion (deflagration) in the 4-inch magazine and that this was visible through the engine room ventilators. This same deflagration would have collapsed the bulkhead that separated the 4-inch and 15-inch magazine, which resulted in a catastrophic explosion that was similar in nature to those that were witnessed at Jutland with the loss of HMS *Indefatigable*, *Queen Mary*, and *Invincible*. This theory was ultimately adopted by the second Board of Enquiry.[4] The findings of this second Board were delivered on 12 September 1941. The findings were, however, little removed from the conclusions of the first board:

(1) That the sinking of *Hood* was due to a hit from *Bismarck*'s 15-inch shell in or adjacent to *Hood*'s 4-inch or 15-inch magazines, causing them all to explode and wreck the after part of the ship. The probability is that the 4-inch magazines exploded first.

(2) There is no conclusive evidence that one or two torpedo warheads detonated or exploded simultaneously with the magazines, or at any other time, but the possibility cannot be entirely excluded. We consider that if they had done so their effect would not have been so disastrous as to cause the immediate destruction of the ship, and on the whole, we are of the opinion that they did not.

(3) That the fire that was seen on *Hood*'s Boat Deck, and in which UP and/or 4-inch ammunition was certainly involved, was not the cause of her loss.

The conclusion of the Board of Enquiry is that the after 4-inch magazine probably exploded first, followed by the after 15-inch magazine, which is only natural as it was so near.[5]

Today, the exact cause of the loss of the *Hood* remains a subject of debate, although the findings of the second Board of Enquiry are generally accepted. The main theories behind the sinking that are debated are as follows:

1. That the *Hood* suffered a direct hit from a shell fired by the *Bismarck* that penetrated her aft magazine. Said shell could only have come from the *Bismarck* as by the point in the battle at which the *Hood* was sunk, the *Prinz Eugen* was no longer firing at the *Hood*. This theory as a version of events was almost taken for granted at the time of the sinking, in part owing to eyewitness testimony which claimed that the explosion that had destroyed the *Hood* had originated near her main mast, well forward of the aft magazine.

2. A shell from the *Bismarck* fell short and struck the *Hood* below her armoured belt where it penetrated the magazine and detonated resulting in the explosion. During the battle, *Prince of Wales* received a similar hit from a 15-inch shell which travelled for approximately eighty feet underwater before striking the battleship 28 feet below the waterline where it penetrated several light bulkheads. While the Second Board discounted this theory as improbable, William Jurens has calculated that one of the *Bismarck*'s shells which fell approximately 20 feet short of the *Hood* could have penetrated the side of the ship beneath the armoured belt in the vicinity of the magazine and detonated it if the fuse worked correctly.[6]

3. The ship's torpedoes were detonated by the fire on the boat deck or by a hit from the *Bismarck*, which blew out the side of the ship allowing a vast influx of water which flooded the ship and broke her back.

4. The fire on the boat deck penetrated a magazine. While the second Board indicated that the 4-inch magazine doors were closed throughout the battle, some have argued that a German shell could have served to open up the magazine doors or the trunking sufficiently to admit flames into the magazine. Within this school of thought, it has also been suggested that flames reached the magazines through the ventilation shafts.

5. This final school of thought suggests that the *Hood* was blown up by the detonation of one of her own shells in one of her guns. At the second Board of Enquiry some witnesses to the battle in the Denmark Strait reported that unusual types of discharge were seen to be emitting from the *Hood*'s 15-inch guns. This has led to some to suggest that a shell could have detonated within one of her guns which caused an explosion within the gun house. This school suggests that it is possible that within the stress and heat of the battle, the safety measures that were introduced in the wake of the Battle of Jutland to prevent gun house explosions reaching the magazines were not enacted correctly or failed.

Discounting the above fifth point, the debate into the loss of the *Hood* by and large centres on whether it was her horizontal or vertical armour that was defeated.

In the summer of 2001, the wreck of the *Hood* was located and filmed by Blue Water Recoveries. At a depth of approximately 9,000 feet (1.70 miles or 2.74 km), the *Hood* was found among three vast debris fields consisting of the bow and stern sections along with a 350-foot-long piece of upturned hull. There is, however, a 225-foot-long area of the ship that is unaccounted for, which covers the approximate area from 'Y' turret to the middle engine room. The images of the *Hood*'s severed bow came as something of a surprise. The ship had been seen to break in two, but not into three. A number of arguments have been advanced for how the bow section broke away from the midsection. According to Bruce Taylor, '[i]t seems probable that the break was owed first to structural weakening when the bow rose out of the water and then to implosion damage once the ship left the surface'.[7] Meanwhile, David Mearns and Rob White have put forward the argument that an explosion in the ship's forward magazines was the root cause, a point which is countered by William Jurens.[8]

One of the standout conclusions that has been drawn is that drawn by Jurens in his 1987 piece, *The Loss of HMS Hood: A Re-Examination*. Jurens's hypothesis is based on the detonation of a 15-inch shell in or near the 4-inch aft magazines:

If this occurred, and ignition of the propellant followed from it, then a large part of the rapidly expanding gas bubble would have taken the path of least resistance and vented into the engineering spaces immediately forward of this area. For a time the sheer inertia of the *Hood*'s structure would have slowed expansion in any other direction. Once the expanding gasses had reached the engine rooms, the quickest exits to the outside would have been the series of massive exhaust vents located on the centreline immediately forward of and aft of the mainmast. These huge ducts, changing in size and shape as they rose through the ship, ended in roughly square vents 1.8 metres [each] side on the boat deck. It was as spectacular, near-vertical columns of flame from these vents near the mainmast, foreshortened to observers on surrounding ships, that the explosion first became visible. Shortly thereafter, the entire stern of the ship exploded. At the time of the blast, the Board of Inquiry calculated the 'X' 15-in magazine contained about 49 tons of cordite, 'Y'

The *Hood*'s severed bow lying on the seabed. Some of the teak decking can still be seen while the degaussing cable is visible around this section of the wreck. (*David Mearns*)

magazine contained 45 tons, and the 4-in magazines contained about 18.5 tons. The uncontrolled burning of this quantity of propellant in the after magazines might have slowed briefly as the volume of the engineering spaces served as a space into which the gasses could expand, and as the vents directed much of the combustion products outboard. But although this expansion and venting could temporarily relieve the pressure, it could never be enough to prevent an explosion from eventually tearing the ship apart.[9]

As Jurens has written, 'The exact origin of the explosion is now, and shall probably always remain, somewhat in doubt'.[10]

Epilogue

Battlecruisers were conceived with a key specific task in mind, and when provided with the opportunity to undertake that task, such as that presented at the Battle of the Falkland Islands, they excelled. Furthermore, battlecruisers were not designed to be used in any engagement with vessels of equal or greater firepower and armour, but were to use their speed to withdraw.

Once HMS *Invincible* had been constructed, the Imperial German Navy was compelled to design and construct its own battlecruisers, and in doing so, served to create vessels that were not only superior to their British counterparts, but also increased the odds that a British battlecruiser would be drawn into an engagement for which it was not designed. Mark Stille has correctly argued that the role of commerce protector and fleet scout could have been carried out by heavy cruisers, which unlike the battlecruisers would not have been drawn into the line of battle if enemy dreadnoughts had sought an engagement.[1]

At Jutland, the predictions that were made in the 1907 *Brassey Naval Annual* came true; the battlecruiser had strayed from its primary role as a cruiser-destroyer and found itself engaged in the line of battle during a fleet-on-fleet action, suffering the consequences. Nicholas Lambert, among others, has stated one point with which there is largely no dispute—that British battlecruisers were inadequately defended.[2] Nevertheless, when deployed in the role for which it had been conceived, the battlecruiser was an incisive, decisive weapon. It was as a result of ill-conceived strategy that the fatal weaknesses of the battlecruisers were exposed.[3] What is more, the British pursuit of the highest possible rate of fire lead to shortcuts being taken, such as the unsafe storage of cordite and the securing open of magazine doors—shortcuts that, in conjunction with inadequate flash protection, would seal the fate of HMS *Invincible* and the other battlecruisers lost at Jutland.

Fortnightly Review has described the hits to the turrets that lead to the destruction of the *Queen Mary* and the *Indefatigable* as an 'unfortunate coincidence which may never happen again in sea engagement'.[4] Given that the *Invincible* was destroyed as the result of a similar strike shortly after the loss of the *Indefatigable* and the *Queen Mary*, not to mention the loss of the *Hood*, this assertion seems hard to justify. It does, however, seem reasonable to suggest that, given their offensive power, the battlecruisers were always likely to be drawn into such engagements as the battle as Jutland or the battle of the Denmark Strait, with the success of the Battle of the Falkland Islands serving only to enhance the reputation of the ships.

One question remains, however, and it concerns the *Hood*. If Jutland highlighted the shortcomings of the battlecruiser concept and demonstrated the vulnerability of the battlecruiser to fire from vessels of equal or greater firepower, against Fisher's conceptualised idea, and given the fact that a large amount of work went into trying to make the *Hood* less vulnerable than her predecessors, why did the Admiralty deploy the *Hood* as a battleship during the Second World War? There are two parts to this answer. The first and predominant reason is the lack of big gun resources available to the Royal Navy. The second part of this answer owes something to the inflated legend of the *Hood*. The *Hood* was renowned and feared the world over. The threat of the *Hood* opening fire had served to deter the Nationalist cruiser *Almirante Cervera* and helped to break the blockade of Bilbao during the Spanish Civil War. Furthermore, during the Abyssinian crisis Mussolini had been fearful of the *Hood* and sought her removal prior to a disengagement in Abyssinia. When launched, the *Hood* was the largest ship in the world and a potent symbol of British might, which all contributed to the legend of 'the Mighty *Hood*'. It is quite possible that this legend may have impaired the judgment of the Admiralty. For over twenty years, she was 'the Mighty *Hood*'; despite her deficiencies, due to this substantial period of time, many may have thought her invincible. Yet her only claim to being 'invincible' comes from that fact that she suffered a similar face to the *Invincible*, with both being lost in an almost identical manner.

The emphatic manner in which HMS *Hood* was destroyed seems to underline that the age of the battlecruiser—if indeed there was such an age—was over. It should also be noted that also coming to a close, more generally, was the era of the big-gun capital ship. On 26 May, Swordfish from the *Ark Royal* undertook a torpedo attack against the *Bismarck*, which damaged her rudder and permitted the Home Fleet to close in and batter her into submission before dispatching her with torpedoes. Without the use of aircraft, the Home Fleet would have failed in their efforts to stop the *Bismarck*. If further evidence was needed, the manner in which the Italian Fleet at Taranto was sunk by aircraft of the Royal Navy's Fleet Air Arm on 12 November 1940; the manner in which bulk of the U.S. Pacific Fleet was destroyed at anchor at Pearl Harbor; the way HMS *Prince of Wales* and the *Repulse* were sunk; and the way in which the Battle of Midway was fought, to name but a few engagements (all by aircraft) showed that navies were moving out of the era of the battleship and big-gun capital ship and into the era of the aeroplane with the aircraft carrier rapidly becoming the new 'mistress of the seas'. The paradigm shift in the way future naval warfare was to be carried out was illustrated by the conversion of the *Courageous*, *Glorious*, and *Furious* (the three battlecruisers ordered by the Royal Navy directly before the order was placed for the *Hood*) to aircraft carriers during the later stages of the First World War, while the United States converted two hulls that had been intended for its battlecruisers into aircraft carriers: the USS *Lexington* and USS *Saratoga*.

Despite Captain Pridham in 1936 being briefed on a planned overhaul and refit of the *Hood* that was scheduled to take place in 1942, it is likely that, if she had survived her encounter with the *Bismarck* on 24 May 1941, the *Hood* would not have undergone the large refit, repair, and modernisation that she required. In late 1938, plans had been discussed with Captain Walker and the crew in which the ship's key deficiencies and shortcomings were highlighted and noted. Based on this, a rough plan was formed, which was officially referred to as the 'large repair', but detailed plans were never drawn up. The sketches that were drawn up are believed to have been lost, but it is likely that the refit would have seen the *Hood* take up a configuration similar to the *Renown*. The refit was expected to cost somewhere in the region of £4.5 million and would have taken between two and three years to complete based on pre-war considerations.

It is likely that, had the *Hood* not been struck by a shell from the *Bismarck*'s fifth salvo and exploded in the catastrophic manner that she did in the Denmark Strait, then she would still not have undergone a large refit. The pre-war 'large repair' plans were based solely on pre-war considerations. With the war raging, resources and finances were severely limited. Resources would more likely have been diverted towards the construction of new vessels and the repair of damaged ones as opposed to being dedicated to a major overhaul. Furthermore, as the war developed and expanded, increasing pressures were placed on the Royal Navy. It is therefore unlikely that the *Hood* could have been spared for long enough to undergo anything other than a minor refit or repair. At best, the *Hood* would likely have had her engines repaired or possibly updated, and saw some slight modifications made to her superstructure in an attempt to save weight and would have had her anti-aircraft armament bolstered.

Romantic images of the *Hood* are conjured up when one thinks of her: the majestic battlecruiser gliding across the sea at high speed. This has led some to believe that had the *Hood* survived the Second World War then she would have been decommissioned and preserved as a museum ship like Nelson's flagship HMS *Victory* in Portsmouth, the cruiser HMS *Belfast* in London, or the battleships USS *Texas* near Houston and the USS *Missouri* at Pearl Harbor. While this is a romantic idea, it is a highly unlikely one. During her career, the *Hood* was well known; however, she was not the icon that she has become since her sinking. Indeed, it was her tragic end and the catastrophic loss of life associated with her sinking that has transformed her from a well-known warship into a maritime icon.

The *Hood* was followed into service by newer and in a number of ways, superior warships such as the vessels of the *King George V*-class and the Royal Navy's last battleship HMS *Vanguard*. At the same time, the *Hood* was outlived by hardened capital ship veterans of the Great War and the Second World War such as HMS *Warspite*, *Queen Elizabeth*, *Iron Duke*, *Valiant*, and *Malaya*. Without exception, following the war, each of these vessels were paid off and sold for scrap. It is worth briefly looking here also at the fate of Britain's battlecruisers.

Up until the Battle of Jutland, the Royal Navy had maintained three squadrons of battlecruisers. The loss of the *Indefatigable*, *Queen Mary*, and *Invincible* served to reduce the number of available battlecruisers sufficiently to warrant a reduction to the maintenance of two squadrons of battlecruisers. After the First World War, many of the Royal Navy's battlecruisers were sold for scrap leaving the navy with just three battlecruisers: HMS *Tiger*, *Repulse*, and *Renown*, with the *Hood* under construction.

In late 1919, the Battlecruiser Squadron was formed consisting of the *Tiger*, *Renown* and *Repulse* and was commanded by Rear Admiral Sir Roger Keyes, who flew his flag in the *Tiger*. In May 1920 with the commissioning of the *Hood*, HMS *Tiger* was removed from an operational role, with the *Hood* becoming the new flagship of the Battlecruiser Squadron on 18 May 1920. When the *Hood* was decommissioned in May 1929 until May 1931 for her major overhaul and refit, flagship duties were transferred to HMS *Renown*. At this time, HMS *Tiger* was returned to active service or order to maintain the three-ship strength of the squadron. When recommissioned in May 1931, the *Hood* resumed the role of flagship of the Battlecruiser Squadron while HMS *Tiger* was decommissioned on 30 March 1931. The *Tiger*, the last battlecruiser to have saw service at Jutland, was finally sold for scrap in February 1932.

HMS *Hood* continued on as flagship throughout the Second World War until her loss during the Battle of the Denmark Strait on 24 May 1941. Following the sinking of HMS *Repulse* on 10 December 1941 by Japanese aircraft, the Battlecruiser Squadron ceased to exist. HMS *Renown* would see service in the Mediterranean, with the Home Fleet and in the Pacific before she was placed in reserve in May 1945. Partially disarmed in July when six of her 4.5-inch turrets and all of her light guns were removed, the *Renown* played host to a meeting between King George VI and President Harry S. Truman on 3 August. The decision to dispose of the *Renown* was announced on 21 January 1948 and she was towed to Faslane for scrapping on 3 August 1948. She was the last of Fisher's battlecruisers to be sent to the scrapyard, outlasting HMS *Furious* (originally designed as a battlecruiser but converted into an aircraft carrier) by days.

In an island nation such as Great Britain with a long naval history, such vessels come and go while others come along to take their places. This pattern, along with Britain's economic state after the war, would have resulted in the *Hood* coming to the very same end as that which ultimately befell the other large capital ships of her era.

The ship's bell manned by the Royal Marines. It was this bell that was recovered in an expedition funded by Microsoft co-founder Paul Allen.

Admirals and Captains

Below is a list of all those who flew their flag in the *Hood* as admiral and those who commanded her as captain.

Admirals

Sir Roger B. Keyes	18 May 1920–31 March 1921
Sir Walter H. Cowan	31 March 1921–15 May 1923
Sir Frederick L. Field	15 May 1923–30 April 1925
Sir Cyril T. M. Fuller	30 April 1925–21 May 1927
Sir Frederic C. Dreyer	21 May 1927–1 May 1929
Wilfred Tomkinson	24 April 1931–15 August 1932
Sir William M. James	15 August 1932–14 August 1934
Sir Sidney R. Bailey	14 August 1934–22 July 1936
Sir Geoffrey Blake	22 July 1936–3 July 1937
Sir Andrew B. Cunningham	3 July 1937–23 July 1938
Sir Geoffrey Layton	23 July 1938–1 June 1939
Sir William J. Whitworth	1 June 1939–11 March 1940
Sir James Somerville	30 June 1940–10 August 1940
Sir William J. Whitworth	10 August 1940–8 May 1941
Lancelot E. Holland	12 May 1941–24 May 1941

Captains

Wilfred Tomkinson	1 January 1920–31 March 1921
Geoffrey Mackworth	31 March 1921–15 May 1923
John K. Im Thurn	15 May 1923–30 April 1925
Harold O. Reinold	30 April 1925–21 May 1927
Wilfred F. French	21 May 1927–1 May 1929
Julian F. C. Patterson	27 April 1931–15 August 1932

Thomas H. Binney	15 August 1932–30 August 1933
Francis T. B. Tower	30 August 1933–1 February 1936
Arthur F. Pridham	1 February 1936–20 May 1938
Harold T. C. Walker	20 May 1938–30 January 1939
Commander William W. Davis	30 January 1939–3 May1939
Irvine G. Glennie	3 May 1939–15 February 1941
Ralph Kerr	15 February 1941–24 May 1941

APPENDIX II

Roll of Honour

Below are the names of the 1,415 men who lost their lives when the *Hood* sank on 24 May 1941.

NAAFI: Navy Army Air Force Institute
PN: Polish Navy
RANVR: Royal Australian Naval Volunteer Reserve
RCN: Royal Canadian Navy
RIN: Royal Indian Navy
RM: Royal Marines
RMB: Royal Marine Band
RN: Royal Navy
RNR: Royal Naval Reserve
RNVR: Royal Naval Volunteer Reserve
RNZN: Royal New Zealand Navy

Abbott, Marine Frederick, RM
Abbott, Ordinary Coder Kenneth, RN
Ablett, Marine Wallace A., RM
Abrams, Cook Robert G., RN
Acton, Able Seaman Percival C. H., RN
Adams, Musician Frank P., RMB
Adams, Corporal Keith H., RM
Adams, Midshipman Nigel N., RNR
Adams, Ordinary Seaman Victor E., RN
Adams, Leading Stoker Victor H., RN
Ainsworth, Able Seaman Frederick J., RN
Akehurst, Stoker 1st Class Rodney G., RN
Aldred, Ordinary Telegraphist Gerald A., RN
Algate, Canteen Assistant Alfred K., NAAFI

Alger, Ordinary Seaman Eric, RN
Alland, Petty Officer Harry C., RN
Allcock, Boy 1st Class William S., RN
Allen, Leading Stoker Arthur F. J., RN
Allen, Leading Seaman Charles W., RN
Allen, Ordinary Seaman Edward B, RN
Allen, Stoker 1st Class James E., RN
Allen, John G, Marine, RM
Allen, Able Seaman William E. S., RN
Allott, Marine George, RM
Almond, Able Seaman Frederick, RN
Altham, Stoker 2nd Class Arthur, RN
Ambridge, Sergeant Walter C., RM
Ambrose, Able Seaman John, RN
Amery, Able Seaman Thomas C. F., RN
Anderson, Ordinary Seaman Arthur D., RN
Anderson, Chief Engine Room Artificer John, RN
Anderson, Ordinary Seaman Joseph M., RN
Andrews, Ordinary Seaman Cecil V., RN
Annis, Stoker 1st Class James E., RN
Applegarth, Leading Signalman Richard, RN
Appleyard, Ordinary Seaman John A. F., RN
Ardley, Boy 1st Class Jack C., RN
Arkinstall, Leading Seaman John, RN
Armstrong, Leading Stoker John C., RN
Armstrong, Able Seaman Norman, RN

Arnold, Stoker Petty Officer, William A., RN

Ashley, Able Seaman Robert G., RN

Assirati, Stoker Petty Officer Albert F., RN

Atkins, Chief Petty Officer Steward William E., RN

Atkinson, Able Seaman John H., RN

Atkinson, Stoker Petty Officer Robert, RN

Austin, Able Seaman Albert G. L., RN

Avery, Able Seaman Albert G., RN

Awdry, Lieutenant-Commander C. D., RN

Ayling, Canteen Assistant Frank R., NAAFI

Ayling, Able Seaman Ronald, RN

Ayres, Ordinary Signalman Henry D., RN

Badcock, Stoker 2nd Class John H., RN

Baildon, Able Seaman Frank, RN

Bailey, Marine Frederick W., RM

Bailey, Ordinary Signalman Leonard W. J., RN

Baines, Leading Seaman Godfrey J., RN

Baker, Ordinary Seaman Andrew L., RN

Baker, Leading Stoker George E., RN

Baker, Petty Officer Telegraphist Kenneth A., RN

Balch, Able Seaman Percy H., RN

Baldwin, Stoker 1st Class Kenneth E. G., RN

Baldwin, Ordinary Seaman Philip R., RN

Ball, Able Seaman Charles F. D., RN

Ball, Stoker 1st Class Philip A., RN

Ball, Leading Stoker William, RN

Ballard, Boy 1st Class Arthur, RN

Balsdon, Stoker 1st Class Ernest F., RN

Bamford, Able Seaman Anthony B. J., RN

Banfield, Boy 1st Class Kenneth J., RN

Banks, Stoker 1st Class George H., RN

Banks, Leading Cook (S) Sidney T., RN

Barclay, Leading Cook (S) Alexander C., RN

Barker, Ordinary Seaman Thomas, RN

Barnes, Stoker Petty Officer Thomas G., RN

Barnes, Able Seaman Walter J., RN

Barnet, Cook (O) William L., RN

Barnett, Stoker 2nd Class Ivor G., RN

Barrie, Able Seaman Walter R., RN

Barringer, Marine William H., RM

Bartley, Signal Boatswain Archibald E. T., RN

Barton, Petty Officer Kenneth C. F., RN

Basham, Ordinary Seaman Howard, RN

Bassett, Petty Officer Charles G., RN

Basstone, Marine Jack, RM

Batchelor, Yeoman of Signals Arthur R., RN

Bates, Leading Seaman Frederick G., RN

Bates, Marine Leonard A., RM

Bates, Wireman Reginald S., RN

Batley, Lieutenant-Commander Anthony R. T., RNVR

Batten, Ordinary Seaman Herbert W. L., RN

Battersby, Clifford, Able Seaman, RN

Baxter, Petty Officer John K., RN

Baylis, Ordinary Signalman Herbert J., RN

Beard, Marine Robert A., RM

Beard, Midshipman Thomas N. K., RCN

Beardsley, Joiner 4th Class Geoffrey V., RN

Belcher, Electrical Artificer 3rd Class Cyril S. V., RN

Bell, Ordinary Signalman Cyril K., RN

Bell, Ordinary Signalman Ronald T. L., RN

Bell, Able Seaman William, RNVR

Belsham, Able Seaman James R., RN

Bembridge, Ordinary Seaman Percy A., RN

Bennett, Marine Ernest, RM

Bennett, Boy 1st Class Percival, RN

Benoist, Able Seaman Donald G., RN

Benwell, Sick Berth Chief Petty Officer Ernest F. T., RN

Berner, Leading Writer Robert V., , RN

Betts, Stoker 1st Class Robert, RN

Beveridge, Ordnance Artificer 4th Class Roy, RN

Biggenden, Chief Stoker Walden J., RN

Binnie, Stoker Petty Officer John E., RN

Bird, Ordnance Artificer 3rd Class Herbert G. A., RN

Bishop, Chief Stoker Charles J., RN

Bishop, Petty Officer Edward J. P., RN

Bispham, Ordinary Seaman Leslie W., RN

Biss, Able Seaman John, RN

Blake, Leading Stoker Harold G., RN

Blann, Able Seaman Kenneth A. F., RN

Bleach, Able Seaman Arthur B., RN

Blondel, Electrical Artificer 4th Class André, RN

Bloodworth, Able Seaman Herbert W., RN

Blow, Ordinary Seaman Leonard, RN

Blunt, Leading Cook (S) William H. T., RN

Boardman, Petty Officer Stanley, RN

Bocutt, Marine Alfred A., RM

Boncey, Petty Officer William L., RN

Bond, Able Seaman Sidney W., RN

Boneham, Marine Norman, RM

Boniface, Able Seaman Jack, RN

Bonner, Able Seaman Colin A., RN

Boone, Engine Room Artificer 4th Class Bernard J., RN

Booth, Stoker 2nd Class George H., RN

Borrer, Able Seaman Harold T., RN

Borsberry, Petty Officer Cook (S) George, RN

Bosley, Leading Sick Berth Attendant Frank W., RN

Bostock, Chief Mechanician Charles W., RN

Bower, Able Seaman Reginald P., RN

Bower, Stoker 1st Class Ronald, RN

Bowers, Ordinary Seaman Leo S., RN

Bowie, Able Seaman Duncan, RNVR

Bowyer, Ordinary Telegraphist Thomas R., RN

Bowyer, Stoker 1st Class Walter F., RN

Bradley, Ordinary Seaman Harold, RN

Bradley, Able Seaman Kenneth J., RN

Bradshaw, Stoker 2nd Class Thomas F., RN

Bramhall, Joiner 4th Class Harold, RNSR

Brand, Corporal William H., RM

Brandon, Ordinary Telegraphist Albert A., RN

Bransden, Able Seaman Paul D., RN

Brett, Ordinary Seaman Benjamin A., RN

Brewer, Ordinary Seaman Arthur W., RN

Brewer, Ordinary Seaman George, RN

Bridge, Telegraphist Arthur T., RN

Bridges, Ordinary Telegraphist Kenneth C., RNVR

Bridges, Wireman Ronald W., RN

Brierley, Leading Steward William L., RN

Bristow, Wireman Harry, RN

Britton, Marine Clarence V., RM

Broadhurst, Wireman Dennis C., RN

Broadley, Leading Seaman William N., RN

Brookes, Telegraphist Donald A., RN

Brooks, Stoker 1st Class Gordon B., RN

Brooks, Stoker 1st Class Jack, RN

Brooks, Marine Terrence L., RM

Broom, Shipwright 3rd Class George W., RN

Brown, Marine Arthur, RM

Brown, Boy 1st Class Eric F., RN

Brown, Stoker 2nd Class Ernest, RN

Brown, Steward George W., RN

Brown, Able Seaman Henry J., RN

Brown, Leading Seaman John L., RN

Brown, Stoker Petty Officer Robert K., RN

Browne, Lieutenant (S) Robert H. P., RN

Brownrigg, Lieutenant-Commander John G. P., RN

Bryant, Midshipman Denis M., RN

Buck, Mechanician 2nd Class Arthur E. J., RN

Buck, Stoker Petty Officer Herbert T. J., RN

Buckett, Midshipman Philip J., RNVR

Bull, Leading Seaman Percival H., RN

Bull, Able Seaman Robert J., RN

Bullock, Able Seaman Edward H., RN

Bullock, Marine Henry W., RM

Bullock, Able Seaman William F., RN

Bulman, Petty Officer Kenneth F., RN

Burckitt, Petty Officer Cook John B. E., RN

Burgess, Warrant Ordnance Officer Henry, RN

Burkin, Marine Robert H., RM

Burnell, Ordinary Seaman Gordon R., RN

Burningham, Chief Petty Officer William F. R., RN

Burns, Able Seaman Albert S., RN

Bussey, Able Seaman Harry F., RN

Butler, Able Seaman Horace A., RN

Butterworth, Able Seaman Alfred N., RN

Byrne, Boy 1st Class Francis, RN

Byrne, Stoker 1st Class Thomas G., RN

Cabell, Chief Petty Officer Cook Percy A., RN

Cabrin, Stoker 2nd Class Roy V., RN

Callon, Boy 1st Class William J., RN

Cambridge, Sub-Lieutenant (E) John H., RNVR

Campbell, Leading Seaman Albert G., RN

Cann, Marine Herbert R., RM

Cantrill, Stoker Petty Officer Joshua, RN

Canty, Yeoman of Signals William D., RN

Capon, Ordinary Seaman Leslie A., RN

Capstick, Marine Arthur J., RM

Carey, Ordinary Seaman Arthur T., RN

Carey, Supply Assistant Daniel A. B., RN

Carlin, Lieutenant-Commander (S)George V., RNVR

Carn, Chief Yeoman of Signals George H. K., RN

Carpenter, Marine Robert S., RM

Carr, Stoker 2nd Class John., RN

Carter, Marine Robert J. W., RM

Cartwright, Captain Thomas D., RM

Cavell, Stoker 1st Class Percy H., RN

Chamberlain, Corporal Henry S., RM

Chandler, Master-at-Arms Alfred J., RN

Chaplin, Boy 1st Class Albert E., RN

Chapman, Commissioned Gunner James A., RN

Chappell, Able Seaman Robert E., RN

Charker, Able Seaman Albert W., RN

Charlton, Able Seaman Robert A., RN

Chatfield, Able Seaman Edwin H., RN

Cheadle, Petty Officer Henry J., RN

Chivers, Engine Room Artificer 3rd Class William A., RN

Choules, Chief Petty Officer Sydney J., RN

Chowney, Chief Petty Officer William H., RN

Churchill, Ordinary Seaman Ronald J., RN

Claringbold, Able Seaman Leon J., RN

Clark, Ordinary Seaman Jack C. P., RN

Clark, Leading Seaman John F., RN

Clark, Marine Leonard A., RM

Clark, Marine Robert G., RM

Clarke, Ordinary Seaman David W., RN

Clarke, Electrical Artificer 4th Class Leslie H., RN

Clarke, Wireman Stanley W., RN

Clayton, Wireman Stanley., RN

Clayton, Ordinary Seaman William A., RN

Cleeter, Able Seaman William G., RN

Clements, Able Seaman Thomas W., RN

Cleton, Engine Room Artificer 4th Class Peter V., RN

Clitherow, Stoker 2nd Class Charles F., RN

Clothier, Ordinary Coder Kenneth R. J., RN

Clout, Able Seaman Cecil G., RN

Cobb, Ordinary Seaman William H., RN

Cockhead, Leading Stoker Alfred J., RN

Cogger, Marine Thomas E., RM

Cole, Ordinary Seaman Albert E., RN

Cole, Marine George D., RM

Cole, Able Seaman John H., RN

Cole, Marine William G., RM

Coleman, Marine Dennis J., RM

Collett, Able Seaman Stanley J., RN

Collings, Midshipman (S) John P., RN

Collins, Petty Officer Arthur R., RN

Collins, Able Seaman Reginald J., RN

Collinson, Boy 1st Class Robert E., RN

Collis, Boy 1st Class Gordon V., RN

Collyer, Boy 1st Class Percy W. L., RN

Comber, Leading Seaman James D., RN

Combes, Ordinary Seaman Richard A. L., RN

Compton, Leading Stoker William A., RN

Conchie, Boy 1st Class William M., RN

Conroy, Stoker 2nd Class Cornelius, RN

Constable, Boy 1st Class Alan R., RN

Cook, Chief Stoker James E., RN

Cook, Able Seaman Joseph R., RN

Cook, Blacksmith 4th Class Vernon., RN

Coombes, Sergeant Gerald E., RM

Cooper, Able Seaman Alan C., RN

Cooper, Mechanician 2nd Class Frederick G. D., RN

Cooper, Able Seaman Geoffrey G., RN

Cooper, Ordinary Coder George W., RN

Cooper, Marine John, RM

Cope, Boy 1st Class George R., RN

Cope, Commissioned Gunner Sidney J., RN

Corddell, Chief Petty Officer Harold L., RN

Corlett, Engine Room Artificer 4th Class John, RN

Cornock, Able Seaman James, RN

Cotton, Stoker 2nd Class Lewis A., RN

Cottrell, Ordinary Seaman Albert E., RN

Coulson, Musician John, RMB

Coulthurst, Stoker 2nd Class Francis B., RN

Court, Able Seaman William R., RN

Cowie, Shipwright 4th Class John E. L., RN

Cox, Ordinary Seaman Arthur J., RN

Cox, Stoker 1st Class Cyril A., RN

Cox, Wireman John F., RN

Cox, Ordinary Coder Leslie L., RN

Cox, Leading Seaman Stanley K., RN

Craft, Able Seaman Thomas E., RN

Cranston, Stoker 1st Class Aylmer N. J., RN

Crawford, Boy 1st Class William M., RN

Crawley, Stoker 1st Class Lawrence, RN

Crawte, Musician Alfred E. J., RMB

Crellin, Stoker 1st Class William, RN

Cresswell, Marine Henry R., RM

Cross, Petty Officer Joseph B., RN

Cross, Cook (O) Robert C., RN

Cross, Commander William K. R., RN

Crouch, Regulating Petty Officer Cecil H., RN

Croucher, Able Seaman Lambert E., RN

Crow, Leading Stoker George L., RN

Crumpton, Leading Stoker Laurence, RN

Cruttenden, Able Seaman John E., RN

Cunningham, Able Seaman John, RN

Cunningham, Ordinary Seaman Richard F., RN

Currie, Stoker 1st Class George, RN

Currie, Stoker 1st Class Robert, RN

Cuthbert, Corporal Albert T., RM

Czerny, Midshipman Stanislaw, PN

D'Abry De L'Arves, Able Seaman Robert, RN

Dade, Petty Officer Steward William F. L., RN

Dakers, Sick Berth Attendant William B., RN

Dale, Lieutenant (E) Richard H., RN

Dall, Able Seaman Francis O., RN

Dalziel, Ordinary Signalman Thomas, RN

Daniels, Stoker 1st Class Charles G., RN

Darby, Ordinary Seaman Leonard, RN

Davey, Leading Telegraphist Frederick G., RN

Davey, Able Seaman Reginald J., RN

Davies, Able Seaman Douglas A., RN

Davies, Able Seaman Frederick M., RN

Davies, Midshipman Hamilton K., RNVR

Davies, Lieutenant Horace D., RM

Davies, Boy Bugler Kenneth J., RM

Davies, Senior Master Com. Warrant Officer Ronald T., RN

Davis, Able Seaman Gordon E., RN

Davis, Marine Herbert A., RM

Davis, Stoker 1st Class Percy J., RN

Dawson, Signal Boy Phillip J., RN

Day, Marine Frederick J., RM

Day, Chief Electrical Artificer William S. W., RN

De Gernier, Able Seaman James B., RNVR

De St George, Able Seaman Edward O., RN

De Ste Croix, Leading Stoker Cyril R., RN

Dean, Stoker 1st Class Cyril A. J., RN

Dean, Signalman George A., RN

Dear, Musician Nelson L., RMB

Dempsey, Able Seaman Martin, RN

Denault, Stoker 2nd Class Benjamin, RN

Dennis, Able Seaman Ronald, RN

Dent, Surgeon Lieutenant Christopher H. C., RNVR

Derrick, Leading Supply Assistant Charles T., RN

Devereaux, Ordinary Seaman Albert, RN

Dewey, Boy 1st Class Edward D. G., RN

Diggens, Able Seaman James B., RN

Dilly, Stoker 1st Class John H. C., RN

Dinsdale, Stoker 1st Class Stanley, RN

Discombe, Musician Archie A. J., RMB

Dixon, Leading Stoker Albert, RN

Dixon, Able Seaman William, RN

Doak, Petty Officer Walter W., RN

Dobeson, Chief Petty Officer Nicholas, RN

Dobson, Able Seaman Charles W., RN

Dodd, Stoker 1st Class Henry, RN

Donaghy, Able Seaman Walter, RN

Donald, Boy 1st Class James H., RN

Donaldson, Ordinary Seaman Walter M. H., RN

Doolan, Stoker 2nd Class Francis, RN

Douglas, Able Seaman Neil H., RN

Douglass, Boy 1st Class Mark R., RN

Dowdell, Leading Seaman William F. S., RN

Dowdles, Able Seaman Malcom M., RNVR

Down, Sub-Lieutenant John R., RNVR

Druken, Ordinary Seaman Valentine, RN

Drury, Ordinary Signalman Ernest, RN

Duckworth, Able Seaman Kenneth R. R., RN

Dudman, Mechanician 1st Class Caleb A. W., RN

Duffield, Stoker 2nd Class John, RN

Dunn, Able Seaman Stephen E., RN

Dunne, Petty Officer Patrick L., RN

Dunnell, Marine Graham G., RM

Dunwell, Able Seaman William S., RN

Dyas, Stoker 2nd Class Richard J., RN

Dyment, Ordinary Seaman Herbert R., RN

Eagles, Midshipman George R., RN

Earl, Stoker 2nd Class Joseph W., RN

Earwaker, Able Seaman Ronald C., RN

Eastwood, Marine Walter C., RM

Eaton, Leading Stoker Raymond K. J., RN

Eaves, Wireman Leonard, RN

Edes, Able Seaman Henry M., RN

Edmiston, Chief Engine Room Artificer Reginald F., RN

Edmonds, Able Seaman Alfred G., RN

Edmonds, Writer Anthony R., RN

Edwards, Marine Melville, RM

Edwards, Stoker 2nd Class Robert, RN

Edwards, Able Seaman Thomas W. G., RN

Eldred, Stoker 1st Class Eric C., RN

Eldridge, Stoker 2nd Class Bertie D. M., RN

Elliott, Stoker Petty Officer John G., RN

Eltis, Ordinary Seaman Donald O., RN

Emery, Musician Lawrence A., RMB

Emery, Stoker Petty Officer Richard C., RN

Erridge, Telegraphist Frank A., RN

Erskine, Lieutenant-Commander (E) John G. M., RN

Erskine, Signalman Roy D., RN

Escott, Stoker 2nd Class Robert W., RN

Evans, Stoker 2nd Class David M., RN

Ewart-James, Ordinary Seaman David E., RN

Eyres, Able Seaman Thomas W. W., RN

Fair, Shipwright 4th Class George W., RN

Fairlie, Stoker 1st Class Percy W., RN

Farmer, Leading Seaman, Albert V.RN

Farnish, Petty Officer Telegraphist Frederick N., RN

Farrar, Marine Clifton, RM

Faulkner, Stoker 1st Class Ronald E., RN

Fenner, Marine Henry J., RM

Field, Ordinary Signalman Edgar C., RN

Fielder, Able Seaman Jack H., RN

Fielding, Surgeon Lieutenant James O., RN

Finch, Boy 1st Class John L., RN

Finlayson, Able Seaman David A., RNVR

Fisher, Blacksmith 3rd Class Leslie, RN

Fitch, Able Seaman Edward G., RN

Fitchew, Ordinary Seaman Cecil A., RN

Fitzgerald, Ordinary Seaman Joseph V., RN

Fletcher, Stoker Petty Officer Peter, RN

Fletcher, Able Seaman Victor W. J., RN

Flint, Able Seaman Sydney G., RN

Floyd, Wireman Charles, RN

Flynn, Stoker 2nd Class John T., RN

Foden, Leading Seaman Leslie J., RN

Foley, Chief Stoker Rodney A., RN

Foot, Leading Stoker Charles, RN

Ford, Midshipman Douglas C., RNR

Ford, Ordinary Seaman Harold E., RN

Ford, Able Seaman Jack, RN

Forrest, Writer Ernest W., RN

Forrest, Wireman George M. D., RN

Forrest, Petty Officer Steward Victor, RN

Forrester, Chief Petty Officer Writer John J., RN

Forster, Engine Room Artificer 4th Class Frederick G., RN

Foster, Able Seaman Algernon T., RN

Foster, Ordinary Seaman Colin E., RN

Foster, Able Seaman Kenneth J., RN

Foster, Ordinary Seaman Ralph, RN

Foster, Able Seaman Reginald, RN

Fotheringham, Marine George, RM

Fowle, Able Seaman Henry J., RN

Fowler, Ordinary Signalman Frank S., RN

Fowler, Musician Robert H., RMB

Francis, Boy 1st Class Charles A., RN

Francis, Leading Stoker Victor R., RN

Freeborn, Warrant Supply Officer Frederick C., RN

Freeman, Ordinary Seaman Douglas E., RN

Freeman, Midshipman Mark H. P., RNR

French, Ordinary Seaman Leslie V., RN

French, Ordnance Artificer 4th Class Ronald M., RN

Friend, Lieutenant Leslie E., RNVR

Frodsham, Sub-Lieutenant Neville H., RN

Fry, Ordinary Coder John C., RN

Fullick, Able Seaman Frederic R., RN

Funnell, Ordinary Seaman Kenneth G., RN

Gabbett, Ordinary Seaman Cecil P., RN

Gale, Stoker 1st Class Ronald M., RN

Gallacher, Ordinary Signalman Cornwall, RN

Gallant, Ordinary Seaman Joseph, RN

Gallant, Ordinary Seaman William, RN

Galliott, Ordinary Seaman Howard W., RN

Galloway, Engine Room Artificer 4th Class Arthur, RN

Gardner, Petty Officer Telegraphist James D., RN

Garman, Leading Stoker Victor G., RN

Garroway, Steward Robert L., RN

Garry, Ordinary Telegraphist Neville W. H., RN

Gascoine, Able Seaman Thomas R., RN

Gaudet, Ordinary Seaman Samuel, RN

Genaway, Ordinary Seaman Victor W., RN

Gibb, Wireman Stanley D., RN

Gibbon, Chief Ordnance Artificer Isaac G., RN

Gibbs, Leading Signalman Charles W. E., RN

Gibson, Stoker 2nd Class James, RN

Gibson, Signalman John H., RN

Gibson, Marine Thomas, RM

Giffen, Stoker 2nd Class John A., RN

Gilbert, Stoker 1st Class Charles E. G., RN

Gilbert, Able Seaman Harold, RN

Gillan, Marine Joseph, RM

Gillett, Ordinary Seaman George P., RN

Gillis, Ordinary Seaman John R., RN

Glass, Able Seaman Leslie G. V., RN

Gledhill, Corporal James E., RM

Glenn, Stoker Petty Officer Robert, RN

Goddard, Able Seaman Sidney, RN

Goff, Boy 1st Class Jack, RN

Goldsmith, Petty Officer Horace W., RN

Gomer, Marine Harry, RM

Gomersall, Ordinary Seaman Royston, RN

Good, Marine Bernard E. C., RM

Good, Petty Officer Frederick A., RN

Goodbody, Stoker 1st Class John W., RN

Goodenough, Cook (S) Herbert H., RN

Gordon, Able Seaman Leslie S., RN

Gough, Colour Sergeant John M., RM

Goulstine, Able Seaman Leonard, RN

Graham, Supply Assistant Donald, RN

Graves, Lieutenant (S) John R., RNVR

Gray, Able Seaman Alfred E. E., RN

Gray, Ordinary Seaman John C., RN

Green, Marine Benjamin L., RM

Green, Able Seaman Harry, RN

Green, Signal Boy Herbert, RN

Green, Ordinary Signalman John H., RN

Green, Ordinary Signalman William J., RN

Green, Leading Stoker William J., RN

Greene, Ordinary Signalman Derek A., RN

Gregory, Leading Seaman Arthur H., RN

Gregory, Marine John, RM

Gregson, Commander Edward H. G., RN

Griffin, Marine Charles A., RM

Griffiths, Ordinary Seaman Leonard F., RN

Grogan, Commander (E) Robert T., RN

Groucott, Able Seaman Roland D., RN

Groves, Musician Stedman B., RMB

Groves, Able Seaman Thomas, RN

Grundy, Wireman Frederick E., RN

Guest, Band Boy Alan, RM

Gulliver, Leading Seaman Edward G. V., RN

Haden-Morris, Supply Assistant Alec B., RN

Hadley, Ordinary Seaman Alan E., RN

Hadow, Ordinary Seaman Norman W. A., RN

Haeger, Sergeant Edward G., RM

Hales, Able Seaman Edward, RN

Hall, Ordinary Seaman David G., RANVR

Hall, Ordinary Seaman George W., RANVR

Hall, Able Seaman Henry G., RN

Hall, Lieutenant-Commander John W., RN

Hall, Signalman Neville T., RNV(W)R

Hall, Stoker 1st Class Norman V., RN

Hall, Marine Thomas, RM

Halls, Ordinary Signalman Wilfred C., RN

Hambley, Able Seaman Thomas H., RN

Hanna, Plumber 3rd Class Robert, RN

Hannaway, Ordinary Telegraphist Edward J., RN

Hannay, Stoker 2nd Class James D., RN

Hanwell, Chief Stoker Tom, RN

Harding, Able Seaman John S., RN

Harding, Stoker 1st Class William, RN

Hardy, Cook (S) Henry F. M., RN

Harkess, Stoker 1st Class Robert W., RN

Harkison, Able Seaman Thomas, RN

Harler, Able Seaman Douglas B., RN

Harmer, Engine Room Artificer 4th Class George, RN

Harris, Chief Mechanician Charles A., RN

Harris, Lieutenant Desmond S. R., RM

Harris, Ordnance Artificer 4th Class Frank R., RN

Harris, Marine James H., RM

Hartley, Boy 1st Class Arthur, RN

Hartley, Stoker 2nd Class Norman, RN

Hartmann, Ordinary Coder Geoffrey H., RN

Harty, Leading Seaman Jack, RN

Harvey, Leading Cook (O) Edward R., RN

Harvey, Stoker 2nd Class Eric O., RN

Hatherill, Marine William H., RM

Haughton, Warrant Engineer Cyril, RN

Hawkey, Signalman Derrick B., RN

Hawkins, Shipwright 1st Class Ernest H., RN

Hawthorne, Wireman Arthur W., RN

Hawthorne, Chief Petty Officer Cook (O) John W., RN

Hayde, Leading Seaman Joseph A., RN

Haynes, Leading Stoker Albert E., RN

Hayton, Able Seaman John W., RN

Heath, Ordinary Seaman David J., RN

Heaton, Able Seaman Albert, RN

Hellens, Engine Room Artificer 4th Class Joseph S., RN

Hemmings, Engine Room Artificer 1st Class Bertie, RN

Henderson, Signalman John, RN

Hendry, Marine William, RM

Hennessy, Boy 1st Class David T., RN

Henshaw, Stoker 1st Class Owen W., RN

Henshaw, Boy 1st Class Ronald, RN

Heptonstall, Able Seaman George A., RN

Herbert, Captain (E) Sidney J., RN

Hermon, Marine Eric D., RM

Herod, Bandmaster Maurice H. E., RMB

Heys, Sick Berth Attendant William W., RN

Hibbs, Corporal Francis H. F., RM

Hibbs, Midshipman Richard A., RNVR

Hickman, Stoker 2nd Class Leonard A., RN

Hickmott, Boy 1st Class William J., RN

Higginson, Stoker 1st Class William, RN

Higgott, Engine Room Artificer 3rd Class John N., RN

Hill, Marine Eric J. R., RM

Hilton, Stoker 1st Class Albert F., RN

Hiscock, Marine Frederick J., RM

Hiscock, Petty Officer William A., RN

Hives, Stoker 1st Class Douglas R., RN

Hoare, Stoker 2nd Class Cyril A., RN

Hoare, Lieutenant (S) Norris H., RNVR

Hobbs, Chief Stoker Frederick J., RN

Hobbs, Engine Room Artificer 4th Class Robert, RN

Hogan, Commander (S) John M., RN

Holdaway, Joiner 1st Class Frank, RN

Holland, Marine Charles, RM

Holland, Stoker 2nd Class Francis H., RN

Holland, Vice-Admiral Lancelot E., RN

Hollis, Ordinary Signalman Bramwell G., RN

Holmes, Boy 1st Class Edward J., RN

Holmes, Leading Stoker George, RN

Holmes, Able Seaman Harold, RN

Holroyd, Sailmakers Mate Arthur, RN

Homer, Chief Mechanician Harold, RN

Honeybun, Chief Stoker Richard J., RN

Hoole, Leading Stoker Horace, RN

Hope, Leading Stoker Ernest J., RN

Horner, Able Seaman Leslie, RN

Horsman, Leading Cook (S) Lawrence, RN

Horton, Petty Officer Steward George W., RN

Howard, Ordinary Seaman Eric S., RN

Howe, Stoker 2nd Class Reginald E., RN

Howie, Marine Robert G. W., RM

Howlett, Ordinary Seaman Patrick, RN

Hows, Marine Gordon, RM

Howse, Leading Seaman Thomas, RN

Hoyle, Ordinary Seaman Sidney, RN

Hughes, Leading Stoker Hugh, RN

Hughes, Marine William F., RM

Hull, Able Seaman Arthur W., RN

Hulme, Wireman Arthur, RN

Hulme, Able Seaman Owen E., RN

Humphrey, Lieutenant (E) Michael S. T., RN

Humphreys, Marine William, RM

Hunns, Marine John A. C., RM

Hunt, Stoker 2nd Class George, RN

Hunt, Ordnance Artificer 1st Class William N., RN

Hunter, Ordinary Seaman John M. J., RN

Huntington, Sergeant Ernest S., RM

Huntley, Plumber 1st Class Henry F., RN

Hurle, Supply Assistant Ronald C., RN

Hurst, Coder Christopher W., RN

Hurst, Commander Surgeon Henry, RN

Huskinson, Able Seaman Sydney, RN

Hutchings, Painter 3rd Class Leslie W. R., RN

Hutchins, Petty Officer Albert J., RN

Iago, Electrical Lieutenant John M., RNVR

Ierston, Ordinary Seaman Kenneth W., RN

Ingram, Able Seaman John W., RN

Ingram, Able Seaman Leslie R., RN

Inkpen, Stoker 1st Class Reginald S., RN

Innes, Able Seaman Alexander, RN

Jack, Ordinary Seaman George, RN

Jackson, Marine George S., RM

Jaggers, Stoker 2nd Class Eric, RN

James, Leading Stoker Leonard A., RN

James, Ordinary Seaman Phillip A., RN

Jarvis, Able Seaman Arthur C., RN

Jarvis, Able Seaman Leonard R., RN

Javan, Ordinary Seaman Kenneth W., RN

Jeffs, Stoker 1st Class Norman, RN

Jelley, Boy 1st Class Stanley A., RN

Jennings, Chief Petty Officer Walter H. W., RN

Jesse, Chief Electrical Artificer Harold, RN

John, Marine Thomas, RM

Johnson, Leading Cook Frederick, RN

Johnson, Stoker 1st Class Ralph, RN

Johnson, Leading Writer Stanley F., RN

Johnson, Petty Officer William F., RN

Johnson, Stoker Petty Officer William C., RN

Johnston, Able Seaman James, RN

Johnston, Assistant Steward William, RN

Jones, Able Seaman Albert J., RN

Jones, Leading Stoker David J., RN

Jones, Midshipman Francis L. L., RCN

Jones, Able Seaman Frederick R., RN

Jones, Stoker 1st Class Gordon H., RN

Jones, Able Seaman Gwilym, RN

Jones, Able Seaman Harold H., RN

Jones, Stoker 1st Class Hayden J., RN

Jones, Stoker Petty Officer James W., RN

Jones, Petty Officer John W., RN

Jones, Ordinary Seaman Kenneth, RN

Jones, Able Seaman Richard, RNR

Jones, Boy 1st Class Robert W., RN

Jones, Ordinary Seaman Ronald G. S., RN

Jones, Boy 1st Class Roy T. R., RN

Jordan, Canteen Assistant Geoffrey W., NAAFI

Jordan, Leading Cook (S) Kenneth F. A., RN

Joyce, Boy 1st Class Leslie R., RN

Julier, Marine Alfred E., RM

Kay, Engine Room Artificer 3rd Class Norman, RN

Kay, Ordinary Seaman Samuel, RN

Keal, Leading Stoker George F., RN

Kean, Petty Officer Telegraphist Albert A., RN

Kearney, Able Seaman Thomas P., RNR

Keating, Able Seaman Kenneth H. W., RN

Keenan, Stoker 2nd Class Robert J., RN

Keens, Boy Telegraphist Eric G., RN

Keers, Boy 1st Class Robert, RN

Keith, Marine Arthur W., RM

Kelly, Ordinary Signalman Cornelius, RN

Kelly, Ordnance Artificer 4th Class John, RN

Kelly, Able Seaman Jack V. K., , RN

Kelly, Stoker Petty Officer Robert, RN

Kemish, Boy 1st Class Colin H. T., RN

Kempton, Ordinary Signalman Sylvius L., RN

Kendall, Able Seaman Albert J., RN

Kerr, Engine Room Artificer 5th Class Alexander, RN

Kerr, Captain Ralph, RN

Kerr, Boy 1st Class Raymond W., RN

Kerridge, Stoker 1st Class Herbert, RN

Kersley, Marine Albert S., RM

King, Able Seaman Ernest H., RN

King, Signalman Howard L. C., RNVR

King, Able Seaman William A., RN

Kingston, Able Seaman Jack, RN

Kinmond, Able Seaman Charles H., RN

Kirk, Ordinary Telegraphist Alfred, RN

Kirk, Marine Russell G., RM

Kirkland, Able Seaman John D., RN

Kitchener, Able Seaman Reginald J., RN

Knapper, Able Seaman Joseph W., RN

Knight, Stoker 1st Class James A. P., RN

Knight, Engine Room Artificer 4th Class John, RN

Knight, Midshipman Roy F., RNR

Knight, Joiner 4th Class Stanley R., RN

Knox, Ordinary Seaman John A., RN

Knox, Stoker 2nd Class John D., RN

Ladd, Stoker 2nd Class Charles J., RN

Laidman, Able Seaman Reginald A., RN

Laing, Ordinary Seaman John, RN

Laking, Stoker 2nd Class Andrew, RN

Lambert, Ordinary Seaman Thomas W., RN

Lancaster, Able Seaman Howard, RN

Lane, Shipwright 2nd Class Cyril F., RN

Lane, Able Seaman Herbert F. W., RN

Langley, Ordinary Coder James, RN

Lansdowne, Canteen Assistant Cecil R. E., NAAFI

Lapthorn, Midshipman Peter R., RNVR

Latimer, Ordinary Seaman Walter S., RN

Laughlin, Boy 1st Class John C. A., RN

Laws, Chief Stoker Albert E., RN

Lawson, Cook (S) Jack, RN

Laycock, Marine Henry, RM

Layton, Marine Sidney G., RM

Le Bosquet, Able Seaman Cecil E., RN

Le Noury, Able Seaman Alfred N., RN

Le Page, Able Seaman Edwin H. G., RN

Leach, Mechanician 1st Class Harold G., RN

Leaney, Boy 1st Class Robert T., RN

Leason, Engine Room Artificer 3rd Class Harry V., RN

Lee, Assistant Steward Wilfred, RN

Leggatt, Stoker 1st Class George F. S., RN

Leggett, Ordinary Seaman Cyril A., RN

Leishman, Chief Stoker William, RN

L'Enfant, Leading Stoker Bertram H., RN

Levack, Marine John S. L., , RM

Lever, Stoker 1st Class Stanley R., RN

Levy, Ordinary Seaman Albert P., RN

Lewington, Yeoman of Signals George C., RN

Lewis, Stoker 1st Class Alfred G., RN

Lewis, Lieutenant Edward P. S., RN

Lewis, Stoker Petty Officer Michael E., RN

Lewis, Able Seaman Thomas, RN

Liddell, Stoker 1st Class Archibald T., RN

Liddle, Leading Seaman Harold, RN

Lifford, Supply Assistant Henry G., RN

Lightbody, Boy 1st Class Robert, RN

Lihou, Able Seaman Owen F. C., RN

Livingstone, Stoker 2nd Class Robert J., RN

Lloyd, Stoker 1st Class Philip, RN

Lock, Stoker Petty Officer Herbert H., RN

Lock, Marine Robert H., RM

Lockhart, Boy 1st Class Archibald W., RN

Locklin, Able Seaman James, RN

London, Sergeant Reginald J. C., RM

Long, Musician George H., RMB

Long, Boy 1st Class Percy C. B., RN

Lott, Able Seaman Frederick C., RN

Love, Leading Stoker Herbert W., RN

Lovegrove, Leading Seaman Herbert E., RN

Lovelock, Stoker 1st Class Charles W., RN

Lownds, Able Seaman John, RN

Luckhurst, Able Seaman John H. J., RN

Lumley, Major Heaton, RM

Luxmoore, Lieutenant (S) Thomas G. P., RN

Luxton, Engine Room Artificer 4th Class Denis W. A., RN

Lyle, Able Seaman James P., RN

Lynch, Able Seaman Augustine P., RN

Lynch, Supply Petty Officer James F., RN

Macdonald, Boy 1st Class Alastair D., RN

Machin, Lieutenant-Commander John L., RN

Mackay, Seaman John, RNR

Mackin, Able Seaman Ronald W., RN

Maclean, Ordinary Coder Hugh W. P., RN

Macnamara, Able Seaman Robert T., RN

Madden, Ordinary Seaman John F., RN

Maidment, Ordinary Seaman Harold L., RN

Maitland, Chief Shipwright John W., RN

Malcolmson, Ordinary Seaman Alexander, RN

Malin, Telegraphist Walter G., RN

Mann, Ordinary Seaman Arthur J., RN

Manser, Marine Richard A., RM

Manton, Cook (S) Ernest P., RN

Markey, Joiner 2nd Class Harold E., RN

Marr, Able Seaman Ian C. C., RN

Marsh, Supply Assistant Eric, RN

Marsh, Leading Seaman Eric, RN

Marsh, Able Seaman Joseph S., RN

Marsh, Marine Percy G., RM

Marsh, Leading Stoker Robert J. A., RN

Martin, Boy 1st Class John W., RN

Martin, Stoker 1st Class Thomas G., RN

Martin, Sergeant William R., RM

Martindale, Boy 1st Class Norman, RN

Maskell, Able Seaman John N., RN

Mason, Boy 1st Class Vernon R. A., RN

Masters, Boy 1st Class Gordon H. T., RN

Matthews, Stoker 2nd Class Albert G., RN

Matthews, Ordinary Telegraphist Stanley G., RN

Matthews, Able Seaman William D., RN

Maycock, Able Seaman Ernest V., RN

McAllen, Stoker 2nd Class John W. F., RN

McAteer, Stoker 1st Class William, RN

McCart, Telegraphist George, RN

McCaughey, Stoker 1st Class Daniel, RN

McCaw, Ordinary Seaman Robert W., RN

McCleary, Able Seaman William, RN

McCormac, Signal Boy John, RN

McCullagh, Engine Room Artificer 4th Class John, RN

McDonald, Able Seaman Ewen, RN

McDonald, Able Seaman Harold, RN

McDonald, Able Seaman Wallace, RN

McDowell, Ordinary Seaman Albert, RN

McDuell, Able Seaman Alfred, RN

McEvoy, Able Seaman Patrick J., RN

McEwan, Assistant Steward Mark, RN

McFadyen, Sergeant Walter E., RM

McGhee, Ordinary Seaman John, RN

McGregor, Stoker 1st Class Alfred, RN

McGuire, Chief Engine Room Artificer Arthur T., RN

McIlwraith, Stoker 1st Class Geoffrey J., RN

McKim, Boy 1st Class William, RN

McLaren, Midshipman John B., RNR

McLatchie, Ordinary Seaman William, RN

McLean, Leading Stoker Alexander, RN

McLeod, Able Seaman Ian M., RN

McNulty, Chief Petty Officer Telegraphist John G., RN

McQuaid, Marine Ernest G., RM

McRae, Boy Telegraphist William R., RN

Meakin, Ordinary Seaman Harry, RN

Mellalieu, Stoker 2nd Class Frank, RN

Melville, Stoker 2nd Class John, RN

Mendham, Boy 1st Class Frederick G., RN

Mepham, Engine Room Artificer 3rd Class Henry J., RN

Metcalfe, Leading Seaman Matthew, RN

Middleton, Petty Officer Frank R., RN

Milburn, Able Seaman Samuel C., RN

Miles, Able Seaman Francis B., RN

Miles, Marine Ronald S., RM

Miles, Chief Petty Officer Vernon G., RN

Millard, Able Seaman David T. H., RN

Millard, Able Seaman George K., RNVR

Miller, Stoker 1st Class James A. K., RN

Miller, Able Seaman Thomas, RNVR

Mills, Ordinary Seaman Campbell R. F., RN

Mills, Ordinary Seaman Harry J., RN

Mills, Marine Montague D., RM

Mills, Stoker 2nd Class Raymond E., RN

Mills, Stoker 1st Class Ronald W., RN

Minard, Leading Signalman André, RN

Mitchell, Electrical Artificer 4th Class Frank, RN

Mitchell, Able Seaman Frederick R., RN

Mitchell, Able Seaman John, RN

Mitchell, Able Seaman Leonard F. W., RN

Moat, Ordinary Seaman Norman, RN

Mochan, Ordinary Seaman John C., RN

Monument, Joiner 4th Class Harry, RN

Moody, Ordinary Signalman Walter, RN

Moon, Petty Officer Jack E., RN

Moon, Able Seaman Walter, RN

Moore, Ordinary Seaman Brian R., RN

Moore, Stoker 2nd Class Edward A. P., RN

Moore, Petty Officer Hugh T. H., RN

Moore, Boy 1st Class James K., RN

Morgan, Marine Albert H., RM

Morgan, Marine Ronald, RM

Morley, Chief Petty Officer Sidney V., RN

Morrell, Stoker 2nd Class Ronald F., RN

Morten, Engine Room Artificer 4th Class Thomas A., RN

Mortimer, Able Seaman Robert E. G., RN

Mortimer, Stoker 2nd Class Stanley E., RN

Mould, Able Seaman Geoffrey J. W., RN

Moultrie, Lieutenant-Commander Edward H. F., RN

Mullen, Telegraphist John, RN

Mulligan, Stoker 1st Class James, RN

Mullins, Ordinary Seaman Edgar W. F., RN

Munday, Wireman Harold J., RN

Murphy, Stoker 1st Class Frank E., RN

Murray, Marine Frederick C., RM

Murray, Able Seaman Hugh, RN

Murray, Electrical Artificer 5th Class Sidney, RN

Murrell, Shipwright 4th Class George P., RN

Myers, Ordinary Seaman Gordon W., RN

Myers, Ordinary Seaman Sidney C. S., RN

Myram, Shipwright 4th Class Maurice A., RN

Nally, Leading Stoker Joseph, RN

Nash, Stoker 1st Class Kenneth R., RN

Naylor, Chief Petty Officer Cook (O) Rodney J., RN

Naylor, Able Seaman Ronald, RN

Neal, Supply Assistant Edward R., RN

Neal, Able Seaman Ronald W., RN

Neale, Marine Robert S., RM

Neave, Able Seaman Peter F. A., RN

Nelson, Stoker 2nd Class William, RN

Nevett, Yeoman of Signals Arthur L., RN

Neville, Petty Officer William A., RN

Newell, Able Seaman Charles J., RN

Newey, Lieutenant Cedric B. N., RNVR

Newnham, Able Seaman Robert, RN

Nicholl, Able Seaman Donald W., RNSR

Nicholls, Stoker 2nd Class Douglas H., RN

Nichols, Ordinary Seaman Thomas F., RN

Nicholson, Petty Officer Alfred F., RN

Nicholson, Cook Thomas W., RN

Noble, Marine Alexander, RM

Norman, Midshipman Christopher J. B., RCN

Norris, Stoker 2nd Class Thomas F., RN

Northam, Able Seaman William A., RN

Nuding, Supply Assistant Albert V., RN

Nugent, Stoker 1st Class William J., RN

Oborne, Petty Officer Steward Reginald G. H., RN

O'Connell, Petty Officer James F., RN

Ogden, Able Seaman Robert, RN

Oldershaw, Leading Stoker Arthur, RN

O'Leary, Stoker 1st Class Leslie S. D., RN

Olive, Cook (O) Ronald M., RN

O'Neil, Ordinary Seaman Owen, RN

O'Reilly, Stoker 2nd Class Dennis P., RN

O'Rourke, Leading Seaman Patrick C., RN

Orrell, Marine Walter J., RM

Ovenden, Canteen Assistant Jack, NAAFI

Owen, Petty Officer Harold, RN

Owens, Lieutenant-Commander George E. M., RN

Pacy, Engine Room Artificer 4th Class Ronald, RN

Paddock, Stoker 1st Class Stanley A., RN

Pae, Able Seaman James, RN

Page, Stoker 2nd Class Victor E. F., RN

Palmer, Stoker 1st Class Frank, RN

Palmer, Regulating Petty Officer Frederick W. J., RN

Palmer, Marine James A., RM

Palmer, Sergeant Reginald W., RM

Palmer, Able Seaman Stephen, RNVR

Papworth, Yeoman of Signals Robert G., RN

Pares, Lieutenant-Commander Anthony, RN

Park, Able Seaman Raymond, RN

Parker, Steward Gordon, RN

Parratt, Stoker 1st Class Albert H., RN

Parton, Stoker 1st Class Stanley G., RN

Passells, Supply Chief Petty Officer Keith C., RN

Passey, Sick Berth Attendant Aubrey R., RN

Patton, Able Seaman Owen, RN

Pay, Able Seaman James L., RN

Payne, Able Seaman Harry T., RN

Payne, Leading Stoker John W., RN

Peace, Marine Denzil S., RM

Peacock, Surgeon Lieutenant (D) John E. C., RN

Peacock, Stoker 2nd Class William, RN

Pearce, Stoker 1st Class Arthur S., RN

Pearce, Engine Room Artificer 3rd Class Harry R., RN

Pearce, Leading Supply Assistant Ronald J., RN

Pearce, Petty Officer William F., RN

Pearse, Electrical Artificer 1st Class John F. F., RN

Pearse, Able Seaman Sidney C., RN

Pearson, Cook (O) George, RN

Peck, Able Seaman Owen O., RN

Peckham, Ordinary Seaman Leonard M., RN

Pedder, Able Seaman Ernest A. J., RN

Peden, Ordinary Seaman David G., RN

Peel, Assistant Steward Reginald K., RN

Peirce, Chief Petty Officer Steward James P., RN

Pemberton, Engine Room Artificer 4th Class Frederick, RN

Pennycook, Stoker 2nd Class William R., RN

Percival, Stoker 2nd Class Stanley E. P., RN

Perkins, Marine William G., RM

Perman, Midshipman Roland G. C., RIN

Perrin, Cook (S) Alfred J., RN

Perry, Steward Aubrey J. W., RN

Perry, Marine Leonard, RM

Perry, Petty Officer Cook (O) William H., RN

Pescod, Boy 1st Class Thomas C., RN

Petch, Able Seaman Roy V., RN

Petty, Able Seaman Edmund J., RN

Phelps, Blacksmith 1st Class Henry F., RN

Phillips, Ordinary Seaman George T. E., RN

Phillips, Leading Seaman Horace E., RN

Phillips, Ordinary Seaman Lancelot J., RN

Phillips, Stoker 2nd Class Norman, RN

Phillips, Ordinary Seaman Raymond T., RN

Phillips, Paymaster Lieutenant (S) Ronald G., RN

Pickering, Stoker Petty Officer Harry, RN

Pierce, Marine Robert D., RM

Pike, Musician William A., RMB

Pink, Able Seaman Harold J., RN

Pinkerton, Wireman Robert R., RN

Piper, Ordinary Signalman Fred H., RNVR

Pitts, Ordinary Seaman Henry G., RN

Plant, Marine Edwin, RM

Plimbley, Leading Steward Edward C., RN

Plumley, Warrant Engineer Reginald A. H., RN

Poar, Marine Reginald J., RM

Pope, Supply Chief Petty Officer Geoffrey C., RN

Porter, Ordinary Signalman Cyril L. D., RN

Porter, Marine Frederick A., RM

Porter, Musician Reginald J., RMB

Porter-Fausset, Lieutenant (S) Frederick A. P., RN

Potts, Writer Frank S., RN

Power, Able Seaman Alfred, RN

Powley, Chief Engine Room Artificer Herbert W., RN

Prangnell, Able Seaman Maurice R., RN

Pratt, Marine Albert W. C., RM

Prescott, Stoker Petty Officer Marcus R., RN

Price, Shipwright 4th Class Alfred C. J. P., RN

Price, Warrant Shipwright William A., RN

Pringle, Stoker 1st Class Robert H. W., RN

Print, Engine Room Artificer 4th Class Dennis C. B., RN

Proudlock, Able Seaman Eric, RN

Pulling, Stoker Petty Officer Edward, RN

Punter, Able Seaman Jack A., RN

Puttick, Stoker 1st Class William F., RN

Puttock, Signalman Maurice J. E., RNVR

Quigley, Ordinary Seaman John J., RN

Radley, Stoker 1st Class Kenneth, RN

Rae, Plumber 3rd Class Hector R., RN

Ramsbotham, Shipwright 4th Class William L., RN

Rance, Leading Stoker John, RN

Randall, Able Seaman Cyril W., RN

Randall, Boy 1st Class Maurice P., RN

Randall, Marine Stanley R., RM

Randall, Stoker 1st Class Victor J., RN

Rannou, Able Seaman Joseph, RN

Rant, Stoker 2nd Class Leonard V., RN

Raw, Engine Room Artificer 4th Class Dennis A., RN

Raw, Able Seaman Irving T., RN

Raw, Stoker 1st Class Roderick M., RN

Rawlinson, Stoker 1st Class Albert G. E., RN

Rawlinson, Able Seaman Leonard, RN

Raynor, Signalman Francis, RN

Read, Ordinary Seaman Anthony V., RN

Read, Boy 1st Class Douglas, RN

Reay, Petty Officer William E., RN

Reddall, Signal Boy Peter E. A., RN

Reed, Corporal Hector L., RM

Rees, Stoker 1st Class Vernon J., RN

Reeve, Leading Steward Robert E., RN

Reeves, Able Seaman Cyril A., RN

Reeves, Ordinary Seaman Stanley E., RN

Rendell, Able Seaman Stewart R. J., RN

Reveler, Engine Room Artificer 4th Class Thomas S., RN

Reynolds, Stoker 2nd Class John A., RN

Rhodes, Steward John, RN

Rice, Stoker 2nd Class Herbert F., RN

Richards, Stoker 1st Class Alfred W., RN

Richardson, Ordinary Signalman Henry F. D., RN

Richardson, Stoker 1st Class Snowden F. O., RN

Richer, Petty Officer Harold E., RN

Ridge, Writer Merlin F., RN

Riding, Ordinary Seaman Walter K., RN

Rigby, Boy 1st Class Benjamin G., RN

Rigglesford, Stoker 1st Class Arthur P., RN

Riley, Stoker 1st Class George P., RN

Ritchie, Petty Officer Telegraphist James S., RN

Ritchie, Electrical Artificer 4th Class Thomas B., RN

Roach, Lieutenant (E) Bryan C. J., RN

Robarts, Ordinary Telegraphist Frederick J., RN

Robb, Able Seaman James G., RN

Robbins, Ordinary Seaman Robert S., RN

Roberts, Mechanician 2nd Class Ernest G., RN

Roberts, Leading Seaman Frederick C., RN

Roberts, Able Seaman Gordon R., RN

Roberts, Able Seaman Lewis G., RN

Roberts, Ordinary Seaman Reginald C., RN

Robins, Sub-Lieutenant Anthony C. R., RNR

Robins, Yeoman of Signals Charles V., RN

Robinson, Able Seaman Arthur E., RN

Robinson, Petty Officer Cook Percival T., RN

Robinson, Boy 1st Class Peter J., RN

Robotham, Able Seaman Charles, RN

Rodgman, Able Seaman Claude B., RN

Rodley, Marine Samuel J., RM

Roe, Commander (S) Donovan C., RN

Rootham, Ordinary Seaman Peter, RN

Rorrison, Boy 1st Class Hugh F., RN

Rose, Stoker 1st Class Reginald T., RN

Rose, Stoker 2nd Class William J., RN

Rose, Leading Seaman William R., RN

Rosenthal, Marine Henry C., RM

Routledge, Boy 1st Class Walter, RN

Rowe, Marine Stanley G. S., RM

Rowlands, Marine Daniel J., RM

Rowntree, Stoker 1st Class George W., RN

Rowsell, Able Seaman Graham H., RN

Rowsell, Boy 1st Class Leslie D., RN

Roy, Boy 1st Class Ian A., RN

Rudd, Ordnance Artificer 4th Class Edwin A., RN

Rundle, Marine Arthur F., RM

Runnacles, Marine Frederick E., RM

Russell, Able Seaman Charles A., RN

Russell, Musician David L., RMB

Russell, Petty Officer John A. G., RN

Russell, Able Seaman Leonard W., RN

Russell, Petty Officer Walter F., RN

Ryder, Petty Officer Telegraphist Leonard, RN

Sadler, Marine Edward R., RM

Saiger, Stoker 1st Class John G., RN

Sammars, Boy 1st Class Thomas J. B., RN

Sanderson, Able Seaman Peter, RN

Sargeaunt, Stoker 2nd Class Henry E. J., RN

Saul, Leading Stoker Charles, RN

Saunders, Marine Albert, RM

Saunders, Engine Room Artificer 4th Class Arthur W., RN

Saunders, Stoker 2nd Class James G., RN

Savage, Chief Engine Room Artificer Edwin J., RN

Sayers, Ordinary Seaman Robert M., RN

Scammell, Leading Stoker Walter G., RN

Scattergood, Stoker 1st Class Frederick J., RN

Scott, Seaman Andrew B., RN

Scott, Ordinary Seaman Jack, RN

Scott, Leading Stoker James, RN

Scott, Marine Robert C., RM

Scott, Stoker 2nd Class William P., RN

Scott-Kerr, Sub-Lieutenant John H. A., RN

Senior, Stoker 2nd Class Reuben, RN

Sewell, Marine Gilbert W., RM

Shadbolt, Marine Maurice H., RM

Shand, Able Seaman Robert, RN

Shannon, Ordinary Seaman John D., RANVR

Sharp, Steward John S., RN

Sharpe, Stoker 2nd Class Albert J., RN

Shawe, Able Seaman Robert B., RN

Shearer, Leading Cook (S) George B. B., RN

Shepherd, Ordinary Seaman Cyril H., RN

Shepherd, Chief Engine Room Artificer George V., RN

Shepherd, Ordinary Seaman Lambert C., RN

Shepherd, Able Seaman Percy R., RN

Sheppard, Petty Officer Leonard F. G., RN

Sherval, Chief Stoker William R., RN

Shiers, Supply Petty Officer William H., RN

Shipp, Stoker 1st Class Leslie F., RN

Shorrock, Able Seaman Stanley H. A., RN

Short, Engine Room Artificer 4th Class Arthur E., RN

Shuck, Ordnance Artificer 5th Class William B., RN

Shuker, Leading Seaman Archibald, RN

Shute, Leading Cook (O) Harry L., RN

Siddall, Able Seaman John, RN

Sidley, Stoker Petty Officer Robert B. P., RN

Silk, Stoker 2nd Class Jack C. R., RN

Sim, Sick Berth Attendant Alexander E., RN

Simmons, Stoker 1st Class Ernest A., RN

Simpson, Ordinary Seaman Peter, RN

Sims, Engine Room Artificer 4th Class William, RN

Sinnott, Able Seaman Frederick W., RN

Skett, Ordnance Artificer 4th Class Raymond L., RN

Skipper, Able Seaman John F., RN

Slade, Able Seaman Ronald A., RN

Slowther, Stoker Petty Officer George, RN

Smart, Able Seaman Leslie E. V., RN

Smith, Steward Alexander G., RN

Smith, Able Seaman Andrew K., RN

Smith, Marine Benjamin T, RM

Smith, Able Seaman Charles L. S., RN

Smith, Able Seaman Dick, RN

Smith, Ordinary Seaman Eric T., RN

Smith, Able Seaman Frederick A., RN

Smith, Stoker Petty Officer Frederick H. S., RN

Smith, Stoker 1st Class George F., RN

Smith, Lieutenant (E) Harold G. E., RN

Smith, Able Seaman James, RN

Smith, Able Seaman James M., RN

Smith, Ordinary Seaman John C., RN

Smith, Chief Petty Officer John H., RN

Smith, Supply Assistant John H., RN

Smith, Regulating Petty Officer John H., RN

Smith, Supply Assistant Peter W. C., RN

Smith, Leading Cook Stanley C., RN

Smith, Able Seaman Stephen R., RN

Smith, Ordinary Seaman Thomas, RN

Smith, Stoker 1st Class Thomas N., RN

Smith, Leading Seaman Walter H., RN

Smith, Able Seaman William G., RN

Smith-Withers, Wireman Stephen J., RN

Snelgrove, Leading Seaman Colin, RN

Snell, Chief Engine Room Artificer John, RN

Snook, Marine George A., RM

Snooks, Ordinary Seaman William H., RN

Snow, Boy 1st Class David J., RN

Solmon, Able Seaman Murdoch M., RN

Southgate, Marine Thomas E., RM

Sowerby, Writer Curzon, RN

Sparkes, Marine Ernest, RM

Spence, Lieutenant (E) Tristram F., RN

Spencer, Mechanician 2nd Class Arthur, RN

Spinner, Stoker 1st Class George D., RN

Sprakes, Chief Stoker John, RN

Spreadbury, Ordinary Seaman Jack F. W., RN

St Clair-Tracy, Electrical Artificer 2nd Class Albert E., RN

Stanley, Able Seaman Leonard, RN

Stannard, Sick Berth Petty Officer George W., RN

Startup, Ordinary Seaman Ian G. E., RANVR

Steel, Commander Douglas M., RN

Steele, Able Seaman Alexander, RN

Steele, Ordinary Seaman Joseph W., RN

Steptoe, Marine John H., RM

Sterne, Able Seaman Benjamin S., RN

Steven, Stoker Petty Officer Arthur, RN

Stevenson, Midshipman Basil P., RNR

Stevenson, Ordnance Artificer 5th Class Noel, RN

Stewart, Able Seaman Albert M., RN

Stewart, Chaplain Robert J. P., RN

Stewart, Able Seaman Thomas, RN

Stibbs, Ordinary Seaman Charles T., RN

Stocker, Boy 1st Class Norman G. L., RN

Stoddard, Marine George H. P., RM

Stokes, Able Seaman John E., RN

Stone, Petty Officer Arthur W., RN

Stothers, Able Seaman Hugh, RN

Stoyles, Chief Stoker Sydney S., RN

Strange, Stoker 1st Class Edward J., RN

Stringer, Able Seaman Cecil A. B., RN

Strong, Leading Writer Arthur J., RN

Stubbings, Marine Douglas H., RM

Stubbs, Lieutenant Charles F. B., RNVR

Sturgess, Able Seaman Cyril L., RN

Sturgess, Boy 1st Class John P., RN

Sulley, Commissioned Ordnance Officer John C., RN

Sullivan, Stoker Petty Officer Albert, RN

Sullivan, Stoker 2nd Class Frank D., RN

Surrey, Chief Petty Officer Writer Archibald H., RN

Swain, Leading Writer James F., RN

Swain, Ordinary Telegraphist Ronald W., RN

Swanborough, Cook (O) Rupert T., RN

Swatton, Petty Officer Bertram C., RN

Swinson, Ordnance Artificer 3rd Class Ernest J., RN

Switzer, Ordinary Seaman Albert, RN

Sylvester, Ordinary Telegraphist James, RN

Symes, Wireman Reginald C., RN

Szymalski, Midshipman Kasimierz, PN

Taggart, Assistant Cook (S) Robert, RN

Tallett, Leading Seaman Ronald L. W., RN

Tamarelle, Electrical Artificer 4th Class Marius, RN

Tapsell, Marine Albert E., RM

Tawney, Musician David R., RMB

Taylor, Ordinary Seaman Arnold E., RN

Taylor, Leading Seaman Charles, RN

Taylor, Telegraphist Charles A., RN

Taylor, Leading Stoker Clifford, RN

Taylor, Wireman David, RN

Taylor, Able Seaman Frederick, RN

Taylor, Stoker 1st Class Henry C., RN

Taylor, Stoker 2nd Class James, RN

Taylor, Marine Lewis J., RM

Taylor, Musician Reginald L., RMB

Taylor, Ordinary Telegraphist William C., RN

Taylor, Commissioned Telegraphist William O., RN

Telford, Marine Charles, RM

Terry, Telegraphist Gordon V., RN

Thomas, Able Seaman Francis J., RN

Thomas, Able Seaman Harold J., RN

Thompson, Able Seaman Harold, RN

Thompson, Boy 1st Class Robert, RN

Thomson, Able Seaman Hugh, RN

Thorpe, Leading Stoker George E., RN

Thorpe, Marine Joseph, RM

Thorpe, Ordinary Seaman Richard, RN

Thurogood, Cook (S) John F., RN

Till, Telegraphist Jack C., RN

Till, Shipwright 3rd Class William E. C., RN

Tipping, Able Seaman Alfred J. E., RN

Titheridge, Canteen Assistant Jack R., NAAFI

Tocher, Ordinary Seaman Edwin, RN

Todd, Stoker 1st Class William C., RN

Tomlins, Leading Seaman George., RN

Tomlinson, Boy 1st Class William T., RN

Toogood, Marine Leslie B., RM

Topham, Able Seaman Thomas, RN

Townley, Stoker 2nd Class William J., RN

Tozer, Commissioned Gunner Harry G. H., RN

Treloar, Leading Seaman/Acting Petty Officer Walter J. B., RN

Trevarthen, Canteen Manager William, NAAFI

Trollope, Stoker 2nd Class Clifton W., RN

Trotter, Petty Officer Telegraphist Ralph W., RN

Trowbridge, Petty Officer William C., RN

Trzebiatowski-Zmuda, Midshipman Leon B. K., PN

Tucker, Ordinary Seaman Leslie, RN

Turnbull, Able Seaman William S., RN

Turner, Stoker 1st Class George F., RN

Turner, Stoker 1st Class George H. F., RN

Turner, Stoker 1st Class John, RN

Tuxworth, Ordinary Signalman Frank A., RN

Twigg, Stoker 1st Class Charles J., RN

Underwood, Stoker 2nd Class John, RN

Upton, Ordinary Telegraphist Roy R., RN

Utteridge, Petty Officer Telegraphist Raymond H., RN

Vacher, Midshipman (S) Geoffrey D. B., RN

Varlow, Commissioned Gunner Albert C., RN

Varndell, Stoker Petty Officer Arthur G., RN

Veal, Chief Petty Officer Cook Richard E., RN

Vickers, Chief Petty Officer Cook Herbert G., RN

Viney, Marine Albert E., RM

Wagstaff, Able Seaman William, RN

Walker, Petty Officer Albert C., RN

Walker, Ordinary Signalman George T., RN

Walker, Stoker 1st Class Thomas, RN

Wallace, Leading Stoker James W., RN

Waller, Stoker 2nd Class William J., RN

Wallis, Marine Michael H. S. J., RM

Walsh, Assistant Cook (S) John F., RN

Walter, Warrant Engineer William F. P., RN

Walters, Assistant Cook (S) Douglas T., RN

Walton, Marine Clifford, RM

Walton, Leading Seaman John, RN

Walton, Chief Stoker Josiah T., RN

Wannerton, Leading Stoker Henry J., RN

Ward, Painter 3rd Class Frederick W., RN

Ward, Signalman George, RN

Ward, Ordinary Telegraphist Joseph, RN

Warden, Kenneth G, Midshipman, RNR

Warrand, Commander Selwyn J. P., RN

Warren, Marine Donald, RM

Warwick, Boy 1st Class Benjamin, RN

Waterhouse, Able Seaman Reginald G., RN

Waterlow, Ordinary Signalman Antony A., RN

Waterman, Able Seaman Albert D., RN

Waters, Stoker 1st Class William F., RN

Waterson, Leading Stoker Thomas J. B., RN

Watkins, Stoker Petty Officer John, RN

Watkinson, Paymaster Sub-Lieutenant Stanley, RNZN

Watson, Able Seaman Alexander, RNR

Watson, Chief Stoker Harry, RN

Watson, Able Seaman John C., RN

Watson, Able Seaman Robert, RNVR

Watt, Stoker 1st Class Charles J. J., RN

Watt, Steward Robert A. E., RN

Watts, Chief Petty Officer Edward A. H., RN

Wearn, Marine Arthur, RM

Wearne, Able Seaman Harry E., RN

Weaver, Marine Henry E., RM

Webb, Able Seaman Albert F., RN

Weddle, Able Seaman William, RN

Welch, Stoker 1st Class Albert C. W., RN

Welch, Petty Officer Reginald A., RN

Welch, Marine Sidney C. T., RM

Weldon, Able Seaman Eric, RN

Wellman, Stoker Petty Officer Arthur C., RN

Wells, Stoker 2nd Class Henry, RN

Wells, Ordinary Seaman Herbert W., RN

Wells, Stoker 1st Class Horace W., RN

Wells, Corporal Philip J., RM

Wells, Able Seaman Ronald D. G., RN

Wells, Boy 1st Class Stanley A., RN

West, Petty Officer Cook (S) Alfred P., RN

West, Chief Engine Room Artificer Robert W., RN

Wharfe, Petty Officer Cyril P., RN

Wheeler, Gunner Ernest F., RN

Wheeler, Able Seaman Francis W., RN

White, Wireman Arthur, RN

White, Petty Officer Telegraphist Edward H., RN

White, Marine Harry, RM

Whitehead, Sergeant Reginald C., RM

Whiteman, Stoker Petty Officer John W., RN

Whitewood, Able Seaman Cyril J., RN

Whitfield, Petty Officer Victor V., RN

Wicks, Able Seaman Hubert G., RN

Wigfall, Engine Room Artificer 3rd Class Leslie A., RN

Wiggett, Stoker 2nd Class James K., RN

Wigzell, Ordinary Coder Norman F. H., RN

Wilcocks, Able Seaman Eric C., RN

Wilcockson, Stoker 1st Class Harry R., RN

Wilkins, Able Seaman George H., RN

Wilkinson, Boy 1st Class Frederick J. R., RN

Wilkinson, Stoker 1st Class James W., RN

Wilkinson, Leading Seaman Stanley, RN

Willetts, Sub-Lieutenant Tom, RNVR

Williams, Ordinary Seaman Frederick P., RN

Williams, Painter 3rd Class Horace A., RN

Williams, Able Seaman Leonard J., RN

Williams, Electrical Artificer 4th Class Lloyd, RN

Williams, Midshipman Roderick G., RNVR

Williams, Writer Roland M., RN

Williams, Able Seaman Tom G. J., RN

Williamson, Leading Stoker Harry, RN

Willis, Stoker 1st Class Albert T., RN

Willis, Marine Herbert, RM

Wilmhurst, Leading Seaman George H., RN

Wilson, Able Seaman George, RN

Wilson, Able Seaman Gordon A. C., RN

Wilson, Leading Seaman Herbert G., RN

Wilson, Ordinary Seaman John V., RN

Wilson, Signalman Walter, RN

Windeatt, Boy Telegraphist Ralph F., RN

Wingfield, Petty Officer Cook (S) Charles H., RN

Winkfield, Leading Stoker Victor M., RN

Wishart, Marine Jack E., RM

Woelfell, Writer Edward J. E., RN

Wood, Able Seaman William E., RN

Woodward, Warrant Electrician Frederick J., RN

Wootton, Boy 1st Class Desmond T., RN

Worboys, Stoker 1st Class Robert M., RN

Worrall, Stoker 2nd Class Arthur, RN

Worsfold, Band Corporal Sydney G., RMB

Worwood, Able Seaman Raymond F., RN

Wright, Ordinary Seaman Alfred W., RN

Wright, Petty Officer Telegraphist Charles E., RN

Wright, Yeoman of Signals George, RN

Wright, Supply Assistant Stanley W. F., RN

Wright, Leading Seaman Thomas C., RN

Wrighting, Stoker 2nd Class Douglas H. W., RN

Wyatt, Marine Jeffrey A. F., RM

Wyldbore-Smith, Lieutenant-Commander Hugh D., RN

Yarrow, Ordinary Seaman Peter M., RN

Yates, Boatswain Robert G., RN

Young, Signalman John O., RN

Young, Boy Bugler Percy A., RM

Younger, Marine Albert, RM

Zurek, Midshipman Kazimierz O., PN

Endnotes

Introduction

1. HRH Queen Elizabeth II, 'The Queen's Speech at the Commissioning Ceremony of HMS *Queen Elizabeth*', www.royal.uk, 7 December 2017
2. Coles, A. and Briggs, T., *Flagship Hood: The Fate of Britain's Mightiest Warship* (London: Robert Hale Limited, 1988), p. 3.

Chapter 1

1. Marder, A. J., *Fear God and Dread Nought: The Correspondence of Admiral of the Fleet Lord Fisher of Kilverstone: Volume II Years of Power, 1904–1914* (Oxford: Jonathan Cape, 1956), p. 149.
2. Howarth, D., *British Sea Power: How Britain Became Sovereign of the Seas* (London: Robinson, 2003), p. 390.
3. *Ibid.*, pp. 390–391.
4. Bourroughs, P., 'The Mid-Victorian Navy and Imperial Defence', *The Journal of Imperial and Commonwealth History*, Vol. 30, No. 2 (2008), p. 103.
5. Marder, A. J., *op. cit.*, p. 181.
6. Marder, A. J., *The Anatomy of British Sea Power: A History of British Naval Policy in the Pre-Dreadnought Era, 1880–1905* (New York: Alfred A. Knopf, 1940), p. 549.
7. Redford, D. and Grove, P. D., *The Royal Navy: A History Since 1900* (London: I.B. Tauris & Co. Ltd, 2014), p. 10.
8. Rose, L. A., *Power at Sea: Volume One: The Age of Navalism, 1890–1918* (Missouri: University of Missouri Press, 2006), p. 31.
9. Marder, A. J., *Fear God and Dread Nought: Volume II*, pp. 151–152.
10. Roberts, J., *The Battleship Dreadnought: Anatomy of the Ship* (Annapolis: Naval Institute Press, 1992), pp. 13 and 16 and Parkes, O., *British Battleships* (Annapolis: Naval Institute Press, 1990), p. 77.
11. Marder, A. J., *op. cit.*, p. 177.
12. *Ibid.*, p. 185.
13. Jane, F. J., 'Are 12-Inch Guns the Best Value for the Weight Entailed? A Plea for Ships Designed to Suit our Strategical Needs', *Royal United Services Institute Journal*, Vol. 47, No. 300 (1903), p. 174.
14. Darwin, J., *Britain and Decolonisation: The Retreat from Empire in the Post-War World* (Basingstoke: Macmillan Press Ltd, 1988), p. 5.
15. Bassett, R., *Battle-Cruisers: A History 1908–48* (London: Macmillan, 1981), p. 7.
16. Backer, S., *Grand Fleet Battlecrusiers* (Barnsley: Seaforth Publishing, 2011), p. 7.
17. Friedman, N., *Naval Firepower: Battleship Guns and Gunnery in the Dreadnought Era* (Maryland: Naval Institute Press, 2008), p. 10.
18. ADM 182/2.

19. Marder, A. J., *op. cit.*, p. 140.
20. CHAR 13/2/124-126.
21. Parkinson, R., *Dreadnought: The Ship that Changed the World* (London: I.B. Tauris & Co., 2015), p. 29.
22. DS.VA/1/29.
23. Saunders, A., *Reinventing Warfare 1914–18: Novel Munitions and Tactics of Trench Warfare* (London: Continuum International Publishing Group, 2012), p. 156.
24. Marder, A. J., *op. cit.*, p. 31.
25. Stille, M., *British Battlecruisers Vs. German Battlecruisers, 1914-16* (Oxford: Osprey publishing Ltd, 2013), p. 31.
26. Marder, A. J., *op. cit.*, p. 187.
27. *The New York Times*, 4 August 1908.
28. Marder, A. J., *op. cit.*, p. 189.
29. Hogg, G., 'Turbinia', National Register of Historic Vessels, 2016, nationalhistoricships.org.uk/register/138/turbinia, accessed 07/04/2018.
30. D'Eyncourt, E. H. W. T., *A Shipbuilder's Yarn: The Record of a Naval Constructor* (London: Hutchinson & Co., 1949), pp. 40–41.
31. Hogg, G., 'Turbinia'.
32. Stille, M., *op. cit.*, pp. 18–19.
33. *Ibid.*, p. 19.
34. *The Evening Chronicle*, 22 March 2004.
35. *The Times*, 28 January 1908.
36. DS.VA 1/12/2.
37. *The Times*, 28 January 1908.
38. *The Times*, 25 February 1908.
39. Browne, B. C., *Selected Papers on Social and Economic Questions* (Cambridge: Cambridge University Press, 1918), p. 155.
40. DS.VA 1/12/2.
41. Stille, M., *op. cit.*, p. 21.
42. Campbell, N. J. M., *Battlecruisers* (London: Conway Maritime Press, 1978), p. 19.
43. Bassett, R., *op. cit.*, p. 11.

Chapter 2

1. Roskill, S., *Admiral of the Fleet Earl Beatty* (London: Collins, 1980), p. 160; Mordal, J., *25 Centuries of Sea Warfare* (London: Abbey, 1973), p. 281; and Wragg, D., *Royal Navy Handbook, 1914–1918* (Stroud: The History Press Ltd, 2006), pp. 83–93.
2. Dick, E., *In the Wake of the Graf Spee* (Southampton: WIT Press, 2015), p. 79.
3. Bassett, R., *Battle-Cruisers*, p. 56.
4. Spencer-Cooper, H., The *Battle of the Falkland Islands 1914* (Driffield: Leonaur, 2011), p. 54.
5. Bassett, R., *op. cit.*, p. 64.
6. Backer, S., *Grand Fleet Battlecrusiers*, p. 22.
7. Massie, R. K., *Castles of Steel: Britain, Germany and the Winning of the Great War at Sea* (London: Vintage Books, 2007), p. 263.
8. Spencer-Cooper, H., *op. cit.*, p. 73.
9. Roberts, J., *Invincible Class* (London: Conway Maritime Press, 1972), p. 40.
10. Spencer-Cooper, H., *op. cit.*, pp. 123–124.
11. Roberts, J., *op. cit.*, p. 40
12. ADM 1/8408/6.
13. *Ibid.*
14. Stille, M., *British Battlecruisers Vs. German Battlecruisers*, p. 25.
15. ADM 186/566.
16. ADM 1/8408/6.
17. *Ibid.*
18. ADM 137/301.
19. *Ibid.*
20. *Ibid.*
21. *Ibid.*
22. *Ibid.*

23. *Ibid.*
24. *Ibid.*
25. ADM 137/1645.
26. *Ibid.*
27. ADM 137/301.
28. *Ibid.*
29. *Ibid.*
30. Bacon, R., *The Jutland Scandal* (London: Hutchinson and Co. Ltd, 1933), p. 90.
31. ADM 137/301.
32. *Ibid.*
33. *Ibid.*
34. *Ibid.*
35. *Ibid.*
36. ADM 137/1645.
37. *Ibid.*
38. *Ibid.*
39. *Ibid.*
40. *Ibid.*
41. *Ibid.*
42. *Ibid.*
43. *Ibid.*
44. *Ibid.*
45. *Ibid.*
46. *Ibid.*
47. *Ibid.*
48. Roskill, S., *op. cit.*, p. 196.
49. Roberts, J., *Battlecruiser* (London: Chatham Publishing, 2003), p. 115.
50. *Ibid.*, p. 117.
51. ADM 137/2027.
52. *Ibid.*

Chapter 3

1.   Hood, J., *The History of Clydebank* (London: The Parthenon Publishing Group Ltd, 1988, pp. 3-5; Buxton, I. and Johnston, I., *The Battleship Builders: Constructing and Arming British Capital Ships* (Barnsley: Pen and Sword, 2013); and Jeffrey, R., *Giants of the Clyde: The Great Ships and the Great Yards* (Edinburgh: Black and White Publishing, 2017).
2.   Raven, A. and Roberts, J., *British Battleships of World War Two: The Development and Technical History of the Royal Navy's Battleship and Battlecruisers from 1911 to 1946* (Annapolis: Naval Institute Press, 1976), p. 60.
3.   Taylor, B., *The End of Glory: War and Peace in HMS Hood, 1916–1941* (Barnsley: Seaforth Publishing, 2012), p. 1.
4.   Johnston, I., *Ships for a Nation: John Brown & Company Clydebank* (Glasgow: West Dunbartonshire Libraries and Museums, 2000), p. 224.
5.   Taylor, B., *The Battlecruiser HMS Hood: An Illustrated Biography 1916–1941* (Barnsley: Seaforth Publishing, 2015), p. 12.
6.   ADM 1/9209.
7.   Taylor, B., *The End of Glory*, p. 3.
8.   Coles, A. and Briggs, T., *Flagship Hood*, pp. 5–8.
9.   *Ibid.*, p. 4.
10. *Ibid.*
11. Johnston, I., *Beardmore Build: The Rise and Fall of a Clydeside Shipyard* (Glasgow: Clydebank District Libraries, 1993), p. 39.
12. GB 248 UGD 348; GB 248 UCS 001 Upper Clyde Shipbuilders Ltd, Clydebank Division; Shipbuilders, Clydebank, West Dunbartonshire (Glasgow: Glasgow University Archives).
13. Roberts, J., *Battlecruisers*, p. 61.
14. Coles, A. and Briggs, T., *op. cit.*, p. 8.
15. *Ibid.*, pp. 9–10.
16. Taylor, B., *op. cit.*, pp. 3–4.

Chapter 4

1. The ships of the *Courageous*-class consisted of three battlecruisers, sometimes referred to as 'large light cruisers' that were built during the First World War. The *Courageous*-class was nominally designed to support Admiral Lord Fisher's Baltic Project, which was intended to land troops on Germany's Baltic coast. Like most battlecruisers of the age, the *Courageous*-class were well armed, fast but lightly armoured. The *Courageous*-class vessels were designed with a shallow draught to allow them to operate in the shallow waters of the Baltic. The first two ships of the class, *Courageous* and *Glorious* were commissioned in 1917 and spent the war patrolling in the North Sea. Their sister ship, a modified *Courageous*-class ship, HMS *Furious* was equipped with a pair of 18-inch guns, the largest guns ever fitted to a Royal Navy vessel. *Furious* was modified to include a deck for launching seaplanes in place of her forward turret and barbette. By July 1918, the rear turret and barbette had been removed and replaced by another flight deck. At the end of the First World War, all three ships were laid up, with the *Glorious* and the *Courageous* being converted to aircraft carriers during the 1920s. As aircraft carriers, all three ships would see service during the Second World War.
2. 'Deep load' is a measurement of a ship's displacement while full of ammunition, stores and fuel.
3. Raven, A. and Roberts, J., *British Battleships of World War Two*, p. 67.
4. HMS *Tiger* was the only battlecruiser authorised in the 1911–12 Naval Programme. As a sole ship, she was not designated as being of a particular class.
5. It should be noted that the *Hood*'s BL 15-inch Mk I naval guns were fitted into Mk II mountings.
6. Norman, A., *HMS Hood: Pride of the Royal Navy* (Stroud: The History Press, 2009), p. 25.
7. Raven, A. and Roberts, J., *op. cit.*, p. 411.
8. ADM 186/249.
9. Roberts, J., *Battlecruisers*, p. 89; Campbell, J., *Naval Weapons of World War II* (Annapolis: Naval Institute Press, 1985), pp. 25–28; and Raven, A. and Roberts, J., *op. cit.*, p. 67.
10. Burt, R. A., *British Battleships 1919–1945* (London: Arms and Armour Press, 1993), p. 297.
11. Raven, A. and Roberts, J., *op. cit.*, p. 67.
12. Campbell, J., *op. cit.*, p. 40.
13. ADM 1/11585.
14. Raven, A. and Roberts, J., *op. cit.*, p. 68.
15. *Ibid.*, p.189.
16. *Ibid.*, pp.189–195.
17. Friedman, N., *Battleship Design and Development 1905–1945* (London: Conway Maritime Press, 1978), pp. 168–172.
18. Roberts, J., *op. cit.*, p. 113.
19. Burt, R. A., *op. cit.*, p. 299 and Raven, A. and Roberts, J., *op. cit.*, pp. 68–69.
20. 1988.421/6, Notes on Handling the 'Hood'.
21. Norman, A., *op. cit.*, p. 25.
22. Cosby, F., *The World Encyclopaedia of Naval Aircraft* (London: Lorenz Books, 2008), p. 84.
23. Taylor, H. A., *Fairey Aircraft Since 1915* (London: Putnam, 1988), p. 147 and Mason, F. K., *The British Bomber Since 1914* (London: Putnam, 1994), p. 178.
24. Taylor, *op. cit.*, p. 166.
25. Brown, D. K., *Nelson to Vanguard: Warship Design and Development 1923 to 1945* (Annapolis: Naval Institute Press, 2000), p. 76.
26. 'H.M.S. HOOD—Notes for Visitors', HMS *Hood Association* (2014), hmshood.com/ship/pamphlet30s.htm, accessed 27/09/2017
27. Norman, A., *op. cit.*, p. 37.

Chapter 5

1. Mearns, D. and White, R., *Hood and Bismarck: The Deep-Sea Discovery of an Epic Battle* (London: Channel 4 Books, 2004), p. 11.
2. *Ibid.*
3. *Ibid.*, p. 12.
4. The findings that resulted from the *Hood*'s speed trials may be found in ADM 226/23.
5. Taylor, B., *The End of Glory*, pp. 28–29.

6. Fairbairn, D., *The Narrative of a Naval Nobody, 1907–1924* (London: John Murray, 1929), pp. 233–234.

7. Keegan, J., *The First World War* (London: Pimlico, 1999), p. 452.

8. Gregory, A., *The Silence of Memory* (Oxford: Berg, 1994), p. 19

9. Allingham, H. and Goodwin, D., *Kitchener's Last Volunteer: The Life of Henry Allingham, the Oldest Surviving Veteran of the Great War* (London: Random House, 2011), p. 132.

10. Taylor, B., *op. cit.*, p. 18.

Chapter 6

1. See Stone, W., *Hero of the Fleet: Two World Wars, One Extraordinary Life—The Memoirs of a Centenarian* (Edinburgh: Mainstream Publishing Company, 2010), Chapter 6.

2. COW/13/2.

3. Taylor, B., *The Battlecruiser HMS Hood*, p. 235; Gröner, E., *German Warships 1815–1945: Major Surface Vessels* (Annapolis: Naval Institute Press, 1990), p. 113.

4. HMS *Hood* Association; Norman, A., HMS *Hood*, pp. 41–42.

5. Connor, W., *To Rio and Back with H.M.S. Hood* (London: The Westminster Press, 1922), pp. 12–13.

6. Taylor, B., *The End of Glory*, p. 20.

7. Ibid.

8. Coles, A. and Briggs, T., *Flagship Hood*, p. 25.

9. Taylor, B., *op. cit.*, p. 21.

10. For more information see: Heathcote, T., *The British Admirals of the Fleet 1734–1995* (Barnsley: Pen & Sword, 2002) and Murfett, M., *The First Sea Lords from Fisher to Mountbatten* (London: Praeger Publishers, 1995).

Chapter 7

1. ADM 116/2219.

2. Harrington, R., '"The Mighty Hood": Navy, Empire, War at Sea and the British Imagination, 1920-60', *Journal of Contemporary History*, Vol. 38, No. 2 (2003), p. 177.

3. O'Connor, V. S., *The Empire Cruise* (London: Riddle, Smith and Duffus, 1925), pp. 5-6.

4. ADM 116/2219.

5. *Ibid.*

6. *Ibid.*

7. *Ibid.*

8. Harrington, R., *op. cit.*, p. 179.

9. ADM 116/2219.

10. Harrington, R., *op. cit.*, p. 179.

11. Most of what follows with regards the movements of the ships has been drawn from records held at the National Archives, Kew. The records consulted are ADM 1/8662, ADM 53/78914, ADM 53/78915, ADM 116/2219, and ADM 116/2220.

12. Benstead, C. R., *Around the World with the Battle Cruisers* (London: Hurst and Blackett, 1925), p. 2.

13. O'Connor, V. S., *op. cit.*, pp. 41–43.

14. *Ibid.*, pp. 70-71.

15. Harrington, R., *op. cit.*, p. 181.

16. Batchelder, A., 'The Mighty Hood and the Melbourne Cricket Club', Courtesy of the HMS Hood Association.

17. O'Connor, V. S., *op. cit.*, p. 179.

18. *The Sporting Globe*, 19 March 1924.

19. *The Argus*, 21 March 1924.

20. *The Sporting Globe*, 21 March 1924.

21. Batchelder, A., *op. cit.*

22. Taylor, B., *The Battlecruiser HMS Hood*, p. 71.

23. Bradford, E., *The Mighty Hood*, (London: Hodder & Stoughton, 1977), p. 78.

24. Cassells, V., *The Capital Ships: Their Battles and Their Badges* (East Roseville: Simon & Schuster, 2000), p. 6.

25. Norman, A., HMS *Hood*, p. 37.

26. *Ibid.*, pp. 37–38.
27. O'Connor, V. S., *op. cit.*, p. 211.
28. Taylor, B., *op. cit.*, p. 72.
29. Bradford, E. *op. cit.*, p. 85.
30. Taylor, B., *op. cit.*, p. 74.
31. Clayton, A., *British Empire as a Superpower, 1919–39* (Athens: University of Georgia Press, 1986), p. 12.

Chapter 8

1. Norman, A., *HMS Hood*, p. 40.

Chapter 9

1. Bell, C. M., 'The Invergordon Mutiny', in Bell, C. M. and Elleman B. (eds), *Naval Mutinies of* the *Twentieth Century: An International Perspective* (London: Frank Cass Publishers, 2003), p. 145.
2. *Ibid.*, pp. 145–146.
3. Coles, A. and Briggs, T., *Flagship Hood*, p.48.
4. *Ibid.*, p. 50.
5. Roskill, S., *Naval Policy Between* the *Wars: Volume II: The Period of Reluctant Rearmament 1930–1939* (Barnsley: Pen and Sword, 2016), pp. 93–94.
6. Bell, C. M., *op. cit.*, pp. 145–146.
7. Ballantyne, I., HMS *Rodney: Slayer of* the *Bismarck and D-Day Saviour* (Barnsley: Pen and Sword, 2016), p. 68.
8. *Ibid.*
9. Taylor, B., *The Battlecruiser HMS Hood*, p. 149.
10. ADM 178/129.
11. MSS/80/098.
12. Bell, C. M., *op. cit.*, p. 147.
13. ADM 178/110.
14. *Ibid.*
15. Divine, D., *Mutiny at Invergordon* (London: MacDonald, 1970), p. 171.
16. *Ibid.*, p. 176.
17. Coles, A. and Briggs, T., *op. cit.*, p. 71.
18. ADM 178/113.

Chapter 10

1. Brown, D. K., *Nelson to Vanguard*, p. 76.
2. Coles, A. and Briggs, T., *Flagship Hood*, p. 73.
3. Taylor, B., *The End of Glory*, p. 110.
4. Coles, A. and Briggs, T., *op. cit.*, pp. xi–xii; Parker, J., *Task Force: Untold Stories of* the *Royal Navy* (London: Headline Book Publishing, 2003), p. 2.
5. Coles, A. and Briggs, T., *op. cit.*, p. xii.
6. Taverner, N., *A Torch Among Tapers: The Life and Career of Captain Rory O'Conor R.N.* (Bramber Bernard Durnford, 2000), p. 10.
7. Taylor, B., *op. cit.*, pp. 112–114.
8. *Ibid.*, p. 116.

Chapter 11

1. *The Times*, 27 February 1935.
2. Coles, A. and Briggs, T., *Flagship Hood*, pp. 84–86.
3. Smith, P. C., *The Battle-Cruiser HMS Renown, 1916–1948* (Barnsley: Pen & Sword, 2008), p. 32.

4. *The Times*, 28 February 1935.
5. Smith, P. C., *op. cit.*, p. 33.
6. *Ibid.*
7. Coles, A. and Briggs, T., *op. cit.*, p. 87.
8. Smith, P. C., *op. cit.*, p. 33.
9. *Ibid.*
10. *Ibid.*
11. *Ibid.*, p. 34.
12. *Ibid.*
13. Coles, A. and Briggs, T., *op. cit.*, p. 88.
14. Smith, P. C., *op. cit.*, pp. 34–35.
15. Taylor, B., *The End of Glory*, p. 20.
16. Smith, P. C., *The Great Ships Pass: British Battleships at War 1939–45* (London: William Kimber, 1977), p. 64.
17. ADM 156/107.
18. Coles, A. and Briggs, T., *op. cit.*, p. 89.

Chapter 12

1. Coles, A. and Briggs, T., *Flagship Hood*, p. 90.
2. Taylor, B., *The Battlecruiser* HMS *Hood*, p. 167.
3. Barker, A. J., *Rape of Ethiopia, 1936* (New York: Ballantyne Books, 1971), p. 17.
4. Taylor, B., *The End of Glory*, p. 120.
5. Coles, A. and Briggs, T., *op. cit.*, p. 92.
6. *Ibid.*, p. 93.
7. Taylor, B., *The Battlecruiser* HMS *Hood*, p. 123.
8. Coles, A., and Briggs, T., *op. cit.*, p. 94.
9. Taylor, B., *The End of Glory*, p. 121.
10. PRID 2.
11. Taylor, B., *op. cit.*, p. 120.
12. PRID 2.
13. Taylor, B., *op. cit.*, p. 121.
14. PRID 2.
15. Taylor, B., *The Battlecruiser* HMS *Hood*, p. 52.
16. James, Admiral Sir W., *The Sky Was Always Blue* (London: Methuen, 1951), p. 184.
17. Marder, A. J., *From the Dardanelles to Oran: Studies of the Royal Navy in War and Peace 1915–1940* (Barnsley: Seaforth Publishing, 2015), pp. 99–100.
18. PRID 2.

Chapter 13

1. IWM 18804.
2. Taylor, B., *The Battlecruiser* HMS *Hood*, p. 172.
3. PRID 2.
4. Coles, A. and Briggs, T., *Flagship Hood*, pp. 102–103.
5. Courtesy of the HMS *Hood* Association.
6. Coles, A. and Briggs, T., *op. cit.*, p. 104.
7. Beevor, A., *The Spanish Civil War* (London: Cassell, 1992), p. 165.
8. Coles, A. and Briggs, T., *op. cit.*, p. 103.
9. Alpert, M., 'The Blockade of Bilbao', *Basque Children of 37 Association UK* (2017), basquechildren.org/-/docs/articles/gen002, accessed 08/04/2018, pp. 5–6.
10. *Ibid.*, pp. 8–9.
11. Coles, A. and Briggs, T., *op. cit.*, p. 107.
12. FO 371/21352.
13. ADM 116/3514.
14. PRID 2.

15. Chatfield Papers.
16. Coles, A. and Briggs, T., *op. cit.*, p. 114.
17. Taylor, B., *op. cit.*, p. 53.
18. Cunningham, A., *A Sailor's Odyssey: The Autobiography of Admiral of the Fleet Viscount Cunningham of Hyndhope* (London: Hutchinson & Co., 1951), p. 186.
19. Murfett, M., *Fool-Proof Relations: The Search for Anglo-American Naval Cooperation During the Chamberlain Years* (Singapore: Singapore University Press, 1984), pp. 130–138.
20. Taylor, B., *op. cit.*, p. 177.
21. PRID 2.
22. Williams, L., *Gone A Long Journey* (Bedhampton: Hillmead Publications 2002), p. 126.
23. Rea, E., *A Curate's Egg* (Durban: Knox Printing Co, 1967), p. 140.
24. Mearns, D. and White, R., *Hood and Bismarck*, p. 27.

Chapter 14

1. Parker, J., *Task Force*, p. 3.
2. Coles, A. and Briggs, T., *Flagship Hood*, pp. 136–137.

Chapter 15

1. Beevor, A., *The Second World War* (London: Back Bay Books, 2013), p. 27.
2. Parker, J., *Task Force*, pp. 3–4.
3. Coles, A. and Briggs, T., *Flagship Hood*, p. 137.
4. Geary, S., *HMS Hood* (London: Robert Ross, 1942), p. 16.
5. Parker, J., *op. cit.*, p. 4.
6. Ballantyne, I., *Bismarck: 24 Hours to Doom* (London: Ipso Books, 2016), p. 53.
7. Williams, *Gone a Long Journey*, pp. 150–151.
8. Taylor, B., The Battlecruiser *HMS Hood*, p. 241.
9. Churchill, W. S., *The Second World War: Volume I: The Gathering Storm* (London: The Folio Society, 2003), p. 603.
10. *Ibid.*, p. 604.
11. For additional information on Operation Primrose, see ADM 202/422. See also Rhys-Jones, G., *Churchill and the Norway Campaign* (Barnsley: Pen and Sword, 2008), pp. 83–84, 86, and 133–134.

Chapter 16

1. Greene, J. and Massignani, A., *The Naval War in the Mediterranean 1940–1943* (London: Chatham Publishing, 1998), p. 57.
2. Jenkins, R., *Churchill* (London: Pan Books, 2002), p. 622.
3. HC Debate 25 June 1940, Vol. 362, cc. 302–305 (Hansard).
4. Parker, T., 'When Winston Churchill Bombed France: The Battle of Mers el-Kabir', *The National Interest*, nationalinterest.org (2018), nationalinterest.org/feature/when-winston-churchill-bombed-france-the-battle-mers-el-17337, accessd 09/04/2018.
5. Rossiter, M., *Ark Royal: The Life, Death and Rediscovery of the Legendary Second World War Aircraft Carrier* (London: Corgi, 2007), pp. 130–131.
6. Jordan, J. and Dumas, R., *French Battleships 1922–1956* (Barnsley: Seaforth Publishing, 2009), p. 126.
7. Coles, A. and Briggs, T., *Flagship Hood*, p. 152.
8. *Ibid.*
9. Jenkins, R., *op. cit.*, p. 622.
10. Brown, R. J., 'Operation Catapult: Naval Destruction at Mers-el-Kebir', *World War II Magazine* (September 1997), reproduced at historynet.com/operation-catapult-naval-destruction-at-mers-el-kebir.htm (2006), Accessed 09/04/2018.
11. Hickman, K., 'World War II: Attack on Mers el Kebir', *ThoughtCo* (2018), thoughtco.com/attack-on-mers-el-kebir-2361435, Accessed 09/04/2018.
12. Coles, A. and Briggs, T., *op. cit.*, p. 154.

13. Rossiter, M., *op. cit.*, pp. 132–133.
14. Churchill, W. S., *The Second World War: Volume II Their Finest Hour* (London: The Folio Society, 2003), p. 189.
15. *Ibid.*
16. *Ibid.*
17. Taylor, B., *The End of Glory*, p. 167.
18. Churchill, W. S., *op. cit.*, p. 191.
19. Brown, D. and Till, G., *The Road to Oran: Anglo-French Naval Relations* (London: Routledge, 2004), p. 182; Smith, C., *England's Last War Against France: Fighting Vichy 1940–42* (London: Phoenix, 2010).
20. In his article published in *World War II* magazine, Robert Brown states that Force 'H' arrived off Mers el-Kébir at 5.30 a.m. Bruce Taylor by contrast states the time as being 8 a.m. Finally, Ted Briggs, who served aboard HMS *Hood* and was present at Mers el-Kébir gives the time of Force 'H's arrival as 8.10 a.m. It is therefore most likely that the time that Force 'H' arrived off Mers el-Kébir was between 8 and 8.10 a.m.
21. Kappes, I. J., 'Mers-el-Kebir: A Battle Between Friends', *Military History Online* (2016), militaryhistoryonline.com/wwii/articles/merselkebir.aspx, Accessed 09/04/2018.
22. Brown, R. J., 'Operation Catapult'.
23. *Ibid.*
24. Rossiter, M., *op. cit.*, p. 133.
25. Brown, R. J., *op. cit.*
26. Taylor, B., *op. cit.*, p. 168.
27. *Ibid.*
28. AIR 234/317.
29. *Ibid.*
30. Taylor, B., *op. cit.*, p. 169.
31. *Ibid.*
32. Brown, R. J., *op. cit.*

Chapter 17

1. Taylor, B., *The End of Glory*, p. 158.
2. Coles, A. and Briggs, T., *Flagship Hood*, p. 191.
3. Taylor, B., *The Battlecruiser HMS Hood*, p. 209.
4. Garzke, W. H., and Dulin, R. O., *Battleships: Axis and Neutral Battleships in World War II* (Annapolis: Naval Institute Press, 1985), p. 158.

Chapter 18

1. Konstam, A., The *Bismarck 1941: Hunting Germany's Greatest Battleship* (Oxford: Osprey Publishing 2011), p. 22.
2. Knowles, D., *Tirpitz: The Life and Death of Germany's Last Great Battleship* (Stroud: Fonthill Media, 2018), pp. 26–27.
3. Taylor, B., *The End of Glory*, p. 183.
4. Knowles, D., *op. cit.*, pp. 63–64; Konstam, A., *op. cit.*, p. 8.
5. Coles, A. and Briggs, T., *Flagship Hood*, p. 198.
6. IWM 15562, Patrick Bernard Jackson (London: Imperial War Museum).
7. Norman, A., *HMS Hood*, p. 75.
8. Rico, J. M., 'Operation Rheinübung', *KBismarck.com* (2013), kbismarck.com/operheini.html, Accessed 09/04/2018.
9. *Ibid.*

Chapter 19

1. Coles, A. and Briggs, T., *Flagship Hood*, p. 204.

2. Ballantyne, I., *Killing the Bismarck: Destroying the Pride of Hitler's Fleet* (Barnsley: Pen and Sword, 2015), p. 66.
3. *Ibid.*, pp. 66–67.
4. Norman, A., *HMS Hood*, pp. 99–100.
5. *Ibid*, p. 100.
6. Ballantyne, I., *op. cit.*, p. 70.
7. Müllenheim-Rechberg, Baron B. von, *Battleship Bismarck: A Survivor's Story* (London: The Bodley Head, 1981), pp. 103–104.
8. Norman, A., *op. cit.*, p. 104.
9. Ballantyne, I., *op. cit.*, p. 72.
10. Grenfell, R., *The Bismarck Episode* (New York: The Macmillan Company, 1949).
11. Kennedy, L., *Pursuit: The Chase and Sinking of the Bismarck* (London: HarperCollins, 1974).
12. Bercuson, D. J., and Herwig, H. H., *Bismarck: The Story Behind the Destruction of the Pride of Hitler's Navy* (London: Pimlico, 2003), p. 102.
13. ADM 116/4309.
14. *Ibid.*
15. Ballantyne, I., *op. cit.*, p. 74.
16. Coles, A. and Briggs, T., *op. cit.*, p. 212.
17. Müllenheim-Rechberg, Baron B. von, *op. cit.*, pp. 105–107.
18. Coles, A. and Briggs, T., *op. cit.*, p. 214.
19. Ballantyne, I., *op. cit.*, p. 77.
20. Coles, A. and Briggs, T., *op. cit.*, p. 215.
21. *Ibid.*
22. *Ibid.*
23. Ballantyne, I., *op. cit.*, pp. 78–79.
24. Müllenheim-Rechberg, Baron B. von, *op. cit.*, pp. 109–110.
25. *Ibid.*, pp. 110–111.
26. ADM 116/4351.
27. *Ibid.*
28. *Ibid.*
29. *Ibid.*
30. *Ibid.*
31. AIR 15/415.
32. Coles, A. and Briggs, T., *op. cit.*, p. 216.
33. *Ibid.*
34. Ballantyne, I., *op. cit.*, p. 81.
35. *Ibid.*
36. Coles, A. and Briggs, T., *op. cit.*, pp. 216–217.

Chapter 20

1. Rhys-Jones, G., *The Loss of the Bismarck* (London: Cassell, 1999).
2. Konstam, A., *The Bismarck 1941*, p. 52.
3. *Ibid.*, pp. 52–53.
4. Ballantyne, I. *Killing the Bismarck*, p. 91.
5. *Ibid.*, pp. 95–96.
6. Courtesy of the HMS *Hood* Association.
7. Coles, A. and Briggs, T., *Flagship Hood*, p. 221.
8. Ballantyne, I., *op. cit.*, p. 97.
9. *Ibid.*

Chapter 21

1. Taylor, B., *The End of Glory*, p. 204.
2. *Ibid.*
3. Ballantyne, I. *HMS Rodney*, p. 133.
4. *Ibid.*
5. Taylor, B., *op. cit.*, p. 203.

6. IWM 90/38/1.

7. Norman, A., *HMS Hood*, p. 35.

8. Bone, D., *Merchantman Rearmed* (London: Chatto & Windus, 1949), p. 95.

9. Bishop, P., *Target Tirpitz: X-Craft, Agents and Dambusters—The Epic Quest to Destroy Hitler's Mightiest Warship* (London: Harper Press, 2012), p. 27.

10. Gilbert, M., *Winston S. Churchill: Volume VI Finest Hour 1939–1941* (London: Heinemann, 1983), p. 1094.

11. Taylor, B., *op. cit.*, p. 205.

12. *Ibid.*

13. Courtesy of the HMS *Hood* Association.

14. Taylor, B., *op. cit.*, p. 206.

15. *Sunday Mirror*, 25 May 1941.

16. *Sunday Times*, 25 May 1941.

17. *Sunday Express*, 25 May 1941.

18. *Sunday Pictorial*, 25 May 1941.

19. *Sunday Dispatch*, 25 May 1941.

20. *Sunday News*, 25 May 1941.

21. *Journal American*, 25 May 1941.

22. *San Francisco Examiner*, 25 May 1941.

23. Taylor, B., *The Battlecruiser HMS Hood*, p. 226.

24. Mearns, D. and White, R., *Hood and Bismarck*, p. 40.

25. *The Times*, 28 May 1941.

Chapter 22

1. ADM 116/4351; Taylor, B., *The End of Glory*, p. 199.

2. ADM 116/4351.

3. For the full findings on the loss of the *Hood* see ADM 1/30817, ADM 116/4351 and ADM 116/4352.

4. Jurens, W., 'The Loss of HMS Hood: A Re-Examination', *Warship International*, Vol. 24, No. 2 (1987), p. 139.

5. ADM 116/4351.

6. Jurens, W. *op. cit.*, pp. 147–151.

7. Taylor, B., *The Battlecruiser HMS Hood*, p. 224.

8. Mearns, D. and White, R., *Hood and Bismarck*, pp. 206–207.

9. Jurens, W., *op. cit.*, pp. 155–157.

10. *Ibid.*, p. 155.

Epilogue

1. Stille, M., *British Battlecruisers Vs. German Battlecruisers*, p. 76.

2. Lambert, N. A., '"Our Bloody Ships" or "Our Bloody System"? Jutland and the Loss of the Battlecruisers, 1916', *Journal of Military History*, Vol. 61, No. 1 (1998), p. 30.

3. Marder, A. J., *From the Dreadnought to Scapa Flow: Volume III: Jutland and After, May to December 1916* (Oxford: Oxford University Press, 1966), pp. 208–214 and Frost, H. H., *The Battle of Jutland* (Annapolis: Naval Institute Press, 1936), p. 213.

4. Hurd, A., 'The Admiralty, The Fleet, and the Battle of Jutland, May 31st 1916', *Fortnightly Review*, Vol. 101, No. 6 (1917), p. 940.

Bibliography

Archival Material

ADM 1/11585, Landing of Naval Wire Barrage equipment from HM Ships after loss of HMS *Hood* (Kew: The National Archives)

ADM 1/8662/111, Special Service Squadron, Empire Cruise (Kew: The National Archives)

ADM 1/8753/219, Report of proceedings of the Battle Cruiser Squadron, Jun– Jul 1931 (Kew: The National Archives)

ADM 1/8770/139, Publication in the Daily Mail of rumours of mutiny on HMS *Hood* (Kew: The National Archives)

ADM 1/9209, Battle Cruisers: Design (Kew: The National Archives)

ADM 1/9210, Hood class: armour and deck protection (Kew: The National Archives)

ADM 1/9555, Battle Cruiser Squadron: transfer to and from the Mediterranean; duties of Rear-Admiral First Battle Squadron, 1935–1938 (Kew: The National Archives)

ADM 1/10633—HMS *Hood* and *Warspite*: report of movements between 9–18 Feb (1940) (Kew: The National Archives)

ADM 1/11726, Loss of the *Hood* in action with German battleship Bismarck: report of Board of Inquiry (Kew: The National Archives)

ADM 1/19140, Sinking of HMS *Hood*: conflicting reports by German officers (Kew: National Archives)

ADM 1/23040, Allocation of first 40 UP projectors (unrotating projectile mountings) (1940) (Kew: The National Archives)

ADM 1/30817, Loss of HMS *Hood* (Kew: The National Archives)

ADM 1/8408/6, Methods of firing used by HM Ships Invincible and Inflexible during the action off the Falkland Islands (Kew: The National Archives)

ADM 53/78910, Ship's Log, 29 Mar 1920–19 Mar 1921 (Kew: The National Archives)

ADM 53/78911, Ship's Log, 20 Mar 1921–10 Mar 1922 (Kew: The National Archives)

ADM 53/78912, Ship›s Log, 11 Mar 1922– 01 Mar 1923 (Kew: The National Archives)

ADM 53/78913, Ship's Log, 02 Mar 1923–15 May 1923 (Kew: The National Archives)

ADM 53/78914, Ship's Log, 16 May 1923– 30 Apr 1924 (Kew: The National Archives)

ADM 53/78915, Ship's Log, 01 May 1924– 18 Apr 1925 (Kew: The National Archives)

ADM 53/78916, Ship's Log, 19 Apr 1925–06 Jan 1926 (Kew: The National Archives)

ADM 53/78917, Ship's Log, 07 Jan 1926–29 Jan 1927 (Kew: The National Archives)

ADM 53/78918, Ship's Log, 30 Jan 1927–21 Feb 1928 (Kew: The National Archives)

ADM 53/78919, Ship's Log, 22 Feb 1928–15 Feb 1929 (Kew: The National Archives)

ADM 53/78920, Ship's Log, 16 Feb 1929–17 May 1929 (Kew: The National Archives)

ADM 53/78921, Ship's Log, 10 Mar 1931–31 Mar 1931 (Kew: The National Archives)

ADM 53/78922, Ship's Log, Apr 1931 (Kew: The National Archives)

ADM 53/78923, Ship's Log, May 1931 (Kew: The National Archives)

ADM 53/78924, Ship's Log, Jun 1931 (Kew: The National Archives)

ADM 53/78925, Ship's Log, Jul 1931 (Kew: The National Archives)

ADM 53/78926, Ship's Log, Aug 1931 (Kew: The National Archives)

ADM 53/78927, Ship's Log, Sep 1931 (Kew: The National Archives)

ADM 53/78928, Ship's Log, Oct 1931 (Kew: The National Archives)

ADM 53/78929, Ship's Log, Nov 1931 (Kew: The National Archives)
ADM 53/78930, Ship's Log, Dec 1931 (Kew: The National Archives)
ADM 53/78931, Ship's Log, Jan 1932 (Kew: The National Archives)
ADM 53/78932, Ship's Log, Feb 1932 (Kew: The National Archives)
ADM 53/78933, Ship's Log, Mar 1932 (Kew: The National Archives)
ADM 53/78934, Ship's Log, Apr 1932 (Kew: The National Archives)
ADM 53/78935, Ship's Log, May 1932 (Kew: The National Archives)
ADM 53/78936, Ship's Log, Jun 1932 (Kew: The National Archives)
ADM 53/78937, Ship's Log, Jul 1932 (Kew: The National Archives)
ADM 53/78938, Ship's Log, Aug 1932 (Kew: The National Archives)
ADM 53/78939, Ship's Log, Sep 1932 (Kew: The National Archives)
ADM 53/78940, Ship's Log, Oct 1932 (Kew: The National Archives)
ADM 53/78941, Ship's Log, Nov 1932 (Kew: The National Archives)
ADM 53/78942, Ship's Log, Dec 1932 (Kew: The National Archives)
ADM 53/78943, Ship's Log, Jan 1933 (Kew: The National Archives)
ADM 53/78944, Ship's Log, Feb 1933 (Kew: The National Archives)
ADM 53/78945, Ship's Log, Mar 1933 (Kew: The National Archives)
ADM 53/78946, Ship's Log, Apr 1933 (Kew: The National Archives)
ADM 53/78947, Ship's Log, May 1933 (Kew: The National Archives)
ADM 53/78948, Ship's Log, Jun 1933 (Kew: The National Archives)
ADM 53/78949, Ship's Log, Jul 1933 (Kew: The National Archives)
ADM 53/78950, Ship's Log, Aug 1933 (Kew: The National Archives)
ADM 53/78951, Ship's Log, Sep 1933 (Kew: The National Archives)
ADM 53/78952, Ship's Log, Oct 1933 (Kew: The National Archives)
ADM 53/78953, Ship's Log, Nov 1933 (Kew: The National Archives)
ADM 53/78954, Ship's Log, Dec 1933 (Kew: The National Archives)
ADM 53/78955, Ship's Log, Jan 1934 (Kew: The National Archives)
ADM 53/78956, Ship's Log, Feb 1934 (Kew: The National Archives)
ADM 53/78957, Ship's Log, Mar 1934 (Kew: The National Archives)
ADM 53/78958, Ship's Log, Apr 1934 (Kew: The National Archives)
ADM 53/78959, Ship's Log, May 1934 (Kew: The National Archives)
ADM 53/78960, Ship's Log, Jun 1934 (Kew: The National Archives)
ADM 53/78961, Ship's Log, Jul 1934 (Kew: The National Archives)
ADM 53/78962, Ship's Log, Aug 1934 (Kew: The National Archives)
ADM 53/78963, Ship's Log, Sep 1934 (Kew: The National Archives)
ADM 53/78964, Ship's Log, Oct 1934 (Kew: The National Archives)
ADM 53/78965, Ship's Log, Nov 1934 (Kew: The National Archives)
ADM 53/78966, Ship's Log, Dec 1934 (Kew: The National Archives)
ADM 53/97652, Ship's Log, Jan 1935 (Kew: The National Archives)
ADM 53/97653, Ship's Log, Feb 1935 (Kew: The National Archives)
ADM 53/97654, Ship's Log, Mar 1935 (Kew: The National Archives)
ADM 53/97655, Ship's Log, Apr 1935 (Kew: The National Archives)
ADM 53/97656, Ship's Log, May 1935 (Kew: The National Archives)
ADM 53/97657, Ship's Log, Jun 1935 (Kew: The National Archives)
ADM 53/97658, Ship's Log, Jul 1935 (Kew: The National Archives)
ADM 53/97659, Ship's Log, Aug 1935 (Kew: The National Archives)
ADM 53/97660, Ship's Log, Sep 1935 (Kew: The National Archives)
ADM 53/97661, Ship's Log, Oct 1935 (Kew: The National Archives)
ADM 53/97662, Ship's Log, Nov 1935 (Kew: The National Archives)
ADM 53/97663, Ship's Log, Dec 1935 (Kew: The National Archives)
ADM 53/97664, Ship's Log, Jan 1936 (Kew: The National Archives)
ADM 53/97665, Ship's Log, Feb 1936 (Kew: The National Archives)
ADM 53/97666, Ship's Log, Mar 1936 (Kew: The National Archives)
ADM 53/97667, Ship's Log, Apr 1936 (Kew: The National Archives)
ADM 53/97668, Ship's Log, May 1936 (Kew: The National Archives)
ADM 53/97669, Ship's Log, Jun 1936 (Kew: The National Archives)
ADM 53/97670, Ship's Log, Jul 1936 (Kew: The National Archives)
ADM 53/97671, Ship's Log, Aug 1936 (Kew: The National Archives)
ADM 53/97672, Ship's Log, Sep 1936 (Kew: The National Archives)
ADM 53/97673, Ship's Log, Oct 1936 (Kew: The National Archives)

ADM 53/97674, Ship's Log, Nov 1936 (Kew: The National Archives)
ADM 53/97675, Ship's Log, Dec 1936 (Kew: The National Archives)
ADM 53/104194, Ship's Log, Jan 1937 (Kew: The National Archives)
ADM 53/104195, Ship's Log, Feb 1937 (Kew: The National Archives)
ADM 53/104196, Ship's Log, Mar 1937 (Kew: The National Archives)
ADM 53/104197, Ship's Log, Apr 1937 (Kew: The National Archives)
ADM 53/104198, Ship's Log, May 1937 (Kew: The National Archives)
ADM 53/104199, Ship's Log, Jun 1937 (Kew: The National Archives)
ADM 53/104200, Ship's Log, Jul 1937 (Kew: The National Archives)
ADM 53/104201, Ship's Log, Aug 1937 (Kew: The National Archives)
ADM 53/104202, Ship's Log, Sep 1937 (Kew: The National Archives)
ADM 53/104203, Ship's Log, Oct 1937 (Kew: The National Archives)
ADM 53/104204, Ship's Log, Nov 1937 (Kew: The National Archives)
ADM 53/104205, Ship's Log, Dec 1937 (Kew: The National Archives)
ADM 53/104206, Ship's Log, Jan 1938 (Kew: The National Archives)
ADM 53/104207, Ship's Log, Feb 1938 (Kew: The National Archives)
ADM 53/104208, Ship's Log, Mar 1938 (Kew: The National Archives)
ADM 53/104209, Ship's Log, Apr 1938 (Kew: The National Archives)
ADM 53/104210, Ship's Log, May 1938 (Kew: The National Archives)
ADM 53/104211, Ship's Log, Jun 1938 (Kew: The National Archives)
ADM 53/104212, Ship's Log, Jul 1938 (Kew: The National Archives)
ADM 53/104213, Ship's Log, Aug 1938 (Kew: The National Archives)
ADM 53/104214, Ship's Log, Sep 1938 (Kew: The National Archives)
ADM 53/104215, Ship's Log, Oct 1938 (Kew: The National Archives)
ADM 53/104216, Ship's Log, Nov 1938 (Kew: The National Archives)
ADM 53/104217, Ship's Log, Dec 1938 (Kew: The National Archives)
ADM 53/109191, Ship's Log, Jan 1939 (Kew: The National Archives)
ADM 53/109192, Ship's Log, Feb 1939 (Kew: The National Archives)
ADM 53/109193, Ship's Log, Mar 1939 (Kew: The National Archives)
ADM 53/109194, Ship's Log, Apr 1939 (Kew: The National Archives)
ADM 53/109195, Ship's Log, May 1939 (Kew: The National Archives)
ADM 53/109196, Ship's Log, Jun 1939 (Kew: The National Archives)
ADM 53/109197, Ship's Log, Jul 1939 (Kew: The National Archives)
ADM 53/109198, Ship's Log, Aug 1939 (Kew: The National Archives)
ADM 53/109199, Ship's Log, Sep 1939 (Kew: The National Archives)
ADM 53/109200, Ship's Log, Oct 1939 (Kew: The National Archives)
ADM 53/109201, Ship's Log, Nov 1939 (Kew: The National Archives)
ADM 53/109202, Ship's Log, Dec 1939 (Kew: The National Archives)
ADM 53/112443, Ship's Log, Jan 1940 (Kew: The National Archives)
ADM 53/112444, Ship's Log, Feb 1940 (Kew: The National Archives)
ADM 53/112445, Ship's Log, Mar 1940 (Kew: The National Archives)
ADM 53/112446, Ship's Log, Apr 1940 (Kew: The National Archives)
ADM 53/112447, Ship's Log, May 1940 (Kew: The National Archives)
ADM 53/11248, Ship's Log, Jun 1940 (Kew: The National Archives)
ADM 53/112449, Ship's Log, Jul 1940 (Kew: The National Archives)
ADM 53/112450, Ship's Log, Aug 1940 (Kew: The National Archives)
ADM 53/112451, Ship's Log, Sep 1940 (Kew: The National Archives)
ADM 53/112452, Ship's Log, Oct 1940 (Kew: The National Archives)
ADM 53/112453, Ship's Log, Nov 1940 (Kew: The National Archives)
ADM 53/112454, Ship's Log, Dec 1940 (Kew: The National Archives)
ADM 53/114434, Ship's Log, Jan 1941 (Kew: The National Archives)
ADM 53/114435, Ship's Log, Feb 1941 (Kew: The National Archives)
ADM 53/114436, Ship's Log, Mar 1941 (Kew: The National Archives)
ADM 53/114437, Ship's Log, Apr 1941 (Kew: The National Archives)
ADM 53/114888, *Prince of Wales*'s Log, May 1941 (Kew: The National Archives)
ADM 116/4309, Termination of Action Between Force H and Italian Forces; Board of Enquiry, (Kew: The National Archives)
ADM 116/1881, Visit of Battle Cruiser Squadron to Scandinavian Ports, 1919–20 (Kew: National Archives)
ADM 116/2219, Empire Cruise of the Special Service Squadron, Volume 1 (Kew: The National Archives)
ADM 116/2220, Empire Cruise of the Special Service Squadron, Volume 2 (Kew: The National Archives)

ADM 116/2254, Special Service Squadron–Letters of Proceedings, Volume 1 (Kew: National Archives)

ADM 116/2255, Special Service Squadron–Letters of Proceedings, Volume 2 (Kew: National Archives)

ADM 116/2256, Special Service Squadron–Letters of Proceedings, Volume 3 (Kew: National Archives)

ADM 116/2257, Special Service Squadron–Letters of Proceedings, Volume 4 (Kew: National Archives)

ADM 116/3514, Proceedings of HM Ships (A-G) in Spanish Waters During Spanish Civil War (Kew: The National Archives)

ADM 116/3516, Spanish Civil War: Proceedings of Rear Admiral 2nd Battle Squadron Apr to Aug 1939 (Kew: The National Archives)

ADM 116/3517, Spanish Civil War: Proceedings of HM Ships in Northern Spanish Waters

ADM 116/4351, Loss of HMS *Hood* in action with German battleship *Bismarck*: Boards of Inquiry (Kew: The National Archives)

ADM 116/4352, Loss of HMS *Hood* in action with German battleship *Bismarck*: Boards of Inquiry (Kew: The National Archives)

ADM 137/301, Jutland. Contains reports of Commander-in-Chief Home Fleets and the Vice-Admiral Commanding Battle Cruiser Fleet, 31 May–1 June 1916 (Kew: The National Archives)

ADM 137/1645, Grand Fleet, Post Jutland changes, 1916 (Kew: The National Archives)

ADM 137/2027, Grand Fleet pack 1187. (Committees formed to consider experience at Jutland), Part I, numbers 1-6 (Kew: The National Archives)

ADM 156/107, Collision between HM Ships the *Hood* and *Renown* (Kew: The National Archives)

ADM 178/110, Invergordon Mutiny Narrative of events by RADM Tomkinson, Senior Officer Atlantic Fleet (Kew: The National Archives)

ADM 178/113, Invergordon Mutiny: men discharged (Kew: The National Archives)

ADM 178/129, Invergordon Mutiny reports (Kew: The National Archives)

ADM 178/171, The Mutiny at Invergordon: Protests from various naval officers (Kew: The National Archives)

ADM 182/2, Admiralty Fleet Orders (Kew: The National Archives)

ADM 186/249, 15» Mark II mountings, HMS Hood, handbook (Kew: The National Archives)

ADM 186/566, Action off the Falkland Islands 8 Dec 1914: report of Vice-Admiral Sir F C D Sturdee (Kew: The National Archives)

ADM 186/797, Operations against French Fleet at Mers el-Kebir, 3–6 Jul 1940 (Kew: The National Archives)

ADM 202/422, Operation 'Primrose' Operations by Royal Marines in Norway (Kew: The National Archives)

ADM 226/23, HMS *Hood* analysis of results of speed trials (Kew: The National Archives)

ADM 234/317, Operations against French Fleet at Mers el-Kebir, 3–6 Jul 1940 (Kew: The National Archives)

ADM 234/509, Sinking of the *Bismarck* 27 May 1941: Official Dispatches (Kew: The National Archives)

ADM 234/510, Sinking of the *Bismarck* 27 May 1941: Plans (Kew: The National Archives)

ADM 267/64, the *Hood*: Board of enquiry into loss (Kew: The National Archives)

ADM 267/111, Damage Reports (Kew: The National Archives)

AIR 15/415, *Bismarck*: Reports on sinking (Kew: The National Archives)

AIR 234/317, Operations Against the French Fleet at Mers-el-Kebir, 03-06 July 1940 (Kew: National Archives)

CHAR 13/2/124-126, Letter From Admiral Fisher to Sir Winston Churchill, 6 December 1911 (Cambridge: The Churchill Archive)

CHT, The Chatfield Papers (Greenwich: National Maritime Museum)

COW/13/2, Papers Witten by Admiral Sir Walter Henry Cowan 1919-45 (Greenwich: National Maritime Museum)

DS.VA 1/12/2 Vickers Armstrong & Co. Ltd Executive Minutes (Newcastle-upon-Tyne: Tyne & Wear Archives)

DS.VA/1/29, 'Sir Andrew Noble Letter to Messers Krupp, 24 November 1898' (Newcastle-upon-Tyne: Tyne & Wear Archives)

FO 371/21352, Spain. Code 41 File 23 Papers 6309-7526 (Kew: The National Archives)

GB 248 UGD 348; GB 248 UCS 001, Records of Upper Clyde Shipbuilders Ltd, Clydebank Division, Shipbuilders, Clydebank, West Dunbartonshire, Scotland (Glasgow: University of Glasgow Archives)

HC Debate 25 June 1940, Vol. 362, cc.302-305 (Hansard)

IWM 90/38/1, Captain G. C. Blundell (London: Imperial War Museum)

IWM 15562, Patrick Bernard Jackson (London: Imperial War Museum)

IWM 18804, Noel Raymond Pugh (London: Imperial War Museum)

MSS/80/098, Commander Harry Pursey/15 (Greenwich: National Maritime Museum)

PRID 1, The Papers of Vice-Admiral Sir (Arthur) Francis Pridham Volume 1 (Cambridge: Churchill College)

PRID 2, The Papers of Vice-Admiral Sir (Arthur) Francis Pridham Volume 2 (Cambridge: Churchill College)
1988.421/6, Notes on Handling the 'Hood' (Portsmouth: Royal Navy Library)

Literature

Allingham, H. and Goodwin, D., *Kitchener's Last Volunteer: The Life of Henry Allingham, the Oldest Surviving Veteran of the Great War* (London: Random House, 2011)
Arthur, M., *The Navy: 1939 to the Present Day* (London: Hodder & Stoughton, 1997)
Backer, S., *British Battlecruisers of the Second World War* (Barnsley: Seaforth Publishing, 2007); *Grand Fleet Battlecruisers* (Barnsley: Seaforth Publishing, 2011)
Bacon, R., *The Jutland Scandal* (London: Hutchinson and Co. Ltd, 1933); *The Life of John Rushworth Earl Jellicoe* (London: Cassell, 1936)
Ballantyne, I., *Bismarck: 24 Hours to Doom* (London: Ipso Books, 2016); HMS *Rodney: Slayer of the Bismarck and D-Day Saviour* (Barnsley: Pen and Sword, 2016); *Killing the Bismarck: Destroying the Pride of Hitler's Fleet* (Barnsley: Pen and Sword, 2015)
Barker, A. J., *Rape of Ethiopia, 1936* (New York: Ballantyne Books, 1971)
Barnett, C., *Engage the Enemy More Closely: The Royal Navy in the Second World War* (New York: W. W. Norton, 1991)
Bassett, R., *Battle-Cruisers: A History 1908–1948* (London: Macmillan, 1981)
Beevor, A., *The Second World War* (London: Back Bay Books, 2013); *The Spanish Civil War* (London: Cassell, 1992)
Bell, C. M. and Elleman, B. (eds), *Naval Mutinies of the Twentieth Century: An International Perspective* (London: Frank Cass Publishers, 2003)
Bennett, G., *The Battle of Jutland* (Barnsley: Pen & Sword Books Ltd, 2015); *The Battles of Coronel and the Falklands, 1914* (Barnsley: Pen & Sword Books Ltd, 2014); *Naval Battles of World War Two* (Barnsley: Pen and Sword, 2004)
Benstead, C. R., *Around the World with the Battle Cruisers* (London: Hurst and Blackett, 1925)
Bercuson, D. J. and Herwig, H. H., *Bismarck: The Story Behind the Destruction of the Pride of Hitler's Navy* (London: Pimlico, 2003)
Bishop, P., *Target Tirpitz: X-Craft, Agents and Dambusters—The Epic Quest to Destroy Hitler's Mightiest Warship* (London: Harper Press, 2012)
Bone, D., *Merchantman Rearmed* (London: Chatto & Windus, 1949)
Boyne, W. J., *Clash of Titans: World War II at Sea* (New York: Simon & Schuster, 1995)
Bradford, E., *The Mighty Hood* (London: Hodder & Stoughton, 1977)
Brown, D. K., *The Grand Fleet: Warship Design and Development 1906–1922* (Barnsley: Seaforth Publishing, 2010); *Nelson to Vanguard: Warship Design and Development 1923 to 1945* (Annapolis: Naval Institute Press, 2000)
Brown, D. and Till, G., The *Road to Oran: Anglo-French Naval Relations* (London: Routledge, 2004)
Browne, B. C., *Selected Papers on Social and Economic Questions* (Cambridge: Cambridge University Press, 1918)
Burroughs, P., 'The Mid-Victorian Navy and Imperial Defence', *The Journal of Imperial and Commonwealth History*, Vol. 30, No. 2 (2008), pp. 102–114.
Burt, R. A., *British Battleships 1919–1945* (London: Arms and Armour Press, 1993)
Buxton, I. and Johnston, I., *The Battleship Builders: Constructing and Arming British Capital Ships* (Barnsley: Pen and Sword, 2013)
Campbell, J., *Naval Weapons of World War II* (Annapolis: Naval Institute Press, 1985)
Campbell, N. J. M., *Battlecruisers* (London: Conway Maritime Press, 1978);
Campbell, N. J. M. and Campbell, J., *Jutland: An Analysis of the Fighting* (Guilford: Lyons Press, 2000)
Cassells, V., *The Capital Ships: Their Battles and Their Badges* (East Roseville: Simon & Schuster, 2000)
Chesneau, R., *Hood: Life and Death of a Battlecruiser* (London: Cassell Publishing, 2002)
Churchill, W. S., *The Second World War: Volume I The Gathering Storm* (London: The Folio Society, 2003); The *Second World War: Volume II Their Finest Hour* (London: The Folio Society, 2003)
Clayton, A., *British Empire as a Superpower, 1919–39* (Athens: University of Georgia Press, 1986)
Coles, A. and Briggs, T., *Flagship Hood: The Fate of Britain's Mightiest Warship* (London: Robert Hale, 1988)
Connor, W., *To Rio and Back with H.M.S. Hood* (London: The Westminster Press, 1922)
Cosby, F., *The World Encyclopaedia of Naval Aircraft* (London: Lorenz Books, 2008)
Cosentino, M. and Stanglini, R., *British and German Battlecruisers: Their Development and Operations* (Barnsley: Seaforth Publishing, 2016)
Crossley, J., *Bismarck: The Epic Chase* (Barnsley: Pen and Sword, 2010)

Cunningham, A., *A Sailor's Odyssey: The Autobiography of Admiral of the Fleet Viscount Cunningham of Hyndhope* (London: Hutchinson & Co., 1951)

D'Eyncourt, E. H. W. T., *A Shipbuilder's Yarn: The Record of a Naval Constructor* (London: Hutchinson & Co., 1949)

Darwin, J., *Britain and Decolonisation: The Retreat from Empire in the Post-War World* (Basingstoke: Macmillan Press Ltd, 1988)

Dick, E., *In the Wake of the Graf Spee* (Southampton: WIT Press, 2015)

Divine, D., *Mutiny at Invergordon* (London: MacDonald, 1970)

Draminski, S., The *Battlecruiser HMS Hood: Super Drawings in 3D* (Lublin: Kagero, 2013)

Edgerton, D., *Britain's War Machine: Weapons, Resources, and Experts in the Second World War* (Oxford: Oxford University Press, 2011)

Fairbairn, D., *The Narrative of a Naval Nobody, 1907–1924* (London: John Murray, 1929)

Friedman, N., *Battleship Design and Development 1905–1945* (London: Conway Maritime Press, 1978); *The British Battleship: 1908–1946* (Barnsley: Seaforth Publishing, 2015); *Fighting the Great War at Sea: Strategy, Tactics and Technology* (Barnsley: Seaforth Publishing, 2014); *Naval Firepower: Battleship Guns and Gunnery in the Dreadnought Era* (Maryland: Naval Institute Press, 2008)

Frost, H. H., *The Battle of Jutland* (Annapolis: Naval Institute Press, 1936)

Garzke, W. H. and Dulin, R. O., *Battleships: Axis and Neutral Battleships in World War II* (Annapolis: Naval Institute Press, 1985)

Geary, S., *HMS Hood* (London: Robert Ross, 1942)

Gilbert, M., *Winston S. Churchill: Volume VI Finest Hour 1939–1941* (London: Heinemann, 1983)

Greene, J. and Massignani, A., *The Naval War in the Mediterranean 1940–1943* (London: Chatham Publishing, 1998)

Gregory, A., *The Silence of Memory* (Oxford: Berg, 1994)

Grenfell, R., *The Bismarck Episode* (New York: The Macmillan Company, 1949)

Gröner, E., *German Warships 1815–1945: Major Surface Vessels* (Annapolis: Naval Institute Press, 1990)

Harrington, R., '"The Mighty Hood": Navy, Empire, War at Sea and the British Imagination, 1920-60', *Journal of Contemporary History*, Vol. 38, No. 2 (2003), pp. 171–185.

Heathcote, T., *The British Admirals of the Fleet 1734–1995* (Barnsley: Pen & Sword, 2002)

Hood, J., *The History of Clydebank* (London: The Parthenon Publishing Group Ltd, 1988)

Hore, P. (ed.), *Dreadnought to Darling: 100 Years of Comment, Controversy and Debate in The Naval Review* (Barnsley: Seaforth Publishing, 2012)

Howarth, D., *British Sea Power: How Britain Became Sovereign of the Seas* (London: Robinson, 2003)

Hoyt, E. P., *Sunk by the Bismarck: The Life & Death of the Battleship HMS Hood* (New York: Stein and Day, 1981)

Hurd, A., 'The Admiralty, The Fleet, and the Battle of Jutland, May 31st 1916', *Fortnightly Review*, Vol. 101, No. 6 (1917)

James, Admiral Sir W., *The Sky Was Always Blue* (London: Methuen, 1951)

Jane, F. T., 'Are 12-Inch Guns the Best Value for the Weight Entailed? A Plea for Ships Designed to Suit our Strategical Needs', *Royal United Services Institute Journal* Vol. 47, No. 300 (1903), pp. 171–175.

Jeffrey, R., *Giants of the Clyde: The Great Ships and the Great Yards* (Edinburgh: Black and White Publishing Ltd, 2017)

Jenkins, R., *Churchill* (London: Pan Books, 2002)

Johnston, I., *Beardmore Build: The Rise and Fall of a Clydeside Shipyard* (Glasgow: Clydebank District Libraries, 1993); *Ships for a Nation: John Brown & Company Clydebank* (Glasgow: West Dunbartonshire Libraries and Museums, 2000)

Jordan, J. and Dumas, R., *French Battleships 1922–1956* (Barnsley: Seaforth Publishing, 2009)

Jurens, W., 'The Loss of HMS Hood: A Re-Examination', *Warship International*, Vol. 24, No. 2 (1987), pp. 122–181.

Kaplan, P., *Battleships: WWII Evolution of the Big Guns* (Barnsley: Pen and Sword, 2015)

Keegan, J., *The First World War* (London: Pimlico, 1999)

Kemp, P. J., *Bismarck and Hood: Great Naval Adversaries* (London: Arms and Armour Press, 1991)

Kennedy, L., *Pursuit: The Chase and Sinking of the Bismarck* (London: HarperCollins, 1974)

Knowles, D., *Tirpitz: The Life and Death of Germany's Last Great Battleship* (Stroud: Fonthill Media, 2018)

Konstam, A., *The Bismarck 1941: Hunting Germany's Greatest Battleship* (Oxford: Osprey Publishing, 2011); *British Battlecruisers 1939–45* (Oxford: Osprey Publishing, 2003)

Lambert, N. A., '"Our Bloody Ships" or "Our Bloody System"? Jutland and the Loss of the Battlecruisers, 1916', *Journal of Military History*, Vol. 61, No. 1 (1998), pp. 29–55.

Levy, J. P., *The Royal Navy's Home Fleet in World War II* (London: Palgrave Macmillan, 2003)

Lightbody, Bradley, *The Second World War: Ambitions to Nemesis* (London: Routledge, 2004)

Mace, M., *The Royal Navy and the War at Sea 1914–1919: Despatches from the Front* (Barnsley: Pen & Sword Books Ltd, 2014).

MacIntyre, D., *Jutland* (London: Pan Books Ltd, 1966).

Marder, A. J., *The Anatomy of British Sea Power: A History of British Naval Policy in the Pre-Dreadnought Era, 1880–1905* (New York: Alfred A. Knopf, 1940); *Fear God and Dread Nought: the Correspondence of Admiral of the Fleet Lord Fisher of Kilverstone: Volume I: The Making of an Admiral, 1854–1904* (Oxford: Jonathan Cape, 1952); *Fear God and Dread Nought: The Correspondence of Admiral of the Fleet Lord Fisher of Kilverstone: Volume II: Years of Power, 1904–1914* (Oxford: Jonathan Cape, 1956); *Fear God and Dread Nought: the Correspondence of Admiral of the Fleet Lord Fisher of Kilverstone: Volume III Restoration, Abdication, and Last Years, 1914–1920* (Oxford: Jonathan Cape, 1959); *From the Dardanelles to Oran: Studies of the Royal Navy in War and Peace 1915–1940* (Barnsley: Seaforth Publishing, 2015); *From the Dreadnought to Scapa Flow: Volume III Jutland and After, May to December 1916* (Oxford: Oxford University Press, 1966)

Mason, F. K., The *British Bomber Since 1914* (London: Putnam, 1994)

Massie, R. K., *Castles of Steel: Britain, Germany and the Winning of* the *Great War at Sea* (London: Vintage Books, 2007); *Dreadnought: Britain, Germany, and the Coming of* the *Great War* (New York: Random House, 1991)

Mearns, D. and White, R., *Hood and Bismarck: The Deep-Sea Discovery of an Epic Battle* (London: Channel 4 Books, 2004)

Melton, G. E., *From Versailles to Mers El-Kébir: The Promise of Anglo-French Naval Cooperation, 1919-40* (Annapolis: Naval Institute Press, 2015)

Mordal, J., *25 Centuries of Sea Warfare* (London: Abbey, 1973)

Müllenheim-Rechberg, Baron B. von, *Battleship Bismarck: A Survivor's Story* (London: The Bodley Head, 1981)

Murfett, M., *The First Sea Lords from Fisher to Mountbatten* (London: Praeger Publishers, 1995); *Fool-Proof Relations: The Search for Anglo-American Naval Cooperation During the Chamberlain Years* (Singapore: Singapore University Press, 1984)

Norman, A., *HMS Hood: Pride of the Royal Navy* (Stroud: The History Press, 2009)

Northcott, M. P., *HMS Hood: Design and Construction* (London: Arms & Armour Press, 1981)

O'Connor, V. S., *The Empire Cruise* (London: Riddle, Smith and Duffus, 1925)

Padfield, P., *The Battleship Era* (London: Pan Books, 1975)

Parker, J., *Task Force: Untold Stories of the Royal Navy* (London: Headline Book Publishing, 2003)

Parkes, O., *British Battleships* (Annapolis: Naval Institute Press, 1990)

Parkinson, R., *Dreadnought: The Ship That Changed the World* (London: I.B. Tauris & Co., 2015)

Preston, A., *Sea Power: A Modern Illustrated Military History*, (London: Phoebus Publishing Company, 1979); *The World's Worst Warships* (London: Conway Maritime Press, 2002)

Raven, A. and Roberts, J., *British Battleships of World War Two: The Development and Technical History of the Royal Navy's Battleship and Battlecruisers from 1911 to 1946* (Annapolis: Naval Institute Press, 1976)

Rea, E., *A Curate's Egg* (Durban: Knox Printing Co, 1967)

Redford, D. and Grove, P. D., *The Royal Navy: A History Since 1900* (London: I.B. Tauris & Co. Ltd, 2014)

Rhys-Jones, G., *Churchill and the Norway Campaign* (Barnsley: Pen and Sword, 2008); *The Loss of the Bismarck: An Avoidable Disaster* (London: Cassell, 1999)

Roberts, J., *Battlecruisers* (London: Chatham Publishing, 2003); *The Battlecruiser Hood: Anatomy of a Ship* (London: Conway Maritime Press, 2013); *The Battleship Dreadnought: Anatomy of the Ship* (Annapolis: Naval Institute Press, 1992); *British Battlecruisers: 1905–1920* (Barnsley: Seaforth Publishing, 2016); *British Warships of the Second World War: Detailed in the Original Builder's Plans* (Barnsley: Seaforth Publishing, 2017); *Invincible Class* (London: Conway Maritime Press, 1972)

Rose, L. A., *Power at Sea: Volume One: The Age of Navalism, 1890–1918* (Missouri: University of Missouri Press, 2006); *Power at Sea: Volume Two: The Breaking Storm, 1919–1945* (Missouri: University of Missouri Press, 2006)

Roskill, S., *Admiral of the Fleet Earl Beatty: The Last Naval Hero* (London: William Collins and Sons & Co., 1980); *Naval Policy Between the Wars: Volume I: The Period of Anglo-American Antagonism 1919–1929* (London: Collins, 1968); *Naval Policy Between the Wars: Volume II: The Period of Reluctant Rearmament 1930–1939* (Barnsley: Pen and Sword, 2016); *The Navy at War 1939–1945* (London: Collins, 1960)

Rossiter, M., *Ark Royal: The Life, Death and Rediscovery of the Legendary Second World War Aircraft Carrier* (London: Corgi, 2007)

Santarini, M., *Bismarck and the Hood: The Battle of the Denmark Strait* (Stroud: Fonthill Media Ltd, 2013)

Saunders, A., *Reinventing Warfare 1914–18: Novel Munitions and Tactics of Trench Warfare* (London: Continuum International Publishing Group, 2012)

Shirer, W. L., *The Sinking of the Bismarck: The Deadly Hunt* (New York: Sterling Publishing Co., 2006)

Smith, C., *England's Last War Against France: Fighting Vichy 1940–42* (London: Phoenix, 2010)

Smith, P. C., *The Battle-Cruiser HMS Renown, 1916–1948* (Barnsley: Pen & Sword, 2008); *The Great Ships Pass: British Battleships at War 1939–45* (London: William Kimber, 1977)

Spencer-Cooper, H., *The Battle of the Falkland Islands 1914* (Driffield: Leonaur Ltd, 2011); *The Battle of the Falkland Islands: Before and After* (London: Cassell, 1919)

Steel, N. and Hart, P., *Jutland 1916: Death in the Grey Wastes* (London: Cassell, 2004)

Stephen, M., *Sea Battles in Close-Up: World War 2* (Annapolis: Naval Institute Press, 1988)

Stille, M., *British Battlecruisers Vs German Battlecruisers 1914–16* (Oxford: Osprey Publishing, 2013)

Stone, W., *Hero of the Fleet: Two World Wars, One Extraordinary Life—The Memoirs of a Centenarian* (Edinburgh: Mainstream Publishing Company, 2010)

Sutherland, J., Canwell, Diane, *The Battle of Jutland* (Barnsley: Pen & Sword Maritime, 2007)

Taverner, N., *Hood's Legacy* (London: Arcturus Publishing, 2001); *A Torch Among Tapers: The Life and Career of Captain Rory O'Conor R. N.* (Bramber: Bernard Durnford, 2000)

Taylor, B., *The Battlecruiser HMS Hood: An Illustrated Biography 1916–1941* (Barnsley: Seaforth Publishing, 2015); *The End of Glory: War and Peace in HMS Hood, 1916–1941* (Barnsley: Seaforth Publishing, 2012)

Taylor, H. A., *Fairey Aircraft Since 1915* (London: Putnam, 1988)

Taylor, T., *HMS Hood vs. Bismarck: The Battleship Battle* (New York: Avon Books, 1989)

Tute, W., *The Deadly Stroke* (Barnsley: Pen and Sword, 2007)

Veronico, N. A., *Hidden Warships: Finding Wold War II's Abandoned, Sunk, and Preserved Warships* (London: Zenith Press, 2015)

Williams, L., *Gone A Long Journey* (Bedhampton: Hillmead Publications 2002)

Winklareth, R., *The Bismarck Chase: New Light on a Famous Engagement* (Annapolis: Naval Institute Press, 1998); *The Battle of the Denmark Strait: A Critical Analysis of the Bismarck's Singular Triumph* (Oxford: Casemate, 2012)

Wragg, D., *Royal Navy Handbook, 1914–1918* (Stroud: The History Press Ltd, 2006)

Zetterling, N. and Tamelander, M., *Bismarck: The Final Days of Germany's Greatest Battleship* (London: Casemate, 2012)

Newspapers

The Argus
The Evening Chronicle
Journal American
London Gazette
New York Times
The Sporting Globe
San Francisco Examiner
Sunday Dispatch
Sunday Express
Sunday Mirror
Sunday News
Sunday Pictorial
Sunday Times
The Times

Websites

www.basquechildren.org
www.historynet.com
www.hmshood.com
www.kbismarck.com
www.militaryhistory.about.com
www.militaryhistoryonline.com
www.nationalhistoricships.org.uk
www.nationalinterest.org
www.royal.uk
www.thoughtco.com

Index